'O' Level

Programming and Problem Solving Through 'C' Language

Module 3

STRICTLY AS PER NEW DOEACC SYLLABUS

M3 – R4

[Also covers syllabus for A3-R4 Paper of DOEACC 'A' Level Examination]

Dr. R. K. Jain

KHANNA BOOK PUBLISHING CO. (P) LTD.

Programming and Problem Solving Through 'C' Language — R K Jain

Published by
Khanna Book Publishing Co. (P) Ltd.

Regd. Office:
1694-95, 1st Floor
Nai Sarak, Delhi - 110 006 (India)
Tel. 011-23283211, 23256658
Telefax: 011-23256658
Website: www.khannabooks.com
E-mail: contact@khannabooks.com

ISBN 978-93-80016-64-1

First Edition 2010

Printed in India by Seth Printers, Noida (U.P.)

Preface

The new syllabus of DOE's various levels of courses, popularly called O-level, A-level, B-level and C-level is out. Keeping in mind the various developments taking place around the world in the field of computers, these syllabus include most of them. While keeping in mind the level of students studying the various levels, the degree of difficulties of the syllabus have been very well designed. I hope that after the new syllabus the courses would be as popular as they were before.

There had been a long struggle between Training Institutes and Government Organizations, since these organizations would not recognize the degree/diploma given by them. Students passing out from these institutions were not given jobs based upon the said diplomas/degrees. Ultimately, the Government formed a society under the Department of Electronics, called DOEACC, who conducts tests and gives grades to the students irrespective of the institutes where they have studied. It is also possible to give the test without having any proper institutional studies. This is more or less on the terms of SAT and GRE conducted by USA. The only difference is that this is not online. There are fixed dates for the exams.

The course for this has been designed for students to appear in the exams at various levels. These levels are O-level, A-level, B-level, C-level. The most popular among these is the O-level, since it is the entry level. Once you have cleared the O-level, you are eligible for a government job. Each course has been divided into various modules. Various books are available for various modules. This book is also made for you to prepare for the O-level course.

This book has been written totally in accordance with the syllabus provided. Each chapter has been embedded with the screen shots for you to know what to expect on the screen, while running the application. Each chapter contains examples which can be attempted to supplement the reading. At the end of the chapter, there is a thorough revision of the text read. Not to mention of the questions provided in the beginning, both in the form of objective and subjective. The book also contains Sample papers which are based on the samples provided by DOEACC society. These would help you in preparing for the exams.

Author

Syllabus

M3-R4: PROGRAMMING AND PROBLEM SOLVING THROUGH 'C' LANGUAGE

The objective of this course are to make the student understand programmng language, programming, concepts of loops, reading a set of data, stepwise refinement, Functon, Control strucutres, Arrays. After completion of this course the student is expected to analyze the real life problem and write a program in 'C' language to solve the problem. The main emphases of the course will on problem solving aspect, i,e., developing proper algorithms.

At the end of the course the students will be able to:

- Develop efficient algorithms for solving a problem.
- Use the various constructs of a programming language viz., conditional, iteration and recursion.
- Implement the algorithm in 'C' language.
- Use simple data structures like arrays, stacks, and linked list in solving problems.
- Handling File in 'C'.

Outline of Course

S.No.	*Topic*	*Minimum No. of Hours*
1.	Introduction to Programming	04
2.	Algorithm for Problem Solving	10
3.	Introduction to 'C' Language	04
4.	Conditional Staements and Loops	07
5.	Arrays	06
6.	Functions	06
7.	Storage Classes	03
8.	Structures and Unions	06
9.	Pointers	06
10.	Self Referential Structures and Linked Lists	04
11.	File Processing	04

Lectures	=	60
Practicals /Tutorials	=	60
Total	=	120

DETAILED SYLLABUS

1. Introduction to Programming **04 Hrs.**

The Basic Model of Computation, Algorithms, Flow-Charts, Programming Languages, Compilation, Linking and Loading, Testing and Debugging, Documentation.

2. Algorithms for Problem Solving **10 Hrs.**

Exchanging values of two variables, Summation of a set of numbers, Decimal Base to Binary Base Conversion, Reversing digits of an integer, GOD (Greatest Common Division) of two numbers, Test whether a number is prime, Organize numbers in ascending order, Find square root of a number, Factorial computation, Fibonacci sequence, Evaluate 'sin x' as sum of a series, Reverse order of elements of an array, Find largest number in an array, Print elements of upper triangular matrix, multiplication of two matrices, Evaluate a Polynomial.

3. Introduction to 'C' Language **04 hrs.**

Character set, Variables and identifiers, Built-in Data Types, Variable Definition, Arithmetic operators, and expressions, Constants and Literals, Simple assignment statement, Basic input/output statement, Simple 'C' programs.

4. Conditional Statements and Loops **07 Hrs.**

Decision making within a program, Conditions, Relational Operators, Logical Connectives, If statement, If-else statement, Loops, While loop, Do while, For loop, Nested loop, Infinite loops, Switch statement, Structured programming.

5. Arrays **06 Hrs.**

One dimensional arrays, Array manipulation; Searching, Insertion, Deletion of an element from an array; Finding the largest/smallest element in an array; Two dimensional arrays; Addition/Multiplication of two matrices, Transpose of a square matrix; Null terminated strings as array of characters, Standard library string functions.

6. Functions **06 Hrs.**

Top-down approach of problem solving, Modular programming and functions, Standard Library of C functions, Prototype of a function; Format parameter list, Return Type, Function call, Block structure, Passing arguments to a Function; call by reference, call by value, Recursive Functions, arrays as function arguments.

7. Storage Classes **03 Hrs.**

Scope and extent, Storage Classes in a single source file; auto, extern and static, register, Storage Classes in a multiple source files; extern and static.

8. Structures and Unions **06 Hrs.**

Structure variables, initialization, structure assignment, nested structure, structures and functions, structures and arrays; arrays of structures, structures containing arrays, unions.

9. Pointers **08 Hrs.**

Address operators, pointer type declaration, pointer assignment, pointer initialization, pointer arithmetic, functions and pointers, Arrays and Pointers, pointer arrays, pointers and structures, dynamic memory allocation.

10. Self Referential Stuctures and Linked Lists **04 Hrs.**

Creation of a singly connected linked list, Traversing a linked list, Insertion into a linked list, Deletion from a linked list.

11. File Processing **04 Hrs.**

Concept of Files, File opening in various modes and closing of a file, Reading from a file, Writing onto a file.

Contents

1. Introduction to Programming 1

1.1 The Basic Model of Computation 1
1.1.1 General Concepts 1
1.1.1.1 Readability 1
1.1.1.2 Efficiency 1
1.1.1.3 Processing 2
1.1.1.4 Memory 2
1.1.1.5 Time 2
1.1.1.6 Realiability 2
1.1.1.7 Meaningfullness 2
1.1.1.8 Portability 2
1.1.1.9 User-friendly 2
1.2 Problem Solving 2
1.2.1 Understanding of the Problem 2
1.2.2 Identifying Minimum number of Inputs required for Output 2
1.2.3 Step by Step Solution for the Problem 3
1.2.4 Breaking Down Solution into Simple Steps 3
1.3 Algorithms 4
1.3.1 Definition 5
1.3.2 Characteristics of an Algorithm 6
1.3.3 Algorithmic Notations 6
1.4 Flow-Charts 9
1.4.1 Advantages of flowcharts 11
1.4.2 Conventions of flowcharts 11
1.4.3 Limitations of flowcharts 12
1.4.4 Expressions in flowcharts 14
1.4.4.1 Addition 14
1.4.4.2 Subtraction 14
1.4.4.3 Multiplication 15
1.4.4.4 Division 16
1.4.4.5 Transfer 16
1.4.4.6 Comparison 16
1.4.4.7 Print 16
1.4.4.8 Feed 16
1.4.5 Types of logic used in flowchart 17
1.5 Programming Languages 18
1.5.1 Machine Language 19
1.5.2 Assembly Language 19
1.5.3 High Level Language 20
1.5.3.1 Readability 20
1.5.3.2 Portability 20

1.5.3.3 Easy debugging 20
1.5.3.4 Easy software development 20
1.5.3.5 Examples of HLL 20
1.6 Compilation 22
1.6.1. Assembler 22
1.6.2. Compilers and Interpreter 23
1.7 Linking and Loading 23
1.7.1 Loader 24
1.8 Testing and Debugging 24
1.8.1 Debugging 24
1.8.2 Syntax Errors 25
1.8.3 Run-Time Errors 25
1.8.4 Logical Errors 26
1.8.5 Methods of Correcting Logical Errors 26
1.8.6 Testing 26
1.9 Documentation 27
1.9.1 External Documentation 28
1.9.2 User's Guide 28
1.9.3 Operators Guide 28
1.9.4 Reference Manual 28
Let us Revise 29
Multiple Choice Questions 29
True/False Questions 31
Match Columns 31
Fill in the Blanks with Appropriate Words 32
Descriptive Type Questions 32

2. Alogrithms for Problem Solving 35

2.1 Exchanging Values of Two Variables 35
2.2 Summation of a Set of Numbers 35
2.3 Decimal Base to Binary Base Conversion 36
2.4 Reversing Digits of an Integer 37
2.5 GOD (Greatest Common Divisor) of Two Numbers 38
2.6 Test Whether a Number is Prime 39
2.7 Organize Numbers in Ascending Order 40
2.8 Find Square Root of a Number 40
2.9 Factorial Computation 41
2.10 Fibonacci Sequence 42
2.11 Evaluate 'Sin x' as Sum of a Series 43
2.12 Reverse Order of Elements of an Array 43
2.13 Find Largest Number in an Array 44
2.14 Print Elements of Upper Triangular Matrix 44
2.15 Evaluate a Polynomial 45
2.16 Multiplication of Two Matrices 45
Let us Revise 46
Multiple Choice Questions 46
True/False Questions 47

Match Columns 47
Fill in the Blanks with Appropriate Words 47
Descriptive Type Questions 47

3. Introduction to 'C' Language 48

3.1 Character set 48
3.2 Variables and identifiers 50
3.3 Built-in Data Types 51
3.3.1 The int 52
3.3.2 The char 53
3.3.3 The float 54
3.3.4 The double 55
3.3.5 The void (Empty data type) 55
3.4 Variable Definition 56
3.5 Arithmetic operators 57
3.6 Expressions 62
3.7 Constants and Literals 64
3.7.1 Enumeration Constants 65
3.8 Simple Assignment Statement 66
3.9 Basic Input/Output Statement 66
3.9.1 Output: the printf family 67
3.9.2 Input: the scanf family 70
Let us Revise 72
Multiple Choice Questions 72
True/False Questions 77
Match Columns 77
Fill in the Blanks with Appropriate Words 77
Descriptive Type Questions 78

4. Conditional Statements and Loops 79

4.1 Decision Making within a Program 79
4.2 Conditions and Relational Operators 79
4.3 Logical Connectives 79
4.5 If statement 80
4.5.1 Nested If Statements 82
4.6 If-else statement 85
4.6.1 The else-if ladder 88
4.7 Loops 92
4.8 While loop 92
4.9 Do while 95
4.10 For loops 97
4.11 Nested Loops 101
4.12 Infinite Loops 102
4.13 Switch statement 103
4.14 Structured programming 110
4.14.1 The break statement 110
4.14.2 The Continue Statement 112
4.14.3 The goto Statement 113

Let us Revise 114
Multiple Choice Questions 115
True/False Questions 121
Match Columns 122
Fill in the Blanks with Appropriate Words 122
Descriptive Type Questions 122

5. Arrays 125

5.1 One Dimensional Arrays 125
5.1.1 One Dimensional Array 126
5.1.2 Multi-dimensional Array 126
5.1.3 One Dimensional Array 127
5.2 Array Manipulation 129
5.2.1 Initialization of one Dimensional Array 129
5.2.2 Initialization of character arrays 130
5.3 Searching 131
5.3.1 Linear Search 131
5.3.2 Binary Search 131
5.4 Insertion 132
5.5 Deletion of an Element from an Array 132
5.6 Finding the Largest/Smallest Element in an Array 133
5.7 Two Dimensional Arrays 133
5.7.1 Initialization Of Multidimensional Arrays 138
5.8 Addition/Multiplication of Two Matrices 141
5.8.1 Addition of Two Matrices 141
5.8.2 Multiplication of Two Matrices 142
5.9 Transpose of a Square Matrix 142
5.10 Null Terminated Strings as Array of Characters 143
5.11 Standard Library String Functions 143
5.11. String Length {strlen()} 143
5.11.2 String Copy {strcpy()} 143
5.11.3 strcmp() 144
5.12 Array Bounds Checking 144
5.13 Arrays and Functions 146
5.14 Visualizing A C String 147
5.15 Vector Operation 148
5.16 Random Access 151
5.17 Multidimensional Arrays and Functions 152
5.18 Multidimensional Arrays 153
Let us Revise 155
Multiple Choice Questions 155
True/False Questions 162
Match Columns 162
Fill in the Blanks with Appropriate Words 162
Descriptive Type Questions 162

6. Functions 165

6.1 Top-down Approach of Problem Solving 165

6.1.1 Step-wise Refnement 165
6.2 Modular Programming and Functions 166
6.2.1 Functions 166
6.3 Standard Library of C Functions 170
6.3.1 Basic I/O Functions 170
6.3.1.1 Console I/O functions 170
6.3.1.2 Disk I/O functions 170
6.3.1.3 Port I/O functions 170
6.3.1.4 Console I/O functions 170
6.3.1.5 Formatted Functions 170
6.3.1.6 UnFormatted functions 171
6.3.1.7 Formatted Console I/O Functions 171
6.3.1.8 Conversion Specifications 172
6.3.2 Escape Sequences 173
6.3.2.1 Escape Characters 173
6.3.3 Scanf() 173
6.3.4 sprintf() function and sscanf() Function 174
6.3.5 Unformatted Console I/O Functions 174
6.3.6 gets( ) and puts( ) 176
6.3.7 Disk Functions 177
6.3.8 Opening A File 177
6.3.9 File Opening Modes 178
6.3.10 Reading from a File 178
6.3.11 Closing The File 179
6.3.12 Writing to A File 179
6.3.12.1 fclose() function 179
6.3.13 Mathematical Functions 179
abs 179
fabs 179
labs 179
fmod 179
cos 179
acos 179
cosh 180
sin 180
asin 180
sinh 180
tan 180
atan 180
tanh 180
6.3.14 String Functions 180
strncat 180
strncpy 180
strncmp 180
stricmp 180
strnicmp 180
strlwr 181

strupr ... 181
strset ... 181
strnset ... 181
strstr ... 181
strchr ... 181
strrchr ... 181
6.3.15 Character Classification Macros ... 181
toupper(c) ... 181
tolower(c) ... 181
toascii(c) ... 181
islower(c) ... 181
isupper(c) ... 181
ispunct(c) ... 181
isspace(c) ... 181
isxdigit(c) ... 181
isalnum(c) ... 182
isalpha(c) ... 182
isdigit(c) ... 182
iscntrl(c) ... 182
isprint(c) ... 182
isgraph(c) ... 182
6.3.16 File Handling Functions ... 182
rename ... 182
unlink ... 182
6.3.17 Directory Control Functions ... 182
chdir ... 182
mkdir ... 182
rmdir ... 182
getcwd ... 182
getcurdir ... 182
getdisk ... 182
fnsplit ... 183
fnmerge ... 183
disable ... 183
enable ... 183
6.3.18 Macros ... 183
FP_OFF ... 183
FP_SEG ... 183
MK_FP ... 183
6.3.19 Graphics Functions ... 183
initgraph ... 183
closegraph ... 183
putpixel ... 183
line ... 183
moveto ... 184
lineto ... 184
circle ... 184

cleardevice ... 184
bar ... 184
bar3d ... 184
arc ... 184
pieslice ... 184
setviewport ... 184
clearviewport ... 184
setcolor ... 184
setbkcolor ... 185
imagesize ... 185
getimage ... 185
putimage ... 185
floodfill ... 185
6.3.20 Time and Date Related Functions ... 185
clock ... 185
ftime ... 185
difftime ... 185
time ... 185
settime ... 185
gettime ... 185
setdate ... 186
getdate ... 186
6.3.21 Miscellaneous Functions ... 186
exit ... 186
_exit ... 186
sleep ... 186
delay ... 186
sound ... 186
nosound ... 186
flush ... 186
kbhit ... 186
system ... 186
abort ... 186
6.4 Prototype of a Function ... 187
6.5 Format Parameter List ... 189
6.6 Return Type ... 189
6.7 Function Call ... 189
6.8 Passing Arguments to a Function ... 189
6.10 Call by Reference ... 190
6.11 Call by Value ... 190
6.12 Recursive Functions ... 190
6.12.1 Types of Recursion ... 193
6.12.2 Exponential ... 194
6.12.3 Elimination of Recursion ... 195
6.13 Arrays as Function Arguments ... 196
Let us Revise ... 200
Multiple Choice Questions ... 200

True/False Questions 203
Match Columns 203
Fill in the Blanks with Appropriate Words 204
Descriptive Type Questions 204

7. Storage Classes 207

7.1 Scope and Extent 207
7.1.1 Types of Scope 207
7.2 Storage Classes in a Single Source File 208
7.3 Auto 208
7.4 Extern 208
7.5 Static 208
7.6 Register 209
7.7 Storage Classes in Multiple Source Files 209
7.7.1 Lifetime 209
7.7.1.1 Automatic Variables 209
7.7.1.2 Static and External Variables 209
7.8 Extern 210
7.9 Static 210
Let us Revise 210
Multiple Choice Questions 211
True/False Questions 211
Match Columns 211
Fill in the Blanks with Appropriate Words 211
Descriptive Type Questions 211

8 Structures and Unions 213

8.1 Structure Variables 213
8.1.1 What is Structure? 213
8.1.2 Defining a Structure with typedef 217
8.2 Initialization 218
8.3 Structure Assignment 223
8.4 Nested Structure 223
8.4.1 Initialization of Nested Structures 227
8.4.2 Structures and Arrays 229
8.4.3 Initialiation of Array of Sructures 231
8.4.4 Pointers to Structures 232
8.5 Structures and Functions 237
8.6 Structures and Arrays 240
8.7 Arrays of Structures 240
8.8 Structures containing Arrays 240
8.9 Unions 241
8.9.1 Initialization of Union 243
8.9.2 Typedef 244
Let us Revise 246
Multiple Choice Questions 246
True/False Questions 247
Match Columns 248

Fill in the Blanks with Appropriate Words 248
Descriptive Type Questions 248

9. Pointers 251

9.1 Address Operators 251
9.2 Pointer Type Declaration 251
9.3 Pointer Assignment 253
9.4 Pointer Initialization 253
9.5 Pointer Arithmetic 258
9.5.1 Addition/Subtraction with Integral values 258
9.5.2 Subtraction of Pointers 259
9.6 Functions and Pointers 259
9.7 Arrays and Pointers 262
9.8 Pointer Arrays 265
9.9 Pointers and Structures 269
9.10 Dynamic Memory Allocation 272
9.10.1 Allocating Memory With malloc 272
9.10.2 Method 1 274
9.10.3 Method 2 275
9.10.4 Method 3 276
9.10.5 Method 4 277
9.10.5 Freeing Memory 282
9.10.6 Reallocating Memory Blocks 283
9.10.7 The sizeof and Storage Allocation 285
9.10.8 The type of sizeof 294
9.10.9 What sizeof cannot do? 295
Let us Revise 296
Multiple Choice Questions 296
True/False Questions 300
Match Columns 300
Fill in the Blanks with Appropriate Words 300
Descriptive Type Questions 301

10. Self Referential Structures and Linked Lists 303

10.1 Creation of a Singly Connected Linked List 303
Linked List 303
10.2 Traversing a Linked List 308
10.3 Insertion into a Linked List 311
10.3.1 Insertion as a First Node 312
10.3.2 Insertion As A Last Node 315
10.3.3 Insertion of a Node at Specific Location 319
10.4 Deletion from a Linked List 322
10.4.1 Deletion of First Node 322
10.4.2 Deletion of Last Node 325
10.4.3 Deletion of a Desired Node 328
Let us Revise 333
Multiple Choice Questions 333
True/False Questions 333

Match Columns 334
Fill in the Blanks with Appropriate Words 334
Descriptive Type Questions 334

11. File Processing 337

11.1 Concept of Files 337
11.2 File Opening in Various Modes 338
11.3 Closing of a File 341
11.4 Reading from a File 342
11.5 Writing onto a File 342
Let us Revise 342
Multiple Choice Questions 342
True/False Questions 343
Match Columns 343
Fill in the Blanks with Appropriate Words 343
Descriptive Type Questions 344

G. Glossary 345

I. Index 349

S1. Sample Paper - 1 351

S2. Sample Paper - 2 355

S3. Sample Paper - 3 359

S4. Sample Paper - 4 363

S5. Sample Paper - 5 367

Introduction to Programming 1

1.1 The Basic Model of Computation

A good programmer is an asset to the company. But, nobody is born to write programs. A good programmer is not born but is developed by his own actions. These actions make him a good programmer. There is a methology which he has to follow to become a good programmer. In this chapter I will discuss this methology, and how it is used while writing programs irrespective of the language he is using.

Programming is a team effort. What can a good programmer do if the inputs to him are given wrong. He has to coordinate between the various users and data providers to cater to their needs and write a good program which would produce the results the user is looking forward to. A manager for example, is not concerned how the problem is solved or how the data is obtained. He is only interested in results which the program is supposed to provide.

For writing any program the programmer has to keep lots of things in mind. Few of them have been mentioned above, the others including problem definition, program design, coding, debugging, testing, documentation, maintenance and redesign. Let us start with the general concepts used for writing any program.

1.1.1 General Concepts

Program writing is definitely a technique. One has to master it by experience. One should always start with writing small and simple programs and then graduate to complex and complicated programs. Whatever he may write, it should be written in a manner which is understood by others. God forbid if he is not around the others should be able to run and modify it. Here the documentation parts becomes very necessary. I will talk about it little later but first let us see what a good program should have.

A good program should have the following characteristics:

1. Readability
2. Efficiency
3. Reliability
4. Meaningfulness
5. Portability
6. User-friendly.

Let us read about them in little details.

1.1.1.1 Readability

As mentioned above the program should be such that it can be read and understood by others. This makes it easy to modify by others.

1.1.1.2 Efficiency

While writing the program the programmer must take care of the following:

1.1.1.3 *Processing*

He should make sure that the program takes the minimum processing time.

1.1.1.4 *Memory*

Mimimum utalization of memory and hard disk space should be used.

1.1.1.5 *Time*

The programmer should be able to produce the program in time frame given.

1.1.1.6 *Realiability*

It goes beyond saying that the program should be reliable and must be in a position to produce good and accurate results. It should take care that the various checks are provided to overcome wrong data and machine malfunctions.

1.1.1.7 *Meaningfullness*

The program should give the meaningful outputs.

1.1.1.8 *Portability*

With the advent of PCs the compatability of one computer with another has been taken care of. But, still there is a possibility that the program may be required to run on a machine which is alien to the program. In this case the program should be such that it needs minimum efforts to be modified to suit the new environments.

1.1.1.9 *User-friendly*

A program should be user-friendly.

1.2 Problem Solving

It is impossible to solve a problem by using a computer, without a clear understanding and identification of the problem. Inadequate recognition of a problem is the key element responsible for poor performance of computers. This step is generally difficult and the programmer should invest a significant portion of his time in problem identification. If he does not spend enough time at this state, he may find that his well-written program fails to solve the real problem.

1.2.1 Understanding of the Problem

Depending on the complexity of the problem, the result of a careful analysis may be simply a testing of the factors with which the program must deal, or it may be a formal written statement of the problem, supported by a description of all the considerations necessary to solve the problem. This step is the process of becoming familiar with the problem that will be solved with a computer program. It starts when the programmer is assigned the task.

This step includes the reviewing of the design document that was prepared for the program, as well as any system-wide information that would be helpful. The process ends when all the programmer's questions have been resolved and the requirements of the program are understood.

Problem definition may, thus, include many factors. Input/Output, time constraints, processing requirements, accuracy, memory limitations, error handling and interfaces with other programs or tables must all be considered.

1.2.2 Identifying Minimum number of Inputs required for Output

In any problem soloving exercise, the computer center receives information from various departments and sends the processed output to various other departments. In most of the cases, the computer center does not have control over the input of the data. Each department which sends the data for processing has to ensure that the data sent is free from errors. But can the computer center make its own checks, yes, they can provide various checks in the data. For example, they can make sure that the number of days worked in never beyond 31, the age of the employee is never less than 18, the basic salary is not less than DA, etc. But still if any error occurs, it is the fault of input and not the processing.

Human factor is also important here. Since the date and time of receiving data is fixed, the department sending the data is under pressure for the same. This results in wrong filling up of the data sheet. This results in wrong results. These data sheets are the results of the various sittings which the computer center has had with both the users and input providers.

1.2.3 Step by Step Solution for the Problem

An often used rule is that a programmer working on a large software project, will write two to ten fully corrected lines of program per day. Since the writing of even ten lines hardly takes just a few minutes, coding is clearly not the most time-consuming stage of software development. So what he does he chalks out the various steps in which the program has to be written. The solution of the problem lies in good steps.

A program writing can be divided into several stages:

1. Program Definition
2. Program Design
3. Coding
4. Debugging
5. Testing
6. Documentation
7. Maintenance

Some of them have been discussed earlier.

Once these steps have been marked down the next step becomes easier.

1.2.4 Breaking Down Solution into Simple Steps

This step is considered complete when a clean compile walkthrough has been held and the program coding has been approved. These steps would not only result in good program but would give satisfactory results.

Stylistic Guidelines: This section presents stylistic guidelines on programming style that will be useful, regardless of the particular language or processor involved.

Using meaningful names and labels: Meaningful names and labels can be helpful in documentation and maintenance as well as in debugging and integrating programs. The names should be as simple and straight forward as possible – PRNTR for the system printer, TTY for a teletypewriter, MAX for a teletypewrite. MAX for the maximum value, START for the beginning of the program. The use of meaningful names will save the programmer endless time and confusion in the various stages of programming.

Clarity and Simplicity of Expressions: Expressions play a key role in the programming. It must be clearly understood by the programmers as far as possible used the standard functions in expressions to improve the readability. There should not be any compromise with the clarity of expressions.

Keep short modules: Divide long modules into sections. Not only will a shorter module be easier to debug and correct, but it is also more likely to be useful in subsequent programs, since its function will be a small one and is more likely to recur. One or two pages of code (50 to 75 lines) is the maximum size for a module. Modules can be implemented as macros or simply copied into the program in order to avoid a massive number of calls and returns.

Keep names and labels distinct: Distinctive names and labels reduce confusion. The use of number 0, 1 and 2 and letter O, I and Z should be kept to a minimum. Certainly the programmer should not, for example, use both MINI and MIN1 as identifiers; the chance for error is too great. Names that, for one reason or another, continually confuse the programmer should be changed; there are always enough errors in programs without inviting additional ones.

Make modules fairly general: Obviously a module that is too specific (for example, one which sorts precisely 30 elements or searches for the letter S) will find little repeated use. Greater generality can often be achieved with little or no extra code; a sort that will handle any number of elements will bono harder to write than one that handles a specific number. General that requires considerable extra code and ingenuity, such as writing a code conversion routine to handle both ASCII and EBCDIC characters, is not worthwhile.

Simple ways to achieve generality have already been mentioned – the use of names instead of specific addresses of data, the collection of definitions at the start of the routine and the use of meaningful names that suggest the purposes or identities of items. All these techniques can produce a program that can be used frequently and easily modified.

Emphasise simplicity and comprehensibility: The first objective of programming is to write a program that works. Saving a few microseconds or few memory locations is seldom important; the code can be optimized later.

Avoid obscure constructions: Examples include the use of offsets from the program counter in computers that have many multiple-word instructions, the use of complex expressions that depend on the order in which operations are performed or operators that are seldom used and complex conditional assemblies. Even if the programmer knows the effects of an obscure construction at that moment, surely a few days or a few months time will return it to obscurity.

Avoid jumps when possible: Jumps make programs difficult to follow and debug. Repeating an instruction is often faster and clearer than jumping to a particular instruction. Programs with a series of jumps should be rewritten before the debugging stage.

Place definitions in groups at the start of the program: Definitions that are grouped at the start of the program can be easily located, checked and changed when necessary. Definitions that are scattered throughout the program can greatly hinder debugging and decomentation.

Use names instead of specific addresses or data: The use of names instead of specific memory addresses, constant, masks, I/O device numbers, or numerical factors, can not only suggest the actual purpose or meaning of the particular address or data but can also make the program easier to change.

Use Comments and Identification: Comments provide the internal documentation of a program. It makes the program easy to understand. The comments, should be included: at the beginning of the program which summarises the purpose of the program, at the beginning of the procedures and functions and to clarify the global and local variables.

Indentation makes program more clear to understand. The statements should be indented in such a manner that nesting of groups of control statement can be matched (i.e. if ….else). The braces pair (…..) should be written in the same column to help in proper matching.

1.3 Algorithms

We have various problems in our life and we try to overcome of those. We have well- defined way to accomplish our work, assignments, etc. If we convert the well-defined way into steps then these steps give rise to the concept of algorithm. Whatever we do in this practical world is based on some well-defined thought. Starting from the civilization, people are used to find the simplest method to fulfill their daily needs and overcome of their problems. This is the origin of algorithm. When a man faces a problem or has some need, he tries to find the solution. It may be that first time he could not find simple solution, but he keeps on trying to get better solution. This is why we have so established society.

In every field, we have well defined means and methods to fulfill our needs. Let us think about computer system. A common man believes that a computer can do anything and everything that he imagines. It is very difficult to make people realize that it is not really the computer but the man behind computer who does everything.

In this Internet world, a man feels that just by entering what he wants to search into the computers, he can get information as desired by him and believes computer does that search. A common man seldom understands that a man made procedure called search has done the entire job and the only support provided by the computer is the executioner and organized storage of information.

In the above instance, a designer of the information system should know what one frequently searches for. He/she should make a structured organization of all those details to store in memory of the computer. Based on the requirement, the right information is brought out. This is accomplished through a set of instructions created by the designer of the information system to search the right information matching the requirement of the users. This set of instructions is termed as program. It should be evident by now that it is not the computer, which generates automatically the program but it is the designer of the information system who has created this. So, a computer can do those things what a designer can programmed. This indicates the limit of a computer system.

Therefore, the program is executed to perform all the activities as desired by a user. This indicates that programming a computer is more important than the computer itself while solving a problem. Even at this stage, one should not quickly jump to conclusion that coding is programming. Coding is perhaps the last stage in the process of programming a computer. Programming involves various activities form the stage of conceiving the problem up to the stage of creating a model to solve the problem. The formal representation of this model as a sequence of instructions is called an algorithm and coded algorithm in a specific computer language is called a program.

One can now experience that the focus is shifted from computer to computer programming and then to creating an algorithm. This is algorithm design which is heart of problem solving in the field of computer.

1.3.1 Definition

An algorithm is named after the ninth century scholar **Abu Jafar Muhammad Ibn Musu Al-Khowarizmi** and simply defined as follows.

(1) An algorithm is a set of well-defined rules for carrying out calculation either by hand or on a machine.

(2) An algorithm is a finite step-by-step procedure to achieve a required result.

(3) An algorithm is a sequence of computational steps that transform the input into the output.

(4) An algorithm is a sequence of operations performed on input (data) that have to be organized in data structures.

(5) An algorithm is an abstraction of a program to be executed on a physical machine (model of Computation).

In more specific way "an algorithm can be classified as a finite sequence of instructions" which has the following basic properties:

- A number of quantities provided to an algorithm initially before the algorithm begins. These quantities are the inputs, which are processed by the algorithm.
- The processing rules specified in the algorithm must be precise and unambiguous and lead to a specific action.
- Each instruction must be sufficiently basic so that a person using paper and pencil can in principle carry it out in a finite time.
- The total time to carry out all the steps in the algorithm must be finite. As algorithms may contain instructions to repetitively carry out a group of instructions, this requirement implies that the total number of repetitions must be finite.

* An algorithm must have one or more outputs.
* Each step of an algorithm should be well-defined, it should not be ambiguous.

The most famous algorithm in history dates well before the time of the ancient Greeks and this is **Euclid's algorithm** for calculating the greatest common divisor of two integers.

1.3.2 Characteristics of an Algorithm

Let us try to present the scenario of a man brushing his own teeth (natural denture) step-by-step and say it is an algorithm.

Step 1. Take the brush
Step 2. Apply the paste
Step 3. Start brushing
Step 4. Rinse
Step 5. Wash
Step 6. Stop

If one goes through all these steps without being aware of the statement of the problem, he/she could possibly feel that this is the algorithm for cleaning a toilet. This is because of several ambiguities while comprehending every step. The step 1 may imply toothbrush, paintbrush, toilet brush, etc. Such an ambiguity should not be an instruction (step) of an algorithmic. Thus, every step should be made unambiguous. An unambiguous step is called definite instruction. Even if the step 2 is rewritten as apply the toothpaste, to eliminate ambiguities yet the conflicts such as, where to apply the toothpaste and where the source of the toothpaste is, need to be resolved. Hence, the act of applying the toothpaste is not mentioned. Although unambiguous, such unrealizable steps can not be included as an instruction (step) of an algorithmic as they are not effective.

The definiteness and effectiveness of an instruction implies the successful termination with desire output of that instruction. However the above two may not be sufficient to guarantee the termination of the algorithm. Therefore, while designing an algorithm care should be taken to provide a proper termination for algorithm.

Therefore, an algorithm can be defined as a sequence of definite and effective instructions, which terminates with the production of correct output from the given input.

In other words, viewed little more formally, an algorithm is a step-by-step formalization of a mapping function to map input set onto an output set.

Thus, every algorithm should have the following five characteristic features.

* Input
* Output
* Definiteness
* Effectiveness
* Termination

Algorithm Design and Analysis (ADA) is a branch of Computer Science that consists of designing and analyzing computer algorithms. The "**Design**" pertains to the description of algorithm at an abstract level by means of a pseudo language, and proof of correctness that is, the algorithm solves the given problem in all cases.

1.3.3 Algorithmic Notations

The pseudo code uses notations used in common languages like PASCAL and C language. For example, if-else structure, for loop structure, while loop structure, do-while loop structure. A conditional statement of an algorithm has the following form.

(1) If-Else Structure:

```
If (condition) then
   Block 1      //     Instruction(s)
Else
   Block 2      //     Instruction(s)
// End of Structure
```

Comments are given with the symbol // for better understanding of the instructions of an algorithm. It is good practice to give comments about the instructions of the algorithm. The above pseudo code executes Block 1 if the condition is true otherwise Block 2 is executed. A block is a set of instructions and it may contain one or more instructions. Sometimes, the If-Else structure is nested and appears as given below.

```
If (condition) then
   Block 1      // Instruction(s)
Else If (condition) then
   Block 2      //Instruction(s)
Else
   Block 3      //Instruction(s)
// End of Structure
```

(2) For loop Structure

We use for loop structure to repeat to certain Block (instructions) up to fixed number of times. There is a counter, which keeps track of the number of repetitions. The structure of **for** loop is given below.

```
For Counter = i to j
{Instruction 1, Instruction 2... Instruction n}
```

There are three things hidden in the for loop structure.

(a) Counter initialization

(b) Condition checking

(c) Increment of Counter

(3) While loop Structure

When we are not sure about the number of repetitions of a block then we use while loop structure as follows.

```
while (condition)
   {Instruction 1, Instruction 2... Instruction n}
```

(4) Do-while loop Structure

When we are not sure about the number of repetitions of a block (instructions) and want that the block could execute at least once then we use do-while loop structure as follows.

```
Do
{Instruction 1, Instruction 2... Instruction n} while (condition)
```

(5) Conditions and Concatenation of Conditions

We use conditions to make the number of execution of a block finite or infinite, some times as there is need. We use some logical operators like AND, OR, NOT, etc to concatenate the conditions. Conditions are expressions, which give the value TRUE (1) or FALSE (0). When we use the logical operators then we evaluate NOT, AND, and OR in sequence. If conditions are concatenated by AND operator then result is TRUE if and only all conditions are TRUE otherwise FALSE and in case of OR operator, result is TRUE if at least one of the conditions is TRUE and FALSE otherwise.

$C=C_1$ AND C_2 AND…AND C_n =TRUE if and only if $C_1=C_2=…=C_n$=TRUE, otherwise FALSE and $C=C_1$ OR C_2 OR…OR C_n =TRUE if at least one the C_1, C_2,…,C_n is TRUE, otherwise FALSE. The NOT operator reverses the value of the condition. If C_1 is TRUE then NOT C_1 is FALSE.

For example, consider the following conditions and show their values after concatenation.

Condition	Value
C_1	1
C_2	1
C_3	0

(a) $C_4=C_1$ AND C_2
(b) $C_5=C_2$ AND C_3
(c) $C_6=C_1$ AND NOT C_3

Solution

(a) C_4= 1 AND 1=1
(b) C_5=1 AND 0=0
(c) C_6=1 AND NOT 0= 1 AND 1=1

The fundamental knowledge necessary to solve problems using a computer is the notation of an algorithm. For example, suppose we have an array **DATA** of numerical values with size **N** in memory. We want to find the location **K** and the value **MAX** of the largest element of **DATA**. An algorithm for this problem can be constructed as illustrated in Figure 1.3.

The execution of an algorithm begins at **Step1** and continues from there in sequential order unless the result of a condition tested or an unconditional transfer specifies otherwise. In the algorithm given next, **Step 1** is executed first if the array **DATA** is empty, the algorithm terminates; otherwise **Step 2** is performed. In this step, **MAX** is initialized to the value of **DATA [I].** Firstly **I** is 1 and variable **I** is incremented by 1. **Step 3** leads to termination of this algorithm if we have already tested the last element of the array **DATA**; otherwise **Step 4** is performed. In this step, the value of **MAX** is compared with the value of next element of the array **DATA.** If **MAX** is less than the next element, **MAX** is assigned this new value (by calling Step 2). If the test fails, no reassignment takes place. The completion of **Step 4** is followed by **Step 5** where control returns to the **Step2** when we assign new value to **MAX** and increment the subscript by 1.

It is very much advisable to the readers that before writing a program design an algorithm for a problem. Do not try hit and trial method. Sometimes it may be costly and may result into damaging the system. Keep in mid that C language is middle-level language. So, any bad instruction can damage the system. Designing an algorithm is simple for any problem when we have some solution for that. Derive the solution step by step considering the flow of processing. If some steps are missing or misplaced then result will be undesirable.

Step 1: [Initialization]
I = 1
K = 1
Step 2: [Increment counter]
MAX = DATA [I]
I = I + 1
Step 3: [Test counter]
If I > N then

Write K, MAX and Exit

Step 4: [Compare and update]

If MAX < DATA [I] then

K = I

Step 5: Go to Step 2:

1.4 Flow-Charts

People always think about the better one and keep on trying. Similar think is true for flowchart. In the previous section we have discussed about the algorithm. An algorithm provides solution for some specific problem in well-defined manner, i.e., step by step processing. Here we have better representation of steps of an algorithm in pictorial manner. Pictorial representation is very much readable and readers can understand the things quickly.

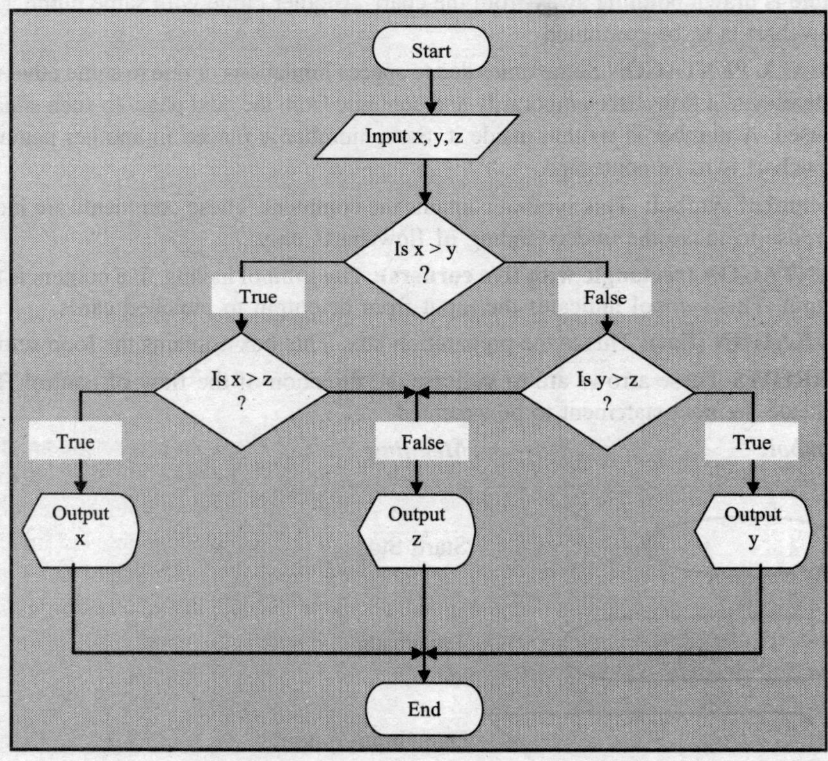

Flowchart is the pictorial representation of the steps involved in solving a problem. It depicts pictorial sequence in which instructions are carried out in an algorithm. Flowchart is used not only as an *aid* in developing algorithms but also to document algorithms. It is the next step towards problem solving. Usually the flowcharts are primarily used as an aid in formulating, writing and understanding the programs. For easy visual recognition, the standard convention is to use only pre-decided and accepted specific symbol for a particular operation only so that every computer professional interprets the flowcharts in the same manner. For example, suppose three numbers are given and we have to find out the largest one. Let **x, y** and **z** are three numbers. Algorithm can be constructed such as:

- Compare **x** with **y** if **x** is larger. Then compare it with **z.** If **x** is found larger than **z** then **x** is the largest; otherwise **z** is the largest.
- If in the first step **x** is smaller than or equal to **y** then **y** is compared with **z.** if **y** is larger than **z** then it is the largest number else **z** is the largest.

This algorithm can be represented by the flowchart shown here. Different symbols used in flowchart are shown next.

Now we define in detail the meaning and significance of each of these symbols. Oval is used for two purposes, to define the starting (START or BEGIN) point of flowchart and to define the ending point (END) of flowchart.

PARALLELOGRAM: Parallelogram is used for input-output. This is the input symbol to indicate the input from standard input or output to standard output device.

RECTANGLE The rectangle is used to indicate the processing. Inside, this processing box statements of processing are specified.

DIAMOND The diamond shaped box is decision box. This has one entry point. There will be at least two exit points depending upon the decision taken inside the symbol. When a condition is tested, if the condition is true, the path for "yes" is followed. If the condition is false, the path for "no" is followed.

CIRCLE- If flowchart is discontinued at some point and continued again at another place, the connector symbol is used. It is a circle with a number written inside it. If a flowchart is discontinued at some point, a circle is drawn pointing away from the chart. Another circle with same number inside it is placed where the flowchart is to be continued.

SMALL PENTAGON Some times due to spaces limitations or due to some other reasons, it becomes necessary to terminate a flowchart temporarily and continue from the next page. In such situations this off page connector is used. A number is written inside it. Same number is placed in another pentagon on next page where the flowchart is to be continued.

Comment symbol: This symbol contains the comment. These comments are included for the documentation purpose to make the understanding of flowcharts easy.

PENTAGON (rectangle with five corners): The symbol having five corners is used for indicating the input-output. This symbol indicates the input from or output to punched cards.

HEXAGON (flat): This is the preparation box. This box contains the loop setting statement, *i.e.*

ARROWS These arrows are to indicate the direction of the flow of control. This means these statements indicate the next statement to be executed.

Symbol	***Meaning***
	Start, Stop
	Terminator
	Data Input/output
	Processing Program Instructions
	Processing Program Instructions
	Alternate Process/ Keying
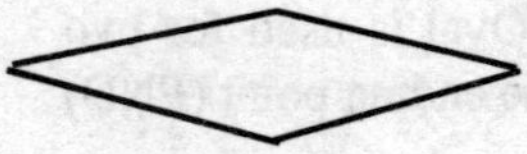	Decision Box

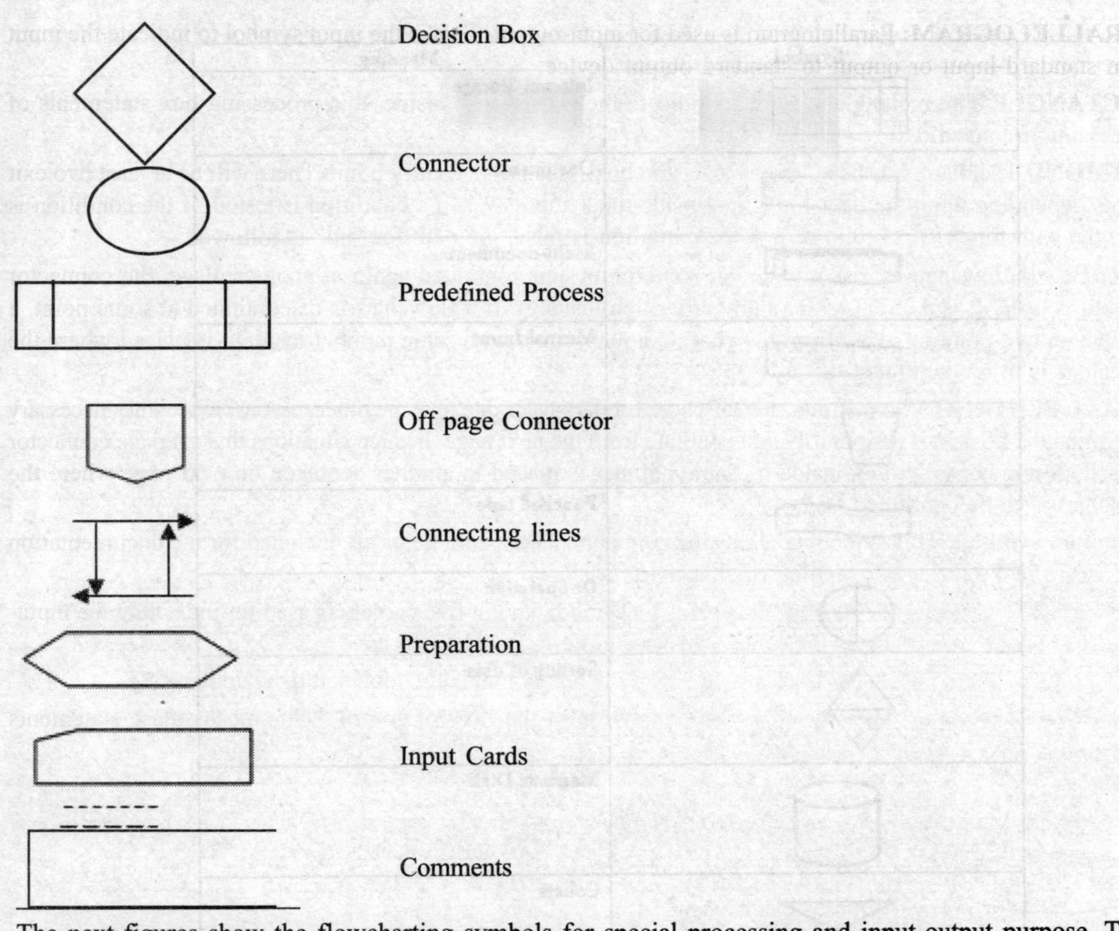

The next figures show the flowcharting symbols for special processing and input-output purpose. These symbols are rarely used in flowcharting.

1.4.1 Advantages of flowcharts

1. Each symbol of flowchart denotes an instruction in a program.
2. Since flowchart is the pictorial representation of the program steps so it becomes easy to understand the problem, as it is easy to explain any thing with the help of pictures instead of printed words.
3. It gives the clear picture of flow of data in any program. Before coding begins, the flowchart assists the programmer to determine the type of logic control to be used in a program.
4. It is easy to detect an error with the help of flowchart.
5. It can be compared in future that if all the steps have been included or not.
6. Flowchart serves as a guiding document for program writing or coding.

1.4.2 Conventions of flowcharts

1. Each symbol of flowchart denotes a particular type of operation.
2. A note is written inside each symbol to indicate the specific function to be performed.
3. Flowcharts are read from top to bottom and left to right.
4. Sequence of operations is performed until a terminate symbol designates the end of the run.

Symbol	Meaning
	Internal Storage
	Documents
	Multi-document
	Manual Input
	Manual Operation
	Punched tape
	Or operation
	Sorting of data
	Magnetic Disk
	Collate
	Extract

5. Crossed lines do not imply any logical relationship.
6. Where two incoming lines join one outgoing line, they should not join at the same point.
7. Annotation should be included with in the symbol to process decision file and input, output giving an indication of the action decision file or document used.
8. Identification of the symbols on a flowchart is aided by numbering the most left top symbols sequentially from 1, so that each symbol can be referred uniquely. Connectors and terminators need to be numbered.
9. Flowcharts are not case-sensitive, so instructions inside the symbols can be written in any case.

1.4.3 Limitations of flowcharts

1. Drawing of flowcharts is a very time consuming process and laborious too especially for large complex problems.

Symbol	Meaning
	Merge two data
	Storage data/ online Storage
	Delay
	Sequential Access Storage/Magnetic Disk
	Summing Junction
	Direct Access Storage
	Display

2. Redrawing of flowcharts is even more difficult and time consuming. It is very difficult to include any new step in the existing flowchart. Only redrawing of the flowchart is the only solution.
3. There are no standards which specify the detail that should be included in any flowchart.
4. If an algorithm has complex branches and loops, flowcharts become very difficult to draw.
5. Some times flowcharts could not be in as detail as desired.

Example: Write an algorithm for the problem of finding the roots of a quadratic equation $ax^2 + bx + c = 0$**.**

Using the formula $\frac{-b \pm \sqrt{b^2 - 4ac}}{2a}$ **or** $\frac{-b \pm \sqrt{D}}{2a}$ **where** $D = b^2 - 4ac$ **. Draw flowchart for this algorithm**

Answer: Algorithm is as follows:

1. Start
2. Read the numeric values for a, b, and c.
3. Calculate the value of D using the formula .
4. if D> 0
   - (a) Calculate one root using the formula .
   - (b) Calculate another root using the formula
   - (c) Display "roots are real and distinct".
   - (d) Display "Root 1 = ", .
   - (e) Display "Root 2 = ",

(f) Exit

5. If D=0, then
   (a) Calculate one root using the formula.
   (b) Display "roots are real and equal".
   (c) Display "Root 1 = ", .
   (d) Display "Root 2 = ",
   (e) Exit
6. If D=0, then
   (a) Calculate one term using the formula .
   (b) Calculate another term using the formula or
   (c) Display "roots are imaginary".
   (d) Display "Root 1 = ", +i.
   (e) Display "Root 2 = ", +i.
   (f) Exit
7. Stop

Details of the flowchart are shown in the next figure.

Flowcharts are designed to facilitate encoding. Following section expresses the representation of different mathematical and logical expressions in flowcharts.

1.4.4 Expressions in flowcharts

This section explains how different type of expressions are formed and expressed in flowcharts. These expressions could be mathematical as well as logical. Also how to initialize the memory location or variables or symbols is another consideration. How to input feed in the values and what is the way of printing or displaying the output.

In flowcharting the memory locations are given a symbolic name and through out the flowchart these symbolic names are used to represent various quantities and figures. Same is done in programs. These symbolic names are known as variables also. One variable can hold one value at a time. As many quantities will be required as input or as temporary processing elements or as output in the flowchart as much will be the variables in that variable.

1.4.4.1 Addition

Addition operation is represented using the symbol (+). Suppose A and B are two memory locations. Add the contents of location A & location B and place the result of this addition in location either A & B or in a new memory location say C. We write these steps while drawing the flowchart as,

C = A + B; Adds the contents of location A & location B and put result in a memory location C.

A = A + B; Adds the contents of A & B and result is stored back to location A.

B = A + B; contents of locations A & B are added and result is stored back to location B.

1.4.4.2 Subtraction

Subtraction operation is represented using the symbol (-). Suppose A and B are two memory locations. Suppose some operations are to be performed on, the contents of there locations. Say, subtract the contents of B from the contents of location A and store the result in B. Then subtract the contents of A from B and store the result in new location C. After that subtract the contents of B from A and store the result in A. Then these will be written in form of mathematical expressions as:

B = A - B; Subtracts the contents of location B from location A and put result back in location B.

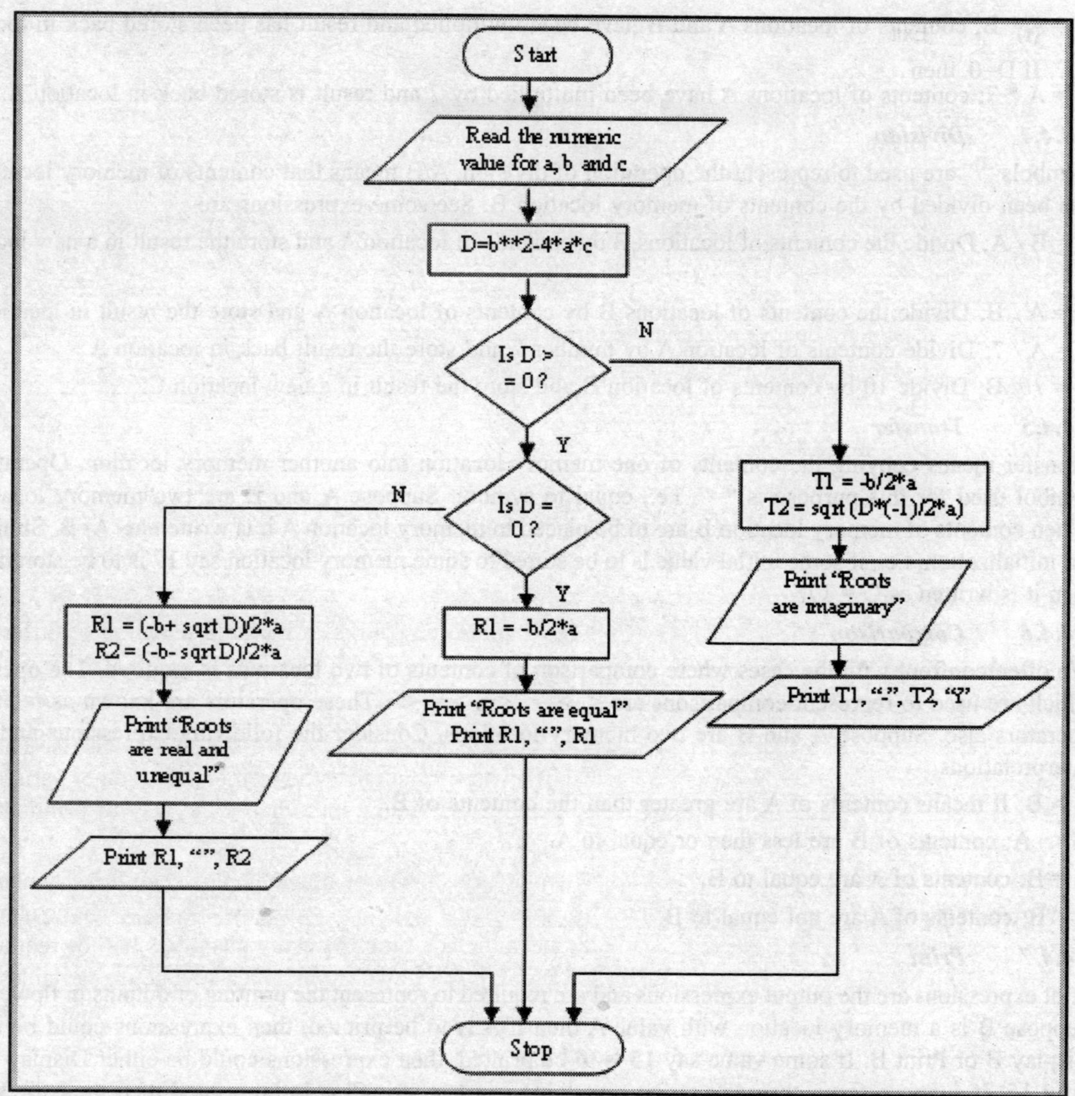

C = B - A; Subtracts the contents of location A from contents of location B and store the result in a new location C.

A = A - B; Subtracts the contents of location B from location A and put result back in location A.

1.4.4.3 Multiplication

Multiplication operation is represented using asterisk (*). Suppose A and B are two memory locations. Now multiply the contents of both A and B and store the result at some new location say C. See how these operations can be expressed.

C = A * B; contents of locations A and B have been multiplied and result has been stored in a new location C.

C = B * A; contents of locations B and A have been multiplied and result has been stored in a new location C.

A = A * B; contents of locations A and B have been multiplied and result has been stored back in location A.

A = A * 7; contents of locations A have been multiplied by 7 and result is stored back in location A.

1.4.4.4 Division

Symbols "/" are used to represent the operation of division. A/B means that contents of memory location A has been divided by the contents of memory location B. See some expressions are

C = B / A; Divide the contents of locations B by contents of location A and store the result in a new location C.

A = A / B; Divide the contents of locations B by contents of location A and store the result in location C.

A = A / 7; Divide contents of location A by number 7 and store the result back in location A.

C = *10/* B; Divide 10 by contents of location B and store the result in a new location C.

1.4.4.5 Transfer

Transfer means copying the contents of one memory location into another memory location. Operator or symbol used for this purpose is "=", i.e., equal to symbol. Suppose A and B are two memory locations. When contents of memory location B are to be placed in memory location A it is written as- A=B. Similarly, for initialization, i.e., if some initial value is to be stored to some memory location say 17 is to be stored at C, then it is written as C = 17.

1.4.4.6 Comparison

We often confront with the cases where comparison of contents of two locations is required. The operators which are used to represent comparisons are <, >, =, <=, >=, <>. These operators are known as relational operators also. Suppose A and B are two memory locations. Consider the following expressions and their interpretations.

A > B; It means contents of A are greater than the contents of B.

B <= A; contents of B are less than or equal to A.

A = B; contents of A are equal to B.

A "'B; contents of A are not equal to B.

1.4.4.7 Print

Print expressions are the output expressions and are required to represent the printing of outputs in flowcharts. Suppose B is a memory location with value A then if A is to be printed, then expressions could be either Display B or Print B. If some value say 15 is to be printed, then expressions could be either Display 15 or Print 15. If suppose some character string says "this is a test string" is to be printed then the expressions could be either Display "this is a test string" or print "this is a test string".

1.4.4.8 Feed

Feeding expressions are the input expressions, i.e., expressions showing the input of values to some locations. If value is to be read into the memory location say B, then expressions could be

Input B or Read B or Read the value of B.

All of the three above written statements will mean that enter some value for memory location B. .

Example: Consider the following problem: Problem is to determine the highest marks obtained by the students in an Examination and the roll no. of the student securing the highest marks. (Assume that only one student has got the highest marks). Write the necessary steps for writing the program to solve the problem.

Answer: Detailed Problem Statement is

We start with the first step of solving this problem that is its detailed statement. We have to write a program which will determine the highest marks obtained by the students in B. Tech 1st year examination.

The input to the programs will be

1. The roll number of a student.
2. The marks obtained by a student.

This process of inputting their roll numbers and marks obtained will be repeated for all the students of the class.

The output to be received from the program is

1. The name of that student who secured the highest marks
2. His/her percentage in class.

The algorithm of problem is

1. Start
2. Read the roll number and marks of number 1 student. This is the highest marks found so far as marks of only one student have been read.
3. Is there any more students in the class?
4. If yes, then go to step 5. If not, then go to step 8.
5. Read next roll number and its marks. Compare the marks of this student (roll no.) previous roll number with the highest marks found so far.
6. If marks read in step V is greater than the highest marks found so far, then erase the previously noted highest marks, and replace it by the marks read in step 5. Also replace the roll number with the new roll number. In this situation other than this, that is, if marks of step 5 are less than the highest marks, then do nothing.
7. Repeat the step 3 thru 6 till all the roll numbers of class have been entered.
8. Calculate the percentage.
9. Print the roll number of the student with highest marks and percentage of the student.
10. Stop.

Shown in figure here is the flowchart for this problem. In this we have used few symbols to represent the memory locations for storing the data. These symbols and their meaning and use are

ROLLNO	store the roll no of a student
MARKS	store the marks of that student
MAXMARKS	store the maximum marks
MAXROLLNO	store the roll no of student who secured maximum marks

All the marks and roll numbers will be input at these locations one by one overwriting the previous one.

1.4.5 Types of logic used in flowchart

There are different logic structures available which are used in the flowchart to represent any construct for iterations of programming language. These constructs are

1. Sequence
2. Selection
3. Iteration

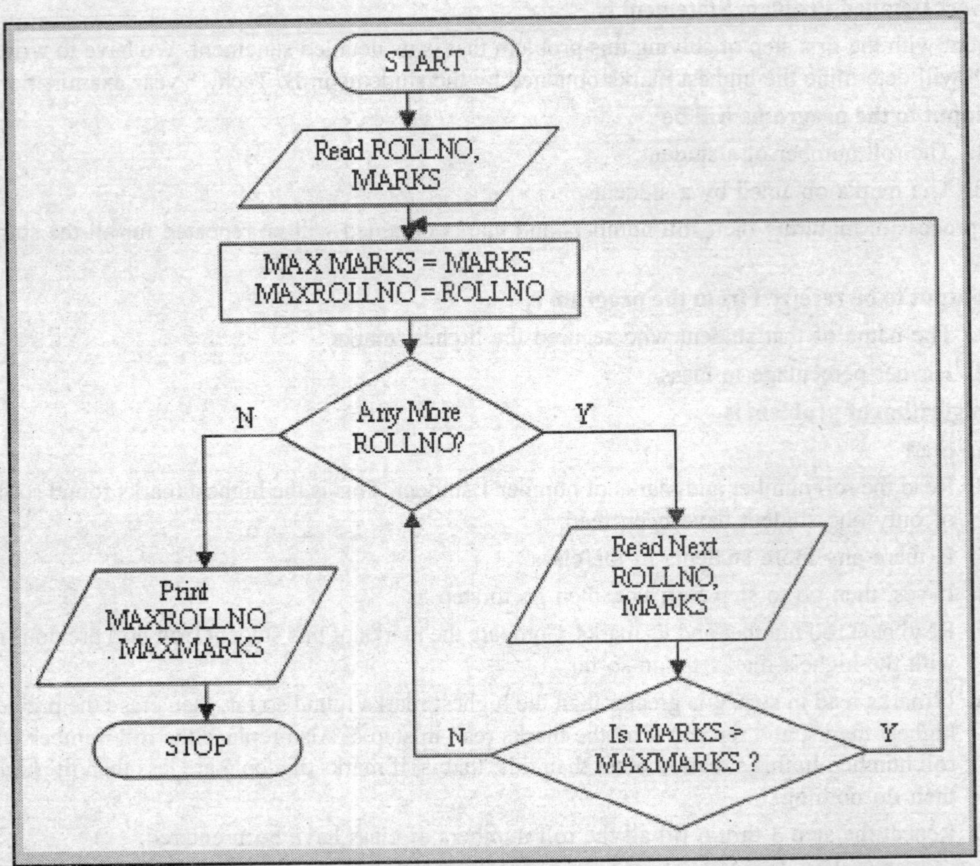

Example 1.7: (i) Prepare the flowchart to calculate the simple interest for the given amount (P) for the given number of years (N) using the formula PNR/100 taking the rate of interest R=13% if P < 10,000 and R = 14% if P >= 10,000.

(ii) Modify the above flowchart to calculate and print the new amount also.

Answer: **(i)** See the figure shown below.

(ii) We introduce one more arithmetic operation P = P+SI in processing box just before the **Print** box and modify the print expression of **Print** box as **"Print 51, POI** (Figure on the next page).

1.5 Programming Languages

A language is a system of communication. In order to communicate with each other, humans need languages like English, Hindi, etc. In the same manner, for communicating with the computer, we use computer language called programming language. A programming language consists of all the symbols, characters and usage rules that permit people to communicate with computers. Learning to program requires learning all these symbols and rules.

There are many programming languages available and each one has its symbols, character set and syntax but each language has an instruction set that permits those familiar operations to be performed.

We know that the computer can neither think nor can make any decision on its own. It needs instructions to understand what to do. A program is a set of logically related instructions that are arranged in a sequence that guides the computer to solve a problem.

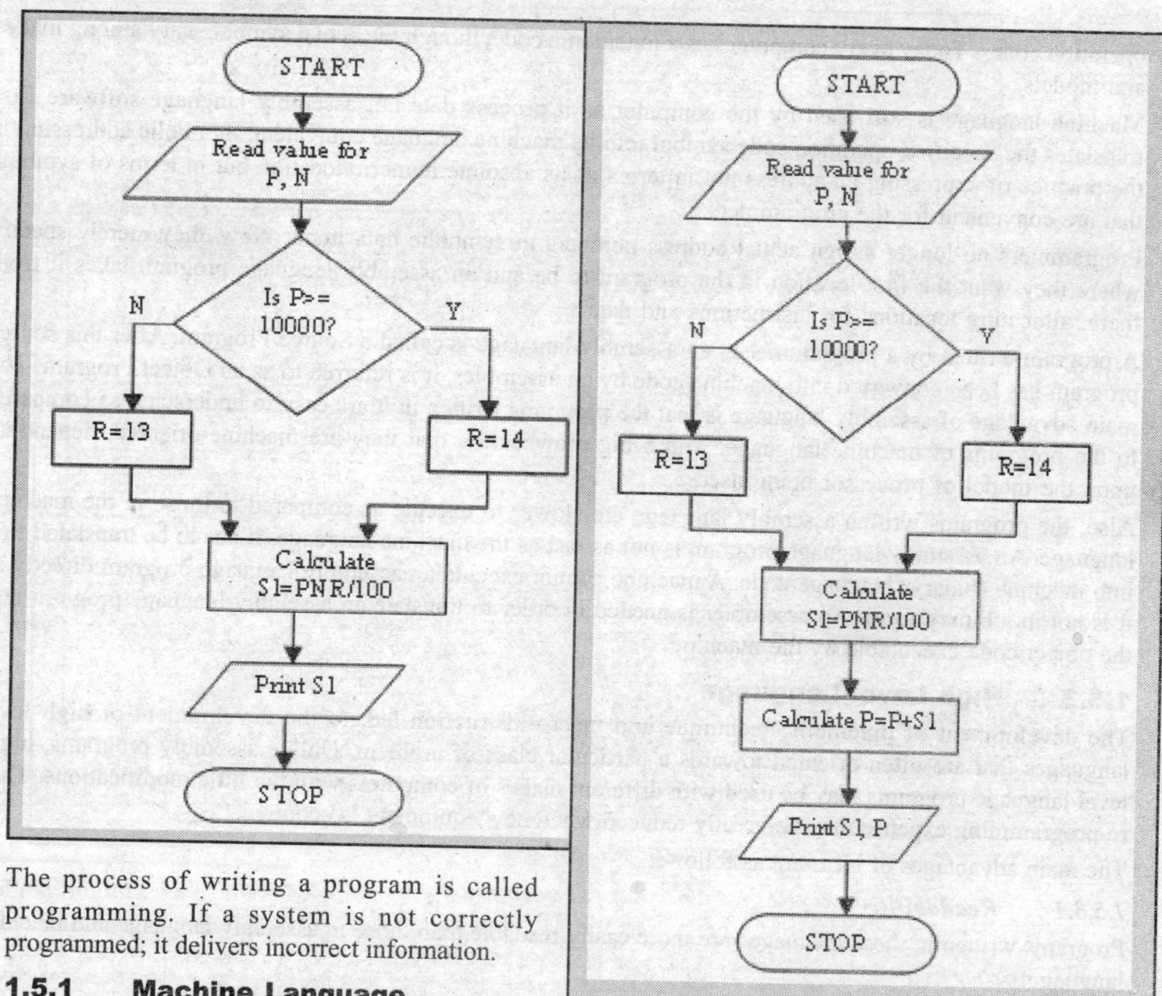

The process of writing a program is called programming. If a system is not correctly programmed; it delivers incorrect information.

1.5.1 Machine Language

This is a sequence of instructions written in the form of binary numbers consisting of 1s and 0s to which the computer responds directly. A machine language would have two parts.

The first part is the command or an operation that tells the computer what functions are to be performed. The second part of the instruction is the operand that tells the computer where to find or store the data on which the desired operation is to be performed.

The machine language is the only one that computer can understand directly. In the earlier computers programmers had to translate instructions directly into machine language from the computers understood. This task was very difficult and very few programmers could do this job. So, this language was very difficult to understand.

But the main advantage of this language is that it is faster in execution as the computer directly starts executing it.

1.5.2 Assembly Language

To ease the burden of the programmer, mnemonic operation codes and symbolic addresses were developed during the early 1950s. The mnemonic refers to a memory aid. One of the first steps for improving the program preparation process was to substitute letter, symbols and mnemonics for the mnemonic machine-language operation codes. Today every computer has a mnemonic code, though the actual symbols vary among makes and models.

Machine language is still used by the computer as it process data but assembly language software first translates the specified operation code symbol into its machine language equivalent. Symbolic addressing is the practice of expressing an address not in terms of its absolute numeric location but in terms of symbols that are convenient for the programmers.

Programmers no longer assign actual address numbers to symbolic data items. Now, they merely specify where they want the first location in the program to be and an assembly language program takes it from there, allocating locations for instructions and data.

A program written by a programmer in an assembly language is called a Source Program. After this source program has been converted into machine code by an assembler, it is referred to as an Object Program. The main advantage of assembly language is that the programs written in it are easy to understand as compared to the programs of machine language. And a big drawback is that they are machine-oriented, depending upon the model of processor being used.

Also, the programs written assembly language are slower to execute as compared to those in the machine language. An assembly language program is not as fast as the machine language. It has to be translated first into machine (binary) language code. A machine cannot execute an assembly language program directly as it is not in a binary form. An assembler is needed in order to translate an assembly language program into the object code executable by the machine.

1.5.3 High Level Language

The development of mnemonic technique and macro-instruction led, to the development of high level languages that are often oriented towards a particular class of problem. Unlike assembly programs, high-level language programs may be used with different makes of computers with the little modifications. Thus re-programming expense may be greatly reduced when new equipment is acquired.

The main advantages of HLL are as follows:

1.5.3.1 Readability

Programs written in these languages are more easily readable than those in assembly language and machine language.

1.5.3.2 Portability

Programs could be run on different machines with little or no changes.

1.5.3.3 Easy debugging

Errors are easy to find and remove.

1.5.3.4 Easy software development

Software could easily be developed using the HLL.

The time and cost of creating machine and assembly languages was quite high. And this was the prime motivation for the development of high level languages.

1.5.3.5 Examples of HLL

There are many High Level Languages available today. The programmer chooses the particular language according to his choice and need of the application. For example, COBOL is best suited for business processing while FORTRAN is suitable for scientific operations.

Some of the programming languages with their main characteristics have been described as follows:

LOGO: LOGO was designed by Seymour Papert who was a teacher in the USA. He designed this language so that the children could learn computers by drawing pictures. Most of its commands enable us to draw pictures. This is one of the reasons why LOGO is called a graphic language. The usage of LOGO is based on a friendly little animal called the TURTLE. It is the name given to the LOGO cursor. It looks like a small triangle. The TURTLE has a head which is the upper tip of the triangle. It can be turned around its center in all direction and it can also move forward and backward.

FORTRAN: It is the short form for FORmula TRANslation. As the name suggests it is used extensively in numeric data types such as an integer, real, float and complex. It was the only language developed by the IBM in 1957. Since then, it has been modified into many versions and the latest version FORTRAN 99, is currently available in the markets. The original work on FORTRAN was started in 1954. As the result of this effort, FORTRAN was introduced in 1957 for IBM 704 computer. FORTRAN is very useful for carrying out scientific and mathematical computations.

The main feature of FORTRAN is very useful for carrying out scientific and mathematical computations. The main feature of FORTRAN is that it can handle the complex numbers very easily. But the syntax of FORTRAN is very rigid. FORTRAN language is not suitable for a large amount of data. But, it is not suitable for a large amount of data. So, it is not used for business programming applications.

COBOL: COBOL stands for Common Business Oriented Language and is one of the popular languages used for business applications. The language has provisions that make computerization of business data processing procedures relatively easy. COBOL is suitable for processing large volumes of data and several reports can generate using COBOL based on the stored data. COBOL programs are characterized by their easy readability due to their verbose syntax and good data organizations ad file handling.

COBOL is an English like language with instruction coded using self-documenting English words rather than short abbreviation. Also, the rules of programming in COBOL conform to many of the rules for writing. Due to its similarity with English, COBOL programs are easy to read and write.

Thus people in business, who rely on computer output but have no computer expertise, can understand the programs written in COBOL. That is why COBOL is called a self-documenting language which is self-explanatory. COBOL was initially developed in 1959 by a group called the CODASYL (Conference On DAta SYstems Languages) Committee with the objectives of developing a standard business-oriented language for which all major manufacturers would provide compilers.

The American National Standards Institute (ANSI) then formed an NASO COBOL committee to develop more satisfactory standards for the language. This led to the availability of ANSI COBOL in 1969. This standard was, however, modified and finally, it approved a standard for COBOL in 1985 and is it is also referred to as COBOL 85.

BASIC: Basic stands for Beginners' All-Purpose Symbolic Instruction Code. It is the most popular computer programming language. He main characteristic of BASIC is to handle both mathematical and business problems; this language was developed specifically for the time-sharing environment but can so be used as a standard programming language in batch-processing environment. This language is easy to understand. But the main problem in BASIC is that most versions of this language do not support indexed files.

PROLOG: Prolog stands for PROgramming in LOGic. Prolog was developed in France in 1973. Prolog is very popular in Japan where it is adopted as the official programming language for the fifth generation computers.

As the name suggests, PROLOG lays stress on the usage of logic to solve problems. PROLOG is basically known as a theorem-providing system, using a formal logic technique known as predicate calculus to prove the truth of propositions from a set of axioms.

PROLOG is a conventional language. It waits for us to type in facts and rules that are related to the program that we want to solve. Then, if we ask the right type of questions, PROLOG would work out and display it on the screen.

So, we can say that the computer programming in PROLOG consists of the following steps:

- Declaring some facts about objects and their relationship.
- Defining some rules about objects and relationship.
- Assuming questions about objects and their relationship.

PASCAL: Pascal is a high Level Language that was developed by the Professor Nickalus Wirth at Eidgenossisehe Technisehe Houcheshule (ETH) in Zurich, Switzerland. The first report on the language appeared in the literature in 1971 and revised reports, describing the language with its improvements, appeared in 1972 and 1973. The first Pascal Reference Manual for Pascal programming was produced in 1974.

Pascal is a general-purpose language that can be used for a wide range of numeric and non numeric applications. The primary objectives behind the development of Pascal were as follows:

- The language should be efficient to implement and easy to execute on modern computers.
- The language should be used for teaching the important concept of computer programming.
- The language should be used for the development of well-structured and well organized programs.

The aforementioned features make Pascal a very good introductory programming language.

C: It is a general-purpose structured programming language. C is characterized by the ability to write very concise source programs. The compiler of C is commonly available for the computers of all sizes. The compilers are usually compact and they generate object programs that are small and highly efficient as compared to the programs written in any other language. The programs written in the C language are high portable; the program written for one computer with very few changes can run on another computer. The reason for this is that C relegates most computer-dependent features in its library functions. Thus every version of C is accomplished by its own set to library functions.

Dennis Ritchie developed C in 1970s at Bell Telephone laboratories. It was the modified versions of two earlier languages, called BCPL and B, which were also developed at Bell Laboratories.

C++: C++ is an object-oriented programming language. As software systems develop into more powerful instruments, they also become more complex. Every new release of a word processor, a database, or a spreadsheet program is longer than the previous one and contains more features. This increasing size and complexity makes it difficult to manage the software development process. As programmers struggle to deal with this complexity, new ideas emerge. One collection of these ideas is based on a philosophy called object-oriented programming.

While object-oriented programs can be written in languages such as C or BASIC, these languages lack some vital features. For example, C provides no mechanism to hide variables from unauthorized access. C also does not enable one class to be declared as a subclass of another. These and other features were added to the C language by Dr. Bjarne Stroustrup at AT &T's Bell Labs in the early 1980s. He called this new language C++. There is no standard definition for the C++ language. At any given time, it is classified into three states-called traditional C++, contemporary C++ and future C++. Traditional C++ is the language as it had existed in release in AT & T versions and which is supported by all the major compilers. Contemporary C++ consists of traditional C++ with some new features which are approved by e committee but implemented by only a few compilers. Future C++ is the language which is under discussion in the committee with new features that have been approved but not yet implemented.

1.6 Compilation

Different type of translators available are: Assembler, Compilers and Interpreters.

1.6.1. Assembler

An assembler is used to convert the program written in assembly language into machine language. Assembly language is much easier to remember as compare to machine language. As machine language use binary (0's and 1's) instruction to write a program whereas assembly language use mnemonic (i.e., meaningful names) which makes assembly language much more easier than machine language.

But computer still understands machine language. So as we need assembler to translate program written in assembly language into the machine code or object code.

1.6.2. Compilers and Interpreter

Compiler: A compiler translates a source program that is usually written in a high level language by a programmer into machine language as a whole. The compiler is capable of replacing single source program statement with a series of machine-language instructions or with a subroutine. For each high level language, the machine requires a separate compiler. A compiler creates a unique object program, i.e., when a source program is compiles, there is not need of that source program because output can be obtained by executing that object program.

Since a high level source program must be translate first into the form of machine can understand, this is done by a software called Compiler which takes the source code as input and produces as output that machine language code of the machine on which it is to be executed. During the process of translation, the compiler reads the source programs statement-wise and checks the syntax (grammatical) errors. Of there is any error, the computer generates a printout of the errors it has detected. This action is known as Diagnostics. The compiler and interpreter have different approaches to translation. The following table lists the differences between a compiler and an interpreter.

Interpreter: Interpreter translates each source program statement into a sequence of machine instructions and executes these machine instructions before translating the next source language statement. Interpreters are also unique for each high level language such as a compiler. Basically, the functions of the compiler and interpreter are the same; the only difference is that compiler provides a separate object program but the interpreter does not. At the time of using interpreter every time the source program is needed. Another difference is that interpreter translates the source program line wise, i.e., it would not execute the next line unless the first one has no error.

Compiler Vs. Interpreter

Compiler	Interpreter
1. Scans the entire program first and translates it into machine code.	1. Translates the program line by line.
2. Converts the entire program to machine code; when all the syntax errors are removed, execution takes place.	2. Each time the program is executed; every line is checked for syntax error and then converted to equivalent machine code.
3. Slow for debugging (removal of mistakes from a program)	3. Good for fast debugging.
4. Execution time is less.	4. Execution time is more.

1.7 Linking and Loading

Usally a longer program is divided into a number of smaller subprograms called modules. It is easier to de velop, test and debug smaller programs. A linker is a program that links (combines) smaller programs to form a single program. While developing a program, subroutines are frequently used. The subroutines are stored in a library file. The linker also links subroutines with main program. The linker links machine codes of the programs. Therefore, it accepts user's programs after editor has editied the program and compiler has produced machine codes of the program. The process is called linking.

1.7.1 Loader

The loader is a program that loads machine cods of a program into he system memory. It accepts programs with in absoute or relocatable format. If a program is in absolute format (*i.e.*, the acutal addresses of the instructions and data are supplied by the programmer), the loader simply loads the program into the system memory. If a program is in relocatable format, the locator assisgns specific addresses to each instruction and data before the loader loads the program into memory. The process performed by the loader is known as loading.

1.8 Testing and Debugging

When the program has been written, it has to be tested. For testing it may be possible that the original data is not available. So you have to make use of the test data which may not contain all the possible options which may be there in the original data. So while testing one has to prepare a data which has all the possible errors which one can expect. Testing of the program can be done in the following steps:

1. Choosing input data whose result (output) is for testing.
2. Testing of modules or submodules.
3. Choose input data which can activate all parts of the program so that any deficiency in any of the parts be judged correctly.
4. Testing whatever program can produce suitable error-message so that the error may be located easily in any of the parts.

1.8.1 Debugging

Checking the program for errors and correcting them is called Debugging. It is not that you will be able to write a program which runs in the first go. You may need to run the program a number of times to find out the various types of errors and correcting them. These errors may occur in the beginning, in the middle or even at the end of the execution. Or even the results produced may have some errors in it. These errors can happen due to the following:

1. Incorrect coding
2. Faults in design
3. Run time errors.
4. Designing errors

These errors may occur together in a program or one at a time. One has to run the program to find out the type of errors. There are various tools available which help you in debugging the program. They are:

Simulators: A simulator is a computer program that simulates the execution of programs on another computer.

Logic analyzers: logic analyzer is a test instrument that is the digital bus oriented version of the oscilloscope. It detects the states of digital signals during each clock cycle and stores them in the memory. It then displays the information on a CRT, much as an oscilloscope does.

Breakpoints: A breakpoint is a place in a program at which execution can be halted, in order to examine the current contents of registers, memory locations and I/O ports.

Trace routines: A trace is a program that prints information concerning the status of the processor at specified intervals. Most simulator programs and some microcomputer development systems have trace facilities.

Memory dumps: A memory dump is a listing of the current contents of a section of the memory. Most simulator programs, microcomputer development systems and monitors can produce memory dumps.

Software interrupts: The software interrupts or trap instruction is frequently used for debugging purposes. The instruction usually saves the current value of the program counter and then branches to a specified memory location.

That memory location can be the starting point of a debugging program that lists of displays status information – breakpoints may be inserted with trap instructions.

Each program has its own unique errors. Nevertheless, some errors are sufficiently common to deserve mention. They include:

1. Failure to initialize variables, particularly counters and pointers. Registers, flags and memory locations should not be assumed to contain zero at the start of the program.
2. Failure to handle trivial cases, such as an array or table with no elements or only one element.
3. Inverting conditions, such as jumping on zero instead of on not zero.
4. Reversing the order of operands, such as moving X to Y when Y to X was meant.
5. Jumping on conditions that have been changed, since they were set to the desired values.
6. Failure to handle fall-through conditions, such as an entry that is never found in a table or a condition that is never met. Such a failure can cause an endless loop.
7. Confusing addresses and values. Memory location 100 does not necessarily contain the number 100.
8. Confusing numbers and characters. ASCII zero or EBCDIC zero is not the same as number zero.
9. Ignoring the direction of noncumulative operations.
10. Ignoring overflow when doing signed arithmetic.

1.8.2 Syntax Errors

Every language whether English, Hindi or otherwise has fixed grammatical rules and these are called syntax rules. Violation of any grammatical rules can cause syntax errors. Similary each programming language has its own fixed rules and syntaxes which have to used properly. If not used in the way they are required to, the syntax error would occur. Syntax errors are also called as compilation errors.

Some common reasons for the syntax errors.

1. Wrong use of statements like, if-else, while, do-while, for.
2. Wrong use of variables and constants or use of those variables which have not been declared in the program.
3. Missing semi-colon.
4. Wrong punctuation.
5. Misspelt keywords.
6. Missing braces.

For example, you may have used two mathematical expressions together in a statement or may have forgotton to add semi colon (;) at the end of the statement. These errors can be detected with the help of compilers which tell the programmer to use the appropriate word in place of wrong usuage.

1.8.3 Run-Time Errors

These errors occur only when the program is run. So you may call them execution errors. The common Run-Time errors are as shown below:

- Dividing a number of zero
- Array indices out of bounds
- Arithmetical Errors like square root of negative number
- Range Errors
- Other Input Errors

1.8.4 Logical Errors

After removing run time errors and syntax errors, we can execute the program to obtain the result. If the results obtained are correct then it is a scuccessful programming. But sometimes the program does not produce the desired results even if there is no run time or syntax error. The errors which occur at this stage are called logical errors. The computer is not capable of recognizing these errors because it cannot present logic on its own. These are hidden errors made by the programmer and the computer flashes no error message for these mistakes.

1.8.5 Methods of Correcting Logical Errors

Some ways to locate and correc logical errors are briefly described below:

1. One approach is to study the source code producing the incorrect results and try to determine the cause of the problem.
2. Put several print or write statements in the program that indicate the values of intermediate computations. Once the errors have been found and corrected, such print or write statements are removed from the program.
3. Use of tracing routines which are software tools provided to the programmer to help in debugging, the program logic. Tracing routines or debug packages assist the programmer in the following logic by printing out intermediate calculated results and field values that are used in making logic decisions in a program. Using these techniques, the programmer can follow the program's execution step by step in order to determine where the logic has an error.
4. Look at a printout of the contents of memory. This printout is called a storage dump or memory dump. The memory dump lists the instructions and data held in the computer's memory in their raw form, that is, their binary or equivalent hexadecimal or octal form. The programmer can then study this listing for possible clues to the cause of the programming error(s). Most programers of high level languages resort to the use of memory dumps only when all other methods of detecting the logical error fail.

1.8.6 Testing

This stage is the validation of the program. Testing ensures that the program performs correctly the required tasks. Program testing and program debugging are closely related. Testing is essentially a later stage of debugging in which the program is validated by trying it on a suitable set of test cases.

Some of the test cases will certainly be the ones used in debugging – the all-zeros case, the various special cases and other obvious cases that must be checked. Program testing is, however, more than a simple matter of exercising the program a few times. Exhaustive testing of all possible cases is the best alternative, but this process is usually impractical. Formal validation methods exist, but are only applicable to very simple programs. Thus, program testing requires a choice of test cases. The situation is further complicated by the fact that many microcomputer programs depend on realtime inputs that are difficult to control or simulate; the microprocessor must interact in a precise manner with a large and complex system. How can the necessary data be generated and presented to the microcomputer?

Several tools are available to help with this task. Clearly, the debugging tools mentioned earlier will be useful. Among the rules that can aid in program testing are the following:

1. Make the test plan part of the program design. Testing should be one of the factors in the problem definition, program design and coding stages.
2. Check all trivial and special cases. Often the simplest can lead to the most annoying and mysterious errors.
3. Select test data on a random basis. Doing so will eliminate any inadvertent bias caused by the programmer selecting test data. Random number tables are widely available and most computers have random number generators.
4. Plan and document software testing just like hardware testing. Obviously, testing can never prove that no errors exist; so good software design, like good hardware design, is an essential part of the testing process.
5. Use the maximum and minimum values of all variables as test data. Extreme values are often use source of special errors.
6. Use statistical methods in planning and evaluating complex tasks. Methods are available for selecting data and evaluating the significance of results. Optimization of techniques may suggest good choices for system parameters and efficient sets of test data.

There are two goals in preparing a test plan. First, a popularly detailed test plan demonstrates that the program specifications are understood completely. Second, the test plan is used during program testing of the program is prepared and documented, indicating the number of tests needed and the purpose of each test. In addition, all input test data is defined in detail and all excepted results, including reporting, are determined and documented.

Program testing includes physically running the tests specified in the test plan as well as correcting errors found in the code during the testing. This step is complete when the test results have been reviewed and approved by the project leader. To build a more consistent history of the time expended to complete each step, the life of the coding step can be defined. The time used in making coding changes needed to correct errors that were detected during the testing step, is recorded as test time.

This eliminates the question of where to record those hours and facilitates consistent recording of time throughout the programming staff. Similarly, it is not allowed to record time in any step that has been previously completed. However, if a flaw is detected, that forces redesign of all or part of a program, this time can be reported in the earlier phases.

In order to test a program properly, test plan development has to be undertaken at some point in the program development process. It has been experienced that performing this step before any logic is constructed ensures that a usable and exhaustive plan for proving the correctness of a program is available when the coding of the program has been completed.

This will most likely provide a more sensible approach to testing all facets of a program with as few test runs as possible. If the development of a test plan is postponed until after the program is coded, it will tend to test only those parts of the program which the programmer has become most concerned with or interested in.

1.9 Documentation

Documentation of a program is a must. One should file all the relative papers relating to that particular program in a file. You never know what would be needed at which time. It may be possible that your results shows something which has not been asked for. If you have the input documentation paper, you can always prove that this was asked for.

Documentation is the proper record of the program. It is definitely needed when the program is to be modified or even if some problem occurs.

Documentation can be divided into 2 parts:

- Externel Documentation and
- Internal Documentation

Let us read about them in details.

1.9.1 External Documentation

It contains program specifications (given by the bosses at the time of writing the program), development history (notes made on the way), proper design of the process of the program including the steps properly explained with the help of flow chart symbols. In totally it is the document which can be called as the User document.

With the help of this you can generate few other documents, if need be. They are:

- User's guide
- Reference manual
- Operators guide

Among the above, I think the user's guide is very important.

1.9.2 User's Guide

It highlights the type of inputs and outputs which the program generates. This helps in planning for their proper disbursement, e.g., which department which report is to be given, etc.

Some of the points of this can be as following:

1. A description of the application area of the program or what will this program do?
2. A description of the input data that the program requires.
3. A descrition of the output produced by the program.
4. A description of the commands needed to start the program.
5. A description of the kinds of interactions that are possible with the program.
6. An explanation of all the messages that the program can produce.
7. A discussion (in nontechnical terms) of the performance capabilities and limitations of the program.

1.9.3 Operators Guide

It contains all the instructions that the operator has to follow while executing the program. It could be:

1. How and when to use the compiler
2. Executing the compiled program
3. What type of errors expected and how to handle them
4. Where to get the input data required by the program
5. How to disburse the output.

1.9.4 Reference Manual

It contains all the instructions about the system specifications of the program, which may include the type of computer used, operating system used, etc. It also has the complete coding of the program.

Let us Revise

1. A good program should have the following characteristics: Readability, Efficiency, Reliability, Meaningfulness, Portability and User-friendly.
2. Instead of running a big program altogether, the program is divided into small parts and they are run independently.
3. There are different ways of using the modular programming. They are: Sequence structure, Decision/ Selection structure and Loop structure
4. Most of the guidelines for writing good programs are based upon following set of norms: Clarity/ Simplicity of Expressions, Names and Functions, Use of comments and Use of Indentation
5. Operator guide contains all the instructions that the operator has to follow while executing the program.
6. User guide highlights the type of inputs and outputs which the program generates.
7. Reference manual contains all the instructions about the system specifications of the program
8. Each program needs maintainance.
9. Program testing is a must before running for final use.
10. Debugging is method of checking errors in the program.
11. Syntax errors are those which occur due to wrong use of language.
12. Run time errors occur at the time of execution.
13. Logic errors are not pointed at the time of execution.
14. Testing ensures that the program performs correctly the required tasks.
15. Set of rules/syntax use for writing programs are called programming languages.
16. Assembly language use mnemonics to write a program.
17. Compilers or interpreters are used to translate high level language into machine code.
18. Interpreter translates the source code written in high level language into the machine code.
19. Machine language is represented in binary form and directly understandable by the computer. No translation is required.
20. Assembler is a program used to convert assembly language into machine code.
21. High-level languages are machine independent. It uses syntax which are easy to remember and meaningful to write the program.
22. In coding phase according to the design of each module, coding for every module is done in any preferred language (such as C, C++, Java, etc).

Multiple Choice Questions

1. In a program, a number has been divided by zero. It is a ______________.
   (a) Logical error (b) Syntax error (c) Run time error
2. Comments are written :
   (a) In the begging of the program
   (b) At the end of the program
   (c) Anywhere in the program
3. Syntax errors include :
   (a) wrong use of statements
   (b) wrong use of manipulators
   (c) wrong use of braces/any missing brace

4. Syntax errors inlcude :
(a) misspelt keywords (b) missing braces (c) missing commas
5. Which are the errors, in spite of which, the program will compile and run?
(a) Logical errors (b) Syntax errors (c) Run time errors
6. Instructions for the operator are there in :
(a) User manual (b) Operators guide (c) Reference manual
7. Checking and removing errors is called :
(a) Checking (b) Removing (c) Debugging
8. Oval is used to represent ________ in flow chart:
(a) terminal symbol (b) connectors (c) flow lines
(d) process symbol
9. Which one is a compiled language:
(a) C (b) Basic (c) machine language
(d) none of these
10. Language which is platform independent is:
(a) machine language (b) assembly language (c) high level language
(d) none of these
11. Language which needs no translation :
(a) machine language (b) assembly language (c) high level language
(d) none of these
12. ________ translates the program line-by-line and generates an object code :
(a) compiler (b) interpreter (c) assembler
(d) none of these
13. C is ________ language:
a) machine language (b) assembly language (c) high level language
(d) none of these
14. Assembler is used to convert ____________ language into the machine code.
(a) machine language (b) C (c) Java
(d) assembly language
15. ________ translates the whole program at once and generates an object code :
(a) assembler (b) compiler (c) interpreter
(d) none of these
16. Coding is followed by :
(a) feasibility study (b) testing (c) design
(d) maintenance
17. Integration testing is done after :
(a) unit testing (b) acceptance testing (c) beta testing
(d) alpha testing
18. Perfective maintenance mean ____________ the software.
(a) debug (b) enhance the functionality of
(c) update the platform of (d) none of these

19. Acceptance testing is done at ___________ site.

(a) customer (b) developer (c) customer and developer

(d) none of these

True/False Questions

1. A good programmer is not born but is developed by his own actions.
2. Wrong input leads to wrong results.
3. A programmer can write big programs at the beginning only.
4. A good program should have the following characteristics: Readability, Efficiency, Reliability, Meaningfulness, Portability and User-friendly.
5. A program can be run in parts.
6. There are different ways of using the modular programming. They are: Sequence structure, Decision/Selection structure and Loop structure.
7. Comments are which you write in the program as some sort of instructions for the operator or user of the program.
8. Operator guide contains all the instructions that the operator has to follow while executing the program.
9. Reference manual contains all the instructions about the system specifications of the program
10. There is no need to maintain any program.
11. Program testing is a must before running for final use.
12. Debugging is method of checking errors in the program.
13. Syntax errors are those which occur due to wrong use of language.
14. Run time errors occur at the time of execution.
15. Logic errors are pointed out at the time of execution.
16. Testing ensures that the program performs correctly the required tasks.
17. Depending on the complexity of the problem, the result of a careful analysis may be simply a testing of the factors with which the program must deal.
18. Meaningful names and labels can be helpful in documentation and maintenance as well as in debugging and integrating programs.
19. The use of number 0, 1 and 2 and letter O, I and Z in a program should be kept to a maximum.
20. Jumps make programs difficult to follow and debug.
21. Comments provide the internal documentation of a program. It makes the program easy to understand.
22. Use of comments reduces the speed of execution of a program.
23. Comments serve as internal documentation for programmers.
24. A comment can be inserted in the middle of a statement.
25. In C, we can have comments inside comments.

Match Columns

Match the matter in Column A with the matter in Column B.

Column A	Column B
A. Divide by zero	1. Modular programming
B. Comments are written	2. Keeping record of the program
C. Wrong use of language	3. Checking the program before actually running
D. Execution error	4. Reference manual

E. Testing program in parts	5. Syntax error
F. Documentation	6. Operators guide
G Testing	7. Logical error
H. System specifications	8. Run time error
I. Instruction for input, output	9. Usually in the beginning of the program

Fill in the Blanks with Appropriate Words

a. Tested	b. Logical	c. Sequence	d. Maintainance
e. Decision	f. Anywhere	g. Programmer	h. Syntax
i. Run time	j. Loop	k. Documentation	l. Operator

1. He who writes the program is called ________.
2. There are 3 types of modular programming structures ____________, ___________ and _______________.
3. To ensure that the program is ok it is _______.
4. Errors which occur due to bad use of the language is called ___________ error.
5. Errors which are pointed out only after receiving the result are called _________ errors.
6. Errors which occur at the time of running are called _________ errors.
7. Comments can be placed ________ in the program.
8. Instructions to run the program are there in the ________ guide.
9. __________ of the program is a must.
10. For long life of the program _________ is done.

Descriptive Type Questions

1. Which are the general concepts of a program?
2. What do you understand by the modular approach of the program?
3. Describe the various types of modular approach.
4. Describe the various type of guidelines which you will keep in mind while writing the program.
5. Describe the various type of documents that are prepared for the program.
6. What steps would you take for maintainance of the program.
7. What sort of errors you get while running the program?
8. How would you test the program?
9. Describe what do you mean by understanding of the problem.
10. How would you break down the problem in steps before actually solving it?
11. Design an algorithm to find the summation of the following series:
    (a) n+(n-1)+(n-2)+(n-3)…+1+0, where n=100
    (b) 1+2+3+…+100
    (c) 1+3+5+…+101
    (d) 0+2+4+…+200
    (e) n! + (n-1)! + (n-2)! +…+1! + 0!, where n=10
12. Construct flowchart to find out summation of the following series:
    (a) n+(n-1)+(n-2)+(n-3)…+1+0, where n=100
    (b) n! + (n-1)! + (n-2)! +…+1! + 0!, where n=10

13. Write an algorithm to find out the value of x^y, where x and y are two positive integers.
14. Draw flowchart to find out the greatest common divisor of two integer numbers.
15. Draw flowchart to find out digits of a number.
16. A Company manufactures three product engines, pumps and fans. It gives a discount of 25 percent on orders for engines, if the order is worth Rs. 10,000 or more. The same discount or more on fan orders of value 5000 or more and on pump orders value Rs. 7000 or more. On all other orders, they do not give any discount. Prepare flowchart for this decision problem.
17. Define the features of C language.
18. Define the algorithm. What is the need of algorithms in computer world?
19. Why flowchart is much expressive as compared to an algorithm?
20. Why and when do we use the #include directive?
21. What does void main(void) mean?
22. Distinguish between the following pairs:

    (a) main() and void main(void)

    (b) int main( ) and void main( )
23. Why the look of a program is important?
24. There are blank spaces permitted in a C program?
25. Describe the structure of a C program.
26. Describe the process of creating and executing a C program under UNIX and DOS system.
27. Given two integers 20 and 10, write a program that uses a function add( ) to add these two numbers and sub( ) to find the difference of these two numbers and then display the sum and difference in the following form: .

    20 + 10 = 30

    20 - 10 = 10
28. How do we implement multiple source program files?
29. Given the values of three variables x, y and z, write a program to compute and display the value of a, where. Execute the program for the following values:

    (a) x = 125, y = 85, z = 25 (b) x = 150, y = 70, z = 70

Programming Question

Given a set of 100 numbers write an algorithm to find the sum and total number of even and odd numbers in list.

Find errors , if any, in the following progam

```
/* A simple program */
    int main( );
    {
        /* Does nothing */
    }
```

Find errors , if any, in the following progam

```
#include (stdio.h)
void main(void)
{
    print("Hello C");
```

```
}
```

Find errors , if any, in the following progam

```
#include <math.h>
void main { }
(
    float X;
    X = 2.5;
    Y = exp(X);
    printf(x, y);
}
```

Answers to Objective Type Questions

Multiple Choice Questions

1. a	2. a	3. a, b	4. a, b, c
5. a	6. b	7. c	8. b
9. a	10. b	11. a	12. b
13. c	14. b	15. c	16. c
17. c	18. b	19. a	

True False Questions

1. T	2. T	3. F	4. T
5. T	6. T	7. T	8. T
9. T	10. F	11. T	12. T
13. T	14. T	15. F	16. T
17. T	18. T	19. F	20. T
21. T	22. T	22. T	23. T
24. T	25. T		

Matching Columns

A. 8	B. 9	C. 5	D. 8
E. 1	F. 2	G 3	H. 4
I. 6			

Fill in the Blanks

1. g	2. c, e, j	3. a	4. h
5. b	6. i	7. f	8. 1
9. k	10. d		

Alogrithms for Problem Solving

2

2.1 Exchanging Values of Two Variables

When you change the values of two variables, it is called exchanging. Let me give you an example for the same:

Let us take two variables x and y and give them values.

x = 22

y = 29

After you interchanging them, you will get the option as:

x = 29

y = 22

Now, let us see how it is done. For this you need a temporary variable called z. Then follow the following steps:

Step1: Copy value of x to z.

z = 22

Step2: Copy value of y to x.

x = 29

Step 3: Copy value of z to y.

y = 22

Finally, you will have:

x = 29

y = 22

This when written in the form of Algorithm, for the computer, will look like the one shown below:

1. Start
2. Get the values of x and y
3. Copy value of x to z
4. Copy value of y to x
5. Copy value of z to y
6. Show the values of x and y
7. Stop.

2.2 Summation of a Set of Numbers

It adds the various values of various values in the series and puts the total value in a new variable. For example,

Summing the following numbers

121

243

50

414

When using computer, we need to construct an algorithm for the same. Computer at a time adds just two numbers. So we add first two numbers and store the value in a new variable. Next in each step add the new number to the total, till you have reached the end.

For this let us assume that the numbers are named as x_1, x_2, x_3, etc., and the total is stored in a new variable called s.

Step1: Copy value of x_1 to s.

Step2: Copy value of x_2 to s.

Step 3: Copy value of x_3 to s.

and so on ....

Finally, you will have the total of all numbers in s.

This when written in the form of Algorithm, for the computer, will look like the one shown below:

1. Start
2. Get the numbers to be added/summed
3. Initialize the sum as 0
4. Copy value of x_1 to s
5. Copy value of x_2 to s
6. Copy value of x_3 to s
7. Repeat this process till you get the last number
7. Stop.

2.3 Decimal Base to Binary Base Conversion

External to computer we use decimal numbers whereas internally we use binary representation, so we have to convert decimal numbers to binary. Also it is sometimes convenient to use a number in a base different from the base currently being used, i.e., to change the number from one base to another.

In a decimal number the value of the

1st digit from R.H.S. = $10^0 = 1$

2nd digit from R.H.S. = $10^1 = 10$

3rd digit from R.H.S. = $10^2 = 100$

Similarly in a binary number the value of the

1st digit from R.H.S. = $2^0 = 1$

2nd digit from R.H.S. = $2^1 = 2$

3rd digit from R.H.S. = $2^2 = 4$

.... and so on.

The process, often called the remainder method, is basically a series of repeated divisions by the number of the base to which you are converting (in our case base is 2). There are two points to remember:

Keep dividing until you reach a zero quotient

Use the remainder in reverse order.

Under the process of conversion we determine which multiples of 2 are present in a given decimal number. Consider the following examples.

Example

$(187)_{10} =$

2	187		
2	93	1	Least significant bit. (L.S.B.)
2	46	1	
2	23	0	
2	11	1	
2	5	1	
2	2	1	
2	1	0	
	0	1	Most significant bit. (M.S.B.)

$(187)_{10} = (10111011)_2$

Another Example

$(330)_{10}$

2	330		
2	165	0	Least significant bit. (L.S.B.)
2	82	1	
2	41	0	
2	20	1	
2	10	0	
2	5	0	
2	2	1	
2	1	0	
	0	1	Most significant bit. (M.S.B.)

$(330)_{10} = (101001010)_2$

The binary equivalent of the decimal number is given by the sequence of remainders obtained during division. L.S.B. of the binary number is the 1st remainder obtained and M.S.B. is the last remainder.

2.4 Reversing Digits of an Integer

Reversing digits basically means changing the digits order backwards. For example, let us use a number.

Number	4 2 6 8
Result after reversing	8 6 2 4

To do this, we divide the number by 10 and print the remainder.

```
                  Dividend
Divisor—10 | 4268 |  426 —— Quotient
             40
             ——
              26
              20
              ——
```

```
 68
 60
 --
  8  ——— Remainder
```

We can get the same remainder by mod() function

r = 4268 mod (10)

8

Now remove 8 from the original integer. So we next get 426, which is the new number to be reversed.

Using the mod() function, again, we get:

r = 426 mod (10)

6

Similarly, we can apply the mod() function on the number 42 which results in 2 as remainder. We can do this till the devidend is less than 10. Let us now place the digits of the remainders in the reverse. So, we can use the integer division by 10 to remove the right most digit from the number being reversed and construct the reversd integer by writing the extracted digits to the right hand side of the last current reversed number representation. At last, when the dividend is less than 10, then add it to the right hand side of the current reversed number representation.

So finally, what we get

Numbers to be changed	Reversed-digits Number
4268	8
426	86
42	862
4	8624

This when written in the form of Algorithm, for the computer, will look like the one shown below:

1. Start
2. Get the numbers to be reversed
3. Extract the right most diit of the number to be reversed by remainder function, i.e., function mod()
4. Construct the reversed integer by writing the extracted digit to right hand side of the current reversed number.
5. Write the integer (dividend which is less than 19)
6. Stop.

2.5 GOD (Greatest Common Divisor) of Two Numbers

To find the greatest common divisor is easy as you will find out next. Divide the greater number with the smaller number. Next, divide divisor by the remainder. Keep on doing this till you get the remainder as 0. Then the divisor is your Greatest Common Divisor Number.

Let me explain this with the help of an example:

For example, let

x = 68

y = 12

As we have to divide the greater number with the smaller number, we will divide x by y.

This is how it will be done.

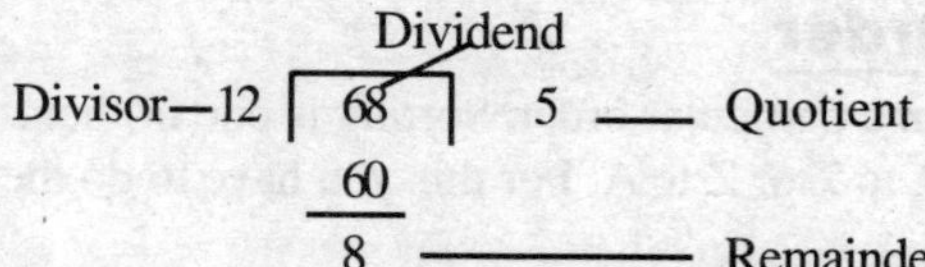

Now the remainder, 8 would become our new divisor.

```
              Dividend
Divisor—8   | 12 |    1 —— Quotient
               8
              ---
               4 ———————— Remainder
```

Thus, 4 is the number which we have been looking for, i.e., the Greatest Common Divisor.

This when written in the form of Algorithm, for the computer, will look like the one shown below:

1. Start
2. Get the numbers for which you have to find the greatest number
3. Divide the greater number with smaller number
4. Make smaller integer be dividend and get the remainder
5. Let remainder by the divisor
6. Repeat the above steps until a zero remainder is obtained. At this stage the divisor is your GCD.
7. Stop.

2.6 Test Whether a Number is Prime

Prime number is a number which can only be divided by itself and number 1. The task here is to find out whether a given number is prime or not. For example, number 2 has two factors 1 and 2, the number 3 has the factors 1 and 3, and so on. A Greek mathematician came out with a formula to find out the prime numbers, the method is known as "Sieve Method". Supposing we have to find out all the prime numbers in the range of 1 to 10. This can be done in the following manner.

1. Strike out 1 because it is not a prime number.
2. Encircle 2 and strike out all the multiples of 2, i.e., 4, 6, 8, 10.
3. Encircle 3 and strike out all the multiples of 3, i.e., 3, 9.
4. The numbers would look like these.

   ~~1~~ ~~2~~ ~~3~~ ~~4~~ 5 ~~6~~ 7 ~~8~~ ~~9~~ ~~10~~
5. This leaves us with just two numbers, i.e., 5 and 7, which are the prime numbers in the range 1 to 10.

This when written in the form of Algorithm, for the computer, will look like the one shown below:

1. Start
2. Get the number range which you want to check whether they are prime numbers or not.
3. Set value of divisor 2.
4. Divide the number by divisor (i.e., 2 in this case). In remainder is zero, then the given number is not prime, else the process is to be continued.
5. Increment divisor by 1, divide the number by he incremented divisor and check if remainder is zero. Keep repeating the process till either the remainder becomes zero or until divisor is equal to the number itself. If remainder becomes zero at any stage, the number is not prime it is prime if carried to last stage, till incremented divisor is number itself.
6. Stop.

2.7 Organize Numbers in Ascending Order

At any given time, the numbers look better if they are arranged in a particular order. Sorting is one of them. You can sort in both ascending and descending order, i.e., from A to Z or Z to A. For this you have to do the following:

1. Let us assume that we have to sort the following numbers.

x_1	x_2	x_3	x_4	x_5	x_6
10	20	8	2	40	30

2. Find the smallest value and place it as first item in the table. At the same time, move the value of the first location of the table to the location where smallest value was stored. It means interchange the value of x_4 and x_1. The current situation would look like the following.

x_1	x_2	x_3	x_4	x_5	x_6
2	20	8	10	40	30

3. Now compare elements of x_2 with other element in the unsorted table and do as before. It means interchange the value of x_3 and x_2. The current situation would look like the following.

x_1	x_2	x_3	x_4	x_5	x_6
2	8	20	10	40	30

4. Again compare elements of x_3 with other element in the unsorted table and do as before. It means interchange the value of x_3 and x_4. The current situation would look like the following.

x_1	x_2	x_3	x_4	x_5	x_6
2	8	10	20	40	30

5. Repeat the steps for the other elements too, to ge the following figure in the end.

x_1	x_2	x_3	x_4	x_5	x_6
2	8	10	20	30	40

This as can be seen is totally in ascending order of the value of x.

This when written in the form of Algorithm, for the computer, will look like the one shown below:

1. Start
2. Read numbers and store them in an array of n elements, i.e., size of array x is n with elements as x_1, x_2, x_3, ... x_9.
3. Find the smallest element within unsorted array.
4. Exchange, or swap smallest value of the array element and store it in 1st element of the unsorted part of array.
5. Repeat steps 3 and 4 until all the elements in the array are arranged in the ascending order.
6. Stop.

2.8 Find Square Root of a Number

Before understanding square root, we must know what we mean by squaring a number. To square a number is to multiply the number by itself.

For example,

$1 \times 1 = 1^2$
$= 1$

$2 \times 2 = 2^2$
$= 4$

However, one of the two equal factors of a number is the square root of that number. Let us read some more examples to understand square root.

1^2	= 1 x 1	The square root of 1 is 1
2^2	= 2 x 2 = 4	The square root of 4 is 2.
3^2	= 3 x 3 = 9	The square root of 9 is 3.

Therefore, if we have to find the square root of 40 then we will see "what number multiplied by itself will give 49". Certainly 7 x 7 = 49. But (–7 x–7) is also gives 49.

So, +7 and also –7 is the square root of 49.

So, we can say that if a is the square root of b then b is the square of. For example,

Square root of 49 is + 7 or –7.

Square root of 64 is + 8 or –8

This when written in the form of Algorithm, for the computer, will look like the one shown below:

1. Place bar over every pair of digits starting with the right hand side (R.H.S). The number of bars indicates the number of digits in the square root.

   529

2. Find the largest square root for the first pair that is less than or equal to the first pair. Take the square root of this number as divisor, and get quotient. Put the quotient above the period. Subtract the product and bring down the next pair of digits to the right of the remainder.

```
  | 2
  |----
2 | 529
  | 4
  |----
  | 129
```

3. Double the quotient as it appears and enter it with a blank on the right for the next digit, as the next possible divisor.

```
   | 23
   |----
2  | 529
   | 4
   |----
43 | 129
```

4. Guess a possible digit to fill the blank and also to become the new digit in the quotient. Enter this digit in both places. Multiply the new digit in the quotient and new divisor. Subtract and bring down the next period.

```
   | 23
   |----
2  | 529
   | 4
   |----
43 | 129
   | 129
   |----
   | 0
```

5. Repeat steps 3 and 4 till the last pair has been used and the remainder comes to zero.
6. Stop.

2.9 Factorial Computation

The product of all positive integers from 1 to n is called the `factorial n' or `n factorial'. It is denoted by n!.

For example,

5! = 1 x 2 x 3 x 4 x 5

= 120

n! = 1 x 2 x 3 . . . . . (n – 2) x (n – 1) x n

where n is a positive integer.

Let us take an example. Suppose we want to find out the value of factorial 5. Assign the value of i = 1 and factorial = 1. So method will be successively go on increasing the value of i by 1 and keep updating the value of factorial by multiplying the current value of i by the value of factorial till the incremented value of i equals to the number desired for finding the factorial.

Thus, factorial = previous value of factorial x i, i.e., start with i = 1, giving factorial 1 = 1 x 1.

Now increment the value of i by 1, giving updated

factorial 2 = 1 x 2

= 2

Again increase the value of i by 1, giving

factorial 3 = 2 x 3

= 6

Increment the value of i until the value of i becomes 5 and corresponding value of factorial is obtained. To summarize, the factorial will be calculated in the following way:

factorial 1 = 1 x 1 = 1

factorial 2 = 1 x 2 = 2

factorial 3 = 2 x 3 = 6

factorial 4 = 6 x 4 = 24

factorial 5 = 24 x 5 = 120

So 5! = 120

This when written in the form of Algorithm, for the computer, will look like the one shown below:

1. Start
2. Get the number of which the factorial is to be calculated, i.e., n.
3. Assign the value of i = 1 and factorial = 1.
4. Calculate factorial n = factorial (n–1) x i.
5. Increment the value of i by 1, i.e., i = i + 1.
6. Repeat steps 4 and 5 till step 4 has been executed with the value of i = n.
7. Write the value of factorial.
8. Stop.

2.10 Fibonacci Sequence

In a Fibonacci sequence, the previous two numbers are added to generate the next Fibonacci number. For example,

$f_1 = 1$ (1st number in the Fibonacci series)

$f_2 = 2$ (2nd number in the Fibonacci series)

$f_3 = f_2 + f_1 = 2 + 1 = 3$

$f_4 = f_3 + f_1 = 3 + 2 = 5$

$f_5 = f_4 + f_1 = 5 + 3 = 8$, and so on

f_1	f_2	f_3	f_4	f_5	f_6	f_7	....
1	2	3	5	8	13	21	....

To get next fibonacci number, we have to do sum of previous two numbers in the series.

This when written in the form of Algorithm, for the computer, will look like the one shown below:

1. Start
2. Assign sum = 0, A = 0, B = 1, i = 1.
3. Get the number of terms up to which you want to generate the Fibonacci number, i.e., n.
4. Add A and B to get next Fibonacci number.
5. Assign the value of B to A, i.e., A = B.
6. Assign the value of sum to B, i.e., sum = B.
7. Write the value of sum to get next Fibonacci number in the series.
8. Increment i with 1, i.e., i = i + 1 and repeat step 3, 4, 5, 6, with the last value of i = n (n is a number of terms up to which we want to enerate Fibonacci number series).
9. Stop.

2.11 Evaluate 'Sin x' as Sum of a Series

Sin as we all know the the angle in radians obtained by dividing Perpendicular over Hypotenuse. To calculate the Sin follow the following steps.

1. Start
2. Read x in radians.
3. Read n where `n' is the number of terms of series which we may like to add-up to get desired precision of sum.
4. For 1st term,

   sum = x

   product = 1 (variable `product' used for denominator)

   num = x (variable `num' used for numerator)

   power = 1.
5. For next terms,

   num = num x $(-x_2)$

   power = power + 2

   product = product x (power – 1) x power

   next_term = num/product.
6. Then,

   sum = sum + next_term
7. Repeat step 5 and 6, looping `n – 1' times to get the sum of first `n' terms of the series.
8. Print sum.
9. Stop.

2.12 Reverse Order of Elements of an Array

Reverse order of elements means value of 1st position of the array is exchanged with last element of the array, 2nd element of array is exchanged with `2nd last' and so on.

To reverse the order of elements follow the following steps.

1. Start
2. Get the values and store them in an array with elements a_1, a_2, a_3, a_4 .... a_n, where n is the number of elements.
3. Compute r, the number of exchange needed to reverse the array r = integer value of n/2.
4. Exchange the ith element with [n – 1 + 1] using temp = a[i]

   a_i = a[n – i + 1]

   a[n – i + 1] = temp
5. Carry step 4, r times increasing i by 1.
6. Print the reversed array elements a_1, a_2, a_3, a_4, ... a_n.
7. Stop.

2.13 Find Largest Number in an Array

In a series of numbers, there is bound to be a number with the largest value. Another number(s) in the set may be equal to this number, but cannot be greater than this number. For example, in the following series:

11, 18, 24, 28, 9, 39

we find that 39 is the largest number.

To find the largest number in an array follow the following steps.

1. Start
2. Get the value of element in an array and store them in the array elements a_1, a_2, a_3, a_4, ... a_n, where n is the number of elements.
3. Set temporary variable and asign the value of 1st array element a_1 to temp.
4. Compare temp with the next element a_2 of the array.
5. If the element is having greater value than temp, assign that value to temp
6. Repeat steps 4 and 5 till last element a_n of the array is encountered.
7. Final value of temp is the largest value stored in the array.
8. Stop.

2.14 Print Elements of Upper Triangular Matrix

Let us consider a 4 x 4 matrix. Now to print last (4 – i + 1) elements in every ith row. In the first row, the last (4 – 1 + 1) = 4 elements has to be printed. In the second row, the last 3 elements have to be printed. Hence the following values will be printed.

1 2 3 4 6 7 8 11 12 16

The matix is:

$$A = \begin{vmatrix} 1 & 2 & 3 & 4 \\ 5 & 6 & 7 & 8 \\ 9 & 10 & 11 & 12 \\ 13 & 14 & 15 & 16 \end{vmatrix}$$

upper triangle

To find the largest number in an array follow the following steps.

1. Start

2. Read the order of square matrix, n.
3. read the contents of the matrix in.
   A [i] [j] form
4. Initiate i to 0 and j to 1.
5. Repeat step 6, and 7, until i is less than or equal to n.
6. Repeat the following steps until j is less than or equal to n.
   (i) print a[i][j]
   (ii) Increment j by 1
7. Stop.

2.15 Evaluate a Polynomial

To evaluate a Polynomial follow the following steps.

1. Start
2. Input name and value of the goods sold.
3. Calculate the total wage. If the value of goods sold is less than or equal to Rs. 1000, then
   wage = 1000 + 25% of value
4. If value of goods sold is greater than Rs. 10,000, then
   wage = 1000 + 25% of value + 50
5. Print the total wages
6. Stop.

2.16 Multiplication of Two Matrices

Let us take the multiplication of two matrix A and B of sizes 2 x 3 and 4 x 2 respectively. They are defined as below:

$$A = \begin{vmatrix} 0 & 2 & 3 \\ 1 & 3 & 1 \\ 2 & 5 & 2 \end{vmatrix} \qquad B = \begin{vmatrix} 1 & 0 \\ 0 & 2 \\ 2 & 2 \end{vmatrix} \quad \text{then}$$

Here A and B are compatible. The product is as follows:

$$A \times B = \begin{vmatrix} 0 \times 1 + 2 \times 0 + 3 \times 2 & 0 \times 0 + 2 \times 2 + 3 \times 2 \\ 1 \times 1 + 3 \times 0 + 1 \times 2 & 1 \times 0 + 3 \times 2 + 1 \times 2 \\ 2 \times 1 + 5 \times 0 + 2 \times 2 & 2 \times 0 + 5 \times 2 + 2 \times 2 \end{vmatrix}$$

$$= \begin{vmatrix} 6 & 10 \\ 3 & 8 \\ 6 & 14 \end{vmatrix}$$

Here 6 is the value of the element lying in the 1st row and 1st column of the product matrix (A x B). This is the sum of the products of the corresponding elements of 1st row of A with 1st column of B.

To multiply two matrices follow the following steps:

1. Start
2. Get 1st and 2nd matrix.

3. Check if numer of columns of 1st matrix is equal to the number of rows in 2nd matrix. Then matrices are compatible for multiplication. Otherwise, product is not possible.
4. If matrices are compatible then find the sum of the product of corresponding element of each row of A with the corresponding element of each column of B and sum the element and equate it to the corresponding position of the product matrix.
5. Stop.

Let us Revise

1. By inter-changing the values of two variables you can change them.
2. For changing from Decimal to Binary we use the process, often called the remainder method, which isis basically a series of repeated divisions by the number of the base to which you are converting.
3. You can sum a number of variables using the summing method.
4. Reversing digits basically means changing the digits order backwards.
5. To find the greatest common divisor, divide the greater number with the smaller number. Next, divide divisor by the remainder. Keep on doing this till you get the remainder as 0. Then the divisor is your Greatest Common Divisor Number.
6. Prime number is a number which can only be divided by itself and number 1.
7. At any given time, the numbers look better if they are arranged in a particular order. Sorting is one of them.
8. Square root is the reverse of squaring, i.e., multiplying with itself.
9. The product of all positive integers from 1 to n is called the `factorial n' or `n factorial'.
10. In a Fibonacci sequence, the previous two numbers are added to generate the next Fibonacci number.
11. Sin as we all know the the angle in radians obtained by dividing Perpendicular over Hypotenuse.
12. Reverse order of elements means value of 1st position of the array is exchanged with last element of the array, 2nd element of array is exchanged with `2nd last' and so on.
13. In a series of numbers, there is bound to be a number with the largest value.
14. You can multiply two matrices to give rise to a new matrix.

Multiple Choice Questions

1. Prime number is a number.
   (a) divisible by 1
   (b) divisible by 1 and by itself
   (c) none of the two
2. GCD of two numbers is:
   (a) the smallest number which is a common factor of the given numbers
   (b) the largest number which is a common factor of two given numbers
   (c) 1 is the GCD for all numbers
3. The product of all natural numbers from 1 to n is called
   (a) n! (b) n x n (c) n^n

4. Sorting an array in the ascending order of numbers is the process of :
   (a) putting the largest number first and smallest in the last
   (b) putting the smallest number first and the largest number in the last
   (c) putting the numbers in any way you desire

True/False Questions

1. In an array of ascending order of numbers, the largest number is the first element of the array and smallest number is the last element of the array.
2. The series 1, 2, 3, 4, 8, 13 is a Fibonacci series.
3. Multiplication of two matrices is possible only when they are compatible.

Match Columns

Match the matter in Column A with the matter in Column B.

Column A	Column B
A. n!	1. Fibonacci series
B. Sin (π/2)	2. Sorted array
C. 1, 1, 2, 3, 5, 8	3. 120
D. 1 3 8 10 12	4. 1

Fill in the Blanks with Appropriate Words

a. 64 b. previous c. Prime d. itself

1. The number 21 is a ________ number since it is divisible by 1 and itself.
2. Square root of a number is that number, which multiplied by ________ gives the original number.
3. The GCD of the number 256 and 64 is ______.
4. In Fibonacci series, the _______ two numbers are added to generate the Fibonacci number.

Descriptive Type Questions

1. Write an algorithm to sort an array in the descending order.
2. Write an algorithm that reads a year and determine whether it is a leap year or not.
3. Write an algorithm to find area of a triangle.

Answers to Objective Type Questions

Multiple Choice Questions

1. b 2. b 3. a 4. b

True False Questions

1. F 2. F 3. T

Matching Columns

A. 3 B. 4 C. 1 D. 2

Fill in the Blanks

1. c 2. d 3. a 4. b

Introduction to 'C' Language 3

3.1 Character set

Characters play a central role in C language. When we write a program, we express C source files as text lines containing characters from the **source character set**. When a program executes in the **target environment**, it uses characters from the **target character set**. These character sets are related, but need not have the same encoding or all the same members. Every character set contains a distinct code value for each character in the **basic C character set**. A character set can also contain additional characters with other code values. For example,

1. The **character constant** 'x' becomes the value of the code for the character corresponding to x in the target character set.
2. The **string literal** "xyz" becomes a sequence of character constants stored in successive bytes of memory, followed by a byte containing the value zero: {'x', 'y', 'z', '\0'}

A string literal is one way to specify a **null-terminated string**, an array of zero or more bytes followed by a byte containing the value zero. **Visible graphic characters** in the basic C character set are shown in Table 3.1.

The code value zero is reserved for the **null character** which is always in the target character set. Code values for the basic C character set are positive when stored in an object of type *char*. Code values for the digits are contiguous, with increasing value. For example, '0' + 5 equals '5'. Code values for any two letters are *not* necessarily contiguous.

Table 3.1 C Character Set

Form	*Members*
Alphabet	A B C D E F G H I J K L M N O P Q R S T U V W X Y Z a b c d e f g h i j k l m n o p q r s t u v w x y z
Numeric	0 1 2 3 4 5 6 7 8 9
underscore	_
punctuation	! " # % & ' ( ) * + , - . / : ; < = > ? [\ ] ^ { | } ~

Escape Sequences: Within character constants and string literals, we can write a variety of **escape sequences**. Each escape sequence determines the code value for a single character. We use escape sequences to represent character codes:

- we cannot otherwise write (such as \n)
- that can be difficult to read properly (such as \t)
- that might change value in different target character sets (such as \a)
- that must not change in value among different target environments (such as \0)

Mnemonic escape sequences help us to remember the characters they represent {Table 3.2}. An escape sequence takes the form as shown in Figure 3.1.

We can also write **numeric escape sequences** using either octal or hexadecimal digits. An **octal escape sequence** takes one of the forms:

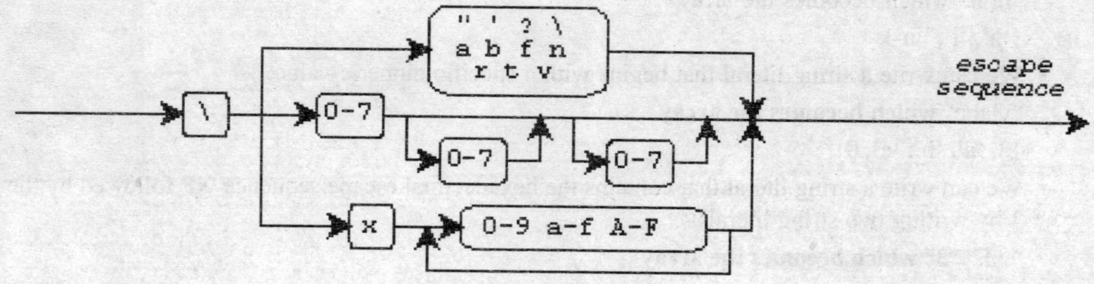

Figure 3.1 Sequence of the escape sequences

Table 3.2 Escape Sequences

Escape Character	*Meaning*	*Short Notation*
\n	New Line	NL
\t	Horizontal Tab	HT
\a	Bell	BEL
\b	Back Space	BS
\f	Form Feed	FF
\r	Carriage Return	CR
\v	Vertical Tab	VT
\\	Back Slash	BAS
\?	Question Mark	QM
\’	Single Quote	SQ
\	Double Quote	DQ
\onnn	Octal Number	ON
\xhhh	Hexadecimal Number	HN
\0	Null Character	NC

d* or *dd* or *ddd

The escape sequence yields a code value that is the numeric value of the 1, 2, or 3-digit octal number following the backslash (\). Each *d* can be any digit in the range 0-7.

A **hexadecimal escape sequence** takes one of the forms:

\x*h* or \x*hh* or ...

The escape sequence yields a code value that is the numeric value of the arbitrary-length hexadecimal number following the backslash (\). Each *h* can be any decimal digit 0-9, or any of the letters a-f or A-F. The letters represent the digit values 10-15, where either a or A has the value 10.

A numeric escape sequence terminates with the first character that does not fit the digit pattern. Here are some examples:

- We can write the null character as ‘\0’.
- We can write a newline character (*NL*) within a string literal by writing:

"hi\n" which becomes the array

{'h', 'i', '\n'}

- We can write a string literal that begins with a specific numeric value:

  "\3abc" **which becomes the array**

  {3, 'a', 'b', 'c', 0}

- We can write a string literal that contains the hexadecimal escape sequence \xF followed by the digit 3 by writing two string literals:

  "\xF" "3" **which becomes the array**

  {0xF, '3', 0}

Trigraphs: A **trigraph** is a sequence of three characters that begins with two question marks (??). We use trigraphs to write C source files with a character set that does not contain convenient graphic representations for some punctuation characters. The resultant C source file is not necessarily more readable, but it is unambiguous. The list of all defined trigraphs is shown in Table 2.3.

These are the only trigraphs. The translator does not alter any other sequence that begins with two question marks. For example, the expression statements:

```
printf("Case ??=3 is done??/n");
printf("You said what????/n");
```

are equivalent to:

```
printf("Case #3 is done\n");
printf("You said what??\n");
```

The translator replaces each trigraph with its equivalent single character representation in an early phase of translation. We can always treat a trigraph as a single source character.

3.2 Variables and identifiers

We have seen in the previous chapter that we use some variable to hold some data and data has some category such as int, float, string, etc. We use names for other purposes also for example, function's name, data structure name, etc.

Variables play an important role in computer programming because they enable programmers to write flexible programs. Rather than entering data directly into a program, a programmer can use variables to represent the data. Then, when the program is executed, the variables are replaced with real data. This makes it possible for the same program to process different sets of data. The names that are used to reference variables, functions, labels and various user-defined objects, etc are called *identifiers (variables),* and a data type. A variable's data type indicates what sort of value the variable represents, such as whether it is an integer, a floating-point number, or a character. For example,

- int number;
- float temp1, temp2;
- int age;

The size of an identifier in C language can vary from 1 to 32 characters. The first character must be a letter or an underscore ('_') character with subsequent characters being letters, numbers or underscores. We can define an identifier in lower case letters or in upper case letters or in combination. But, the keywords of C language are always in small letters. For example,

- char Left_right;
- int __date123;

  :

- int year_2006;
- int January_2006;

One can think that what the need of underscore character in identifiers is. It is good practice that we use names (identifiers) such that these reflect some sense or carry some meaning. For example,

- lont int date_of_birth;
- char Company_Name[100];
- char father_name[50];
- char mother_name[40];
- int Flat_no;
- float Square_root_of_integers;

Following are **incorrect declarations**:

- int 2number;
  /*Leading character is numeric */
- float;
  /* Keyword */
- char .right;
  /* Leading character is special character dot */
- char father.name[50];
  /*In the middle there is a special character dot */
- int num&num'
  /* In the middle there is a special character & */
- float Tem;p;
  /* character semicolon is special character */
- char My_flat_No_street_no_city_name_ country_name[150];
  /*Invalid identifier name, more than 32 characters are used */

If we declare function names according to the above definition, following are valid function names:

- float _function_square_root( );
- int set_xy_value( );
- char function1( );
- int Finding_date( );

Following are **invalid function names**:

- int 2fun();
- float 2_fun_();
- .int integer_to_integer();
- int length.calculation();
- char !function();
- double yes_function_$_function();
- char *function_is_a_feature_of_c_language();

3.3 Built-in Data Types

We have discussed that each variable which is used in the program required to be declared first. It means, when we declare a variable within a program, it is required to tell **C** compiler about the variables' name and its data type. A data type defines the set of values the variable can store, as well as the set of operations that can be performed on the data.

For example, integer, character, float, etc. we cannot perform division on characters. So, for each data type variable there are set of permissible operations in C language. **C** language supports *five primary data* types which are shown in Table 3.4.

Table 3.4 Data Types in C

Data Type (Keyword)	*Meaning*
int	Integer
char	Character or String
float	Floating-point
double	Used with int and float data types for larger numbers
void	Accept any type of data based on cast operator it returns the value

3.3.1 The int

The keyword **int** in C language is used to define integer data type. **C** uses the type **int** to store integer data that may be positive or negative. **C** compiler normally allocates 16-bit to store data of the type **int**, but it is compiler dependent and may vary from compiler to compiler, viz., under windows and DOS it allocates 16-bit, Window-NT allocates 32-bit because it is 32-bit Operating System, similarly UNIX and LINUX allocates 32-bit in normal case. A variable of type **int** can store data in the range of –32,768 to 32767. Out of 16-bit the most significant bit (MSB) is used for sign representation. It means 15-bit are used for magnitude representation. The **int** data type always stores integer data and used to operate integer arithmetic operations. For example, following declarations are *correct* in C language:

- int number1, number2, Temp=0;
- int integer_no = 15;
- int first_num, second_num;

Following declarations are incorrect:

- int first_num=2.0;
- int temp = harry;

We use string "**%d**" with printf() function to print an integer data type as given below:

- printf("%d", number1);
- printf("number1 = %d", number1);
- printf("The first number is: %d", first_number);

We can see that we have used *printf* function differently. Suppose *number1 = 20*, *first_number = 100*, then outcome of the above statements are in the following sequence:

20

Number1=20

The first number is: 100

The conclusion is that we can use the *printf* ( ) function as per our convenience with some appropriate message. Go through the Example 3.1 which is implementing the above discussion.

Example 3.1: Write a C program which receives a floating point number and prints an integer.

Answer: In the following program segment, the variable num is int type but we have assigned data 50.5

which is real number. The compiler will only allocate the integer part of this data, i.e., num=50.

```
#include<stdio.h>
  main( )
  {
     int num;
     num = 50.5 ;
     printf("Value of num = %d", num);
  }
```

OUTPUT

Value of num = 50

3.3.2 The char

The **char** data type is used to hold **ASCII** (American Standard Code for Information Interchange) characters and there is generally 8-bit or 1 byte memory reservation for it. The compiler normally allocates 8-bits to store data of type **char**. A variable of type **char** can store data in the range –128 to 127, but storage of a character data type is dependent on a compiler. The most significant bit in 8-bit memory is reserved for sign and remaining 7-bit is used for representing binary value of character. The syntax to declare **char** type variable is given below:

char var1, var2, var3, …, varn;

For example,

- char ch, x, y, z ;
- char str, temp;
- char ch ='Y', x='N'; /* in this declaration we have assigned values to character type variable during declaration, i.e., ch is assigned value 'Y' and x will receive value 'N' */
- char A='a', b='B'; /* A receives 'a' and b receives 'B' */
- char name='Z'; /* name is assigned value 'Z' */

We can print a character using printf( ) function in the similar way as we have for integer type; we put "%c" in place of "%d" as given below:

- printf("%c", x);
- printf(" Entered Character is: %c", ch);
- printf("First character is: %c and second character is: %c", x, y);

Go through the Example 3.2 which is implementing the above discussion.

Example 3.2: Write a 'C' code to print a character and also its ASCI value.

Answer: We will discuss this problem in two steps. In the first part of the code we implement the character printing and in next part ASCI code of the character.

In the following program segment, identifier **ch** is defined as **char** type. In next statement it assigns character 'Y' to **ch** and finally prints the information associated with the variable **ch**.

```
/* The char type data can be processed */
   #include<stdio.h>
   main()
   {
```

```
    char ch ;
    ch = 'Y' ;
  printf("Value of ch  = %c", ch);
  }
```

OUTPUT

Value of ch = Y

A character quoted within a single quote is used to assign a character constant value to a parameter. In the above example, we have assigned character **Y** to variable **ch**. Here, **ch** will store **ASCII** value of character **c**. Consider the following program segment that outputs the ASCII value of character **c**.

```
/* ASCII value associated with a char type parameter */
  #include<stdio.h>
  void main()
  {
     char ch='c' ;
     printf("ASCII value of ch = %d",ch);
  }
```

OUTPUT

ASCII value of ch = 99

The output 99 is **ASCII** value of character c. From this example, it can be seen that if we change the output format we get the **ASCII** value of a character. It means if we use "%d" in place of "%c" then we can get ASCII value of a character.

3.3.3 The float

C language provides keyword **float** to store floating-point data. An identifier to declare a floating-point data follows the keyword float. **C** compiler normally allocates 32-bits to store floating-point data; it is dependent on a compiler. A variable of type **float** can store data with 6 to 7 of precision in the range of 3.4E-38 to 3.4E+38 (value of E is 10). The MSB is used for sign, next 8-bit is used for exponent and remaining 23-bit is used for mantissa. We declare a float type as follows:

- float real_number;
- float num=12.99;
- float number= 20;

If we assign integer value to a float type variable then C compiler stores it as a floating-point number. We can print the value of a float type variable by using "%f" with the help of *printf* function. For example,

- printf("The value of real_number is: %f ", real_number);
- printf("Value of num = %f ", num);
- printf("You have entered the value of number = %f ", number);

Go through the Example 3.3 which is implementing the above discussion.

Example 3.3: Write a 'C' code which takes input real (floating point) number and prints the same.

Answer: The following program segment prints the value of real_number.

```
/* The float data type declaration */
#include<stdio.h>
void main()
{
   float real_number ;
   real_number = 130.7 ;
   printf("Value of real_number = %f",x);
}
```

OUTPUT

Value of real_number = 130.7

3.3.4 The double

We have discussed that C compiler allocates 16-bit for **int** data type, 8-bit for char, and 32-bit for float data type. Sometimes in arithmetic operations we need more storage to store larger data. To solve this problem, C provides the type **double** to store floating-point data up to **64-bit storage**, i.e., double storage of what a float data type has. A variable of type double can store data with 14 digits of precision, in the range **–1.7E-308** to **1.7E+308** (value of E is 10). The MSB is used for sign, next 8-bit is used for exponent, and remaining 52-bit is used for mantissa. See Example 3.4 which is implementing the above discussion.

Example 3.4: Write a 'C' code which demonstrates double.

Answer: In the following program segment identifier **larger_number** is defined **double** type and is assigned a value 3012345.78888. We can print the value of this identifier in same way as float data is printed.

```
/* The double type declaration of a variable */
 #include<stdio.h>
main()
{
   double  larger_number ;
   larger_number = 3012345.78888 ;
   printf("Value of larger_number is %f", larger_number);
}
```

OUTPUT

Value of larger_number is 3012345.78888

3.3.5 The void (Empty data type)

The keyword **void** is used in two contexts: function declarations and pointers. The **void** data type is associated with functions in C language. The pointer type void* is a generic pointer type: any pointer can be assigned to a void*, and a void* can be assigned to any pointer. In function definitions and declarations, it is used to indicate either that the function has no return value, or that it takes no arguments. A function is a program segment that solves some specific work. The **main ()** is also a function defined in C language. The function main() can also uses void to changes its return type. The data type **void** has three uses:

- To declare explicitly a function returning no value.
- To declare explicitly a function having no arguments.
- To create a generic pointer.

When used as a function return type, void means that the function does not return a value. For example,

```
void hello (char *name)
{
    printf("Hello, %s.", name);
}
```

When found in a function heading, void means the function does not take any parameters. For example,

```
int init (void)
{
    return 1;
}
```

This is not the same as defining

```
int init ()
{
    return 1;
}
```

Because in the second case the compiler will not check whether the function is really called with no arguments at all; instead, a function call with arbitrary number of arguments will be accepted without any warnings (this is implemented only for the compatibility with the old-style function definition syntax).

Pointers can also be declared as **void**. They cannot be de-referenced without explicit casting. This is because the compiler cannot determine the size of the object the pointer points to. See Example 3.5 which is implementing the above discussion.

Example 3.5: Write a 'C' code which demonstrates the void pointer type variable.

Answer: Following is the void_pointer() function which is **void** type and demonstrates the different stage of a **void** pointer data type.

```
void void_pointer()
{
    int x;
    float f;
    void *p = &x;           /* p points to x */
    *(int*)p = 2;           /* p holds 2 */
    p = &r;                 /* p points to r*/
    *(float*)p = 1.1;       /* p holds 1.1 */
}
```

In this program segment we have declared p as void type variable. First it is receiving address of variable x. The p further takes an integer value 2. Then in the next statement p receives address of the r. Finally p holds a float value 1.1.

3.4 Variable Definition

A variable is a name that C language compiler associates with a storage location in the main memory of the computer. Variable holds data that can be modified during program execution. After you declare a variable in a program, you can assign a value tc it.

Variables can be allotted using the following rules:

1. Variable cna consit of any sequnece of letters, digits and underscores (_).

2. No other special characters such as +, $, –, etc, are allowed, while giving a name to a variable.
3. The first character of a variable should be a letter or an underscore (_). It can be followed by letters, ditits or underscore.
4. Variable name is case sensitive. That is, Num, and NUM and num are three different variables. Though uppercase letters are allowed, usually variable in C language are written in lowercase.
5. Reserve words called keywords which convey specific meaning to the compiler of C language cannot be used as names of identifiers or variables.

Table 3.5 shows some valid and invalid variable names. It is better to name variables with descriptions that convey the idea of what values they hold. For example, if root of a quadratic equation is to be calculated, the variable in which the value of the root is to be stored can be named as 'root_1' rather than naming it as 'a', 'b', or by any other name.

Table 3.5 Valid and invalid variable names

Valid variable name	*Invalid variable names*
j	5j—a variable name cannot begin with a digit.
j5_system_name	$name—a variable name cannot contain a $ sign.
UpPer_and_Lower_cAse	int—because int is a reserved name or a keyword bad%#*n—a variable name cannot contain any special character except an underscore.

3.5 Arithmetic operators

The **C** language provides +, -, /, *, **%** operators. The **%** operator is modulus division operator and results the value of the remainder, e.g., **8 % 3 = 2** because the remainder is two and **6%3 = 0**, as the remainder is zero. In case of division operator if both operands are **int** type we get integer result e.g., **6/3 = 2, 7/3=2.** If one operand is **float**, the division will be **float** type because float data type comes before the **int** data type in hierarchy. The result of the division also depends on the variable to which we assign the result of evaluated expression. If two operands are integer type but variable to which the expression is assigned is **float** type, the result is **float** type. Generally computed value depends on the data type of the recipient variable. For example, see the following,

1. int x = 30 ;
   int y = 9 ;
   float z = x/y ;
   Then value of z will be 3.333333
2. int x = 30 ;
   int y = 9 ;
   int z = x/y;
   Then the value of z will be 3
3. float x = 30.04 ;
   int y = 9 ;
   int z = x/y;
   Then the value of z will be 3
4. int x = 30 ;
   float y = 9.2 ;
   int z = x/y;

Then the value of z will be 3

5. int x = 30 ;

   float y = 9.2 ;

   float z = x/y ;

   Then value of z will be 3.260869

Similar case is for addition, subtraction, and multiplication operations. For examples,

1. int z, w, x=32, y=20;

   z= x-y;

   w=x+y;

   Then values of z and w are 12 and 52, respectively.

2. int z, w, x=32;

   float y=20.22;

   z= x-y;

   w=x+y;

   Then values of z and w are 11 and 42, respectively.

3. float x=32.55, z, w;

   int y=20;

   z=x-y;

   w=x+y;

   Then values of z and w are 12.55 and 42.55, respectively.

4. int x=20, y=32, z;

   z=x-y;

   Then value of z= -12.

5. float y=32.55;

   int x=20, z;

   z=x-y;

   Then value of z is -12.

6. int x=25, y= - 5, z;

   z= x*y;

   Then value of z is –125.

7. int x=25, z;

   float y=10.5;

   z=x*y;

   Then value of z is 262.5.

We can try other combinations also for arithmetic operators. We may get warning from compiler that data types are not compatible, but finally we can run programs. Sometimes we can print the value of an integer variable as float and float variable as integer by placing the appropriate "%d" or "%f". See Example 3.6 which is implementing the above discussion.

Example 3.6: Write a program segment for demonstrating the different types of arithmetic operators.

Answer: Following code segment demonstrates different types of arithmetic operators available in C.

For example, let us see the following program segment which demonstrates the arithmetic operators.

```
/* Test of the arithmetic operators */
/*arithopt.c*/
#include<stdio.h>
#include<conio.h>
void main()
{
   int x, y, z;
   float x1 , y1 , z1 ;
   printf("\n Division Operator'/' ") ;
   printf("\n——————————————");
   x = 100 ;
   y = 30 ;
   z = x / y ;
   printf("\n x = %d",x);
   printf("\n x = %d",y);
   printf("\n x/y(integer value) = %d ",x/y);
   printf("\n x/y (float value) = %f ", (float) a/b);
   x1 = 15.5 ;
   y1 = 5.0 ;
   z1 = x1 / y1 ;
   z = x1 / y1 ;
   printf("\n x1 = %f",x1);
   printf("\n y1 = %f",y1);
   printf("\n x1/y1(integer value) = %d ",z);
   printf("\n x1/y1 (float value) = %f ", z1);
   printf("\n Addition Operator '+'") ;
   printf("\n——————————————");
   x = 100 ;
   y = 30 ;
   z = x + y ;
   printf("\n x = %d",x);
   printf("\n y = %d",y);
   printf("\n x+y(integer value) = %d ",x+y);
   printf("\n x+y (float value) = %f ", (float) x+y);
   x1 = 15.5 ;
   y1 = 5.0 ;
   z1 = x1 + y1 ;
   z = x1 + y1 ;
   printf("\n x1 = %f",x1);
   printf("\n y1 = %f",y1);
   printf("\n x1+y1(integer value) = %d",z);
   printf("\n a1+b1 (float value) = %f ", z1);
```

```
    printf("\n Multiplication Operator '*'") ;
    printf("\n------------------");
    x = 100 ;
    y = 30 ;
    z = x * y ;
    printf("\n x = %d",x);
    printf("\n y = %d",y);
    printf("\n x*y(integer value) = %d ",x*y);
    printf("\n x*y (float value) = %f ", (float) x*y);
    x1 = 15.5 ;
    y1 = 5.0 ;
    z1 = x1 * y1 ;
    z = x1 * y1 ;
    printf("\n x1 = %f",x1);
    printf("\n y1 = %f",y1);
    printf("\n x1*y1(integer value) = %d ",z);
    printf("\n x1*y1 (float value) = %f ", z1);
    getch( );
}
```

OUTPUT

Division Operator '/ '

x=100

y=30

x/y (integer value) = 3

x/y (float value) = 3.333333

x1=15.500000

y1=5.0000000

x1/y1 (integer value) = 3

x1/y1 (float value) =3.1000000

Addition Operator '+'

x=100

y=30

x+y (integer value) = 130

x+y (float value) = 130.000000

x1=15.5000000

y1=5.0000000

x1+y1 (integer value) = 20

x1+y1 (float value) = 20.500000

Multiplication Operator '*'

----

x=100

```
y=30
x*y (integer value) = 3000
x*y (float value) = 3000.00000
x1=15.50000
y1=5.00000
x1*y1 (integer value) = 77
x1*y1 (float value) = 77.50000
```

We have used the printf ( ) as:

```
printf("\n x*y (float value) = %f ", (float) x*y);
```

There is escape sequence "\n" and then the message "x*y (float value) =" and then type casting "(float) x*y". Why we need such type of casting? We have two integer variables x and y and we want to print x*y as float value. So, here we need to type cast the x*y to float value. Similarly, we can type cast a float value into integer value to avoid the compiler warning/error message.

Now recall the previous examples of the arithmetic operators {arithopt.c}. We can use type casting as given below to avoid the incompatibility of the operands used:

```
·  float y=32.55;
      int x=20, z;
      z=(int) x-y;
·  int x = 30 ;
      float y = 9.2 ;
float z = (float) x/y ;
·  int x = 30, y=9 ;
      float z = (float) x/y ;
```

See Example 3.7 which is implementing the above discussion.

Example 3.7: Following program segment demonstrates the mode '%' operator.

```
#include <stdio.h>
void main()
{
  int i,j;

  /* The modulo is the remainder of after an integer division
     */
  printf("14 modulo 7 (14%%7) is %i\n", 14%7);   /* answer is 0
     */
  printf("15 modulo 7 (15%%7) is %i\n", 15%7);   /* answer is 1
     */
  i=10; j=6;
   printf("%i modulo %i (%i%%%i) is %i\n",i,j,i,j,i%j);      /*
     answer is 4   */
}
```

3.6 Expressions

Logical operators are used to combine multiple relational or logical tests. They allow compound conditions to be evaluated. *Logical operators* are mainly used to control program flow. The logical operators along with their syntax are shown in Table 3.6.

Table 3.6 Logical Operators

Operator	*Expression*	
&&	Logical AND	exp1 && exp2
||	Logical OR	exp1 || exp2
!	Logical NOT	!exp1

The logical AND operator (&&) and the logical OR (||) operator evaluate the truth or falsehood of pairs of expressions. The AND operator evaluates to 1 if and only if both expressions are true. The OR operator evaluates to 1 if *either* expression is true. To test whether y is greater than x and less than z, we would write

```
(x < y) && (y < z)
```

The logical negation operator (!) takes only one operand. If the operand is true, the result is false; if the operand is false, the result is true. The operands to the logical operators may be integers or floating-point objects. The expression

```
1 && -5
```

results in 1 because both operands are nonzero. The same is true of the expression

```
0.5 && -5
```

Logical operators (and the comma and conditional operators) are the only operators for which the order of evaluation of the operands is defined. The compiler must evaluate operands from left to right. Moreover, the compiler is guaranteed not to evaluate an operand if it is unnecessary. For example, in the expression

```
if ((a != 0) && (b/a == 6.0))
```

if a equals 0, the expression (b/a == 6) will not be evaluated. This rule can have unexpected consequences when one of the expressions contains side effects.

In C, true is equivalent to any *nonzero* value, and false is equivalent to 0. Table 3.7 shows the logical tables for each operator, along with the numerical equivalent. All of the operators return 1 for true and 0 for false.

Table 3.7 Truth Table for C's Logical Operators

Operand	*Operator*	*Operand*	*Result*
Zero	&&	zero	0
nonzero	&&	zero	0
Zero	&&	nonzero	0
nonzero	&&	nonzero	1
Zero	||	zero	0
nonzero	||	zero	1
Zero	||	nonzero	1
nonzero	||	nonzero	1
not applicable	!	zero	1
	!	nonzero	0

Table 3.8 shows a number of examples that use relational and logical operators. The logical NOT operator has a higher precedence than the others. The AND operator has higher precedence than the OR operator. Both the logical AND and OR operators have lower precedence than the relational and arithmetic operators.

Logical operators (and the conditional and comma operators) are the only operators for which the order of evaluation of the operands is defined. For these operators, operands must be evaluated from left to right. However, the system evaluates only as much of a logical expression as it needs to determine the result. In many cases, this means that the system does not need to evaluate the entire expression. For instance, consider the following expression:

```
if ((a < b) && (c == d))
```

The system begins by evaluating (a < b). If a is not less than b, the system knows that the entire expression is false, so it will not evaluate (c == d). This can cause problems if some of the expressions contain side effects:

Table 3.8 Examples of Expressions Using the Logical Operators

Given the following declarations:int j = 0, m = 1, n = -1;float x = 2.5, y = 0.0;

Expression	*Equivalent Expression*	*Result*
j && m	(j) && (m)	0
j < m && n < m	(j < m) && (n < m)	1
m + n || ! j	(m + n) || (!j)	1
x * 5 && 5 || m / n	((x * 5) && 5) || (m / n)	1
j <= 10 && x >= 1 && m	((j <= 10) && (x >= 1)) && m	1
!x || !n || m+n	((!x) || (!n)) || (m+n)	0
x * y < j + m || n	((x * y) < (j + m)) || n	1
(x > y) + !j || n++	((x > y) + (!j)) || (n++)	1
(j || m) + (x || ++n)	(j || m) + (x || (++n))	2

```
if ((a < b) && (c == d++))
```

In this case, d is only incremented when a is less than b. This may or may not be what the programmer intended. In general, we should avoid using side effect operators in logical expressions. See Example 3.8 which is implementing the above discussion.

Example 3.8: Write a C program to enjoy your vacation in Europe by winning lottery.

Answer: This program shows how logical operators are used in the implementaion of above problem.

```
#include <stdio.h>
int main(void)
{
int won_lottery, enough_vacation, money_saved;
char answer;

won_lottery = enough_vacation = money_saved = 0;

printf("\nThis program determines whether you can ");
printf("take your next vacation in Europe.\n");
printf("Have you won the lottery? y or n: ");
fflush(stdin);
scanf("%c", &answer);
if (answer == 'y')
won_lottery = 1;

printf("Do you have enough vacation days saved? y or n: ");
fflush(stdin);
scanf ("%c", &answer);
if (answer == 'y')
enough_vacation = 1;
```

```
printf("Have you saved enough money for the trip? y or n: ");
fflush(stdin);
scanf("%c", &answer);
if (answer == 'y')
money_saved = 1;

printf("\n");

if (won_lottery)
{
     printf("Why do you need a program to decide if you");
     printf(" can afford a trip to Europe?\n");
} /* end if */

if (won_lottery || (enough_vacation &&money_saved))
printf("Look out Paris!\n");
else if (enough_vacation &&(!money_saved))
printf("You've got the time, but you haven't got \the
      dollars.\n");
else if (!enough_vacation || (!money_saved))
{
     printf("Tough luck. Try saving your money and ");
     printf("vacation days next year.\n");
} /* end else/if */
}
```

3.7 Constants and Literals

We have seen data types in C and we know that a variable can hold some data. The data can be assigned while writing a program or inputted through keyboard also. The data can be modified as per need of a programmer. But sometimes we need to make some data constant and it should not be alter during the program execution. A data may be modified knowingly or unknowingly. We have a special feature in C that makes a data constant throughout the execution of a program. For this, we use keyword const defined in C language. We can also make a data constant by using *define* directive in C. For example, the following directive creates a constant named Size and assigns value 25 to it.

```
#define Size 25
```

This directive (define) is instruction for the C preprocessor; the preprocessor will replace the constant name with its value.

There is a keyword **const** available in **C**, which is also used for the same purpose. With this keyword, one requires to use prefixes/suffixes, which are given in **Table 3.9**. The **const** ensures that the parameter defined and value associated will not alter during the lifetime of the program. The constants can be classified into five categories:

- Character Constants
- Integer constants
- Floating-point constants

Table 3.9 Constant suffixes/prefixes

Constant suffix/prefix	*Example*
L, l are used for long integer and double as suffix	6599L, 35471
F, f are used for float constant as suffix	46578F, 54328f
For hexadecimal constant 0x is used as prefix	0x35536
Single quote is used for character constant	'Y'
For integer constant simply const keyword is placed	const in num =7674

- Literal constants (Strings, group of characters)
- Enumeration constants

For example, the program *constant.c* discusses the constant declarations with the help of keyword **const**.

```
/* constant.c */
#include<stdio.h>
void main()
{
   const int num = 345;
   const long int LONG =999678647L;
   const float Float_num = 1234.30045f;
   const int Octal = 012345;
   const int Hex = 0x1abc;
   const int Unsigned_num = 1236u;
   printf ("\n Integer %d,num);
   printf ("\n Long integer %ld ,LONG);
   printf ("\n Float %f,Float_num);
   printf ("\n Octal %o,Octal);
   printf ("\n Hexadecimal %X,Hex);
   printf ("\nUnsigned integer: %u ,Unsigned_num);
}
```

OUTPUT

Integer 234
Long integer 999678647
Float 1234.30045
Octal 12345
Hexadecimal 1ABC
Unsigned integer 1236

3.7.1 Enumeration Constants

These fall into the category of 'half baked'. They are not proper enumerated types, as in Pascal, and only really serve to help we reduce the number of #define statements in a program. For example,

```
enum e_tag
{
```

```
        a, b, c, d=20, e, f, g=20, h
}var;
```

Just as with structures and unions, the e_tag is the tag, and var is the definition of a variable.

The names declared inside the enumeration are constants with int type. Their values are these:

a = 0

b = 1

c = 2

d = 20

e = 21

f = 22

g = 20

h = 21

So we can see that, in the absence of anything to the contrary, the values assigned start at zero and increase. A specific value can be given if we want, when the increase will continue one at a time afterwards; the specific value must be an *integral constant* that is representable in an int. It is possible for more than one of the names to have the same value. The only use for these things is to give a better-scoped version of this:

```
#define a 0
#define b 1
/* and so on */
```

It is better scoped because the declaration of enumerations follows the standard scope rules for C, whereas #define statements have file scope details about #define. Not that we are likely to care, but the C states that enumeration types are of a type that is compatible with an implementation-defined one of the integral types. So what? For interest's sake here is an illustration:

```
enum ee{a,b,c}e_var, *ep;
```

The names a, b, and c all behave as if they were int constants when we use them; e_var has type enum ee and ep is a pointer to enum ee. The compatibility requirement means that (amongst other implications) there will be an integral type whose address can be assigned to ep without violating the type-compatibility requirements for pointers.

3.8 Simple Assignment Statement

The process of giving initial values to variables is known as initialization. We can initialize more than one variable in a single statement. This type of initializaation would need more number of assignment operators. Hence, the name multiple assignment statements.

For exmple,

(i) int x = y = z = 20;

(ii) float a = b = c = d = 3.65

The first statement initializes the three int variables x, y, and z to 20. The second statement initializes the four float variables a, b, c, and d to 3.65.

3.9 Basic Input/Output Statement

There are a number of related functions used for formatted input/output (I/O), each one determining the format of the I/O from a *format string*. For output, the format string consists of plain text, which is output unchanged, and embedded *format specifications* which call for some special processing of one of the remaining arguments to the function. On input, the plain text must match what is seen in the input stream; the format specifications again specify what the meaning of remaining arguments is? Each format specification is introduced by a % character, followed by the rest of the specification.

3.9.1 Output: the printf family

printf's name comes from **print** formatted. It generates output under the control of a *format string* (its first argument) which consists of literal characters to be printed and also special character sequences- *format specifiers* which request that other arguments be fetched, formatted, and inserted into the string. Our very first program was nothing more than a call to printf, printing a constant string. For those functions performing output, the format specification takes the following form, with optional parts enclosed in brackets:

```
%<flags><field width><precision><length>conversion
```

The meaning of *flags*, *field width*, *precision*, *length*, and *conversion* are given in Table 3.10, although tersely. For example, see the following code:

```
printf("Hello, world!\n");
```

Table 3.10 Format flags

Flags	*Meaning*
-	Left justify the conversion within its field.
+	A signed conversion will always start with a plus or minus sign.
‘’ *space*	If the first character of a signed conversion is not a sign, insert a space. Overridden by + if present.
#	Forces an alternative form of output. The first digit of an octal conversion will always be a 0; inserts 0X in front of a non-zero hexadecimal.
0	Pad d, i, o, u, x, X, e, E, f, F and G conversions on the left with zeros up to the field width. Overridden by the - flag. If a precision is specified for the d, i, o, u, x or X conversions, the flag is ignored. The behaviour is undefined for other conversions.
field width	A decimal integer specifying the minimum output field width. This will be exceeded if necessary. If an asterisk is used here, the next argument is converted to an integer and used for the value of the field width; if the value is negative it is treated as a - flag followed by a positive field width. Output that would be less than the field width is padded with spaces (zeros if the *field width* integer starts with a zero) to fit. The padding is on the left unless the left-adjustment flag is specified.
precision	This starts with a period ‘.’. It specifies the minimum number of digits for d, i, o, u, x, or X conversions; the number of digits after the decimal point for e, E, f conversions; the maximum number of digits for g and G conversions; the number of characters to be printed from a string for s conversion. The amount of padding overrides the field width. If an asterisk is used here, the next argument is converted to an integer and used for the value of the field width. If the value is negative, it is treated as if it were missing. If only the period is present, the precision is taken to be zero.
length	h preceding a specifier to print an integral type causes it to be treated as if it were a short. (Note that the various sorts of short are always promoted to one of the flavours of int when passed as an argument.) l works like h but applies to a long integral argument. L is used to indicate that a long double argument is to be printed, and only applies to the floating-point specifiers. These are cause undefined behaviour if they are used with the ‘wrong’ type of conversion see Table 3.11.

Our second program also featured a call to printf:

```
printf("i is %d\n", i);
```

In this case, whenever printf "printed the string "i is %d", it did not print it verbatim; it replaced the two

Table 3.11 DATA formatters

Specifier	Effect	Default precision
D	signed decimal	1
I	signed decimal	1
U	unsigned decimal	1
O	unsigned octal	1
X	unsigned hexadecimal (0–f)	1
X	unsigned hexadecimal (0–F)	1
Precision	*Precision* specifies minimum number of digits, expanded with leading zeros if necessary. Printing a value of zero with zero precision outputs no characters.	
f	Print a double with *precision* digits (rounded) after the decimal point. To suppress the decimal point use a *precision* of explicitly zero. Otherwise, at least one digit appears in front of the point.	6
e, E	Print a double in exponential format, rounded, with one digit before the decimal point, *precision* after it. A *precision* of zero suppresses the decimal point. There will be at least two digits in the exponent, which is printed as 1.23e15 in e format, or 1.23E15 in E format.	6
g,G	Use style f, or e (E with G) depending on the exponent. If the exponent is less than "4 or e" *precision*, f is not used. Trailing zeros are suppressed, a decimal point is only printed if there is a following digit.	unspecified
c	The int argument is converted to an unsigned char and the resultant character printed.	
s	Print a string up to *precision* digits long. If *precision* is not specified, or is greater than the length of the string, the string must be NUL terminated.	infinite
p	Display the value of a (void *) pointer in a system-dependent way.	
n	The argument must be a pointer to an integer. The number of characters output so far by this call will be written into the integer.	
%	A %	—
'['']'	String char []* (character selection)	
%ud	Unsigned integer	
%uc	Unsigned character	
%uf	Unsigned floating point number	
%ld	Long integer	

characters %d with the value of the variable i. There are quite a number of format specifiers for printf which are given in Table 3.11.

It is also possible to specify the width and precision of numbers and strings as they are inserted (somewhat like FORTRAN format statements). A notation like %3d means to print an int in a field at least 3 spaces wide; a notation like %5.2f means to print a float or double in a field at least 5 spaces wide, with two places to the right of the decimal.) To illustrate with a few more examples: the call

```
printf("%c %d %f %e %s %d%%\n", '1', 2, 3.14, 56000000., "eight",
        9);
```

would print

```
1 2 3.140000 5.600000e+07 eight 9%
```

The call

```
printf("%d %o %x\n", 100, 100, 100);
```

would print

```
100 144 64
```

Successive calls to printf just build up the output a piece at a time, so the calls

```
printf("Hello, ");
printf("world!\n");
```

would also print Hello, world! (on one line of output).

Earlier we learned that C represents characters internally as small integers corresponding to the characters' values in the machine's character set (typically ASCII). This means that there is not really much difference between a character and an integer in C; most of the difference is in whether we choose to interpret an integer as an integer or a character. printf is one place where we get to make that choice: %d prints an integer value as a string of digits representing its decimal value, while %c prints the character corresponding to a character set value.

So the lines

```
char c = 'A';
int i = 65;
printf("c = %c, i = %d\n", c, i);
```

would print c as the character A and i as the number 65. But if, on the other hand, we called

```
printf("c = %d, i = %c\n", c, i);
```

We had see the decimal value (printed by %d) of the character 'A', followed by the character (whatever it is) which happens to have the decimal value 65.

We have to be careful when calling printf. It has no way of knowing how many arguments we have passed it or what their types are other than by looking for the format specifiers in the format string. If there are more format specifiers (that is, more % signs) than there are arguments, or if the arguments have the wrong types for the format specifiers, printf can misbehave badly, often printing nonsense numbers or (even worse) numbers which mislead us into thinking that some other part of a program is broken.

Because of some automatic conversion rules which we have not covered yet, we have a small amount of latitude in the types of the expressions we pass as arguments to printf. The argument for %c may be of type char or int, and the argument for %d may be of type char or int. The string argument for %s may be a string constant, an array of characters, or a pointer to some characters (though we have not really covered strings or pointers yet). Finally, the arguments corresponding to %e, %f, and %g may be of types float or double. But other combinations do *not* work reliably: %d will not print a long int or a float or a double; %ld will not print an int; %e, %f, and %g will not print an int.

Table 3.12 Functions performing formatted output	
Name	***Purpose***
fprintf	General formatted output as described. Output is written to the file indicated by stream.
printf	Identical to fprintf with a first argument equal to stdout.
sprintf	Identical to fprintf except that the output is not written to a file, but written into the character array pointed to by s.
vfprintf	Formatted output as for fprintf, but with the variable argument list replaced by arg which must have been initialized by va_start. va_end is not called by this function.
vprintf	Identical to vfprintf with a first argument equal to stdout.
vsprintf	Formatted output as for sprintf, but with the variable argument list replaced by arg which must have been initialized by va_start. va_end is not called by this function. Note (va_start and va_end will discussed later on).

The functions that use these formats are described in Table 3.12. All need the inclusion of <stdio.h>. Their declarations are:

```
#include <stdio.h>

int fprintf(FILE *stream, const char *format, ...);
int printf(const char *format, ...);
int sprintf(char *s, const char *format, ...);

#include <stdarg.h>      /* as well as stdio.h */
int vfprintf(FILE *stream, const char *format, va list arg);
int vprintf(const char *format, va list arg);
int vsprintf(char *s, const char *format, va list arg);
```

All of the above functions return the number of characters output, or a negative value on error. The trailing null is *not* counted by sprintf and vsprintf.

3.9.2 Input: the scanf family

A number of functions exist analogous to the printf family, but for the purposes of input instead. The most immediate difference between the two families is that the scanf group needs to be passed *pointers* to their arguments, so that the values read can be assigned to the proper destinations. Forgetting to pass a pointer is a very common error, and one which the compiler cannot detect—the variable argument list prevents it. The format string is used to control interpretation of a stream of input data, which generally contains values to be assigned to the objects pointed to by the remaining arguments to scanf. The contents of the format string may contain:

white space: This causes the input stream to be read up to the next non-white-space character.

ordinary character: Anything except white-space or % characters. The next character in the input stream *must* match this character.

conversion specification: This is a % character, followed by an optional * character (which suppresses the conversion), followed by an optional nonzero decimal integer specifying the maximum field width, an optional h, l or L to control the length of the conversion and finally a non-optional conversion specifier. Note that use of h, l, or L will affect the type of pointer which must be used.

Except for the specifiers c, n and [, a field of input is a sequence of non-space characters starting at the first non-space character in the input. It terminates at the first conflicting character or when the input field width is reached.

The result is put into wherever the corresponding argument points, unless the assignment is suppressed using the * mentioned already. The conversion specifiers shown in Table 3.13 may be used. The size specifiers have the effect shown in Table 3.14. The functions are described below, with the following declarations:

Table 3.13 Conversion specifiers

Specifier	Effect
d i o u x	Convert a signed integer, a signed integer in a form acceptable to strtol, an octal integer, an unsigned integer and a hexadecimal integer, respectively.
e f g	Convert a float (*not* a double).
s	Read a string, and add a null at the end. The string is terminated by whitespace on input (which is not read as part of the string).
[	Read a string. A list of characters, called the *scan set* follows the [. A] delimits the list. Characters are read until (but not including) the first character which is *not* in the scan set. If the first character in the list is a circumflex ^, then the scan set includes any character not in the list. If the initial sequence is [^] or [], the] is not a delimiter, but part of the list and another] will be needed to end the list. If there is a minus sign (-) in the list, it must be either the first or the last character; otherwise the meaning is implementation defined.
c	Read a single character; white space is significant here. To read the first non-white space character, use %1s. A field width indicates that an array of characters is to be read.
p	Read a (void *) pointer previously written out using the %p of one of the printfs.
%	A % is expected in the input, no assignment is made.
n	Return as an integer the number of characters read by this call so far.

Table 3.14 Size specifiers

Specifier	Modifies	Converts
l	d i o u x	long int
h	d i o u x	short int
l	e f	double
L	e f	long double

```
#include <stdio.h>
int fscanf(FILE *stream, const
       char *format, ...);
int sscanf(const char *s, const char *format, ...);
int scanf(const char *format, ...);
```

fscanf takes its input from the designated stream, scanf is identical to fscanf with a first argument of stdin, and sscanf takes its input from the designated character array. If an input failure occurs before any conversion, EOF is returned. Otherwise, the number of successful conversions is returned: this may be zero if no conversions are performed. An input failure is caused by reading EOF or reaching the end of the input string (as appropriate). A conversion failure is caused by a failure to match the proper pattern for a particular conversion.

Let us Revise

1. Characters play a central role in C language.
2. Variables play an important role in computer programming because they enable programmers to write flexible programs.
3. The keyword **int** in C language is used to define integer data type.
4. We use string "**%d**" with printf() function to print an integer data type.
5. The **char** data type is used to hold **ASCII** (American Standard Code for Information Interchange) characters and there is generally 8-bit or 1 byte memory reservation for it.
6. **C** language provides keyword **float** to store floating-point data.
7. C provides the type **double** to store floating-point data up to **64-bit storage.**
8. The keyword **void** is used in two contexts: function declarations and pointers.
9. A variable is a name that C language compiler associates with a storage location in the main memory of the computer.
10. The **C** language provides **+, -, /, *, %** operators.
11. The logical AND operator (&&) and the logical OR (||) operator evaluate the truth or falsehood of pairs of expressions.
12. The **const** ensures that the parameter defined and value associated will not alter during the lifetime of the program.
13. There are a number of related functions used for formatted input/output (I/O), each one determining the format of the I/O from a *format string*.
14. printf's name comes from **print** formatted.
15. A computer program consists of two parts: ***code*** and ***data***.

Multiple Choice Questions

1. How many bits are reserved for int data type by a C compiler?
   (a) 16-bit (b) 32-bit (c) 64-bit
   (d) Depends on Compiler
2. How many bits are reserved for float data type by a C compiler?
   (a) 16-bit (b) 32-bit (c) 64-bit
   (d) Depends on Compiler
3. How many bits are reserved for char data type by a C compiler?
   (a) 8-bit (b) 16-bit (c) 32-bit
   (d) Depends on Compiler
4. Suppose a C compiler reserves 16-bit for a signed int data type. What is the range of the integer number represented by a signed integer variable?
   (a) –32768 to 32767 (b) -32768 to 32768 (c) -2^{15} to 2^{15}-1
5. Suppose a C compiler reserves 16-bit for a unsigned int data type. What is the range of the integer number represented by an integer variable?
   (a) 0 to 65536 (b) 0 to 65535 (c) 0 to 65537
6. Suppose a C compiler reserves 16-bit for a char data type. What is the total number of characters that can be represented and stored by compiler?
   (a) 127 (b) 128 (c) 256
   (d) 255

7. Consider the following program:

```
#include<stdio.h>
void main( )
{
int number =16;
printf("The value of number is: %f ", number);
}
```

What is output of the above program?

(a) The value of number is: 16

(b) Syntax error: Opening curly bracket is missing

(c) Syntax error: number cannot be printed as float

(d) None

8. Consider the following program:

```
#include<stdio.h>
void main( )
{
const int number =16;
printf("The value of number is: %u ", number);
}
```

What is output of the above program?

(a) The value of number is: 16

(b) Syntax error: Opening curly bracket is missing

(c) Syntax error: number cannot be printed as unsigned

(d) None

9. Consider the following program:

```
#include<stdio.h>
void main( )
{
const int number =16;
number = number +1;
printf("The value of number is: %d ", number);
}
```

What is output of the above program?

(a) The value of number is: 16

(b) Syntax error: Value of number cannot be modified

(c) The value of number is: 17

(d) None

10. Consider the following program:

```
#include<stdio.h>
void main( )
{
```

```
        printf(" C is a middle-level
        language");
    }
```

What is output of the above program?

(a) C is a middle-level language (b) Syntax error (c) C is a middle-level Language

11. Consider the following integer type variables in C language:

(i) number (ii) number_132 (iii) ingeter.number

(iv) intger_number (v) data_of_birth

which one is incorrect variable name?

(a) (ii), (iv), (v) (b) (ii) (c) (iii)

12. Consider the following program:

```
#include<stdio.h>
void main( )
{
    int num1=25, num2=30;
    num1=num1+num2;
    num2=num1- num2;
    num1=num1-num2;
    printf("\n Value of Num1= %  and value of num2= %d",
num1, num2);
}
```

What does the above program do?

(a) Swap the value of num1 and num2
(b) Add the num2 with num1
(c) Add num1 with num2
(d) None

13. How many temporary variables are needed to swap two data type?

(a) One (b) Two (c) Zero
(d) At most one

14. Is the following declaration incorrect?

```
char ch= "Y";
```

(a) Yes (b) No (c) Depends on Compiler
(d) Cannot decide

15. How many symbols can be placed in a variable name in C language?

(a) 16 (b) 32 (c) 64

16. What is the output of following program?

```
#include<stdio.h>
void main( )
{
        printf("\n C language is middle-level language");
}
```

(a) C language is middle-level language (b) Syntax error

(c) No output (d) None

17. What is the output of following program?

```
#include<stdio.h>
void main( )
{
   int number;
   printf("\n number is : %d", number) ;
 }
```

(a) 256 (b) 0 (c) Garbage

(d) None

18. What is the output of following program?

```
#include<stdio.h>
void main( )
{
   int num1, num2;
   num1=10;  num2=15;
   printf("\n number are : %d", num1, num2) ;
}
```

(a) 10 (b) 10 15 (c) Error

(d) None

19. What is the output of following program?

```
#include<stdio.h>
void main( )
{
   int number = 011;
   printf("\n number is : %d", number) ;
}
```

(a) 9 (b) 011 (c) Garbage

(d) None

20. What is the output of following program?

```
#include<stdio.h>
void main( )
{
   float number = 7/3;
   printf("\n number is : %f", number) ;
 }
```

(a) 2.333333 (b) 2.00000 (c) Garbage

(d) None

21. What is the output of following program?

```
#include<stdio.h>
void main( )
{
    float number = 5.0/2;
    printf("\n number is : %f", number) ;
}
```

(a) 2.50000 (b) 2.00000 (c) Garbage
(d) None

22. What is the output of following program?

```
#include<stdio.h>
void main( )
{
    int number = 7/3;
    printf("\n number is : %d", number) ;
}
```

(a) 2.333333 (b) 2 (c) Garbage
(d) None

23. What is the output of following program?

```
#include<stdio.h>
void main( )
{
    float number;
    number = (float) 2+5/2;
    printf("\n number is : %f", number) ;
}
```

(a) 3.555555 (b) 4.00000 (c) Garbage
(d) None

24. What is the output of following program?

```
#include<stdio.h>
void main( )
{
    float number;
    number = 2+(float) 5/2;
    printf("\n number is : %f", number) ;
}
```

(a) 3.555555 (b) 4.50000 (c) Garbage
(d) None

25. What is the output of following program?

```
#include<stdio.h>
```

```
void main( )
{
    float number;
    number = (float) 2+5/2;
    printf( ) ;
}
```

(a) 3.555555 (b) 4.00000 (c) Error

(d) None

True/False Questions

1. Any valid printable ASCII character can be used in an identifier.
2. All variables must be given a type when they are declared.
3. Declarations can appear anywhere in a program.
4. C treats the variables name and Name to be same.
5. The underscore can be used anywhere in an identifier.
6. The keyword void is a data type in C.
7. Floating point constants, by default, denote float type values.
8. Like variables, constants have a type.
9. Character constants are coded using double quotes.
10. Initialization is the process of assigning a value to a variable at the time of declaration.
11. All static variables are automatically initialized to zero.
12. The scanf function can be used to read only one value at a time.

Match Columns

Match the matter in Column A with the matter in Column B.

Column A	Column B
A. \n	1. carriage return
B. %	2. assignment operator
C. &&	3. bitwise operator
D. \r	4. Escape sequence
E. &	5. logical operator
F. +=	6. mod operator

Fill in the Blanks with Appropriate Words

a. different	b. object	c. reserved	d. 2
e. multiply	f. conditional	g. \n	h. one's complement

1. The run time library is a collection of _________ files.
2. ________ is called newline character.
3. ?: is ______________ operator.
4. Operators &, ^, == have _________ precedence.
5. The unary operator - can be used for performing ___________ on a variable.
6. In 'C' while is _________ word.

7. Number of bytes occupied by a zero terminated string “a” is __________.
8. The operator i << 2 is equivalent to __________ i by 4.

Descriptive Type Questions

1. What is precedence of an operator? Explain with the help of suitable examples.
2. Write a C program, which prints all **ASCII** values.
3. Given the values of the variables a, b and c, write a program to rotate their values such that a has the value of b, b has then value of c, and c has the value of a.
4. Write a program that reads a floating-point number and then displays the right-most digit of the integral part of the number.
5. Modify the above program to display the two right-most digits of the integral part of the number.
6. Write a program that will obtain the length and width of a rectangle from the user and compute its area and perimeter.
7. The total distance travelled by a vehicle in *t* seconds is given by

   distance = $u*t + (a*t^2)/2$

   Where *u* is the initial velocity (meters per second), *a* is the acceleration (meters per second^2). Write a program to evaluate the distance traveled at regular intervals of time, given the val-ues of *u* and *a*. The program should provide the flexibility to the user to select his own time intervals and repeat the calculations for different values of *u* and *a*.

Answers to Objective Type Questions

Multiple Choice Questions

1. a	2. b	3. c	4. a
5. c	6. b	7. a	8. c
9. b	10. a	11. a	12. c
13. b	14. c	15. a	16. b
17. a	18. c	19. a	20. b
21. c	22. b	23. a	24. c
25. b			

True False Questions

1. F	2. F	3. T	4. T
5. T	6. T	7. T	8. T
9. T	10. T	11. T	12. T

Matching Columns

A. d	B. f	C. e	D. a
E. c	F. b		

Fill in the Blanks

1. b	2. g	3. f	4. a
5. h	6. c	7. d	8. e

Conditional Statements and Loops

4

4.1 Decision Making within a Program

It is an instruction to the computer to perform a specific operation. It may be a declaration, an input-output action, arithmetic and logical operation, assignments or it may be a control statement. You will be studying all about these statements sebsequently. Normally, the statements in a program are executed in the order in which they appear in the program. This type of execution is called a sequential execution. But, in most of the programs, it is necessary to:

- Select a set of statements from several alternatives.
- Skip certain statements depending on some conditions in the program and continue the execution from some other point.
- Repeat a set of statementss for a known number of times or until a specified condition is fulfilled

Under such situations, we make use of control statements. They are generally called control structures. They define the order of execution of statements in a program.

4.2 Conditions and Relational Operators

A program consists of a number of statements which are usually executed in sequence. Programs can be much more powerful if we can control the order in which statements are run. Statements fall into three general types:

- Assignment, where values, usually the results of calculations, are stored in variables.
- Input / Output, data is read in or printed out.
- Control, the program makes a decision about what to do next.

Generally, statements of a program are executed one by one starting from the first instruction. This is known as serial or sequential execution. The order in which statements are written and executed in a program is extremely important. In other words when a particular statement is executed, the statements on next line of the program are taken up for the execution and then next and so on. But sometimes it is desirable to skip or jump some statements (block code), which is based on some specified condition. There are some other situations like loops that are not normal sequential execution. So, C language provides looping and jumping facilities also and this makes the C language different from other low-level languages.

We can categorize the statements of C based on the order of execution. **ANSI C** standard statements can be grouped into categories as given in **Table 4.1.** This chapter will discuss the use of control statements in C. We will show how they can be used to write powerful programs.

4.3 Logical Connectives

We can restrict the flow of execution based on the certain condition what we have. To control the flow of execution of programs, **C** language provides very powerful facilities in the form of selection (conditional) statements. **C** supports two types of selection statements; **if** and **switch**. The **?:** operator is an alternative to

if statement in certain circumstances as discussed in the previous chapter. The **if** statement can be further classified into two categories:

- if
- if - else

Now, let us see the both if statements.

Table 4.1 Category of C statements

Statement Category	Statement Sub-category
Block	Begins with {and ends with}
Expression	All valid C language expressions
Selection	1. if
	2. switch
Iteration	1. for
	2. while
	3. do-while
Jump or Loop	1. break
	2. goto
	3. continue
	4. return
Labels	1. case
	2. default

4.5 If statement

If a set of statements is executed based on a condition's validity, i.e., **if** the given condition is evaluated true then set of statements is executed otherwise not. The syntax for **if** statement is given below:

```
if (condition
)
{
  Statement 1;
  Statement 2;
  ...
  ...
  ...
  Statement n;
}
```

The statements outside if-block do not affected by the validity of condition of if statement, i.e., whether the control enters into the **if** block or not. The condition is opposed in form of expressions like:

```
· if(number > 10)
{
  ...
  ...
}
· if(character = = 'y' || character = = 'Y')
{
  ...
  ...
}
```

Here we have used OR operator to combine two simple conditions; character = = 'y' and character = = 'Y'. If any one of these conditions is evaluated TRUE then statements of if-block are evaluated. We can use other operators also. If condition of if statement is TRUE then control enters into the if-block and statements of if-block are executed and then after the next statement of the if-block is executed. Even if the condition of if statement is found FALSE, the next statement of the if-block is evaluated automatically due to sequential nature of C language. Let us see a simple Example 4.1 that illustrates the above discussion.

Example 4.1: Write a C program to find average of five subject marks of a student. Using if statement state whether students has secured more than 50% or not.

Answer: Following is the implementation.

```
#include<stdio.h>
void main()
{
int num1, num2, num3, num4, num5;
float sum;
printf("\n Enter the marks of five subjects:");
scanf("%d%d%d%d%d", &num1, &num2, &num3, &num4, &num5);
sum = (num1+num2+num3+num4+num5)/500;
sum=sum*100;
if(sum >50)
   printf("\n You have scored more than 50% marks");
getch();
}
```

OUTPUT

Enter the marks of five subjects: 56 65 70 45 82

You have scored more than 50% marks

In the above program segment we are taking five input data from the standard device. It finds the summation and divides the summation with 500 and resulting value is multiplied with 100 to get the percentage. This percentage is checked whether it is greater than 50% or not. If greater than 50% then output is displayed otherwise not.

If the condition is true, the statements enclosed in the braces are executed or if braces are not present after if statement then single statement after if statement is executed. After the if-block statement, next statements to if-block are executed. One thing should be noted here that if there is more than one statement in if-block then we place braces otherwise for single statement there is no need of braces. The control-flow of if-statement is shown in Figure 4.1. This is shown here:

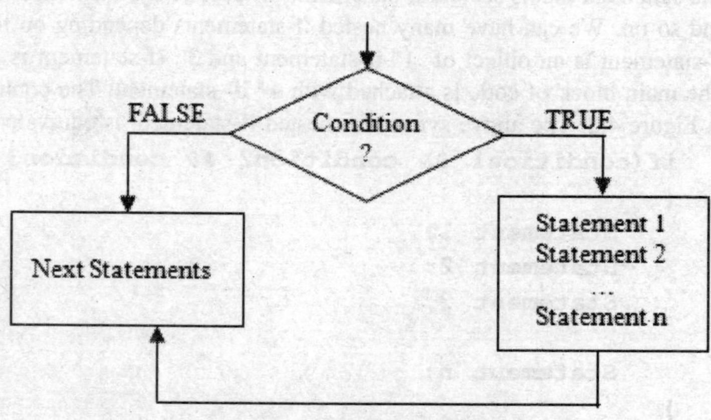

Figure 4.1 Control-flow of if-statement

```
· if(condition)
    {
    Statement1;
    Statement 2;
    ...
    Statement n;
  }

· if(condition)      /*No need of braces for single statement */
    statement;
```

4.5.1 Nested If Statements

We have seen in the previous section that if statement is evaluated if the condition is found TRUE otherwise not. There are certain situations where more than single condition is there. For example, let us consider the previous program. We have printed the marks which is above 50% only. There is no provision of printing other marks that are above or below 50%. We can do it by placing nested if-statements like given below:

```
                if ( condition1 )
                    if (condition2 )
                        if (condition3 )
                            if (condition4 )

...
        {
    Statement 1;
        Statement 2;
        ...
    Statement n;
        }
```

We can have braces after an if-statement, if more than single statements are there. The first if-statement has one statement that is second if-statement; the second if-statement has one statement that is third if-statement, and so on. We can have many nested if-statements depending on the requirement. In the above syntax 2nd **if**-statement is an object of 1st **if**-statement and 3rd **if**-statement is an object of 2nd **if**-statement and so on. The main block of code is attached with 4th **if**- statement. The control-flow of nested if-statement is shown in Figure 4.2. The above syntax for nested **if**-statement is equivalent to the following syntax:

```
if(condition1 && condition2 && condition3 && condition4)
{
   Statement 1;
   Statement 2;
   Statement 3;
   ...
   Statement n;
}
```

Go through the Example 4.5 and Example 4.6 which are implementing the above discussion.

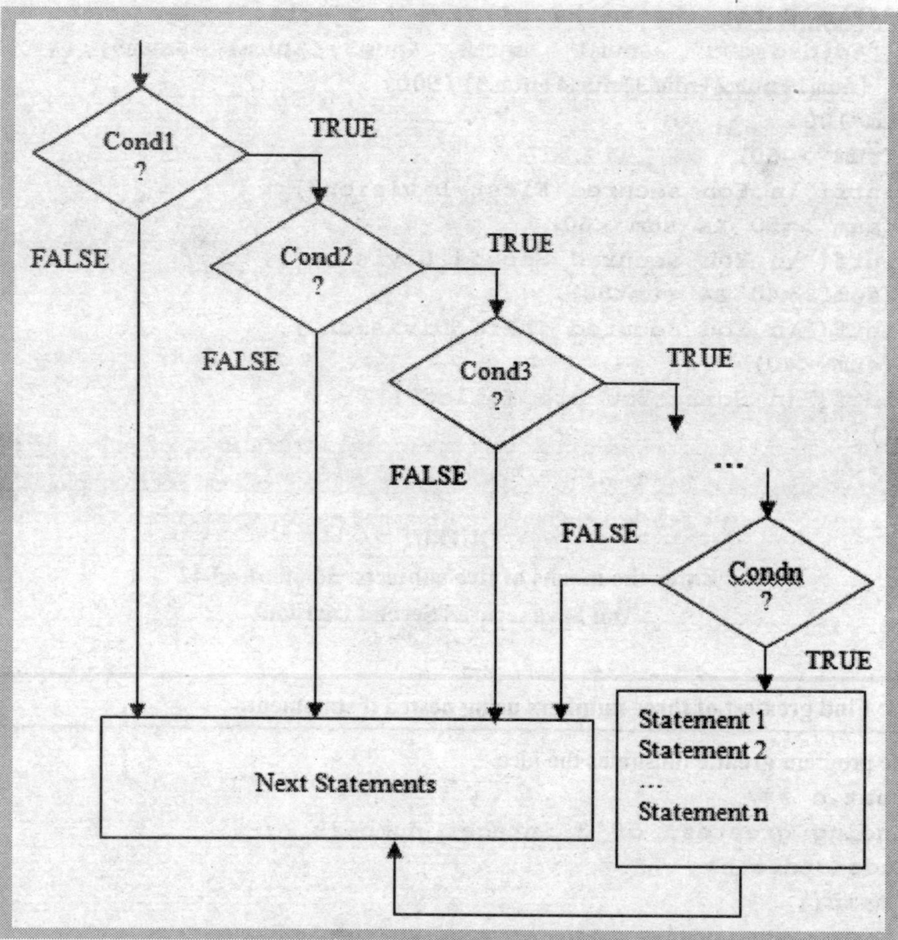

Figure 4.2 Control-flow of Nested if-statement

Example 4.2: Let us consider the Example 4.1 and modify to get first division, second division, third division, and fail. Use the following conditions:

- If percentage of marks > = 60 then first division
- If percentage of marks > = 50 and marks <60 then second division
- If percentage of marks >= 40 and marks <50 then third division
- If percentage of marks <40 then fail

Answer: The following program segment implements the above discussion:

```
#include<stdio.h>
void main()
{
int num1, num2, num3, num4, num5;
float sum;
```

```
printf("\n Enter the marks of five subjects:");
scanf("%d%d%d%d%d", &num1, &num2, &num3, &num4, &num5);
sum = (num1+num2+num3+num4+num5)/500;
sum=sum*100;
   if(sum >=60)
   printf("\n You secured First Division");
   if(sum >=50 && sum <60)
   printf("\n You secured Second Division");
   if(sum >=40 && sum<50)
   printf("\n You secured Third Division");
   if(sum <40)
   printf("\n Sorry…You are failed");
getch();
}
```

OUTPUT

Enter the marks of five subjects: 56 60 61 45 42

You have secured Second Division

Example 4.3: Find greatest of three numbers using nested if statement.

Answer: The program **great.c** illustrates the idea.

```
/* great.c **/
/* Finding greatest of 3 integer numbers */
#include<stdio.h>
void main()
{
   int x , y , z ;
   printf("\n Enter value for x , y ,z :") ;
   scanf("%d %d %d", &x, &y, &z) ;
   if ( x >y)
      if(x > z )
         printf(" \n x is greatest = %d", x) ;
   if ( x < y)
      if( y > z )
         printf(" \n y is greatest = %d", y) ;
   if ( x < y)
      if(z > y )
         printf(" \n z is greatest = %d", z) ;
   if ( x >y)
      if( y < z)
         if(x < z )
               printf(" \n z is greatest  = %d", z) ;
}
```

4.6 If-else statement

Sometimes placing nested if-statements results in a long series of if-statements and it appears complex also. We have seen that statements of a if-block are evaluated if and only if condition is TRUE. But in case of FALSE validity of the condition there is no block such as if-block. C language provides this facility to place else-block after an if-block. If condition of if-statement is found FALSE then statements of else-block are evaluated. So, in this way we use the both values of the opposed condition, i.e., if condition is TRUE then if-block otherwise else-block. The control-flow of if-else statement is shown in Figure 4.3. The syntax for **if-else** statement is given below:

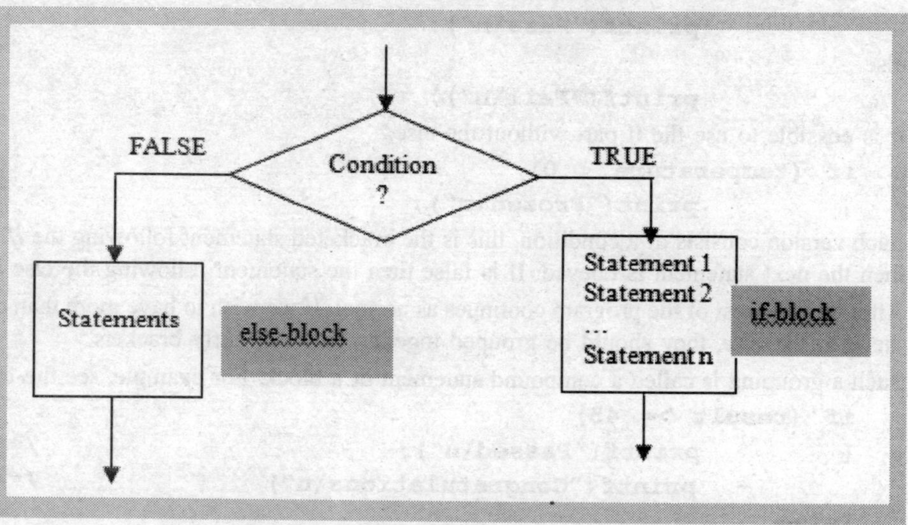

Figure 4.3 Control-flow of if-else statement

```
if(condition)
{
  Statement 1;
  Statement 2;
  Statement 3;
    ...
  Statement n;
}else
{
  Statement 1;
  Statement 2;
  Statement 3;
    ...
  Statement m;
}
```

In the above syntax, if **condition** is TRUE then the code of the first block (following the if statement) is executed else code of the second block is executed. Execution of both blocks is mutually exclusive.

This statement generally is used to decide whether to do something at a special point, or to decide between two courses of action. The following condition decides whether a student has passed an examination with a pass mark of 45.

```
   if  (result >= 45)
            printf("Pass\n");
else
            printf("Fail\n");
```

It is possible to use the if part without the else.

```
   if  (temperature < 0)
            print("Frozen\n");
```

Each version consists of a condition, this is the bracketed statement following the *if*. If the condition is true then the next statement is obeyed. If is false then the statement following the else is obeyed if present. After this, the rest of the program continues as normal. If we wish to have more than one statement following the *if* or the *else*, they should be grouped together between curly brackets.

Such a grouping is called a compound statement or a block. For example, see the following code segment

```
   if  (result >= 45)
   {        printf("Passed\n");                            /*   A*/
            printf("Congratulations\n")                    /* B */
   }else
   {        printf("Failed\n");                            /* C */
            printf("Good luck in the reappear \n"); /* D */
   }
```

In the above code segment if the value of result is greater or equal to 45 lines A and B are executed otherwise lines C and D are executed.

Sometimes we wish to make a multi-way decision based on several conditions. The most general way of doing this is by using the *else* if variant on the *if* statement. This works by cascading several comparisons. As soon as one of these gives a true result, the following statement or block is executed, and no further comparisons are performed. In the following example we are awarding grades depending on the examination result.

```
   if  (result >= 75)
            printf("Passed: Grade A\n");
   else if  (result >= 60)
            printf("Passed: Grade B\n");
   else if  (result >= 45)
            printf("Passed: Grade C\n");
   else
            printf("Failed\n");
```

In this example, all comparisons test a single variable called **result**. In other cases, each test may involve a different variable or some combination of tests. The same pattern can be used with more or fewer else if's, and the final lone *else* may be left out. It is up to the programmer to devise the correct structure for each programming problem. Go through the Example 4.4 which is implementing the above discussion.

Example 4.4: Write a program which computes summation of even and odd numbers between 0 and 100. Put a choice to select whether interest is in even or odd.

Answer: The program segment **ifelse.c** implements the above discussion.

```
/**         ifelse.c          **/
/* Find summation even and odd numbers between 0 and 100 */

# include<stdio.h>
# include<ctype.h>
# include<stdlib.h>
void main()
{
   int even , i ;
   int odd ;
   char choice ;

   /* Initialization section */

   even = 0 ;
   odd  = 0 ;

   /*       end           */

   printf("\nEnter choice O = odd , E = even: ") ;
   choice = getchar() ;
   choice = toupper(choice) ; /* change in upper case */

   /* This section find Summation of even number */

   if ( choice == 'E' )
   {
   for( i = 0 ; i <= 100 ; i += 2 )
   {
      even += i ;
   }
   printf("\n Summation of even number between 0 and 100 = %d",
      even);
}
   /*      end          */

   /* This section find summation of odd numbers */

   else
   if ( choice == 'O' )
   {
      for( i = 1 ; i <= 100 ; i += 2 )
```

```
        {
           odd += i  ;
        }
        printf("\n Summation of odd number between 0 and 100 = %d",
        odd);
    }
    /*     end */

    else
    {
        printf("\n Wrong Choice ")  ;
        exit(0)  ;     /* Transfer control to prompt */
    }
}
```

In the above program segment we have defined variable choice which is used to pick choice option from the standard input device (keyboard). If we want to find summation of even number we need to select option 'E' and for odd 'O'. For any other choice it displays "Wrong Choice". In this program segment we have used **for** loop statement, this will be discussed later in this chapter. In **for** loop we have used increment by 2 in both the case (even and odd). Because whether summation is for even or odd numbers depends on initialization of counter, i.e., value of **i** in the **for** loop. For even numbers summation i=0 and for odd i=1.

4.6.1 The else-if ladder

We have discussed the if-else statement in the previous section. In some situation the else-statement is followed by if-statement and then further else-statement is followed by if-else statement. This looks like a ladder. The syntax for the **else-if** ladder is given below:

```
if ( condition1 )
 {
    Statement 1;
     Statement 2;
     Statement 3;
        ...
    Statement n;
        }else if ( condition 2 )/* else-statement is corresponding
        to just above if-statement*/
    {
    Statement 1;
    Statement 2;
    Statement 3;
        ...
    Statement m;
        }else if ( condition 3 ) /* else-statement is corresponding
        to just above if-statement*/
        {
```

```
    Statement 1;
    Statement 2;
    Statement 3;
    ...
    Statement o;
    }else if ( condition 4 ) /* else-statement is corresponding
    to just above if-statement*/
       {
       Statement 1;
       Statement 2;
       Statement 3;
       ...
       ...
         ...
         Statement p;
    }else    /* else-statement is corresponding to just above if-
    statement*/
      {
    Statement 1;
    Statement 2;
    Statement 3;
    ...
    ...
    ...
    Statement q;
      }
```

For example, consider the following algorithm which is used to categories the rank of the students in a class.

```
if marks >=60% then first division
else if marks >40% and marks <=50% then second division
   else if marks >=40% and marks<50% then third division
      else failed
```

Due to the sequential nature of C language, the conditions are evaluated from top to bottom and as soon as a true condition is found, the statements associated with it are executed and rest of the ladder is bypassed. If none of the conditions is true, the code of final **else**-block is executed. Generally this is called **default condition**. If all other conditions are false and final **else** is not present, no action takes place. In the above algorithm if no condition will be true student will be declared failed. Go through the Example 4.5 and Example 4.6 which are implementing the above discussion.

Example 4.5: Write a C code to implement the above algorithm for grading a student.

Answer: The above notion is illustrated in the following program segment.

```
/*** result.c.c    **/
#include<stdio.h>
void main()
{
int num1, num2, num3, num4, num5;
float sum;
printf("\n Enter the marks of five subjects:");
scanf("%d%d%d%d%d", &num1, &num2, &num3, &num4, &num5);
sum = (num1+num2+num3+num4+num5)/500;
sum=sum*100;
   if(sum >=60)
      printf("\n You secured First Division");
   else if(sum >=50 && sum <60)
      printf("\n You secured Second Division");
   else if(sum >=40 && sum<50)
      printf("\n You secured Third Division");
   else
   printf("\n Sorry...You are failed");
getch();
}
```

OUTPUT

Enter the marks of five subjects: 56 60 61 75 52

You have secured First Division

Example 4.6: Implement a four-function arithmetic calculator for the addition, subtraction, multiplication and division operations.

Answer: Following implementation receives one operand then operator and then second operand for manipulating the said calculator.

```
/* calc2.c */
/* Four-function calculator */
#include <stdio.h>

void main(void)
{
   float num1=1.0, num2=1.0;
   char op;

   while ( !(num1==0.0 && num2==0.0) )
   {
      printf("\n\n Enter expression having number, operator,
```

```
number\n");
scanf("%f %c %f", &num1, &op, &num2);
if ( op == '+')
   printf(" Summation = %f", num1 + num2);
else if (op == '-')
   printf(" Subtraction = %f", num1 - num2);
else if (op == '*')
   printf("Multiplication  = %f", num1 * num2);
else if (op == '/')
   printf(" Quotient = %f", num1 / num2);
}
}
```

In the above program segment, there are three **else-if** stairs. The **if-else** statement has only one alternative to be used but it is not always applicable. Simple **if-else** statement has the syntax:

```
if(condition)
   expression 1 ;  /* must be a single statement */
else
   expression 2 ;  /* must be a single statement */
```

If both expressions are single statement, it can be represented with the help of ternary operator (**? :**). Otherwise there is no alternative available in **C** language. The syntax for ternary operator is:

```
result = condition ? expression 1 : expression 2;
```

For example, consider the following code segment.

```
·  char string ;
int x;
printf("\n enter value of x:");
scanf("%d", &x);
   string =  x < 14 ? 'Y' : 'N' ;
·  int number;
char ch;
printf("\n enter your choice (Y or N:");
scanf("%c", &ch)
   number = ch= = 'Y' ? 400 : 200;
```

In the first example, if value of x is entered less than 14 then **string** is assigned 'Y' otherwise 'N'. In the second example, if character 'Y' is entered then **number** holds 400 otherwise 200.

Let us see one more example,

```
a = 16 ;
   b = a < 19 ? a * a : a /4 ;
```

Here, the value of **b** is 256. If **a** is greater than or equal to 19, **b** will receive the value 4. The replacement of the same code with the help of **if - else** statement can be written as:

```
a = 16 ;
if ( a < 19 )
b = a * a ;
else
b = a / 4 ;
```

The use of **ternary** operator to replace **if-else** statements is not limited to only assignment statement and it can also be used with functions when functions return some values. If functions are declared as void, this operator is not useful.

4.7 Loops

In all programming languages, iteration statements allow a set of instructions to be repeatedly performed until a certain condition is reached. This condition may be predefined or open ended (as in the while and do-while loop), i.e., either we can provide the value of a condition when program is written or when program is executed. C gives us a choice of three types of loop, while, do while and for.

- The **while** loop keeps repeating an action until an associated test returns false. This is useful where the programmer does not know in advance how many times the loop will be traversed.
- The **do - while** loops is similar, but the test occurs after the loop body is executed. This ensures that the loop body is run at least once.
- The **for** loop is frequently used, usually where the loop will be traversed a fixed number of times. It is very flexible and novice programmers should take care not to abuse the power it offers.

4.8 While loop

The syntax of **while** statement is given below:

```
while( condition )
{
  Statement 1;
  Statement 2;
   ...
  Statement n;
}
  Statement 1;
  Statement 2;
   ...
  Statement m;
```

Here, the condition may be any expression having nonzero value. The loop continues until the condition is true else the body of the loop will not be executed any more. There is no initialization and modification of counter variable as we have in **for** loop. Go through the Example 4.7 which is implementing the above discussion.

Example 4.7: Write C code which is implementing user controlled while loop.

Answer: Consider the following program segment that implements this idea:

```
/**      whiletst1.c          **/
# include<stdio.h>
void main()
{
char choice='\0' ;  /* Initializing choice as NULL*/
while ( choice != 'B' )
 {
 printf("\n Enter choice (B) to break the while loop:");
 choice = getchar();
 printf("\n Your choice is: %c", choice );
 }
}
```

This program run until we input B. When we input B, the condition becomes false and program is terminated. Like **for** loop, the **while** loop conditions are checked at the beginning. If the condition is true the control is transferred to the program body of the **while** loop otherwise the control is transferred out of the while loop. With **while** loop, it is possible to use several conditions to terminate the loop as illustrated in Example 4.8.

Example 4.8: Write C code which is implementing several conditions controlled while loop.

Answer: Consider the following program segment that implements this idea:

```
/**              whiletst2.c            **/
/* Multiple condition checking in while loop*/
#include<stdio.h>
  void demonstration() ;  /* Prototype */
  void main()
  {
   demonstration() ;
  }

/* Definition of the function load() */
void load()
 {
   int condition ;
   condition = 1 ;
     /* any value other than NULL means condition is true */
   while(condition)
   {
     condition = function1() ;  /* Returned value of function
     assigned to condition */
     if(condition)
      condition = function2() ;
     /* Returned  value of function assigned to condition */
```

```
    if(condition)
      condition = function3() ;
     /* Returned  value of function assigned to condition */
    if (condition)
      condition = function4() ;
    /* Returned  value of function assigned to condition */
            }    /*End of the while loop*/
} /* End of load () function*/

/* Definition of function1() */
int function1()
 {
  int cond1 ;
  printf("\n enter the first condition:");
  scanf("%d", &cond1);
  return(cond1);
 }

/* Definition of function2() */
int function2()
 {
     int cond2 ;
     printf("\n enter the second condition:");
     scanf("%d", &cond2);
     return(cond2);
 }

/* Definition of function3() */
int function3()
 {
     int cond3 ;
     printf("\n enter the third condition:");
     scanf("%d", &cond3);
     return(cond3);
 }

/* Definition of function4() */
int function4()
 {
     int cond4 ;
     printf("\n enter the fourth condition:");
     scanf("%d", &cond4);
     return(cond4);
}
```

In the above program, any of the four functions return false value and cause the loop to exit. It is also possible to define **while** loop without program body. In this case, it is possible to include any valid statement of C in parenthesis. For example, consider the following statement:

```
while((ch = getchar ()) != '\n' )
```

Here, **ch** = **getchar** () is a statement which is included the parenthesis of while loop and also the condition is mentioned. This loop continues until we press the enter key.

4.9 Do while

We have discussed for loop and while loop that are executed only if the condition is found TRUE. If condition is FALSE, no statement in these loops will be executed. It is look like very much restricted provision in C. But C provides another less restrictive loop also. This is **do-while** loop. Whatever condition is there, the statements of do-while loop are executed at least once. This loop is used when some condition is found valid for its initial value and may or may not valid for other values. The syntax of a **do-while** statement is given below:

```
do
{
        Statement 1;
        Statement 2;
          ...
        Statement n;
} while(condition) ;

     Statement 1;
     Statement 2;
     Statement 3;
       ...
     Statement m;
```

From the above syntax it is clear that the body of the loop will be executed at least once because first the body of the loop is executed and then the condition is checked. Figure 4.5 illustrates the above discussion. Statement 1, statement 2, Statement 3, …, and Statement n is executed and then condition is checked for its validity. If condition is found valid then Statement 1, statement 2, Statement 3, …, and Statement n are executed until the invalid condition. It is unique feature of the **do-while** loop that its body is executed at least once as compared to for loop and while loop. Go through the Example 4.9 which is implementing the above discussion.

Example 4.9: Write C code which is implementing the notion of do-while loop.

Answer: Consider the following program segment that implements this idea:

```
/**   dowhile.c **/
# include<stdio.h>
void main()
{
 int number =1;
 char choice='\0';   /*Initially choice =NULL*/
 do
```

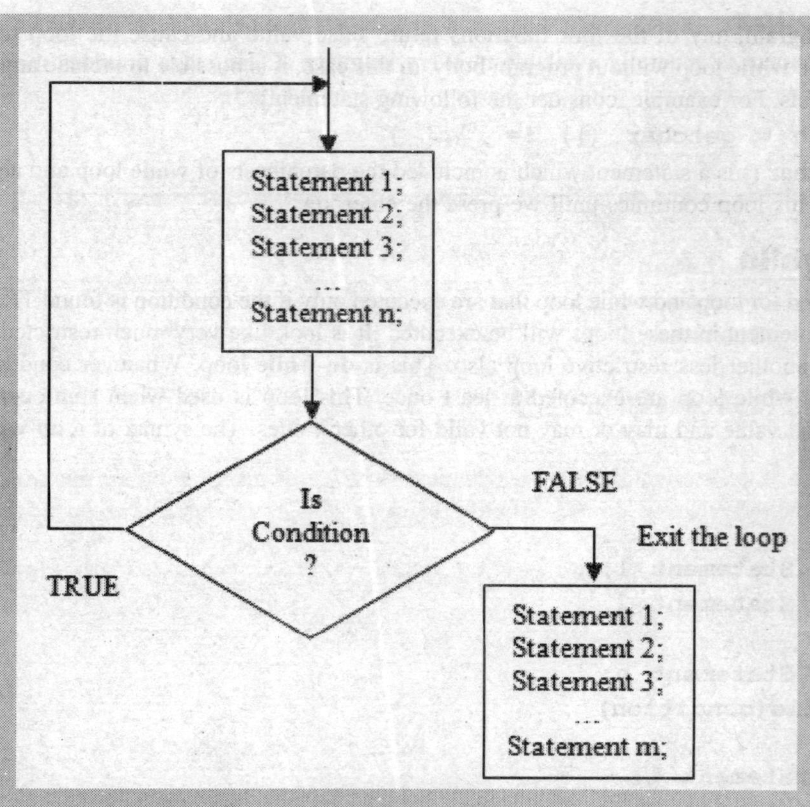

Figure 4.4 Control-flow of do-while Loop

```
  {
    printf("Enter character y:
    scanf("%c", &choice);
    printf("\n This is %d time…", number++);
  }while(choice=='y'||choice=='Y');    /*end of do-while loop*/
 printf(" You are exit the do-while loop");
}
```

OUTPUT

Enter character y: Y

This is 1 time…

Enter character y: y

This is 2 time…

Enter character y: n

You are exit the do-while loop

4.10 For loops

This looping statement is generally available in every language. **C** language provides more powerful and flexible looping statement. One example of looping statement in C is **for** loop. The syntax of **for** statement is given below:

```
for(Initialization; Condition; Increment/Decrement )
        {
            Statement 1;
            Statement 2;
            Statement 3;
                ...
            Statement n;
        }
```

From above syntax, it is clear that there are **n** statements which are controlled by the **for** loop. When number of statements is one then there is no need of curly brackets. The above syntax can be represented with the help of Figure 4.5.

The for loop starts with the initialization of counter that is used to set the condition TRUE or FALSE. Initialization of counter can be done in for-statement or outside before for-statement. After the initialization the condition is checked for its validity and if it is TRUE then statements in for-block are executed in serial order. After this execution counter is modified (generally incremented or decremented). Now, condition is further checked whether it is valid or not; if valid then statements in **for** loop are executed. This is carrying on till the condition is found TRUE (valid). When the condition is found FALSE then **for** loop terminated without executing the statement in **for** loop. It should be noted here that we use **for** loop in a program when the value of counter is well known in advance.

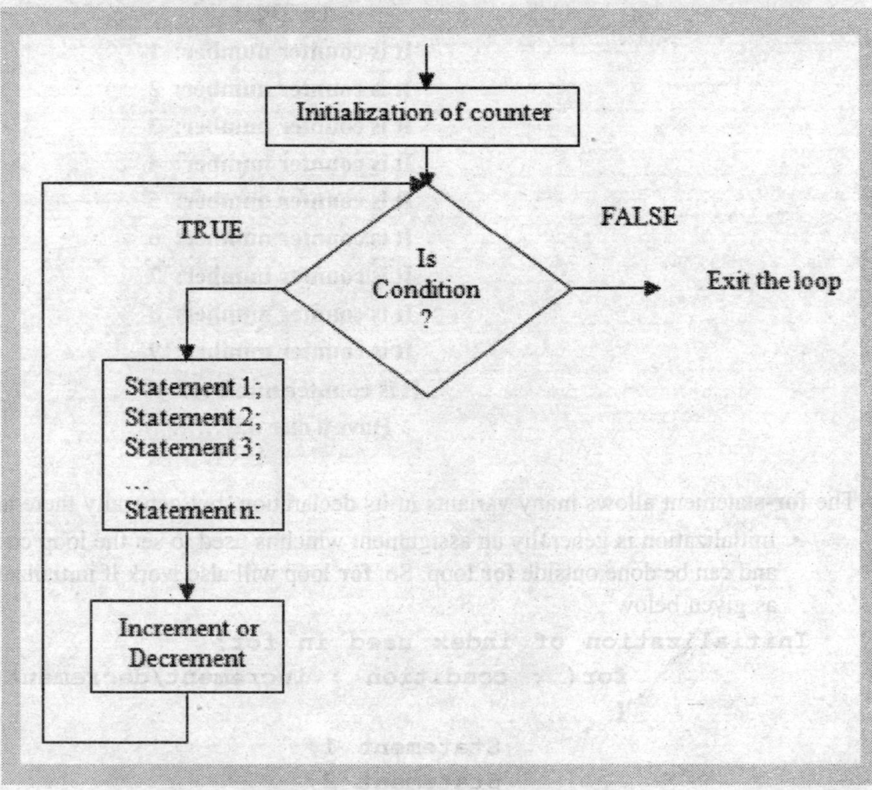

Figure 4.5 Control-flow of for Loop

Go through the Example 4.10 which is implementing the above discussion.

Example 4.10: Write C code for implementing simple for loop based program.

Answer: Consider the following program segment which demonstrates *for* statement.

```
/**   fortest.c **/
# include<stdio.h>
void main()
{
int counter ;
for (counter = 0 ;  counter < 10 ; counter++ ) /* Initialization
     inside the loop */
{
 printf("\n It is counter number:   %d time", counter+1 );
}
 printf("\n Have a nice day...... ");
}
```

OUTPUT

It is counter number: 1
It is counter number: 2
It is counter number: 3
It is counter number: 4
It is counter number: 5
It is counter number: 6
It is counter number: 7
It is counter number: 8
It is counter number: 9
It is counter number: 10
Have a nice day.....

The **for**-statement allows many variants in its declaration, but generally there are three:

- Initialization is generally an assignment which is used to set the loop control variable that is counter and can be done outside **for** loop. So, **for** loop will also work if initialization is done outside for loop as given below:

```
Initialization of index used in for;
          for( ; condition ; increment/decrement )
          {
                 Statement 1;
                 Statement 2;
                 Statement 3;
                 ...
```

```
        Statement n;
    }
```

- Condition in a **for** loop is always a *relational expression* that determines when to exit the loop. The relational expression may be a part of arithmetic statements. For example, consider the following **for**-statement:

```
        for( i = 0 ; i < ( a + 10 ) ;   i++ )
```

Here, **(a + 10)** is an arithmetic expression where variable a is compatible with variable i, first it is evaluated then the value of this expression is compared with the value of **i** to check the validity.

- The increment/decrement defines how the loop control variable (counter) will be changed each time when loop is repeated. This cannot be done outside the for loop as initialization but it can defined in the for loop any where as given below:

```
for(counter=10, counter>=10; )
{
        Statements;
        counter =counter - 1;
        statements;
}
```

Another thing is to be taken care that the **initialization, condition** and **increment/decrement** must be separated by semicolon (;) otherwise compiler raises error(s). In **C** language semicolon (;) is a statement terminator operator which means **for** loop may contain many statements. The **for** loop continues to execute as long as the condition is found TRUE. Once the condition becomes FALSE, program execution resumes on the statement following the **for**-statement. Go through the Example 4.11 which is implementing the above discussion.

Example 4.11: Write a program to generate table of square of 10-20 integer numbers.

Answer: Following program segment (**fortest2.c**) evaluates square of the numbers 10 to 20 and displays the result in tabular form.

```
/** fortest2.c **/
# include<stdio.h>
void main()
{
   int number ;
   for (number = 10 ; j <= 20 ; number++ )
      /*Single Statement, no need of curly brackets*/
      printf("\n Square %d of %d ", number*number, number );
   printf("\n Have more fun.... ");
}
```

In the above program segment initially the value of number is set to 10. Since number is less than 20, the **printf( )** function is called, number is incremented by 1 and the condition is tested to see if it is still less than or equal to 20. This process is repeated until number is greater than 20 and at this point, the loop is terminated. In this example number is loop control variable that is also known as counter, which controls **for** loop. In the above example, there is a single statement so that opening and closing braces are not required.

In **for** loop, the condition is always tested at the beginning of the loop. It means the code inside the loop block may not be executed at all if the condition is false at the beginning of the loop. Go through the Example 4.12 which is implementing the above discussion.

Example 4.12: Write C code using for loop which is not in normal.

Answer: Consider the following program.

```
/** fortest3.c    **/
# include<stdio.h>
void main()
{
   int x=10 ,y;
   y=10;
   for (; y != x ; y++ )
      printf("\n Value of y = %d ", y );
   printf("\n Have a nice day.... ");
}
```

In the above example, **for** loop is never executed because x and y are equal when the condition is initially tested and condition is found FALSE. So, control does not enter the body of for loop, even the counter y does not incremented.

In **for** loop, several variants in its declaration are allowed that increase its power, flexibility and applicability, formally programming situations, e.g., a very powerful facility is achieved with the help of comma (,) operator. With the help of this operator, it is possible to use more than one variable to control the loop. For example, see the following program segment:

```
   for( x = 1 , y = 1 ; x*y < 100  ; x++)
   {
   printf("\n enter the value of counter y:",);
     scanf("%d", &y);
  othe executable Statements;
  }
```

Here in this syntax two-initialization variables are used, viz. x and y. Further, setting of control is done with the help of keyboard by providing the value of y. Conditional expressions may be relational or logical statement. Following example implements many loop control variables:

```
void fun()
  {
     int x, y ;
     for( x = 10 , y = 0 ; x != y ; y++, x- - )
     printf("\n WELCOME in era of multiple counters....");
     printf("\n Number of loop computations = %d", j-);
 }
```

4.11 Nested Loops

Sometimes misuse of the conditional expression or without conditional statement in **for** loop results in infinite loop. In other words, if the condition of a for loop is not set properly or there is no conditional statement to terminate the for loop, there is infinite loop situation and computer may be in hang situation. So, one should take care about the conditional statement in for loop. The control-flow of infinite for loop is shown in Figure 4.6. Now, let us see the syntaxes of **for** loop that normally causes infinite loop:

Figure 4.6 Control-flow in Infinite for loop

- ```
  for( ; ; )          /* Without the
     conditional expression*/
  {
       Statement 1;
       Statement 2;
       ...
       Statement n;
  }
  ```
- ```
  for( i=0; ;i++ )          /*
     Without the conditional
     expression*/
  {
       Statement 1;
       Statement 2;
       ...
       Statement n;
  }
  ```
- ```
  for( i=1 ; i>0 ;i++ )          /* Wrong condition is set*/
  {
       Statement 1;
       Statement 2;
       ...
       Statement n;
  }
  ```
- ```
  for( i=0; i<=10;i- - ) /* Modification of counter variable i is
     incorrect */
  {
       Statement 1;
       Statement 2;
       ...
       Statement n;
  }
  ```
- ```
  for( i=0;number=5 ;i++ )          /* Without the conditional
     expression*/
  {
  ```
  ```

```
        Statement 1;
        Statement 2;
        ...
        Statement n;
    }
```

There are many variations of the above syntax that result in infinite loop. We should be careful about the following:

- Which one is the counter variable(s),
- What is the condition at which program terminates,
- How counter variable(s) is modified (incremented or decremented),
- Termination point of **for** loop is well defined or not?

Go through the Example 4.13 which is implementing the above discussion.

Example 4.13: Write C code using for loop which is executed for infinite length of time.

Answer: Now, let us see one program that falls in infinite loop:

```
/** fortest4.c **/
# include<stdio.h>
void main()
{
  for ( ; ; )
     printf(" I am in infinite loop");
}
```

When we run the above program, the computer displays string "I am in infinite loop" infinitely. To quit from this program, one is required to press interrupt key, which is **CTRL-BREAK** in **DOS** environment and **DEL** in **SCO UNIX, Linux,** and **AIX-L** environments.

4.12 Infinite Loops

When we put statement terminator with **for**-statement, the program body of the loop is executed for infinite length of time and no output is displayed as shown below:

```
#include<stdio.h>
 void main()
 {
   int number ;
  for ( ; ; );
  {
     printf("Enter Value of number:");
      scanf("%d",&number);
     printf(" Value of x = %d", number);
  }
 }
```

The above notion can be used as delay in many programs. Suppose somebody has initialized the counter value 500 or more without for loop body. This provides only the delay, not any other thing. We can use this idea to improve the efficiency of certain algorithms or to construct time delay loops. Removing spaces from an input stream is a common programming task. For example, a database program may allow a query such as "show all balances less than Rs 600.00". The database and to have each word fed to it separately, without spaces. That is, the database input processor recognizes "*show*" but not "*sh   ow*". We can remove the spaces between the character 'h' and 'o' using pointer or character array in a **for** loop as given below:

```
for (; *string == ' ' ; string++);
```

Other application is to construct delay loops. For example, following function creates a delay function.

```
    Delay_in_display(int counter)
{
    for (; counter; counter- -);      // Delay
}
```

The value of variable counter is provided to the function Delay_in_display ( ) and depending on the value function provides delay. Generally, the value of counter is larger like 500 or more.

4.13 Switch statement

We use **if–else** statements if number of decisions are small. When number of decision is very large and it is required to select too many decisions, it is not possible with the help of **if-else** statements. **C** language provides a multiple branch selection statement called **switch** statement, which successively tests the value of a condition (expression) against a list of **integer** or **character** constants only. When a match is found, the statements associated with that constant are executed. With the help of **switch** and **case** statements, one may choose any number of decisions. The syntax of switch-case statement is given below:

```
switch ( condition )
 {
 case constant1:
    Statement 1;
    Statement 2;
    Statement 3;
    ...
    Statement p;
 case constant 2:
    Statement 1;
    Statement 2;
    Statement 3;
    ...
    Statement q;
 case constant 3:
    Statement 1;
    Statement 2;
    Statement 3;
    ...
```

```
        Statement r;
    default:
        Statement 1;
        Statement 2;
        Statement 3;
        ...
        Statement s;
    }
```

The **switch** statement is well structured, but can only be used in certain cases where;

- Only one variable is tested, all branches must depend on the value of that variable. The variable must be an integral type (int, long, short or char).
- Each possible value of the variable can control a single branch. A final, catch all default branch may optionally be used to trap all unspecified cases.

Hopefully an example will clarify things. This is a function which converts an integer into a vague description. It is useful where we are only concerned in measuring a quantity when it is quite small.

```
estimate(int number)
/* Estimate a number as none, one, two, several, many */
{       switch(number) {
        case 0 :
                    printf("None\n");
                    break;
        case 1  :
                    printf("One\n");
                    break;
        case 2  :
                    printf("Two\n");
                    break;
        case 3  :
        case 4  :
        case 5  :
                    printf("Several\n");
                    break;
        default  :
                    printf("Many\n");
                    break;
        }
}
```

Each interesting case is listed with a corresponding action. The break statement prevents any further statements from being executed by leaving the switch. Since case 3 and case 4 have no following break, they continue on allowing the same action for several values of number. Both if and switch constructs allow the programmer to make a selection from a number of possible actions.

The **switch** statement tests whether an expression matches with the integer or character constants specified in the case statements. We label each case or with integers valued constants, constant expression or character constant only. If a case matches the expression value, execution starts from that case. All case expressions, integer constants value or character constant must be different. The case labeled default is executed if none of the case match is found. The default case is optional and if it is not available, control comes out of the switch case statement. Other cases and default case may be placed in any order. The **ANSI-C** standard specifies that a switch can have at most 256 case statements. Go through the Example 4.14 which is implementing the above discussion.

Example 4.14: Implement Example 4.9 using switch and case statement.

Answer: Consider the following program segment which is a five function calculator shows operations performed on two numbers depending on inputting the operators.

```
/** switch1.c **/
# include<stdio.h>
void main()
{
   int x , y, result ;
   char choice ;
   x = 100 ;
   y = 25 ;
   printf("\n Enter an arithmetic operator: ") ;
   choice = getchar() ;
      switch(choice)
      {
      case '-' :
         printf("\n x = %d", x);
         printf("\n y = %d", y);
         printf("\n Demo of '-' operator");
         result = x - y ;
         printf("\n Difference of two numbers = %d", result);
         getch();
         break ;
      case '+' :
         printf("\n x = %d", x);
         printf("\n y = %d", y);
         printf("\n Demo of '+' operator");
         result = x + y ;
         printf("\n Addition  of two numbers = %d", result);
         getchar();
```

```
        break ;
    case '*' :
        printf("\n x = %d", x);
        printf("\n y = %d", y);
        printf("\n Demo of multiplication operator");
        result = x * y ;
        printf("\n Multiplication of two numbers = %d", result);
        break ;

    case '/' :
        printf("\n x = %d", x);
        printf("\n y = %d", y);
        printf("\n Demo of '/' operator ");
        result = x / y ;
        printf("\n Division of two numbers = %d", result);
        getch( );
        break ;

    case '%' :
        printf("\n x = %d", x);
        printf("\n y = %d", y);
        printf("\n Demo of '%; operator ");
        result = x % y ;
        printf("\n Remainder  = %d", result);
        getch( );
        break ;
    default :
        printf(" \n Wrong choice of operator… ");
        getch();
    }
}
```

OUTPUT
Enter an arithmetic operator: +
Addition of two numbers = 125

When character constants are used, their integer **ASCII** values are automatically obtained. The **break** statement is optional. This is used to terminate the statement sequence associated with each constant. If **break** statement is missing, the execution will continue to next **case** statements until a **break** statement is encountered or the end of **switch** statement reaches. This type of representation can be implemented with the help of or **case** statement. The syntax for **switch-case** statement without break is given below:

```
switch (condition)
{
     case constant1: /* No break statement*/
      statements;

     case constant2: /* No break statement*/
      statements;

     case constant3: /* No break statement*/
      statements;

     case constant4: /* No break statement*/
      statements;

      case constant5:     /* No break statement*/
      statements;
      ...
    default: statements;
}
```

Consider the next Example in which four case statements case 1, 2, 3 and 4 are combined in one due to absence of **break** statement.

Example 4.15: switch-case statement with some missing break statement.

Answer: Go through the following code segments for different variants of switch-case statement.

```
/**         switch2.c          **/
# include<stdio.h>
void main()
{
   int choice ;
   printf(" \n Enter your choice (integer value up to 5): ");
   scanf("%d", &choice);

   switch(choice)
   {
   case 1:     printf("\n Your Choice is: %d", choice) ;
   case 2:     printf("\n Your Choice is: %d", choice) ;
   case 3:     printf("\n Your Choice is: %d", choice);
   case 4:     printf("\n Your Choice is: %d", choice);
        break;
   case 5:     printf("\n Your Choice is: %d", choice);
```

```
        break ;
    default  :   printf("\n Your Choice is invalid");     }
}
```

In the above program, if we enter **choice = 1**, case **1, 2,** 3 and **4** are executed because case 1, case 2 and case 3 have no break statement.

Another form of **switch-case** statement is:

```
 switch(choice)               /* Correct declaration */
 {
     case 'A' : ...
                        char ch ;    /* Valid Declaration of char
     variable in C++*/
                        ...
                        statements;  /*No break statement*/
     case 'B':
     statements;    /*No break statement*/
     case 'C':
     statements;    /*No break statement*/
   ...
default:
  statements;
 }

/* Incorrect declaration of a variable */
        switch(choice)
        {
         char ch ;/*incorrect declaration*/
         case 'A'  :   ..
       statements;
  }
```

Let us see a program that illustrates the above notion.

```
#include<stdio.h>
   void main()
     {
        int choice ;
        printf("\n Enter your choice (integer): ");
        scanf("%d",&choice);
        switch(choice)
          {
            case 1 : char ch ;       /* Incorrect declaration and
     correct for C++*/
```

```
                              ch = getchar();
                              break ;
                default : break ;
              }
          }
```

In the above program segment **ch** is outside of the block. When one compiles this program segment compiler generates the following errors.

- Expression syntax incorrect
- ch not defined.

If we define variable **ch** inside a block, this format is correct and does not generate compile time errors. ***It should be noted that in block variable's declaration is generally permitted in C++ not in C.*** Consider the following syntax that gives correct form of the declaration. The implementation of this syntax is just below the syntax.

```
switch(choice)
   {
    case 'A' :
                 if( condition )
                 {
     char ch;    /* Correct because declared char ch; in block of
     if statement */
                                  ...
                 }
    case 'B' : statements;
       ...
   }
```

Go through the Example 4.16 which is implementing the above discussion.

Example 4.16: Write C code for demonstrating block variable declaration.

Answer: Let us see the following program segment that illustrates the above idea.

```
#include<stdio.h>
   void main()
      {
         int choice ;
         printf("\n Enter Your choice (integer): ");
         scanf("%d", &choice);
      switch(choice)
            {
       case 1  :
         if (choice < 12)
```

```
                {
        char ch ;
        ch = getchar();
        printf("\n No Error in Declaration");
                }
            break ;
      default : break ;
   }
}
```

4.14 Structured programming

We have discussed about condition in for loop, while loop, and do-while loop. These loops have different notion in declaring the condition, checking condition and modifying the condition. Sometimes we need to bypass normal loop condition. C provides this facility. We can terminate a normal loop by using if-statement and break statement.

4.14.1 The break statement

We have already met break in the discussion of the switch statement. It is used to exit from a loop or a switch, control passing to the first statement beyond the loop or a switch. With loops, break can be used to force an early exit from the loop, or to implement a loop with a test to exit in the middle of the loop body. A break within a loop should always be protected within an **if** statement which provides the test to control the exit condition. When the **break** statement is encountered inside a loop, the loop is immediately terminated and the program control resumes from the next statement following the loop. The **break** statement terminates the execution of the nearest enclosing **do**, **for**, **switch**, or **while** statement in which it appears. Syntax of break statement is

***jump-statement*:**

break;

Go through the Example 4.17 which is implementing the above discussion.

Example 4.17: Write C code which is implementing the notion of break statement.

Answer: Consider the following program segment illustrates the idea of break statement.

```
/**       break1.c    **/
# include<stdio.h>
void main()
{
int num1=420, num2=422, num3=424, num3=426, num4=428, num5=430,
      num6=432, num7=434, num8=436, num9=438, num10=440;
   int choice_number, i, flag=0;
   printf("\n Enter a number to be searched:");
   scanf("%d", &choice_number);

   for ( i = 0 ; i <= 10 ; i++ )
   {
```

```
        if(choice_number== num1+2*i)
        {
           printf("\n Number is not found in the list");
           flag=1;           /*Indicates successful search*/
           break;
        }
     } /* end of for loop*/
     if (flag==0)
        printf("\n Search is unsuccessful");
     getch();
  }
```

The above program runs successfully, but we will get some warning from compiler that we have not used the value of num2, num3, etc.

The **break** statement is frequently used to terminate the processing of a particular case within a **switch** statement. Lack of an enclosing iterative or **switch** statement generates an error. Within nested statements, the **break** statement terminates only the **do-while**, **while**, **for**, or **switch-case** statement that immediately encloses it. We can use a **return** or **goto** statement to transfer control elsewhere out of the nested structure

In the program break2.**c**, the nesting of **for** loop is done and the inner **for** loop contains the **break** statement. When the **break** statement is encountered, the control is transferred to the outer for loop. Go through the Example 4.18 which is implementing the above discussion.

Example 4.18: Write C code which is implementing the break statement for controlling the execution of loop controlled program.

Answer: Consider the following program segment that implements this idea:

```
/**      break2.c          **/
#include<stdio.h>
void main()
{
   int i , number;
   for( i = 0 ; i < 10 ; i++ )
   {
      number = 10 ;
      for ( ; ; )
      {
         printf(" \n number = %d", number) ;
         number ++;
         if( number == 50)
               break;
      }
   }
}
```

In this program segment value of number is reaches as 50 condition of if statement is satisfied and inner for loop is terminated and control is transferred to outer for loop.

4.14.2 The Continue Statement

We have seen in the previous section that a break statement can be used to terminate a normal loop. One must thing that there should be reverse of the break statement, yes there is. C provides the **break** statement. The function of this statement is reverse of **break** statement. The **continue** statement forces the next iteration of the loop to be executed skipping code following the **continue** statement. This is similar to break but is encountered less frequently. It only works within loops where its effect is to force an immediate jump to the loop control statement.

- In a while loop, jump to the test statement.
- In a do while loop, jump to the test statement.
- In a for loop, jump to the test, and perform the iteration.

Like a break, continue should be protected by an if statement. We are unlikely to use it very often.

In continue.c, if any negative number is entered then continue statement forces the control to the previous statements without following the statements after the continue statement. It is very much surprise package in a middle-level language. Go through the Example 4.19 which is implementing the above discussion.

Example 4.19: Write C code which is implementing the notion of continue statement for executing code based on some consition.

Answer: Consider the following program segment that implements this idea:

```
/*          continue.c          */
# include<stdio.h>
void main()
{
    int number ;
    do
    {
      printf("\n Input number 101 to break: ");
      scanf("%d", &number) ;
         if(number < 0 )
               continue;
            /* if Condition is true then control back to previous
      printf( ) statement*/
      printf("\n You Number is = %d", number);
    } while(number !=101) ;
}
```

OUTPUT

Input number 101 to break: 400

You Number is = 400

Input number 101 to break: 23

You Number is = 23

```
Input number 101 to break: -3
Input number 101 to break: 10
You Number is = 10
Input number 101 to break: 101
You Number is = 101
```

The do-while loop runs until the number 101 is entered. Whenever the input number is negative then control is transferred to "printf("\n Input number 101 to break: ");" statement.

4.14.3 The goto Statement

This feature in C language is similar to the **goto** statement in assembly languages. It also indicates that C language is a successor of low-level languages. We have discussed about the continue statement in the previous section that forces the control to the skip the following statements in block and execute the previous statements. The continue statement is equipped with if-statement. C provides the similar functionality of the continue statement. Using a goto statement we can make the control to be transferred at any point in a program. It is more powerful than a continue statement but dangerous also. As a good programming style, we must avoid the use of **goto** statement. A label always follows a **goto** statement. The label may be an identifier declared, constant, character constant or a string constant. No special characters are allowed in the label but single character is allowed. A label decides the position where the control jumps and be followed by colon (:). A label may be constant as well as a variable. The syntax of goto statement is given below:

```
    Label:
                    Statement 1;
                    Statement 2;
                    ...
                    Statement n;
    if(condition ) goto Label ;
                    Statement 1;
                    Statement 2;
                    Statement 3;
                    ...
                    Statement p;
```

Consider the program segment **goto.c** which implements the use of **goto** statement given below. Go through the Example 4.20 which is implementing the above discussion.

Example 4.20: Write C code which is implementing the notion of goto statement for transferring control of a program from one statement to another whenever required.

Answer: Consider the following program segment that implements this idea:

```
/**   goto.c   **/
#include<stdio.h>
void main()
{
   int number ;
   do
```

```
    {
        printf("\n Input a number 101 to break loop: ");
        scanf("%d",&number) ;
          if(number < 0 )
               continue ;
          /* if Condition is true then control back
          to previous printf( ) statement*/
        printf(" Your Number is= %d", number);
        goto number ;
    } while(number !=20) ;

    number:     /*label */
        printf("\n WELCOME AT SCO UNIX 'C...'");
}
```

OUTPUT

Input number 101 to break: -3
Input number 101 to break: 10
You Number is = 10
WELCOME AT SCO UNIX 'C...'

Let us Revise

1. A good program should have the following characteristics: Readability, Efficiency, Reliability, Meaningfulness, Portability and User-friendly.
2. Instead of running a big program altogether, the program is divided into small parts and they are run independently.
3. There are different ways of using the modular programming. They are: Sequence structure, Decision/ Selection structure and Loop structure
4. Most of the guidelines for writing good programs are based upon following set of norms: Clarity/ Simplicity of Expressions, Names and Functions, Use of comments and Use of Indentation
5. Operator guide contains all the instructions that the operator has to follow while executing the program.
6. User guide highlights the type of inputs and outputs which the program generates.
7. Reference manual contains all the instructions about the system specifications of the program
8. Each program needs maintainance.
9. Program testing is a must before running for final use.
10. Debugging is method of checking errors in the program.
11. Syntax errors are those which occur due to wrong use of language.
12. Run time errors occur at the time of execution.
13. Logic errors are not pointed at the time of execution.
14. Testing ensures that the program performs correctly the required tasks.
15. Set of rules/syntax use for writing programs are called programming languages.

16. Assembly language use mnemonics to write a program.
17. Compilers or interpreters are used to translate high level language into machine code.
18. Interpreter translates the source code written in high level language into the machine code.
19. Machine language is represented in binary form and directly understandable by the computer. No translation is required.
20. Assembler is a program used to convert assembly language into machine code.
21. High-level languages are machine independent. It uses syntax which are easy to remember and meaningful to write the program.
22. In coding phase according to the design of each module, coding for every module is done in any preferred language (such as C, C++, Java, etc).

Multiple Choice Questions

1. How many times will the following program print WELCOME?

```
#include< stdio.h>
void main()
{
    int count;
    for(count=-15; count>=-1; count- -)
    prinft("\n WELCOME");
    getch();
}
```

(a) 1 (b) 0

(c) 14 (d) None

2. How many times will the following program print WELCOME?

```
#include< stdio.h>
void main()
{
    int count;
    for(count=-15; count>=-1; count++)
    prinft("\n WELCOME");
    getch();
}
```

(a) Infinite (b) 0

(c) 14 (d) None

3. How many times will the following program print WELCOME?

```
#include< stdio.h>
void main()
{
    int count;
    for(count=-15; count<=-1; count++)
    prinft("\n WELCOME");
    getch();
```

```
}
```

(a) 15 (b) 0

(c) 14 (d) None

4. What is the output of following program?

```
#include< stdio.h>
void main()
{
    int i;
    char ch='a';
    for(i=0; i<=25; i++)
    prinft("\n %c", ch+i);
    getch();
}
```

(a) Error (b) a

(c) abcd....z (d) None

5. What is the output of following program?

```
#include< stdio.h>
void main()
{
    char ch='a';
    while(ch<='z')
prinft("\n %c", ch++);
    getch();
}
```

(a) Error (b) a

(c) abcd....z (d) None

6. What is the output of following program?

```
#include< stdio.h>
void main()
{
    int i=5;
printf("\n %d %d", i++, ++i);
    getch();
}
```

(a) 5 5 (b) 5 6

(c) 6 5 (d) 6 6

7. What is the output of following program?

```
#include< stdio.h>
void main()
{
    int i;
for(i=3;  i<18; i+=3);
```

```
prinft("\n %d", i);
    getch();
 }
```

(a) 15 (b) Error

(c) 18 (d) None

8. What is the output of following program?

```
#include<stdio.h>
void main()
{
    int counter=12;
    do
    {
       printf("Its do-while loop..);

    } while(count<=12);
```

(a) No output (b) Its do-while loop..

(c) Error (d) None

9. Select the correct statement.

(a) If condition is missing in for loop, it is assumed to be TRUE

(b) If condition is missing in for loop, it is assumed to be FALSE

(c) If condition is missing in for loop, it results in syntax error

(d) If condition is missing in for loop, it will terminate the program

10. Select the correct statement.

(a) Body of for loop executed at least once

(b) Body of while loop executed at least once

(c) Body of do-while loop executed at least once

(d) Body of none for, while, and do-while executed without condition

11. If condition is missing in a loop written in C language then infinite loop can be avoided by placing

(a) break statement (b) goto statement

(c) return statement (d) All

12. Choose the correct statement(s).

(a) Any non-zero value represents TRUE condition

(b) 0 represents FALSE condition

(c) 0 and negative values represents FALSE condition

(d) None

13. Select the incorrect statement.

(a) for loop cannot be nested

(b) while loop cannot be nested

(c) switch-case statement can be nested and any value can be supplied to case statement

(d) do-while loop cannot be bested

14. In case of switch-case statement
    (a) default case must be there
    (b) default case may or may not be there
    (c) if default case is there then it should be last statement
    (d) default case can be placed any where in the body
15. A break-statement in C language can be replaced by
    (a) exit-statement (b) return-statement
    (c) goto-statement (d) Cannot be replaced by any one
16. A switch-case statement can be replaced by
    (a) if-else statement (b) do-while loop
    (c) if-statement (d) None
17. Choose the correct statement a for loop.
    (a) counter can be initialized outside the loop body
    (b) counter cannot be initialized outside the loop body
    (c) counter must be modify inside the loop body
    (d) body of loop cannot be empty
18. Which one of the following is syntactically correct?
    (a) for(;) (b) for(; ;)
    (c) For(; ;) (d) None
19. What is the output of the following program?

```
#include<stdio.h>
void main()
{
    int number=0;
    printf("\n %d", number+=(number+=3, 10, 25));
    getch();
}
```

    (a) 6 (b) 0
    (c) 3 (d) Error
20. What is the output of following program?

```
#include<stdio.h>
void main()
{
    int number =25;
    switch(number)
    {
        case 'x':
              if(number>20)
        case 'y':
              number =0;
        printf("\n %d", number);
```

```
    }
    printf("\n %d", number);
}
```

(a) Error (b) 25

(c) 0 (d) None

21. What is the output of following program?

```
#include<stdio.h>
void main()
{
    char choice = x;
    switch(choice)
    {
        case 'x':
              if(choice>20)
        case 'y':
              choice  = 97;
        printf("\n %c", choice);
    }
}
```

(a) c (b) b

(c) a (d) None

22. What is the output of following program?

```
#include<stdio.h>
void main()
{
    int number =25;
    switch(number)
    {
        int temp=10;
case 25:
              printf("%d", temp);
              number++;
        case 26:
              printf("\n %d", number);
    }
}
```

(a) Error (b) 25

(c) 0 (d) None

23. What is the output of following program?

```
#include<stdio.h>
void main()
{
    int i, j;
```

```
    for(i=0, j=0, i<=2; i++, j++)
    printf(" %d", j);
}
```

(a) Error (b) 012

(c) 0 (d) None

24. What is the output of following program?

```
#include<stdio.h>
void main()
{
    int i, j=0;
    for(i=0, j++, i<=2; i++, printf("%d", j))
}
```

(a) Error (b) 012

(c) 11 (d) None

25. What is the output of following program?

```
#include<stdio.h>
void main()
{
    int i, j=0;
    for(i=0, ++j, i<=2; i++, printf("%d", j))
}
```

(a) Error (b) 012

(c) 11 (d) None

26. What is the output of following program?

```
#include<stdio.h>
void main()
{
    int i, j=0;
    for(i=0, printf("%d", ++j), i<=2; i++)
}
```

(a) Error (b) 1

(c) 11 (d) 012

27. What is the output of following program?

```
#include<stdio.h>
void main()
{
    int i, j=0;
    for(i=0, printf("%d", j++), i<=2; i++)
}
```

(a) Error (b) 1

(c) 0 (d) 012

28. Choose the correct statement about do-while loop.
    (a) the condition is evaluated first
    (b) body is evaluated first
    (c) condition is initialized first
    (d) None
29. Distinguish between the following pairs:
    (a) getchar and scanf functions.
    (b) %s and %c specifications for reading input from standard input device.
    (c) %s and %[ ] specifications for reading input from standard input device.
    (d) %g and %f specification for printing on standard output device.
    (e) %f and %e specifications for printing on standard output device.
30. Write scanf statements to read the following data lists:
    (a) 78 A 95.89.
    (b) 123 1.2345 C
    (c) 15-10-2002
    (d) 10 TRUE 20
31. State the outputs produced by the following printf statements.
    (a) printf (“%d%c%f”, 10, ‘x’, 1.23);
    (b) printf (“%2d %c %4.2f”, 1234 ‘x’, 1.23);
    (c) printf (“%d\t%4.2f”, 1234, 456);
    (d) printf (“\”%08.2f\””, 123.4);
    (e) printf (“%d%d %d”, 10, 20);
32. State errors, if any, in the following input statements.
    (a) scanf(“%c%f%d”, city, &price, &year);
    (b) scanf(“%s%d”, city, amount);
    (c) scanf(“%f, %d”, &amount, &year);
    (d) scanf(\n”%f”, root);
    (e) scanf(“%c %d %ld”, *code, &count, Root);
33. What will be the values stored in the variables year and code when the data 1988, x is keyed in as a response to the following statements:
    (a) scanf(“%d %c”, &year, &code); .
    (b) scanf(“%c %d”, &year, &code);
    (c) scanf(“%d %c”, &code, &year);
    (d) scanf(“%s %c”, &year, &code);
34. State what (if anything) is wrong with each of the following output statements:
    (a) printf(%d 7.2%f, year, amount};
    (b) printf(“%-s, %c”\n, city ,code);
    (c) printf(“%f, %d, %s, price, count, city);
    (d) printf(“%c%d%f\n”, amount, code, year);

True/False Questions

1. The purpose of the header file <studio.h> is to store the programs created by the users.
2. The C standard function that receives a single character from the keyboard is getchar.
3. The getchar cannot be used to read a line of text from the keyboard.
4. The input list in a scanf statement can contain one or more variables.
5. When an input stream contains more data items than the number of specifications in a scanf statement, the unused items will be used by the next scanf call in the program.
6. Format specifiers for output convert internal representations for data to readable characters.
7. Variables form a legal element of the format control string of a printf statement.
8. The scanf function cannot be used to read a single character from the keyboard.
9. The format specification %+-8d prints an integer left-justified in a field width of 8 with a plus sign, if the number is positive.
10. If the field width of a format specifier is larger than the actual width of the value, the value is printed right-justified in the field.

11. The print list in a printf statement can contain function calls.
12. The format specification %5s will print only the first 5 characters of a given string to be printed.

Match Columns

Match the matter in Column A with the matter in Column B.

Column A	Column B
A. while (0)	1. 2
B. while (1)	2. 1
C. 5/2	3. forces exit from a program
D. 5%2	4. assignment never takes place
E. The exit function	5. forces immediate exit from any loop
F. The break statement	6. infinite loop

Fill in the Blanks with Appropriate Words

a. test b. 3 c. reserved d. goto
e. do while f. continue

1. The ___________ statement is used to skip some statements within a loop and start next iteration.
2. The _________ is executed at least once always before it evaluates the test expression.
3. In C while is ____________ word.
4. An infinite for loop has missing _______ expression.
5. Nesting can be done upto ________ level for while loop.
6. ___________ is an unconditional jump statement.

Descriptive Type Questions

1. Write a program that counts numerical digits in a given number.
2. Write a program that works like a five-function calculator. The operations are:
   (a) addition (+) (b) subtraction (-)
   (c) multiplication (*) (d) division (\)
   (e) mod (%)
   Use **while** and **if-else** statements only.
3. Write a four-function calculator with the help of **while** and **switch** statements.
4. Write a program that calculates the factorial of an input integer number using **for** and **if** statements only.
5. With the help of **while** statement, write a program that calculates the factorial of an integer number? Repeat the same with the help of **do-while** statement.
6. See the beauty of the mathematics in the following series and write programs for generating the series.
   (a) 1*8+1=9
   12*8+2=98
   123*8+3=987
   1234*8+4=9876
   ...
   123456789*8+9=987654321
   (b) 1*9+2=11
   12*9+3=111

123*9+4=1111

1234*9+5=11111

...

123456789*9+10=1111111111

(c) 9*9=7=88

98*9+6=888

987*9+5=8888

9876*9+4=88888

...

987654321*9+0=888888888

(d) 1*1=1

11*11=121

111*111=12321

1111*1111=1234321

...

111111111 * 111111111=12345678987654321

7. Write a program that splits a number into its constituent digits.
8. Write a program that finds ASCII code for each character inputted by user.
9. Write a program that prints table of ASCII codes.
10. Write a function **itob(n,s,b)** that converts the integer **n** into a base of **b** character representation in the string **s**.
11. Write a program that will read **n** number (integer) from keyboard and display should be in text. For example 113 number entered and can be written as

    (a) One hundred thirteen

    (b) One one three
12. A Government has a particularly simple system of taxation. Income above rupees 60,000 is taxed at 20 percent and income greater than or equal to Rs 1,50,000 is taxed at 33 percent. Write a program that reads incomes and prints the taxes due. The program should read incomes until the user wants. Assume that the income is an integer. Drop the fractional part of the tax, so that it is written as an integer.
13. Read a series of floating point numbers from the keyboard and print a statistical summary of the data that includes

    (a) the largest value input,
    (b) the smallest value input,
    (c) the sum of all values read,
    (d) the mean of all values input,
    (d) the population variance and the standard deviation. The population variance measures the spread of the values and given by the formula

$$\frac{\sum_{i=1}^{n} x_i^2 - \overline{x^2}}{n}$$

where is the mean of the **n** values x_1, x_2, x_3 ..., x_n read. The standard deviation is the square root of the variance.

14. Write a program that prints a calendar for a year. Prompt the user for which day of the week **January** 1 is on and whether the year is a leap year. The day that **January** 1 is on is coded as given below:

    1 Sunday

    2 Monday

    3 Tuesday

    4 Wednesday

    5 Thursday

    6 Friday

    7 Saturday

The leap year condition is coded as

    1 leap year

    0 no leap year

Answers to Objective Type Questions

Multiple Choice Questions

1. a	2. b	3. c	4. a
5. c	6. b	7. a	8. c
9. b	10. a	11. a	12. c
13. b	14. c	15. a	16. b
17. a	18. c	19. a	20. b
21. c	22. b	23. a	24. c
25. b	26. a	27. c	28. a
29. b	30. c	31. b	32. a
33. c	34. b		

True False Questions

1. F	2. F	3. T	4. T
5. T	6. T	7. T	8. T
9. T	10. T	11. T	12. T

Matching Columns

A. c	B. d	C. e	D. a
E. f	F. b		

Fill in the Blanks

1. f	2. e	3. c	4. a
5. b	6. d		

Arrays 5

5.1 One Dimensional Arrays

The C language provides some widely used **compound** or **derived** data types together with mechanisms which allow the programmer to define variables of these types and access the data stored within them. We have also discussed about the memory allocation for a data type. For example, generally C compiler reserves two bytes for **int** data type, one byte for **char** data type, etc. Let us take one problem here. Suppose we have 50 integer numbers and we have to use these numbers in a program. How these numbers will be identified? For a moment, we can use 50 identifiers of **int** data type to represent these numbers. But declaring and using 50 identifiers are not easy solution. The same problem may be there with char and float data types. To overcome of this type problem, C provides array data structure.

A programmer is concerned with developing and implementing algorithms for a variety of tasks. As tasks become more complex, algorithm development is facilitated by structuring or organizing data in specialized ways. There is no best data structure for all tasks; suitable data structures must be selected for the specific task. Some data structures are provided by programming languages; others must be derived by the programmer from available data types and structures. A **data structure** is a *logical* or *mathematical* way of storing data in a computer so that it can be used efficiently. Often a carefully chosen data structure will allow a more efficient operation. There are two types of data structures: (i) **Linear**: For example, Arrays, Linked Lists, Stacks, Queues, etc, and (ii) **Non-linear**: For example, Trees (like B Trees, B+ Trees, B* Trees, etc), Graph, etc.

Many tasks require storing and processing a list of data items. For example, we may need to store a list of examination scores and to process it in numerous ways: find the maximum and minimum, average the scores, sort the scores in descending order, search for a specific score, etc. Data items in simple lists are usually of the same scalar type; for example a list of examination scores consists of all integer type items. We naturally think of a list as a data structure that should be referenced as a unit. C provides a derived data type that stores such a list of objects where each object is of the same data type - the array.

The data elements in an array are represented in linear manner, i.e., there is linear relationship among the elements and these elements are stored in consecutive memory locations and this is why an array is known as linear data structure. In other words, an array is a compound data type which allows a collection of data of the same type to be grouped into a single object. As with any data type, to understand how to use an array, one must know how such a structure can be declared, how data may be stored and accessed in the structure, and what operations may be performed using this new type.

In computer programming world, an **array** is a linear data structure also known as a **vector** or **list** (for one-dimensional arrays) or a **matrix** (for two-dimensional arrays). A linear relationship among the elements is represented by means of sequential memory locations. Arrays hold a series of data elements of same data type. We can simply say that an array is a finite list of elements of same data type. Individual elements are accessed by their position in the array. The position is given by an **index**, which is also called a **subscript**.

The index usually uses a consecutive range of integers (like 0, 1, 2, 3, …, 50), but the index can have any ordinal set of values. Some arrays are *multi-dimensional*, meaning they are indexed by a fixed number of integers, for example by a tuple of four integers. Generally, one- and two- dimensional arrays are the most common. For example, let us consider five data elements of integer type.

```
int num1=101;
int num2-201;
int num3=301;
int num4=401;
int num5=501;
```

The list of five integer data elements can be simply represented by an array as given below:

```
integer_number[5]={101, 201, 301, 401, 501};
```

It becomes more difficult to keep track of this as the number of variables increases. Arrays offer a solution to this problem. Arrays, like other variables in C, must be declared before they can be used. The number 5 within the square bracket represents the size of the declared array. This also represents the maximum number of data elements to be stored. We can use an index or subscript to access the elements of an array. In C language **index starts with zero**. In the above example, if *i* is an index, then

```
integer_number[0]=101,
integer_number[1]=201,
integer_number[2]=301,
integer_number[3]=401, and
integer_number[4]=501
```

The index i varies between 0 to 4.

Two points must be kept in mind while discussing arrays:

- The elements of an array are accessed by means of an **index** or **subscript** set consisting of **n** consecutive numbers, where **n** represents the size of array.
- The elements of an array exist in consecutive memory locations.

Arrays are of different dimension. Here we are discussing only one and two dimensional arrays other dimensional arrays we see later on.

5.1.1 One Dimensional Array

It is also known as vector or list. It is an n-ordered set of n elements. Suppose we have n elements namely a_1, a_2, a_3, …, a_n of same data type (**homogeneous**) and we have an array named A holds these elements. Mathematically A is represented by:

$$A=(a_1, a_2, a_3, \ldots, a_n) \text{ or}$$
$$A(a_1, a_2, a_3, \ldots, a_n)$$

Due to the ordering property elements are put in consecutive manner and we can access any element by its index of subscript. For example,

$$A(1)=a_1 \text{ or } A[1]=a_1,$$
$$A(3)=a_3 \text{ or } A[3]=a_3,$$
$$A(i)=a_i \text{ or } A[i]=a_i \text{ for } 1<=i<=n$$

5.1.2 Multi-dimensional Array

Two-dimensional, three-dimensional, four-dimensional, etc are known as multi-dimensional array. A two-dimensional array is an array in which each element is itself a one-dimensional array. Two-dimensional array is also known as **table**. A two-dimensional array named X is shown in Figure 6.1. It has m rows and n columns.

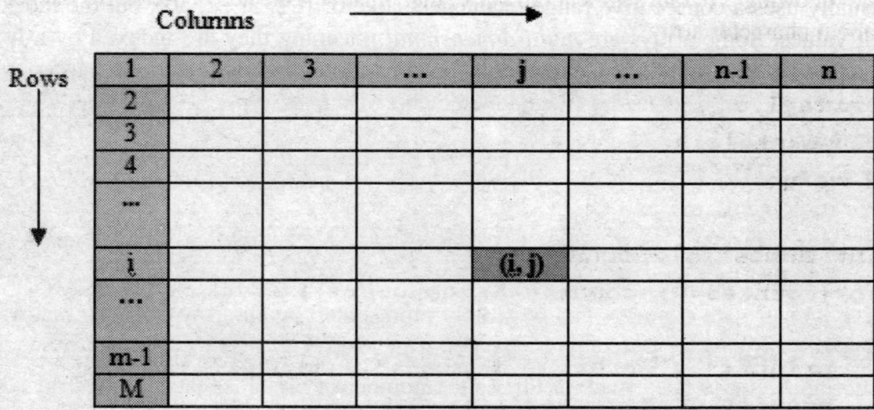

Figure 6.1 Two-dimensional Array

We use two subscripts to identify an element of two-dimensional array. For example, in the Figure 6.1 element **X(i, j)** is highlighted. The row number is i and column number is j. The total number of elements in a table of m rows and n columns is **m*n**.

5.1.3 One Dimensional Array

An *array* is a collection of objects of the same data type, allocated contiguously in memory. Individual objects in an array, called *elements*, are accessed by their position in the array. The subscripting operator ([]) provides the mechanics for creating an index to array elements. This form of access is called *indexing* or *subscripting*. An array facilitates the coding of repetitive tasks by allowing the statements executed on each element to be put into a loop that iterates through each element in the array.

The C language provides limited built-in support for an array type: reading and writing individual elements. Assignment of one array to another, the comparison of two arrays for equality, returning self-knowledge of size is not supported by this language.

The type of an array is derived from the type of its elements, in what is called *array type derivation*. If array objects are of incomplete type, the array type is also considered incomplete. Array elements may not be of type void or of function type. However, arrays of pointers to functions are allowed. The syntax to represent subscripted variables of an array in C language is given by:

```
Data type name_of_array [size of array];
```

For example, see the following declaration.

- int number[5];
- int list[13] ;
- char string[20];
- float real_numbers[6];

In the above example, **number** is an array of size 5, **list** is an array of size 13. Arrays **number** and **list** are **int** type. The array **string** is **char** data type of size 20 and **real_number** is an array of size 6 of **float** data type. These all arrays are one-dimensional arrays. We will discuss about the two-dimensional arrays later in this chapter. Example 5.1 demonstrates simple implementation of an array.

Example 5.1: Write a program to read into (integer and character) and display the contents of an array.

Answer: See the following program segment (array1.c) that illustrates the above notion fro integer and array2.c explores idea about character array.

```
/** array1.c   **/
#include<stdio.h>
void main()
{
   int number[5], counter;
   for(counter=0; counter<5; counter++)
   {
      printf("\n Enter %d Number:", counter+1);
      scanf("%d", &number[i]);
   }
   printf("\n You have entered following numbers:");
   for(counter=0, counter<5;counter++)
   printf("\t %d", number[counter]);
getch();
}  // end of the main
```

OUTPUT

Enter 1 Number:25

Enter 2 Number:35

Enter 3 Number:45

Enter 4 Number:55

Enter 5 Number:65

You have entered following numbers:

25 35 45 55 65

In the above program, **number** is an **int** data type array of size 5. The **int** variable **counter** is used as index when five numbers are inputted through keyboard. We have used two **for** loops for accepting and displaying five integer numbers in first loop and second loop, respectively.

Let us see another program which takes the name of a person and display it, i.e., it demonstrates char array.

```
/** array2.c   **/
#include<stdio.h>
 void main()
 {
     char name[20];
     printf("\n Enter your  good name (not more than 20
     characters):");
     scanf("%s", name);
```

```
    printf("\n Your good name is: %s", name);
    getch();
  }
```

In the above program, name of a person is taken as input which is not greater than 19 characters, and it is displayed. One thing is noticeable here that when *name* is scanned the symbol '&' is not used as prefix which has been used through out in scanning any data type so far. This symbol '&' used to get the address of a variable. The name of any **char** type array itself represents its address (i.e., base address or starting address of an array from where onwards storage reserved for the data elements of the array). So, whenever a **char** array is scanned, there is no need of using '&' symbol.

5.2 Array Manipulation

Most of the arithmetical operations can be done on the elements of an array. The Table 5.1 summarises these manipulations on the elements of an array declared say double x[8]. The word double here means that all the values stored in the array x are of double precision.

Table 5.1 Statements manipulating Array x

Statement	Explanation
print x[0]	Displays the value of x[0]
x[3] = 25	Stores the value 25 in x[3]
sum = x[0] +x[1]	Stores the sum of x[0] and x[1]
sum += x[2]	Adds x[2] to sum
x[3] += 1.0	Adds 1.0 to previous value of x[3]
x[2] = x[0] + x[1]	Stores the sum of x[0] and x[1] in x[2]

5.2.1 Initialization of one Dimensional Array

The initializer for an array is a comma-separated list of constant expressions enclosed in braces ({ }). The initializer is preceded by an equal sign (=). We do not need to initialize all elements in an array. If an array is partially initialized, elements that are not initialized receive the value 0 of the appropriate type. The same applies to elements of arrays with static storage duration. All file-scope variables and function-scope variables declared with the static keyword have static storage duration. The following definition shows a completely initialized one-dimensional array:

```
static int number[3] = { 5, 7, 2 };
```

The array number contains the following values: number[0] is 5, number[1] is 7; number[2] is 2. When we have an expression in the subscript declarator defining the number of elements in this case 3, we cannot have more initializers than the number of elements in the array.

The following definition shows a partially initialized one-dimensional array :

```
static int number1[3] = { 5, 7 };
```

The values of number1[0] and number1[1] are the same as in the previous definition, but number1[2] is 0.

A designated initializer, or designator, points out a particular element to be initialized. A designator list is a comma-separated list of one or more designators. A designator list followed by an equal sign constitutes a designation. Designated initializers allow for the following flexibility :

- Elements within an aggregate can be initialized in any order.
- The initializer list can omit elements that are declared anywhere in the aggregate, rather than only at the end. Elements that are omitted are initialized as if they are static objects: arithmetic types are initialized to 0; pointers are initialized to NULL.
- Where inconsistent or incomplete bracketing of initializers for multi-dimensional arrays or nested aggregates may be difficult to understand, designators can more clearly identify the element or member to be initialized.

The following definition shows how we can use designated initializers to skip over elements of the array that we do not want to initialize explicitly. The array number contains the following values: number[0] is 5; number[1] is implicitly initialized to 0; number[2] is 7.

```
static int number[3] = { [0] = 5, [2] = 7 };
```

In the following example, the third and second elements of the one-dimensional array aa are initialized to 3 and 6, respectively:

```
int aa[4] = { [2] = 3, [1] = 6 };
```

Designated initializers can be combined with regular initializers, as in the following example:

```
int a[10] = {2, 4, [8]=9, 10};
```

In this example, a[0] is initialized to 2, a[1] is initialized to 4, a[2] to a[7] are initialized to 0, and a[9] is initialized to 10. In the following example, a single designator is used to "allocate" space from both ends of an array:

```
int a[MAX] = {1, 3, 5, 7, 9, [MAX-5] = 8, 6, 4, 2, 0};
```

The designated initializer, [MAX-5] = 8, means that the array element at subscript MAX-5 should be initialized to the value 8. If MAX is 15, a[5] through a[9] will be initialized to zero. If MAX is 7, a[2] through a[4] will first have the values 5, 7, and 9, respectively, which are overridden by the values 8, 6, and 4. In other words, if MAX is 7, the initialization would be the same as if the declaration had been written:

```
int a[MAX] = {1, 3, 8, 6, 4, 2, 0};
```

Instead of an expression in the subscript declarator defining the number of elements, the following one-dimensional array definition defines one element for each initializer specified:

```
static int item[ ] = { 1, 2, 3, 4, 5 };
```

The compiler gives item the five initialized elements, because no size was specified and there are five initializers.

5.2.2 Initialization of character arrays

We can initialize a one-dimensional character array by specifying :

- A brace-enclosed comma-separated list of constants, each of which can be contained in a character
- A string constant (braces surrounding the constant are optional)

Initializing a string constant places the null character (\0) at the end of the string if there is room or if the array dimensions are not specified. The following definitions show character array initializations:

```
static char name1[ ] = { 'J', 'a', 'n' };
static char name2[ ] = { "Jan" };
static char name3[4] = "Jan";
```

These definitions create the following elements:

Element	Value	Element	Value	Element	Value
Name1[0]	J	name2[0]	J	name3[0]	J
Name1[1]	a	name2[1]	a	name3[1]	a
Name1[2]	n	name2[2]	n	name3[2]	n
		name2[3]	\0	name3[3]	\0

Note that the following definition would result in the null character being lost:

```
static char name3[3]="Jan";
```

When we initialize an array of characters with a string, the number of characters in the string - including the terminating '\0' - must not exceed the number of elements in the array.

Whenever the initial values are assigned to an array then the size is automatically determined by C compiler. Initializing the size of an array may result in wastage of memory.

5.3 Searching

Search is there in all the computer programs. It allows you to search for a character, word, string of characters, sometimes even the graphics too. In C also we have the search command. Supposing a specific information is given in an array. Searching refers to the operation of finding the location of Info in an array and displaying an appropriate message. The search is said to be successful, if Info arrears in the array elese it known as unsuccessful search. There are some simple techniques for searching, which are:

1. Linear search
2. Binary search

5.3.1 Linear Search

Here each of an array element is compared one by one with given ITEM to be searched. Until either the desired element is found or the end of the list is reached. This method, which traverses the array sequentially to locate the given ITEM is called linear search. The algorithm shown in Figure 5.2 searches the ITEM in a linear array, using Repeat until loop.

```
[Linear Search] LINEAR [DATA, N, ITEM, LOC]
Here DATA is a linear array with N elements, and ITEM is given item
of information. The algorithm finds the location LOC of ITEM in DATA,
or sets LOC := 0 if the search is unsuccessful.
Step 1   [Insert ITEM at the end of DATA.]
         Set DATA[N + 1] := ITEM
Step 2   [Initialize counter.] get LOC := 1
Step 3   [Search for ITEM.]
         Repeat while DATA[LOC] ≠ ITEM;
              Set LOC := LOC + 1
         [End of loop]
         [End of loop in step 2]
Step 4   [Successful?] If LOC = N + 1, then: Set LOC := 0
Step 5   Exit
```

Figure 5.2 Algorithm for linear search in an array using Repeat loop

5.3.2 Binary Search

If you want to locate an item in an ordered list for a particular number then, this can be done efficiently by using a binary search. This is a searching technique in which each comparison either locates an item for the target value or divides the remaining list in half. Because the array (list) is in the order (ascendng or descending), it will only be necessary to repeat this process on one of the two segments, thereby reducing the remaining search operation very rapidly.

Suppose we are required to locate 29 in the array shown in Figure 5.3 using binary search techniques, take the following steps:

Step 1 Split the ten element list into half (10/2 = 5), and check the fifth element. The result is 23. But 29 > 23. Thus the searched value is higher in the list, i.e., a larger subscript is needed.

Step 2 Split the five elements in the second half of the list into half, i.e., [(10 – 5)/2 +5] = 7.5 (rounded to

8). Check the 8th element. The result is 52 but 29 < 52. Thus, search is lower in the list, i.e., a lower subscript is needed.

Step 3 Split the distance between the fifth and the eight into half (8 – 5)/2 + 5 = 6.5 (rounded to 7). So check the seventh element. The result is 35 and 29 < 35. So check still lower in the list, i.e., a lower subscript is needed.

Step 4 Split the distance between the fifth and the seventh element into half ([(7 – 5)/2 + 5]. So check the sixth element which is 29. That is the match.

```
    N
1   1
2   5
3   11
4   17
5   23      Comp 1 (29 > 23)
6   29      Match comp 4
7   35      Comp 3 (29 < 35)
8   52      Comp 2 (29 < 52)
9   71
10  93
```

Figure 5.3 Locating an array element containing 29

5.4 Insertion

Insertion is the process of addng a new element to the array. The following algorithm inserts a data element ITEM into the array LA[] at the Kth position. We assume that the array LA[] has N elements

```
INSERT (LA,N,K,ITEM)
Step 1   Set J := (initialise the counter)
Step 2   Repeat steps 3 and 4 while J >= K
Step 3   Set LA[J + 1] := LA[J]
         (move to the jth element down)
Step 4   Set J := J - 1 (decrease the counter)
         [End of loop in step 2]
Step 5   Set LA[K] := ITEM (copy ITEM to Kth element of array LA)
Step 6   Set N := N + 1
Step 7   Exit
```

5.5 Deletion of an Element from an Array

Deletion is the process of removing an element from the array. The algorithm shown below deletes the Kth element from the linear array LA[] and assigns it to a variable ITEM.

```
INSERT (LA,N,K,ITEM)
Step 1   Set J := (initialise the counter)
Step 2   Repeat steps 3 and 4 while J >= K
Step 3   Set LA[J + 1] := LA[J]
         (move the jth element down)
Step 4   Set J := J - 1 (decrease the counter)
         [End of loop in step 2]
Step 5   Set LA[K] := ITEM (copy ITEM to Kth element of array LA)
Step 6   Set N := N + 1
Step 7   Exit
```

5.6 Finding the Largest/Smallest Element in an Array

In a series of numbers, there is bound to be a number with the largest value. Another number(s) in the set may be equal to this number, but cannot be greater than this number. For example, in the following series:

11, 18, 24, 28, 9, 39

we find that 39 is the largest number.

To find the largest number in an array follow the following steps.

1. Start
2. Get the value of element in an array and store them in the array elements a_1, a_2, a_3, a_4, ... a_n, where n is the number of elements.
3. Set temporary variable and asign the value of 1st array element a_1 to temp.
4. Compare temp with the next element a_2 of the array.
5. If the element is having greater value than temp, assign that value to temp
6. Repeat steps 4 and 5 till last element a_n of the array is encountered.
7. Final value of temp is the largest value stored in the array.
8. Stop.

5.7 Two Dimensional Arrays

C does not have true multidimensional arrays. However, because of the generality of C's type system, we can have *arrays of arrays*, which are almost as good. Multi-dimensioned arrays have two or more index values which specify the element in the array. For example, two-dimensional array has two indices; three-dimensional array has three indices, and so on. Two-dimensional arrays are a little more complicated to use than one-dimensional ones. We will use two-dimensional arrays as examples in this section, although the techniques can be extended to three or more dimensions. The syntax for two-dimensional array is as follows:

```
Data type array_name [size of row] [size of column];
```

For example, let us consider some declaration given below:

- int a2[5][7]; /* 5 represent row and 7 represents column*/
- char string[3][10]; /* 3 rows and 10 column, i.e., three strings of 10 characters each*/
- float real_number[5][4]; /* 5 rows and 4 column */
- int temp[5][10][5] /* Three-dimensional array */

In the above declaration, a2 is an array of 5 elements, each of which is an array of 7 ints. We usually think of it as having 5 rows and 7 columns, although this interpretation is not mandatory. Just as we declared a two-dimensional array using two pairs of brackets, we access its individual elements using two pairs of brackets:

```
int i, j;
for(i = 0; i < 5; i++)
{
    for(j = 0; j < 7; j++)
        a2[i][j] = 0;
}
```

Make sure to put each subscript in its own, correct pair of brackets. Neither

```
int a2[5, 7];            /* XXX WRONG */
```

nor

```
    a2[i, j] = 0;          /* XXX WRONG */
```

would do anything remotely like what we wanted.

Two-dimensional arrays are used when it is required to process the matrices, tabular data, etc. Go through the Example 5.2 for implementation of basic concept of two-dimensional array.

Example 5.2: Write C code which demonstrates the two-dimensional array. You are also required to present memory address of the elements in the array.

Answer: Let us see the following program segment (array6.c) which demonstrates the notion of two-dimensional array. In this program segment we defined number[5][3] a two dimensional array with size 5*3, i.e., 5 rows and 3 columns. We have used two **for** loops to readout data into number[][]. Finally with the help of two for loops we displayed the array **number** contents onto the standard output device. Further we consider **array20.c** which demonstrates how elements of the array are located into the system memory.

```
/** array6.c **/
# include<stdio.h>
void main()
{
          int number[5][3] ;
 int i, j;
 for( i = 0 ; i < 5 ; i ++ )
 {
    for ( j = 0; j < 3 ; j ++ )
   {
     printf("\nEnter row: %d element: %d:", i+1, j+1);
                   scanf("%d", &number[i][j]) ;
   }
    }
    printf("\n You have entered:");
    for( i = 0 ; i < 5 ; i ++ )
   {
      printf("\n Row = %d:",i+1);
      for ( j = 0; j < 3 ; j ++ )
         printf("\t          %d ", number[i][j]);
   }
} /*End of main function*/
```

OUTPUT

Enter row: 1 element: 1 : 2
Enter row: 1 element: 2 : 4
Enter row: 1 element: 3 : 6
Enter row: 2 element: 1 : 3
Enter row: 2 element: 2 : 6

Enter row: 2 element: 3 : 9
Enter row: 3 element: 1 : 4
Enter row: 3 element: 2 : 8
Enter row: 3 element: 3 : 12
Enter row: 4 element: 1 : 5
Enter row: 4 element: 2 : 10
Enter row: 4 element: 3 : 15
Enter row: 5 element: 1 : 6
Enter row: 5 element: 2 : 12
Enter row: 5 element: 3 : 18
You have entered:

Row = 1: 2	4	6
Row = 2: 3	6	9
Row = 3: 4	8	12
Row = 4: 5	10	15
Row = 5: 6	12	18

Here, a question may arise about the organization of the above data in computer memory and the clarification is given in **Figure 5.4**. We assume that 2-byte is reserved for an int data type.

Now let us see another program that prints the addresses of the elements of a two-dimensional array.

```
/**   array20.c **/
# include<stdio.h>
void main( )
{
   int number[5][3] ;
   int i ;
   int j ;
   for( i = 0 ; i < 5 ; i ++ )
      for ( j = 0; j < 3 ; j ++ )
         number[i][j] = i*j ;
   printf("\nAddress  Element  Value \n");
   for( i = 0 ; i < 5 ; i ++ )
   for ( j = 0; j < 3 ; j ++ )
   printf("\n 0%x  | number[%d][%d]  | %d  ", &number[i][j], i,j,
      number[i][j]);
```

OUTPUT

Address	Element	Value
0ffd8	| number[0][0] |	0

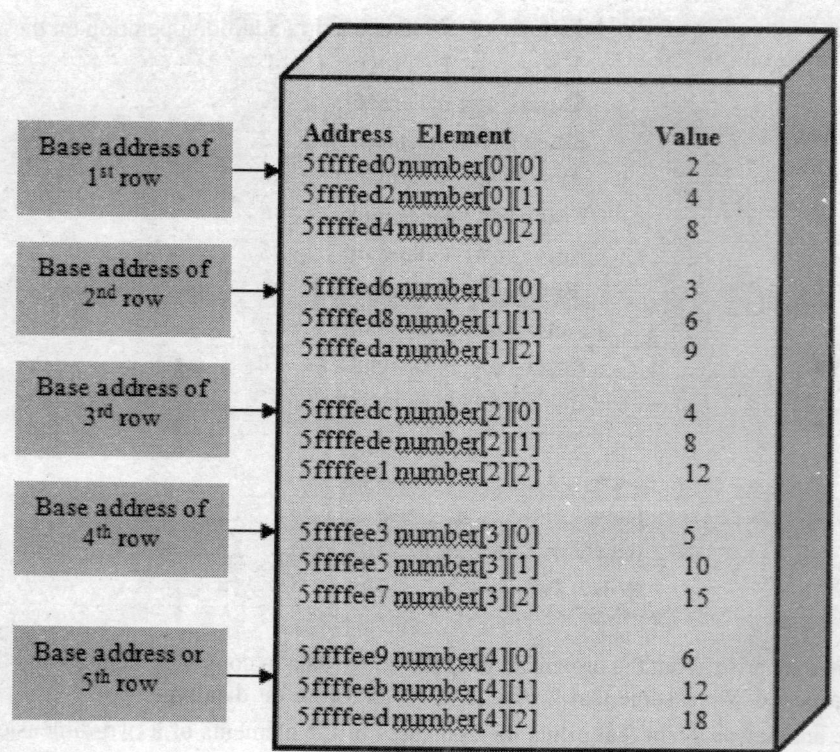

Figure 5.4 Two-dimension arrays in memory

0ffda	**number[0][1]**	**0**
0ffdc	**number[0][2]**	**0**
0ffde	**number[1][0]**	**0**
0ffe0	**number[1][1]**	**1**
0ffe2	**number[1][2]**	**2**
0ffe4	**number[2][0]**	**0**
0ffe6	**number[2][1]**	**2**
0ffe8	**number[2][2]**	**4**
0ffea	**number[3][0]**	**0**
0ffec	**number[3][1]**	**3**
0ffee	**number[3][2]**	**6**
0fff0	**number[4][0]**	**0**
0fff2	**number[4][1]**	**4**
0fff4	**number[4][2]**	**8**

Go through the Example 5.3 which demonstrates one use of two dimensional arrays, matrix operation.

Example 5.3: Write C code which computes summation of two-matrices.

Answer: From the following program it is clear that one application of the two dimensional array is the development of random data for two matrices of 3x4 and perform addition operation on these data. The data is finally displayed on the screen.

```
/** array21.c **/
#include<stdio.h>
#include<stdlib.h>
void main()
{
long  matrix1[3][4], matrix2[3][4], result[3][4], i , j ;
 printf("\nGeneration of Matrix of Size 3x4 in Progress");
 printf("\n————————————");
   printf("\n MATRIX ONE:");
   for( i = 0 ; i < 3 ; i++ )
   {
      printf("\n") ;
      for ( j = 0 ; j < 4 ; j++ )
      {
         matrix1[i][j] = rand( )*10/100;
         printf("%6d    ", matrix1[i][j] ) ;
      }
   }
   printf("\n MATRIX SECOND: ");
   for( i = 0 ; i < 3 ; i++ )
   {
      printf("\n") ;
      for ( j = 0 ; j < 4 ; j++ )
      {
         matrix2[i][j] = rand( )*10/100;
         printf("%6d    ", matrix2[i][j] ) ;
      }
   }
   /* Summation Section */
   for( i = 0 ; i < 3 ; i++ )
     for ( j = 0 ; j < 4 ; j++ )
      result[i][j] = matrix1[i][j] + matrix2[i][j];
      /* Output Section*/
   printf("\n\n\n Summation of two  Matrices:");
   printf("\n Output Matrix of Size 3x4");
   for( i = 0 ; i < 3 ; i++ )
   {
      printf("\n") ;
      for ( j = 0 ; j < 4 ; j++ )
      printf("%8d  ", result[i][j]) ;
```

```
    }
    printf("\n Press a key");
    getch() ;
}
```

OUTPUT

Generation of Matrix of Size 3x4 in Progress

MATRIX ONE:

34	13	-212	109
-145	56	-206	-13
-326	-164	245	145

MATRIX SECOND:

-298	321	-116	136
-114	50	280	-116
90	-132	63	87

Summation of two Matrices:

Output Matrix of Size 3x4

-264	334	-328	245
-259	106	74	-129
-236	-296	308	232

Press a key

5.7.1 Initialization Of Multidimensional Arrays

Like one-dimensional array, two-dimensional arrays can also be initialized. To initialize two-dimensional array, data are provided in set form. The size of each set must be equal to size of the row and each set must be enclosed into braces. We can initialize a multidimensional array using any of the following techniques:

- Listing the values of all elements we want to initialize, in the order that the compiler assigns the values. The compiler assigns values by increasing the subscript of the last dimension fastest. This form of a multidimensional array initialization looks like a one-dimensional array initialization. The following definition completely initializes the array month_days:

```
static month_days[2][12] =
{
 31, 28, 31, 30, 31, 30, 31, 31, 30, 31, 30, 31,
 31, 29, 31, 30, 31, 30, 31, 31, 30, 31, 30, 31
};
```

- Using braces to group the values of the elements we want initialized. We can put braces around each element, or around any nesting level of elements. The following definition contains two elements in the first dimension; we can consider these elements as rows. The initialization contains braces around each of these two elements:

```
static int month_days[2][12] =
{
```

```
    { 31, 28, 31, 30, 31, 30, 31, 31, 30, 31, 30, 31 },
    { 31, 29, 31, 30, 31, 30, 31, 31, 30, 31, 30, 31 }
  };
```

- Using nested braces to initialize dimensions and elements in a dimension selectively. In the following example, only the first eight elements of the array **grid** are explicitly initialized. The remaining four elements that are not explicitly initialized are automatically initialized to zero.

```
static short grid[3] [4] = {8, 6, 4, 1, 9, 3, 1, 1};
```

The initial values of grid are:

Element	Value	Element	Value
grid[0] [0]	8	grid[1] [2]	1
grid[0] [1]	6	grid[1] [3]	1
grid[0] [2]	4	grid[2] [0]	0
grid[0] [3]	1	grid[2] [1]	0
grid[1] [0]	9	grid[2] [2]	0
grid[1] [1]	3	grid[2] [3]	0

- Using *designated* initializers: The following example uses designated initializers to explicitly initialize only the last four elements of the array. The first eight elements that are not explicitly initialized are automatically initialized to zero.

```
static short grid[3] [4] = { [2][0] = 8, [2][1] = 6, [2][2] =
   4, [2][3] = 1 };
```

The initial values of **grid** are:

Element	Value	Element	Value
grid[0] [0]	0	grid[1] [2]	0
grid[0] [1]	0	grid[1] [3]	0
grid[0] [2]	0	grid[2] [0]	8
grid[0] [3]	0	grid[2] [1]	6
grid[1] [0]	0	grid[2] [2]	4
grid[1] [1]	0	grid[2] [3]	1

Go through the Example 5.4 which demonstrates initialization of two dimensional arrays.

Example 5.4: Write C code which initializes two two-dimensional arrays.

Answer: Consider the following program segment, which has initialized two two-dimensional array **matrix1** and **matrix2**. And on the choice basis, perform the addition and subtraction on these arrays.

```
/** array22.c **/
# include<stdio.h>
# include<stdlib.h>
void main()
{
   int matrix1[5][5] = { { 1,1,1,1,1 },
                         { 2,2,2,2,2 },
```

```
                        { 3,3,3,3,3 },
                        { 4,4,4,4,4 },
                        { 5,5,5,5,5 } };
   int matrix2[5][5] = { { 0,0,0,0,0 },
                        { 6,6,6,6,6 },
                        { 7,7,7,7,7 },
                        { 8,8,8,8,8 },
                        { 9,9,9,9,9 } };
   int i , j ;
   int result[5][5] ;
   char choice ;
   do
   {
      printf("\nEnter Choice \n A=Addition \n S=Subtraction \n
      N=Break \n Choice is:");
      choice = getchar() ;
      choice = toupper(choice) ;/*Convert into Upper case*/
      if(choice = = 'A')  /*Addition*/
      {
         printf("\n");
         for( i = 0 ; i < 5 ; i++ )
               for ( j = 0 ; j < 5 ; j++ )
                    result[i][j] = matrix1[i][j] + matrix2[i][j] ;
          /* Output */
         printf("\n Output Matrix Addition of Two Matrices  ");
         printf("\n");
         for( i = 0 ; i < 5 ; i++ )
         {
               printf("\n") ;
               for ( j = 0 ; j < 5 ; j++ )
               printf("%5d", result[i][j]) ;
         }
         printf("\n");
         printf("\n Press a key ");
         getch() ;
         }elseif(choice = = 'S')     /*Subtraction*/
         {
               printf("\n");
               for( i = 0 ; i < 5 ; i++ )
                     for ( j = 0 ; j < 5 ; j++ )
                           result[i][j] = matrix1[i][j] -
      matrix2[i][j] ;

               /* Output */
```

```
                printf("\n Output Matrix Subtraction of Two Matrices
        ");
                printf("\n");
                for( i = 0 ; i < 5 ; i++ )
                {
                        printf("\n") ;
                        for ( j = 0 ; j < 5 ; j++ )
                            printf("%6d", result[i][j]) ;
                   }
                printf("\n");
                printf("\n Press a key ");
                getch() ;
           }else if(choice = = 'N')
           {
                printf("\n Choice is wrong");
                printf("\n Press a key to exit");
                getch() ;
                exit(0) ;   /*Terminates the program*/
           }
      } while (choice !='N');
  }  // End of main function
```

Run the above program segment and perform the desired action.

5.8 Addition/Multiplication of Two Matrices

Matrix is a two dimensional array represented as $[A_{ij}]$ where i is the number of row and j is the number of columns. Even though the elements of a two dimensional array are represented as a matrix. They are stored in adjacent locations like a one dimenstional array inside he memory of a computer. The elements may be stored row-by-row (row major) or column-by-column (column major). The choice ofthe arrangement is not with the user and depends on the programming language.

5.8.1 Addition of Two Matrices

Let A and B are two matices of the same order. Then thier sum, A + B is defined as another matrix, each element of which is summation of the corresponding elements of A and B. For example if we have:

$$A = \begin{matrix} 9 & 8 \\ 7 & 5 \end{matrix}$$

$$B = \begin{matrix} 2 & 4 \\ 3 & 4 \end{matrix}$$

then,

$$A + B = \begin{matrix} 9+2 & 8+4 \\ 7+3 & 5+4 \end{matrix}$$

	11	12
or A + B =	10	9

i.e., if A = $[a_{ij}]$ and $[b_{ij}]$ then A + B = $[a_{ij}] + [b_{ij}]$

5.8.2 Multiplication of Two Matrices

Let us take the multiplication of two matrix A and B of sizes 2 x 3 and 4 x 2 respectively. They are defined as below:

	0	2	3		1	0	
A =	1	3	1	B =	0	2	then
	2	5	2		2	2	

Here A and B are compatible. The product is as follows:

	0 x 1 + 2 x 0 + 3 x 2	0 x 0 + 2 x 2 + 3 x 2
A x B =	1 x 1 + 3 x 0 + 1 x 2	1 x 0 + 3 x 2 + 1 x 2
	2 x 1 + 5 x 0 + 2 x 2	2 x 0 + 5 x 2 + 2 x 2

	6	10
=	3	8
	6	14

Here 6 is the value of the element lying in the 1st row and 1st column of the product matrix (A x B). This is the sum of the products of the corresponding elements of 1st row of A with 1st column of B.

To multiply two matrices follow the following steps:

1. Start
2. Get 1st and 2nd matrix.
3. Check if numer of columns of 1st matrix is equal to the number of rows in 2nd matrix. Then matrices are compatible for multiplication. Otherwise, product is not possible.
4. If matrices are compatible then find the sum of the product of corresponding element of each row of A with the corresponding element of each column of B and sum the element and equate it to the corresponding position of the product matrix.
5. Stop.

5.9 Transpose of a Square Matrix

A transpose of a matrix is obtained by interchanging the rows with corresponding columns of a given matrix. The transpose of matrix A is denoted by A^T. If matrix A is an m x n then after transposing it we will get an n x m matrix which is the transpose of matrix A and represented as A^T. For example,

	1	2	3	4
A =	5	6	7	8
	9	6	7	8

Then transpose of matrix A is

	1	5	9
	2	6	6
A^T =	3	7	7
	4	8	8

5.10 Null Terminated Strings as Array of Characters

In programming language C, a string is not a formal data type but it is an array of type char. A character can be a single letter, numeral, punctuation marks, or other such symbol or a special character. A string is any sequence of all these different types of characters. For example Sachin Tendulkar is a string and is tored in memory using the ASCII codes of the characters. The string is represented using ASCII coded form in he memory as shown in Figure 5.5. A string is a series of characters, terminated by a null character. Null character is a character with a numeric value of zero and it is represented by '\0' in C.

S
A
C
H
I
N
T
E
N
D
U
L
K
A
R

Figure 5.5 String representation of "Sachin Tendulkar" in memory

5.11 Standard Library String Functions

The file string.h available in the library of C has several built in functions such as strlen(), stcpy(), strcmp(), etc., for string manipulation. To use thee functions, the header file string.h must be included at the begining of a program as shown below:

```
#include<string.h>
```

Let us have a look at each one of them.

5.11. String Length {strlen()}

The strlen() function is used to find the length of the string or the number of characters in a given string, excluding the end-of-string character (null). The following program 5.5 demonstrates this function.

Example 5.5: Write C code to find the length of the string.

Answer: Here the length of the string includes any special or blank characters also.

```
#include<stdio.h>
#include<string.h>
void main()
  {
     char name[25];
     int nch;
     printf("\n Enter name);
     gets(name);
     nch = strlen(name);
     printf(Length of the string name = %d \n", nch);
  }
```

```
OUTPUT
Enter name: Sachin
Length of the string name = 6
```

5.11.2 String Copy {strcpy()}

The strcpy() function is used to copy the contents of one string to another, i.e., source string is copied to destination string.

```
strcpy(s1, s2)
```

copies string s2 to string s1.

The following program 5.6 demonstrates this function.

Example 5.6: Write C code to copy a string to another string.

Answer: Here the length of the string includes any special or blank characters also.

```
#include<stdio.h>
#include<string.h>
void main()
   {
      char str1[15], str2[15];
      printf("Enter a string str1 to be copied into str2 ; ");
      gets(str1);
      strcpy(str2, str1);
      puts(str2);
   }
```

```
OUTPUT
Enter a string str1 to be copied into str2: Sachin
Sachin
```

5.11.3 strcmp()

The strcmp() function is used to compare two strings, character by character. It accepts any two strings as parameters and returns an integer value.

```
strcmp(s1, s2)
```

the following conditions apply.

If s1 < s2 /* If the first string is less than the second string it returns –1 */

If s1 = s2 /* If both are identical it returns 0 */

If s1 > s2 /* If the first string is greater than the second string it returns 1 */

5.12 Array Bounds Checking

We know that C language is used as system programming language due to its variety of features that are very much powerful. But so far we have not discussed any weakness. Since C provides many features that provides low-level features of a computer system. For example, memory and registers can be accessed directly. These features come along with some lacuna also. One of the routed weaknesses of **C** language is the lack of array bounds checking. This weakness is due to frugal use of memory although it is strength of a language. Lack of bounds checking simply means that no safeguards exist to prevent an array from being overwritten. If a character array is declared with a subscript of 10 sequential bytes, only 10 sequential bytes of memory are reserved for array. However, if a program miscalculates and writes more than 10 characters (including NULL) to this array, the excess characters are written into the memory locations that immediately follow the block that was allocated for the array. The 10-element boundary of the array is exceeded and bytes are written into memory locations not set aside exclusively for this array. When this occurs, what happens? It is programmer responsibility to take care of this.

There is no single answer to this question. If there are a few declared variables in the program, there is a good chance that the unreserved portion of memory that was overwritten by the offending string is not being used anyway and the program may run in a normal fashion.

However, if there are many variables, the exclusive storage allocated to these, others may be overwritten by the unwarranted long string. This will certainly cause an improper execution sequence. In a worst-case scenario, those extra string elements may overwrite a management portion of memory or even interact with other variables to do the same thing.

The result can be a crash where the computer simply locks up in a continuous loop and must be rebooted/restarted. This is very much dangerous situation if somebody is using C language carelessly. However, there have been cases where hard disk drives have been erased by disastrous overwrites to interrupt addresses (in DOS). Go through the Example 5.7 for implementation of this discussion.

Example 5.7: Write a C program for demonstrating the limitation of C in respect to using array without implementing the array checking.

Answer: Following program segment illustrates the above discussion.

```
/** array13.c **/
# include<stdio.h>
# include<string.h>
void main ()
{
    char str1[10] = {"Eish itaa"};
    char str2[5];
    str2[0]=str1[0];
    str2[1]=str1[1];
    str2[2]=str1[2];
    str2[3]=str1[3];
    str2[4]=str1[4];
    str2[5]=str1[5];
    str2[6]=str1[6];
    str2[7]=str1[7];
    str2[8]=str1[8];
    str2[9]=str1[9];
    printf("\n The given string is: %s", str1);
    printf("\n Copied string is: %s", str2);
    getch();
}
```

OUTPUT

The given string is: taa

Copied string is:Eish itaa

We can see here that even the size of array str2 is declared 5; it contains string constant "Eish itaa" having 10 characters. In the above program, null character is not assigned to indicate the termination of string. This is a weak point of using C language. So, we are required use the memory allocation and initialization very carefully. Pointers add more power and flexibility in memory allocation and data accessing which we will discuss later on.

In the above program the array bounds are exceeded, but there will be no error message or warning when the program compiles. The different types of compilers will generate different type of output. The reason for this aberration lies in the way storage is managed.

5.13 Arrays and Functions

We know that an array is a variable capable of storing multiple values of the same data type. Like other variables, arrays can be passed to functions. When a function receives an array as a parameter the compiler does not have to specify the array size in the parameter declaration. Go through the Example 5.8 for implementation of this discussion.

Example 5.8: Write a C program which finds summation of elements of an array. Use of function for finding the summation is essential.

Answer: In following program the function **display(),** the square brackets follow the variable name **int_array** inform the compiler that the parameter is an array. Other than knowing that the parameter is an array, the compiler does not care about the size of an array passed to the function.

```
/** array14.c    **/
# include<stdio.h>
int display(int integer_array[], int number_of_element)
{
    int count;
    int sum =0;
    for (count =0; count < number_of_element; count++)
    {
        printf("\n    value[%d] = %d", count, integer_array[count]);
        sum += integer_array[count];
    }
    return (sum);
}

void main()
{
    int numbers[5] = {1, 2, 3, 4, 5};
    int result;
    result = display(numbers, 5);
    printf("\n Summation = %d", result);
}
```

In the function **display(),** two parameters are required. They are an array parameter **integer_array** to catch the array passed and a parameter **number_of_element** to catch the index of the last element (information) in the array to be processed.

5.14 Visualizing A C String

Storing a single **ASCII** character requires a byte of memory. We know that a string is a sequence of **ASCII** characters. When we declare a string constant, **C** automatically assigns **NULL** ('\0') character. When we create strings with the help of programs by reading character from standard input device, it is required to assign **NULL** character at the end of the string to indicate the end of the string. The best way to visualize a string is simply a collection of bytes (ASCII characters) terminated by a **NULL.** The above discussion is illustrated in **Figure 5.6.**

When functions work with strings, they normally care about the location at which the string starts (base address). Once the function knows the base address, it can traverse the successive memory locations until it encounters the **NULL** ('\0' end of the string indicators).

In **C**, a character string is a **NULL** or zero terminated arrays of characters. To create a character string, we simply declare a character array to create a character string. We declare a character array such as:

```
char string [15];
```

Suppose char array string has value "Prit Gupta", i.e.,

```
char string[12]={"Prit Gupta"};
```

The memory map of the above array string is shown in Figure 5.6.

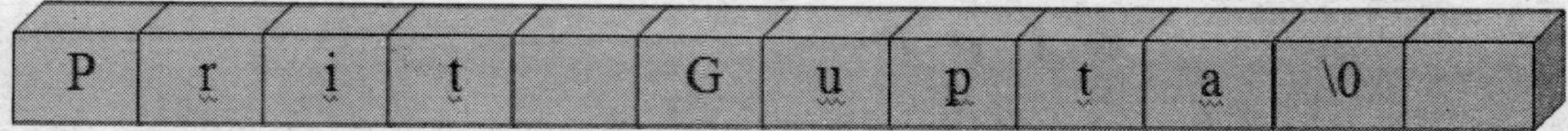

Figure 5.6 Consecutive memory allocation for char array string

In this case **C** compiler will create a string capable of storing 12 characters that is index from **string [0]** through **string [11]. C** compiler does not typically place the **NULL** character after the last character in the string. Instead, functions such as **gets ( )** and **fgets ( )** place the **NULL** character at the end of string. When we manipulate strings, it is programmer's responsibility to ensure that the **NULL** character is present. Go through the Example 5.9 for implementation of this discussion.

Example 5.9: Write C code which demonstrates the formation of string from character array.

Answer: For example, consider the following program segments (array15.c and array16.c) that manipulate the above discussion:

```
/** array15.c **/
# include<stdio.h>
void main()
{
   char string[27];
          int i;
   for(i =0; i < 26; i++)
      string[i] = 'a'+i;
   string[i] = '\0'; /*assigning null character*/
   printf("\n The string is: %s", string);
   getch();
}
```

The program uses **for** loop to assign the letter a to z to **string**. The program then places the **NULL** character after the letter z to indicate the string's end. The **printf** () function then displays each character in the string up to the **NULL** character. As we have discussed, **C** functions that work with strings use the **NULL** character to determine the string's end. For example, consider the following program segment and guess the output.

```
/** array16.c **/
# include<stdio.h>
void main()
{
   char string[27];
   int i;
   for(i =0; i < 26; i++)
   {
      string[i] = 'A'+i;
   }
   string[15] = '\0';
   printf("\n The string is : %s", string);
   getch();
}
```

A character string is a sequence of zero or more characters that is typically terminated by a **NULL** character ('\0'). When we work with characters in **C**, we can use the character's numeric **ASCII** value or we can place the character within single quotes, such as 'x'. When we use the double quotes, on the other hand, such as "x", **C** creates a character string that contains the letter (or letters) specified and is terminated by **NULL** character.

5.15 Vector Operation

One-dimensional arrays are also known as vectors or lists. The operations, which are possible on vectors, are given below:

- Addition
- Subtraction
- Multiplication

Go through the Example 6.8 for implementation of this discussion.

Example 5.10: Write C code which demonstrates the operation on one dimensional array.

Answer: In the program segment **array17.c** vector operations on one-dimensional array is given. This program performs above three operations provided in the list on the choice basis given by the user. Following list of characters are used to indicate an operation:

A for addition

S for subtraction

M for Multiplication

```
/** array17.c **/
```

```
# include<stdio.h>
void main()
{
    int vector1 [5] = {4, 5, 6, 7, 8};
    int vector2 [5] = {1, 2, 3, 4, 5};
    int result [5 ] ;
    char choice ;
    int i ;
    do
    {
        printf("\n Enter Choice \n A = Addition \n
        S = Subtraction \n M= Multiplication \n Choice is:");
        choice = getchar() ;/*receive the characater*/
        choice = toupper(choice) ;/*convert in upper case*/
        switch(choice)
        {
        case 'A' :
            printf("\n Addition operation:");
            for( i = 0 ; i < 5 ; i++ )
                result [i] = vector1[i] + vector2[i] ;
            for( i = 0 ; i < 10 ; i++ )
                printf("\n %d",result [i] );
                printf("\n Press a key.....");
                getch() ;
                break ;

        case 'S' :
            printf("\n Subtraction operation");
            for( i = 0 ; i < 10 ; i++ )
                result [i] = vector1[i] - vector2[i] ;
            for( i = 0 ; i < 10 ; i++ )
                printf("\n %d",result [i] );
                printf("\n Press a key");
                getch() ;
                break ;
        case 'M' :
            printf("\n Multiplication operation:");
            for( i = 0 ; i < 10 ; i++ )
                result [i] = vector1[i] * vector2[i] ;
            for( i = 0 ; i < 10 ; i++ )
                printf("\n %d",result [i] );
                printf("\n Press a key");
                getch() ;
```

```
                break ;
        default :
            printf("\n Choice of operation is wrong....");
            printf("\n Press a key");
            getch() ;
            exit(0);            /*program is terminated here*/
        }
    } while (( choice = = 'A' || choice = = 'S'  || choice = =
      'M') ;
}  /*End of main function*/
```

The above program segment performs addition, subtraction, and multiplication of two vectors {4, 5, 6, 7, 8} and {1, 2, 3, 4, 5}. The user enters the choice from list {A, S, M} and accordingly operation is performed. If choice is other than the said list then program terminates after raising message "Choice of operation is wrong..."

OUTPUT
Enter Choice
A=Addition
S=Subtraction
M=Multiplication
Choice is: M
Multiplication operation:
4
10
18
28
40
Press a key
Enter Choice
A=Addition
S=Subtraction
M=Multiplication
Choice is: a
Addition operation:
5
7
9
11
13
Press a key
Enter Choice

```
A=Addition
S=Subtraction
M=Multiplication
Choice is: s
Subtraction operation:
3
3
3
3
3
Press a key
Enter Choice
A=Addition
S=Subtraction
M=Multiplication
Choice is: e
Choice of operation is wrong....
```

5.16 Random Access

Random accessing of the elements in an array is possible. This simple operation is used to find the information stored at any position in the array by using the index. For example, let int **List [10]** be an array. Here, the list contains 10 elements, if one wants to see an element at the 9th position in the array, he/she will simply write the following code:

```
printf("\n %d", List [8]);
```

It will show the 9th element of the array List. For the better details, readers are advised to go through the Example 5.11.

Example 5.11: Write C code which demonstrates the random operation on an array.

Answer: For example, consider the following program segment that implements the above discussion:

```
/** array6.c **/
# include<stdio.h>
void main()
{
   int choice ;
   char List [ ] = {"ANAMICA"};

   printf("\n Enter Choice of character(0-6): ") ;
   scanf("%d", &choice) ;
   printf("\n Position : %d Value : %c", choice, List[choice]);
}
```

OUTPUT
Enter Choice of character(0-6): 2
Position: 2 Value: A

This program will randomly display information existing in the **List**. Here the **List** contains 7 characters. If one gives **choice = 6**, it will display **position**: 6 **Value**: A. Similarly, any choice one may enter as an input.

5.17 Multidimensional Arrays and Functions

The most straightforward way of passing a multidimensional array to a function is to declare it in exactly the same way in the function as it was declared in the caller. If we want to call

```
func(a2);
```

then we might declare

```
func(int a[5][7])
{
    ...
}
```

and it is clear that the array type which the caller passes is the same as the type which the function func accepts. If we remember what we learned about simple arrays and functions, however, two questions arise. First, in our earlier function definitions, we were able to leave out the (single) array dimension, with the understanding that since the array was really defined in the caller, we did not have to say (or know) how big it is. The situation is the same for multidimensional arrays, although it may not seem so at first. The hypothetical function func above accepts a parameter a, where a is an array of 5 things, where each of the 5 things is itself an array. By the same argument that applies in the single-dimension case, the function does not have to know how big the array a is, overall. However, it certainly does need to know what a is an array *of*. It is not enough to know that a is an array of "other arrays"; the function must know that a is an array of *arrays of 7* int*s*. The upshot is that although it does not need to know how many "rows" the array has, it *does* need to know the number of columns, i.e., if we want to leave out any dimensions, we can only leave out the first one:

```
func(int a[][7])
{
...
}
```

The second dimension is still required. (For a three- or more dimensional array, all but the first dimension is required; again, only the first dimension may be omitted.)

The second question we might ask concerns the equivalence between pointers and arrays. We know that when we pass an array to a function, what really gets passed is a pointer to the array's first element. We know that when we declare a function that seems to accept an array as a parameter, the compiler quietly compiles the function as if that parameter were a pointer, since a pointer is what it will actually receive. What about multidimensional arrays? What kind of pointer is passed down to the function?

The answer is, a pointer to the array's first element. And, since the first element of a multidimensional array is another array, what gets passed to the function is a *pointer to an array*. If we want to declare the function func in a way that explicitly shows the type which it receives, the declaration would be

```
func(int (*a)[7])
{
    ...
}
```

The declaration int (*a)[7] says that a is a pointer to an array of 7 ints. Since declarations like this are hard to write and hard to understand, and since pointers to arrays are generally confusing, we recommend that when a programmer writes functions which accept multidimensional arrays, needs to declare the parameters using array notation, not pointer notation. What if we do not know what the dimensions of the array will be? What if we want to be able to call a function with arrays of different sizes and shapes? Can one say something like

```
func(int x, int y, int a[x][y])
{
    ...
}
```

where the array dimensions are specified by other parameters to the function? Unfortunately, in C, we cannot. Finally, we might explicitly note that if we pass a multidimensional array to a function:

```
int a2[5][7];
func(a2);
```

We cannot declare that function as accepting a pointer-to-pointer:

```
func(int **a)                    /* WRONG */
{
...
}
```

As we said above, the function ends up receiving a pointer to an array, not a pointer to a pointer. More details over pointer and function we take in the Chapter 18.

5.18 Multidimensional Arrays

One obvious question here, how many dimensions are supported by a C compiler in a definition. This question is accurately answered by the designer of a compiler. So, **C** supports many numbers of subscripted variables to manipulate an array and it is compiler dependent. A multi-dimensional array can be logically converted in one-dimensional arrays. The syntax for multidimensional array is given below:

```
Data type array name [size1][size2]...        [size n];
```

For example, consider the following three-dimensional array **number**. In this array any expression can be written with the help of three subscript variables:

```
int number[5][3][4];
```

The **number** is a three dimensional array declaration. The total number of elements stored in this array will be 5x3x4 = 60 and total memory space required = 60 x 2 = 120 bytes. The following example gives the demonstration of a three dimensional array. This shows representation how any element of array can be accessed by three subscripts. If we want to access the third element of the list, the declaration will be **number[0][0][2].** This array can be logically converted into one-dimensional array that has 60 elements of same data type as multi-dimensional array has. For example, consider the following declarations which have same effect.

```
int  num1[3][3][3]={{1, 2, 3}, {4, 5, 6},{7, 8, 9} };
   int num2[3][3]={1, 2, 3, 4, 5, 6, 7, 8, 9};
         char string[2][3][16] = {
              "TOM ALTER",
              "JERRY",
```

```
                    "TILLY",
                    "MONGIA",
                    "S TENDULKAR"
                        };
char str2[4][10]={  "TOM ALTER",  "JERRY",  "TILLY", "MONGIA",  "S
    TENDULKAR"};
```

The memory representation for three-dimensional array is similar to one-dimensional and two-dimensional arrays. Go through the Example 5.12 for the better illustration.

Example 5.12: Write C code for implementing three-dimensional arrays.

Answer: Following program segment illustrates the above discussion:

```
/* array25.c */
# include<stdio.h>
void main()
{
   char string[2][3][16] = {      "TOM ALTER",
                    "JERRY",
                    "TILLY",
                    "MONGIA",
                    "S TENDULKAR"};
   int i , k;
   printf("\n Subscript Variable Starting Address String");
   for ( k = 0 ; k < 2 ; k++ )
   for ( i = 0 ; i < 3 ; i++ )
   {
      printf("\n");
      printf("string[%d][%d][16]",k,i);
      printf("%18x",&string[k][i]);
      printf(" %12s",string[k][i]);
   }
   printf("\n Press a key");
   getchar() ;
}
```

OUTPUT

Subscript Variable	Starting Address	String
string[0][0][16]	ff96	TOM ALTER
string[0][1][16]	ffa6	JERRY
string[0][2][16]	ffb6	TILLY
string[1][0][16]	ffc6	MONGIA

string[1][1][16]	ffd6	S TENDULKAR
string[1][2][16]	ffe6	
Press a key		

From the output of the program segment array23.c and array25.c it is clear that output is same, means any dimension of arrays processed as single dimension.

Let us Revise

1. Many tasks require storing and processing a list of data items.
2. In computer programming world, an **array** is a linear data structure also known as a **vector** or **list** (for one-dimensional arrays) or a **matrix** (for two-dimensional arrays)
3. Two-dimensional, three-dimensional, four-dimensional, etc are known as multi-dimensional array.
4. Individual objects in an array, called *elements*, are accessed by their position in the array.
5. The initializer for an array is a comma-separated list of constant expressions enclosed in braces ({ }).
6. Initializing a string constant places the null character (\0) at the end of the string if there is room or if the array dimensions are not specified.
7. The search is said to be successful, if Info arrears in the array elese it known as unsuccessful search.
8. Insertion is the process of addng a new element to the array.
9. Multi-dimensioned arrays have two or more index values which specify the element in the array.
10. To initialize two-dimensional array, data are provided in set form.
11. Matrix is a two dimensional array represented as $[A_{ij}]$ where i is the number of row and j is the number of columns.
12. A transpose of a matrix is obtained by interchanging the rows with corresponding columns of a given matrix.
13. In programming language C, a string is not a formal data type but it is an array of type char.
14. The strcpy() function is used to copy the contents of one string to another, i.e., source string is copied to destination string.
15. The strcmp() function is used to compare two strings, character by character.
16. Random accessing of the elements in an array is possible

Multiple Choice Questions

1. An array is a
   (a) Collection of homogeneous elements (b) Collection of data types
   (c) Data type (d) None
2. What is the output of following program?

```
#include<stdio.h>
void main()
{
    int array[size], size=5;
    array[0]=1;
    array[1]=2;
    array[2]=3;
    array[3]=4;
```

```
        array[4]=5;
        for(size=0; size<5; size++)
printf("%d", array[size]);
        getch();
    }
```

(a) 1 2 3 4 5 (b) Error

(c) 23451 (d) None

3. What is the output of following program?

```
    #include<stdio.h>
    #define size 5
    void main()
    {
        int array[size], i=5;
        array[0]=1;
        array[1]=2;
        array[2]=3;
        array[3]=4;
        array[4]=5;
        for(size=0; size<5; size++)
printf("%d", array[size]);
        getch();
    }
```

(a) 1 2 3 4 5 (b) Error

(c) 23451 (d) None

4. What is the output of following program?

```
    #include<stdio.h>
    #define size 5;
    void main()
    {
        int array[size], i=5;
        array[0]=1;
        array[1]=2;
        array[2]=3;
        array[3]=4;
        array[4]=5;
        for(size=0; size<5; size++)
printf("%d", array[size]);
        getch();
    }
```

(a) 1 2 3 4 5 (b) Error

(c) 23451 (d) None

5. Consider the following program.

```
#include<stdio.h>
void main()
{
    char name[30];
    printf("\n Enter your name:");
    scanf("%s", name);
    printf("\n %s", name);
    getch();
}
```

Suppose you have entered your name as given below:

Enter your name: Prem Nath

What is the output of above program?

(a) Prem Nath (b) PremNath

(c) Prem (d) Nath

(Hint: Space from keyboard taken as termination of a string)

6. Consider the following program. What is the output?

```
#include<stdio.h>
void main()
{
    char name[]="Prem Nath";
    printf("\n %s", name);
    getch();
}
```

(a) Prem Nath (b) Prem

(c) Nath (d) Error

7. Consider the following program. What is the output?

```
#include<stdio.h>
void main()
{
    char name[]="Prem Nath";
    name[4]='\0';
printf("\n %s", name);
    getch();
}
```

(a) Prem Nath (b) Prem

(c) Nath (d) Error

8. Consider the following program. What is the output?

```
#include<stdio.h>
void main()
{
    char name[]="Prem Nath";
    printf("\n %s", name[5]);
```

```
        getch();
    }
```

(a) Prem Nath (b) Prem

(c) N (d) Error

9. Consider the following program. What is the output?

```
    #include<stdio.h>
    void main()
    {
        char name[10]="Prem";
        name[4]='N';
        name[5]='a';
        name[6]='t';
        name[7]='h'
        name[8]='\0'
printf("\n %s", name);
        getch();
    }
```

(a) Prem Nath (b) PremNath

(c) Prem (d) Error

10. What is the output of following program?

```
    #include<stdio.h>
    void main()
    {
        int number[5];
        number[-3]=3;
        printf("%d", number[-3]);
        getch();
    }
```

(a) Error (b) Garbage

(c) 3 (d) None

11. What is output of following program?

```
 #include<stdio.h>
    void main()
    {
        int number[5];
        number[-3]=3;
        printf("%d", number[3]++);
        getch();
    }
```

(a) Error (b) 4

(c) 3 (d) Garbage

12. What is output of following program?

```
#include<stdio.h>
   void main()
   {
      int number[5]={1, 2, 3, 4, 5};
      printf("%d", number[5]);
      getch();
   }
```

(a) Error (b) 4

(c) 5 (d) Garbage

13. What is output of following program?

```
#include<stdio.h>
   void main()
   {
      int number[5]={1, 2, 3, 4, 5};
      printf("%d", 4[number]);
      getch();
   }
```

(a) Error (b) 4

(c) 5 (d) Garbage

14. What is output of following program?

```
#include<stdio.h>
   void main()
   {
      int number[5]={a, b, c, d, e};
      printf("%d", 0[number]);
      getch();
   }
```

(a) Error (b) 4

(c) 5 (d) Garbage

15. What is output of following program?

```
#include<stdio.h>
   void main()
   {
      int number[5]={'a', 'b', 'c', 'd', 'e'};
      printf("%d", 0[number]);
      getch();
   }
```

(a) Error (b) 4

(c) 5 (d) 97

16. What is output of following program?

```
#include<stdio.h>
   void main()
```

```
{
    int number[5]={'a', 'b', 'c', 'd', 'e'};
    printf("%c", 0[number]);
    getch();
}
```

(a) Error (b) Garbage

(c) a (d) 97

17. What is output of following program?

```
#include<stdio.h>
void main()
{
    char number[]={'a', 'b', 'c', 'd', 'e'};
    printf("%s", number);
    getch();
}
```

(a) Error (b) Garbage

(c) abcde (d) 97

18. What is output of following program?

```
#include<stdio.h>
void main()
{
    char number[]={'a', 'b', 'c', 'd', 'e', '\0'};
    printf("%s", number);
    getch();
}
```

(a) Error (b) Garbage

(c) abcde (d) 97

19. What is output of following program?

```
#include<stdio.h>
void main()
{
    char number[]={'1', '+', '3', '=', '4'};
    number[5]='\0';
    printf("%s", number);
    getch();
}
```

(a) Error (b) 1+3=4

(c) 134 (d) None

20. What is output of following program?

```
#include<stdio.h>
void main()
{
```

```
    int number[5], i;
    number[0]=printf("");
    number[1]=printf("A");
    number[2]=printf("AB");
    number[3]=printf("ABC");
    number[4]=printf("ABCD");
    for(i=0; i<5; i++)
printf("%d", number[i]);
    getch();
  }
```

(a) Error (b) Garbage

(c) AABABCABCD01234 (d) None

21. What is output of following program?

```
#include<stdio.h>
  void main()
  {
    int number[]={'a', 1, 2, 3, 4}, i;
    number[1]+=number[0];
    number[2]+=number[0];
    number[3]+=number[0];
    number[4]+=number[0];
    for(i=0, i<5; i++)
printf("%d", number[i]);
    getch();
  }
```

(a) Error (b) 979899101102

(c) abcde (d) None

22. What is output of following program?

```
#include<stdio.h>
  void main()
  {
    int number[]={'a', 1, 2, 3, 4}, i;
    number[1]+=number[0];
    number[2]+=number[0];
    number[3]+=number[0];
    number[4]+=number[0];
    for(i=0, i<5; i++)
printf("%c", number[i]);
    getch();
  }
```

(a) Error (b) 979899101102

(c) abcde (d) None

True/False Questions

1. If A[10] is an array, then A+2 points to the third element of the array.
2. "A" is a string but 'A' is a character.
3. Is this a correct array definition? int num(25);
4. A string is an array of characters
5. If you want to initialize an array it must be a static array or an external array.
6. Automatic arrys cannot be initialized.
7. An array is a collection of variable of different data types scattered throughout memory.
8. The array index must be an integer data type.
9. An array may contain elements of different types.
10. The name of array represents addresses.

Match Columns

Match the matter in Column A with the matter in Column B.

Column A	Column B
A. Sorting	1. removing an item from the list
B. Transpose	2. combining two lists
C. Deletion	3. row-major
D. Array	4. joins two strings
E. Merging	5. interchanging rows with columns
F. strcat()	6. arranging in some order

Fill in the Blanks with Appropriate Words

a.	arrays	b.	string.h	c.	division	d.	ctype.h
e.	commas	f.	brackets				

1. The ____________ indicates to the compiler that we are dealing with an array.
2. The values used to initialize an array are separated by __________ and surrounded by braces.
3. _________ can be stored in the memory column major order or in row major order.
4. Right shifting an unsigned integer is equivalent to its ________ by 2.
5. String function strcpy() belongs to ________ headed file.
6. _________ header file declares various character manipulation routines.

Descriptive Type Questions

1. Can we change the value of the control variable in for statements? If yes, explain its conse-quences.
2. What is a null statement? Explain a typical use of it.
3. Use of go to should be avoided. Explain a typical example where we find the application of goto becomes necessary.
4. How would you decide the use of one of the three loops in C for a given problem?
5. How can we use for loops when the number of iterations are not known?

6. How would we search a word in a given text? Write a program to search a word of five characters in a text of 100 characters.
7. Write a program to delete an element at position p in a given array.
8. Write a program to fill in a two-dimensional array of Boolean values by setting mat[i][j] to 1 if the greatest common divisor of i and j is 1 and to 0 otherwise.
9. Why do array subscripts start at 0 instead of 1 in C language?
10. Is it possible to use a character as an array subscript? Explain your answer.
11. First load an array numbers with 10 integers between 1 and 100 and then write the code to perform a frequency distribution on the numbers in the array numbers. The output should list the numbers in ascending order and their corresponding frequency as follows:

Numbers	2	13	17	33	56	62	66	70	80	90
Frequency	2	1	4	5	1	3	1	4	2	1

12. Write programs, which will generate the following output:

(a)	9	8	7	6	5	4	3	2	1
	9	8	7	6	5	4	3	2	
	9	8	7	6	5	4	3		
	9	8	7	6	5	4			
	9	8	7	6	5				
	9	8	7	6					
	9	8	7						
	9	8							
	9								
(b)	1	2	3	4	5	4	3	2	1
	1	2	3	4		4	3	2	1
	1	2	3				3	2	1
	1	2						2	1
	1	1							
(c)	1	2	3	4	5				
	1	2	3	4					
	1	2	3						
	1	2							
	1								
(d)	1	2	3	4	5	6	7	8	9
	1	2	3	4	5	6	7	8	
	1	2	3	4	5	6	7		
	1	2	3	4	5	6			
	1	2	3	4	5				
	1	2	3	4					
	1	2	3						
	1	2							

Answers to Objective Type Questions

Multiple Choice Questions

1. a	2. b	3. c	4. a
5. c	6. b	7. a	8. c
9. b	10. a	11. a	12. c
13. b	14. c	15. a	16. b
17. a	18. c	19. a	20. b
21. c	22. b		

True False Questions

1. F	2. T	3. F	4. T
5. F	6. T	7. F	8. T
9. F	10. T		

Matching Columns

A. 6	B. 5	C. 1	D. 3
E. 2	F. 4		

Fill in the Blanks

1. f	2. e	3. a	4. c
5. b	6. d		

Functions 6

6.1 Top-down Approach of Problem Solving

Top down design is a strategy in which the solution to a huge computation problem is developed from a vague outline to a precisely defind algorithm. This way of design provides a method to handle the complexity of the problem by breading them into easy and understandable sub-modules. The process of repeatedly breaking a task down into sub-tasks should continue until we entially end up with sub-tasks that can be easily implemented. The following figure describes how top-down design is implemented.

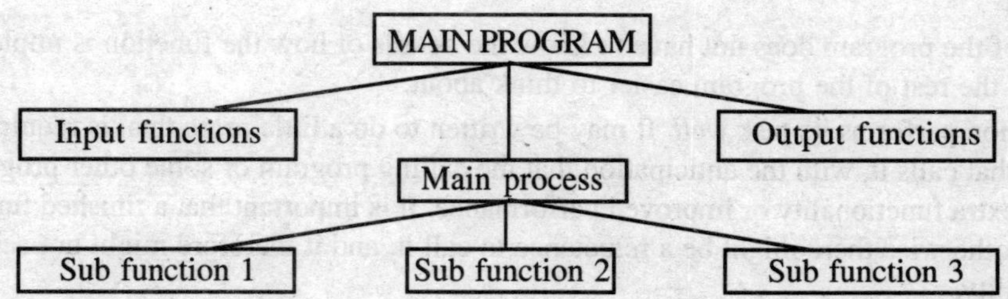

Fig. 6.1 Top down design deelopment

Advantages of integrated top-down developement include:

- The ability to experiment with successive prototypes as the system evolves
- The gradual integration of sub-systems
- Easy handling of the job at hand

The main disadvantage of integrated top-down development is the necessity for back tracking and the potential for considerable re-writing of code. Also, the evolving system may bcome too large for new modeules being integrated into the system.

6.1.1 Step-wise Refnement

Step-wise refinement is a top-down technique for decomposing a system from high-level specifications into more elementary elements. Step-wise refinement is also known as successive refinement. The problem is first decomposed into few major processing steps that will solve the problem abstractly. The process is then repeated for each part of the system until is decomposed to sufficient detail so that implementation in a programming language is straightforward.

The major benefits of step-wise refinement as a design technique are:

- Top-down decomposition
- Incremental addition of details
- Postponment of decisions

- Continual verificaion of consistency

6.2 Modular Programming and Functions

It is a method in which long programs are divided into smaller programs or modules that can be designed, coded and debugging separately with a minimum amount of interaction.

6.2.1 Functions

A function is a "black box" that we have locked part of our program into. It is a subprogram which performs a well-defined task. It may be developed separately and tested. We may then name each such subprogram and specify the method of sending data to each of them and getting processed results from them. Once the subprograms are tested, they are linked together to do a specified task. The idea behind a function is that it *compartmentalizes* part of the program and in particular the code within the function has some useful properties:

1. It performs some well-defined task, which will be useful to other parts of the program.
2. It might be useful to other programs as well, i.e., we might be able to reuse it (and without having to rewrite it).
3. The rest of the program does not have to know the details of how the function is implemented. This can make the rest of the program easier to think about.
4. The function performs its task *well*. It may be written to do a little more than is required by the first program that calls it, with the anticipation that the calling program or some other program may later need the extra functionality or improved performance. It is important that a finished function does its job well, otherwise there might be a reluctance to call it, and it therefore might not achieve the goal of reusability.
5. By placing the code to perform the useful task into a function, and simply calling the function in the other parts of the program where the task must be performed, the rest of the program becomes clearer: rather than having some large, complicated, difficult-to-understand piece of code repeated wherever the task is being performed, we have a single simple function call, and the name of the function reminds us which task is being performed.
6. Since the rest of the program does not have to know the details of how the function is implemented, the rest of the program does not care if the function is re-implemented later, in some different way as long as it continues to perform its same task, of course. This means that one part of the program can be rewritten, to improve performance or add a new feature without having to rewrite the rest of the program.
7. It is a good idea to break up a big problem into a number of small sub-programs. Divide and conquer is the name given to a method for breaking up a complicated problem into smaller parts and solving each separately and is a well known problem solving method.
8. A program written as sequence of functions with each function carrying out a specified task is easy to understand.
9. It is easy to test small compact functions.
10. Commonly used functions may be generalized, tested and added in the library for future use.
11. Functions developed by others may be used. For example, a larger number of efficient, well-tested programs for common problems like matrix manipulation; statistical computation, sorting and searching, etc are normally available.

The functions are main building blocks of **C** Language. Functions are probably the most important weapon in our battle against software complexity. The syntax for declaring a user defined function is

Data type name of function (Datatype1 parameter1, Datatype2 parameter2,…, Datatypen parameter1n)

```
{
    Data type specifies list of parameters;
    Statement 1;
    Statement 2;
                    ...
                    ...
                    ...
    Statement n;
}
```

Function has a *name* that is used to call (invoke) it and a list of zero or more *arguments* or *parameters* that we hand to it for it to act on or to direct its work; it has a *body* containing the actual instructions (statements) for carrying out the task the function is supposed to perform; and it may give us back a *return value*, of a particular type. For example, consider the following code segment which defines a very simple function multibytwo() and accepts one argument, multiplies it by 2, and returns the computed value.

```
int multbytwo(int x)
{
    int retval;
    retval = x * 2;
    return retval;
}
```

On the first line we see the return type of the function (int), the name of the function (multbytwo), and a list of the function's arguments, enclosed in parentheses. Each argument has both a name and a type; multbytwo() accepts one argument, of type int, named x. The name x is arbitrary, and is used only within the definition of multbytwo(). The caller of this function only needs to know that a single argument of type int is expected; the caller does not need to know what name the function will use internally to refer to that argument. In particular, the caller has to pass the value for variable named x.

Next we see, surrounded by the familiar braces, the body of the function itself. This function consists of one declaration of a local variable retval and two statements. The first statement is a conventional expression statement, which computes and assigns a value to retval, and the second statement is a return statement, which causes the function to return to its caller, and also specifies the value which the function returns to its caller. The return statement can return the value of any expression, so we do not really need the local retval variable; the function could be collapsed to

```
int multbytwo(int x)
{
    return x * 2;
}
```

Go through Example 6.1 which demonstrates above discussion.

Example 6.1: How do we call a function?

Answer: See the following program segment which is calling to multbytwo() function defined above.

```
#include <stdio.h>
extern int multbytwo(int);
```

```
int main()
{
    int i, j;
    i = 3;
    j = multbytwo(i);
    printf("%d\n", j);
    return 0;
}
```

In the above program segment we have defined an *external function prototype declaration*. It is an external declaration, in that it declares something which is defined somewhere else. We have already seen the defining instance of the function multbytwo, but maybe the compiler has not seen it yet. The function prototype declaration contains the three pieces of information about the function that a caller needs to know: the **function's name**, **return type**, and **argument type**(s). Since we do not care what name the multbytwo function will use to refer to its first argument, we do not need to mention it. On the other hand, if a function takes several arguments, giving them names in the prototype may make it easier to remember which are so names may optionally be used in function prototype declarations. Finally, to remind us that this is an external declaration and not a defining instance, the prototype is preceded by the keyword extern.

The presence of the function prototype declaration lets the compiler know that we intend to call this function, multbytwo. The information in the prototype lets the compiler generate the correct code for calling the function, and also enables the compiler to check up a code segment. Down in the body of main, the action of the function call should be obvious: the line

```
j = multbytwo(i);
```

calls multbytwo, passing it the value of i as its argument. When multbytwo returns, the return value is assigned to the variable j. The value of main's local variable i will become the value of multbytwo's parameter x; this is absolutely not a problem, and is a normal sort of affair. The variable i is not really needed, since we could just as well call

```
j = multbytwo(3);
```

and the variable j is not really needed, either, since we could just as well call

```
printf("%d\n", multbytwo(3));
```

The call to multbytwo is a subexpression which serves as the second argument to printf. The value returned by multbytwo is passed immediately to printf. In general, we see the flexibility and generality of expressions in C. An argument passed to a function may be an arbitrarily complex subexpression, and a function call is itself an expression which may be embedded as a subexpression within arbitrarily complicated surrounding expressions.

We should say a little more about the mechanism by which an argument is passed down from a caller into a function. Formally, C is *calling by value*, which means that a function receives *copies* of the values of its arguments. We can illustrate this with an example. Suppose, in implementation of multbytwo, we had gotten rid of the unnecessary retval variable like this:

```
int multbytwo(int x)
{
    x = x * 2;
    return x;
}
```

We might wonder, if we wrote it this way, what would happen to the value of the variable i when we called

```
j = multbytwo(i);
```

When implementation of multbytwo changes the value of x, does that change the value of i up in the caller? The answer is no. x receives a copy of i's value, so when we change x we do not change i. For example, consider the following code segment which is a function that raises a double to the power of an unsigned, and returns the result.

```
double power(double val, unsigned pow)
{       double ret_val = 1.0;
        unsigned i;

        for(i = 0; i < pow; i++)
                ret_val *= val;

        return(ret_val);
}
```

This function power() is multiplying the **val** by itself **pow** times. A for loop is used to control the number of multiplications, and variable ret_val stores the value to be returned. Careful programming has ensured that the boundary condition is correct too, i.e., let us examine the details of this function.

```
double power(double val, unsigned pow)
```

This line begins the function definition. It tells us the type of the return value, the name of the function, and a list of arguments used by the function. The arguments and their types are enclosed in parenthesis, each pair separated by commas. The body of the function is bounded by a set of curly brackets. Any variables declared here will be treated as local unless specifically declared as static or extern types.

```
return(ret_val);
```

When execution of a function reaches to a return statement, control of the function returns to the calling function. The bracketed value is the value which is returned from the function. If the final closing curly bracket is reached before any return value, then the function will return automatically, any return value will then be meaningless. The example function can be called by a line in another function which looks like this

```
result = power(val, pow);
```

This calls the function power assigning the return value to variable result. Here is an example of a function which does not return a value.

```
void error_line(int line)
{
      fprintf(stderr, "Error in input data: line %d\n", line);
}
```

The definition uses type void which is optional. It shows that no return value is used. Otherwise the function is much the same as the previous example, except that there is no return statement. Some void type functions might use return, but only to force an early exit from the function, and not to return any value. This is rather like using break to jump out of a loop.

When the argument which is being passed to a function is not a single variable, but is rather an array, the function does *not* receive a copy of the array, and it therefore *can* modify the array in the caller. The reason is that it might be too expensive to copy the entire array, and furthermore, it can be useful for the function to write into the caller's array, as a way of handing back more data than would fit in the function's single return value.

6.3 Standard Library of C Functions

Every compiler of C comes with its own set of library functions. These function perform file access, mathematical computations, graphics, memory managment, and data conversion, etc. Let us read more about them.

6.3.1 Basic I/O Functions

C has no provisions for reading and writing the input and output. In fact there is no command for writing to the floppy or reading from it. On the other hand it has no provision for sending the data to the monitor for displaying the results. Only commands available with C are print() and scan().

Each Operating System has it's own facility for inputting and outputting data from and to the files and devices. It's simple matter for a system programmer to write a few small programs that would link the C compiler for particular Operating system's I/O facilities. The developers of C Compilers do just that. They write several standard I/O functions and put them in libraries.

Though these functions are not part of C's formal definition, they have becme a standard feature of C language and hae been initiated more or less faithfully by every designer of a DOS based or a UNIX based C Compilers. Whatever version of C you are using it's almost certain that you have access to such a library of I/O functions.

In fact, the way DOS displays an output on screen is different than the way UNIX does it. Fortunately, the printf( ) function that we use on a DOS based C compiler works even with a UNIX based C compiler. This is because, the standard library function printf( ) for DOS based C compiler has been written keeping in mind the way DOS output characters to screen.

Similarly, the printf( ) function for a UNIX based compiler has been written keeping in mind the way UNIX outputs characters to screen. We, as users do not have to bother about which printf( ) has been written in what manner. We should just use printf( ) and it would take care of the rest of the details. Same is true about all other standard library functions available for I/O.

The various library functions available for input output in C can be classified into 3 broad categories:

6.3.1.1 Console I/O functions

These functions are there to receive input from keyboard and to write output to VDU.

6.3.1.2 Disk I/O functions

These functions are there to perform I/O operations on a floppy disk or hard disk.

6.3.1.3 Port I/O functions

These functions are there to perform I/O operation on various ports of the computer.

Let us now take a close look at each of these.

6.3.1.4 Console I/O functions

Console I/O functions can be further classified into two categories:

formatted and

unformatted console I/O functions.

The main difference between them is that the formatted functions allow the input read from the keyboard or the output displayed on the VDU to be formatted as per our requirements. For example, if values of average marks and percentage marks are to be displayed on the screen, then the details like where this output would appear on the screen, how many spaces would be present between the two values, the number of places after the decimal points, etc., can be controlled using formatted functions.

6.3.1.5 Formatted Functions

Type	*Input*	*Output*
char	scanf()	printf()

int	scanf()	printf()
float	scanf()	printf()
string	scanf()	printf()

6.3.1.6 UnFormatted functions

Type	*Input*	*Output*
char	getch()	putch()
	getche()	putchar()
	getchar()	
int	—	—
float	—	—
string	gets()	puts()

Now let us discuss these console I/O functions in detail.

6.3.1.7 Formatted Console I/O Functions

The functions printf( ) and scanf( ) fall under the category for formatted console I/O functions. These functions allow us to supply the input in a fixed format and let us obtain the output in the specified form. Let us discuss these functions one by one. But, first of all let us understand printf( ) and its use in C. In its general form this command looks like this….

```
printf ("format string", list of variables);
```

The format string can contain:

- characters that are simply printed as t hey are
- conversion specifications that begin with a % sing
- escape sequences that begin with a \ sing

For example, look at the following program:

```
main()
{
    int avg = 643;
    float per = 39.6;
    printf ("Average=%d\nPercentage=%f", avg, per);
}
```

The output of the program would be…..

```
Average = 643
Percentage = 39.600000
```

How does printf() functions interpret the contents of the format string. For this it examines the format string form left to right. So long as it doesn't come across either a % or a \, it continues to dump the characters that it encounters, on to the screen.

In this example Average = is dumped on the screen. The moment it comes across a conversion specification in the format string, it picks up the first variable in the list of variables and prints its value in the specified format. In this example, the moment %d is met the variable avg is picked up and its value is printed.

Similarly, the moment an escape sequence is met it takes the appropriate action. Here, the moment \n is met it places the cursor at the beginning of the next line. This process continues till the end of format string is reached.

6.3.1.8 Conversion Specifications

The %d %f used in the printf() are called conversion characters. They tell /printf() to print the value of avg as a decimal integer and the value of per as a float. Following is the list of conversion characters that can be used used with the printf() functions.

Data type		*Conversion character*
Integer	short signed	%d or %i
	short unsigned	%u
	long signed	%ld
	long unsigned	%lu
	unsigned hexadecimal	%x
	unsigned octal	%o
Real	float	%f
	double	%lf
character	signed character	%c
	unsigned character	%c
string		%s

We can provide following optional specifiers in the conversion specifications.

Specifier	*Description*
dd	digits specifying field width
.	decimal point separating field width from precision (precision stands for the number of places after the decimal point)
dd	digits specifying precision
–	minus sign for left justifying the output in the specified field width

The field width specifier tells printf() how many columns on screen should be used while printing a value. The following example would make it more clear.

```
main()
{
    int weight = 36;

    printf ("\nweight is %d kg", weight);
    printf ("\nweight is %2d kg", weight);
    printf ("\nweight is %4d kg", weight);
    printf ("\nweight is %6d kg", weight);
    printf ("\nweight is %-6d kg", weight);
}
```

The output of the program would look like this.......

```
columns  0123456789012345678901234567890
         weight    is 36 kg
```

```
weght      is 36 kg
weight     is     36 kg
weight     is             36 kg
weight     is 36          kg
```

6.3.2 Escape Sequences

In the last example, we had seen that \n creates a new line, when inserted in a printf()'s format string. It is called the newline character. The newline character is an 'escape sequence', so called because the backslash symbol (\) is considered an 'escape' character characters. It causes an escape from the normal interpretation of a string, so that the next character is recognised as one having a special meaning.

This is demonstrated in the following example.

```
main()
{
    printf ("You\are\definitely\going\to\like\it");
}
```

the output would look like.

```
01234567890123456789012345678901234567890
You  are    definitely      going
to          like  it
```

The cursor jumps over eight columns when it encounters the "\t" character. This is another useful technique for lining up columns of output. Most compilers allow the user to change the number of print zones available on the screen, thereby changing the tab width.

The following escape characters are in use.

6.3.2.1 Escape Characters

Esc. Seq.	*Purpose*
\n	New line
\b	Backspace
\f	Form feed
\'	Single quote
\\	Backslash
\t	Tab
\r	Carriage return
\a	Alert
\"	Double quote

You can use these escape characters whenever needed.

6.3.3 Scanf()

Let us now leave print() and see how scanf() is used. It allows us to enter data from keyboard that will be formatted in a certain way.

The general form of scanf() statement is as follows:

```
scanf ("format string", list of addresses of variables);
```

For example:

```
scanf ("%d %f %c", &c, &a, &ch);
```

Note that we are sending addresses of variables (addresses are obtained by using '&' the 'address of' operator) to scanf() function. This is necessary because the values received form keyboard must be dropped into variables corresponding to these addresses. The values that are supplied through the keyboard must be separated by either blank(s), tab(s) or newsline(s). Do not include these escape sequences in the format string.

All the format specifications that we learnt in printf() function apply for scanf() function as well.

6.3.4 sprintf() function and sscanf() Function

The sprintf() function works similar to the printf() function except for one small difference. Instead of sending the output to the screen as printf() does, this function writes the output to an array of characters.

The following program illustrates this.

```
main()
(
    int i = 10;
    char ch = `A'
    float a = 3.14
    char str[20]
        printf("\n%d %c %f", i, ch, a);
        sprintf(str, "%d %c %f", i, ch, a);
        printf("\n%s", str);
}
```

Here the values of I, cha and a and printed on the screen. Also sprintf() stores these values in the character array str. Since the string str is present in memory what is written into str using sprintf() doesn't get displayed on the screen. After str has been built, its contents can be displayed on the screen. The second printf() statement does this.

Then there is a function called sscanf(), which is counterpart of sprinttf(). It allows us to read characters from a string and to convert and store them in C variables according to specified formats. The sscanf() function comes in handy for in-memory conversion of characters to values.

You may find it convenient to read in strings from a file and then extract values from a string by using sscanf(). The usage of sscanf() is same as scanf(), except that the first argument is the string from which reading is to take place.

6.3.5 Unformatted Console I/O Functions

In this category you will find the various standard library functions. A complete list of these functions are given in a later chapter. So far for input we have consistently used the scanf() function. However, for some situations the scanf() function has a drawback. You have to hit the Enter key before the function can accept what you have typed.

On the other hand, we often want a function that will read a single character the instant it is typed without waiting for the Enter key to be hit. getch() and gerche() are two such functions which serve this purpose. These functions return the character that has been most recently typed. The 'e' in getche() function means it displays the character that you typed on the screen.

As against this getch() just returns the character that you typed without displaying it on the screen. getchar() works similarly and displays the character that you typed on the screen, but unfortunately requires Enter key to be typed following the character that you typed. The difference between getchar() and fgetchar () is that the former is a macro whereas the letter is a function.

Here is a sample program which illustrates the use of these functions.

```
main()
{
   char ch;

   print  ("\nPress any key to continue");
   getch() ; /* will not echo the character */

   printf  ("\nType any character") ;
   ch = getche() ; /* will echo the character typed */

   printf  ("\nType any character") ;
   gechar() ; /* will echo character, must be followed by enter key
*/
   printf  ("\nContinue Y/N") ;
   fgetchar() ; /* will echo character, must be followed by enter key
*/
}
```

And here is a sample run of this program....

```
   Press any key to continue

   Type any character B

   Type any character W

   Continue Y/N Y
```

putch() and putchar() on the other hand print a character on the screen. Thought the working of putch(), putchar() and fputchar() is concerned, it is exactly the same.

The following program illustrates this.

```
main()
{
   char ch = 'R';

   putch (ch);
   putchar (ch);
   fputchar (ch);
   putch ('B');
```

```
    putchar ('B');
    fputchar ('B');
}
```

This will give the output as:

```
RRRBBB
```

All of these putch( ), putchar( ) and fputchar( ) output only one character at a time.

6.3.6 gets( ) and puts( )

In C gets() is used to receive a string of data from the keyboard. Well scanf() function can be used for the same, but it has its own limitations, as shown in the following program.

```
main()
{
    char name[40] ;

    printf ("\nEnter name") ;
    scanf ("%s, name) ;
    printf ("%s, name) ;
}
```

And here is the output

```
Enter name Amitabh Bachchan

Amitabh
```

It is now be understood that Bachchan was never stored in array name[], because after Amitabh you had given a space. The momemnt this space is given C assumes that the word has been completed. So you get only half the result of what was expected.

Now you understand why scanf() is not used to get the data. The solution to this problem is to use gets( ) function. It is terminated when a Enter key is hit. Thus, spaces and tabs are perfectly acceptable as part of the input string.

Moreover, gets( ) gets a newline (\n) terminated string of characters from the keyboard and replaces the \n and a \0. The puts( ) function works exactly opposite to gets( ) function. It outputs a string to the screen. Let us understand this by means of a program.

```
main()
{
    char cricketer[40];
    puts ("Enter name") ;
    gets (cricketer) ; /*sends base address of array */
    puts ("Happy cricketing!") ;
    puts (cricketer) ;
}
```

Following is the sample output:

```
    Enter name
```

```
Sachin Tendulkar

Happy cricketing!

Sachin Tendulkar
```

Did you notice anything here. The puts() function has been used twice, once for the name and then for Happy cricketing!. This is so because puts() can output only one string at a time. If we attempt to print two strings using puts( ), only the first one gets printed. Similarly unlike scanf( ), gets( ) can be used to read only one string at a time.

6.3.7 Disk Functions

Disk operations are performed on entities called files. There are a large number of standard library functions available for performing Disk or file Input/Output. These functions can be broadly divided into two categories:

(a) High level file I/O functions (also called standard I/O or stream I/O functions)

(b) Low level file I/O functions (also called system I/O functions)

High level Disk I/O functions are more commonly used in C programs, since they are easier to use than low level disk I/O functions. There is one basic difference between high level and low level disk I/O functions. High level disk I/O functions do their own buffer management, whereas in low level disk I/O functions, buffer management has to be done explicitly by the programmer.

6.3.8 Opening A File

For all the file operations, like reading and writing, you have to open the file. Opening a file establishes a link between the program and the operating system, about, which file we are going to access and how. We provide the operating system with the name of the file and whether we plan to read or write to it.

The link between our program and the operating system is a structure called FILE which has been defined in the header file "stdio.h" (standing for standard input/output header file). Therefore, it is necessary to always include this file when we are doing high level disk I/O. When we request the operating system to open a file, what we get back (fi the request is indeed granted), is a pointer to the structure FILE. That is why, we make the following declaration before opening the file.

```
FILE *fp;
```

For each file which is opened there is a FILE structure, which contains information about the file being used, such as its current size, its location in memory, etc.

More importantly it contains a character pointer which points to the character that is about to get read.

To understand this, look at the followng statements,

```
FILE *fp ;

fp = fopen ("RB1.C", "r") ;
```

where,

fp — It is a pointer variable, which contains address of the structure FILE which has been defined in the header file "stdio,h".

fopen( ) — It will open a file "RB1.C" in 'read' mode, which tells the C compiler that we would be reading the contents of the file. Note that "r" is a string and not a character; hence the double quotes and not single quotes. In fact, fopen( ) performs 3 important taks when you open the file in "r" mode:

(a) Firstly it searches on the disk the file to be opened.

(b) If the file is present, it loads the file from the disk into memory. Of course if the file is very big, then it loads the file part by part.

If the file is absent, fopen( ) returns a NULL. NULL is a macro defined in "stdio.h" which indicates that you failed to open the file.

(c) It sets up a character pointer (which is part of the FILE structure) which points to the first character of the chunk of memory where the file has been loaded.

6.3.9 File Opening Modes

We had earlier used read ("r") mode. However, "r" is but one of the several modes in which we can open a file. Following is a list of all possible modes in which a file can be opened. The tasks performed by fopen() when a file is opened in each of these modes are also mentioned.

"r" Searches file. If the file exists, loads it into memory and sets up a pointer which points to the first character in it. If the file doesn't exist it returns NULL.

Operations possible – reading from the file.

"w" Searches file. If the file exists, its contents are overwritten. If the file doesn't exist, a new file is created. Returns NULL, if unable to open file.

Operations possible – writing to the file.

"a" Searches file. If the first exists, loads in to memory and sets up a pointer which points to the first character in it. If the file doesn't exist, a new file created. Returns NULL, if unable to open file.

Operation possible – appending new contents at the end of file.

"r+" Searches file. If it exists, loads it into memory and sets up a pointer which points to the first character in it. If file doesn't exist it returns NULL.

Operations possible – reading existing contents, writing new contents, modifying existing contents of the file.

"w+" Searches file. If the file exists, its contents are destroyed. If the file doesn't exist a new file is created. returns Null, if unable to open file.

Operations possible – writing new contents, reading from back and modifying existing contents of the file.

"a+" Searches file. If the file exists, loads it into memory and sets up a pointer which points to the first character in it. If the file doesn't exist, a new file is created. Returns NULL, if unable to open file.

Operations possible – reading existing contents, appending new contents to end of file. Cannot modify existing contents.

6.3.10 Reading from a File

When you open the file its contents are brought into memory (partly or wholly) and a pointer points to the very first character. To read the file's contents from memory there exists a function called fgetc( ). This has been used in our sample program through,

```
ch = fgetc ( fp ) ;
```

fgetc( ) reads the character from current pointer position, advances the pointer position so that it now points to the next character and returns the character that is read, which we collected in the variable ch.

Note that once the file has been opened, we no longer refer to the file by its name, but through the file pointer fp.

6.3.11 Closing The File

When we have finished reading from the file, we need to close it. This is done using the function flcose() through the statement,

```
fclose( fp ) ;
```

This deactivates the file an hence it can no longer be accessed using getc(). Once again we don't use the filename but the file pointer fp.

6.3.12 Writing to A File

For this we use the function called fputc. The fputc() function is similar to the putch() function, in the sense that both output characters. However, putch() function always writes to the VDU, whereas, fputc() writes to the file.

The writing process continues till all characters from the source file have been written to the target file, following which the while loop terminates.

6.3.12.1 fclose() function

When you send a character off to a file by using fputc(), the character is actually stored in a buffer – an area in memory, rather than being immediately written to the disk. When the buffer is full, its contents are written to the disk at once.

Or if the program knows that the last character to be written to the disk has been received in the buffer, but it is still not full, it forces the buffer to be written to the disk by 'closing' the file. Another purpose that fclose() servers is, it frees the link used by the particular file and the associated buffers, so that these are available for other files.

Other functions are:

6.3.13 Mathematical Functions

abs

```
int abs(int x);
```

Returns absolute value of a integer number x.

fabs

```
double fabs(double x);
```

Returns absolute value of a real number x.

labs

```
long labs(long x);
```

Returns absolute value of a long integer number x.

fmod

```
doble fmod(double x, double y);
```

Returns x module y, the remainder of x/y.

cos

```
double cos(double x);
```

Returns the cosine of x, where is angle x is in radians.

acos

```
double acos(double x);
```

Returns cosine inverse of x.

cosh

```
double cosh(double x);
```

Returns hyperbolic cosine of x.

sin

```
double sin(double x);
```

Returns the sine of x, where is angle of x is in radians.

asin

```
double asin(double x);
```

Returns sine inverse of x.

sinh

```
double sinh(double x);
```

Returns hyperbolic sine of x.

tan

```
double tan(double x);
```

Returns the tangent of x, where angle x is in radians.

atan

```
double atan(double x);
```

Returns tangent inverse of x.

tanh

```
double tanh(double x);
```

Returns hyperbolic tangent of x.

6.3.14 String Functions

strncat

```
void *strncat(char *dest, const char *src, size_t maxlen);
```

Appends at most maxlen characters of src to dest.

strncpy

```
void *strcpy(char *dest, const char *src, size_t maxlen);
```

Copies at most maxlen characters of src to dest.

strncmp

```
int strncmp(const char *dest, const char *src, size_t maxlen);
```

Compares at most first maxlen characters of src and dest.

stricmp

```
int stricmp(const char *dest, const char *src);
```

Compares two strings src and dest without regard to case.

strnicmp

```
int strnicmp(const char *dest, const char *src, size_t maxlen);
```

Compares at most first maxlen characters of src and dest without regard to case.

strlwr

```
char *strlwr(char *s);
```

Converts a string to lowercase.

strupr

```
char *strupr(char *s);
```

Converts a string to uppercase.

strset

```
char *strset(char *s, int c);
```

Sets all characters of s to c.

strnset

```
char *strnset(char *s, int c, size_t n);
```

Sets first n characters of s to c.

strstr

```
char *strstr(const char *s1, const char *s2);
```

Finds the occurrence substring s1 in s2.

strchr

```
char *strchr(const char *s, int c);
```

Returns a pointer to the first occurrence of c in s.

strrchr

```
char *strrchr(const char *s, int c);
```

Returns a pointer to the first occurrence of c in s.

6.3.15 Character Classification Macros

toupper(c)

Converts character c to uppercase, if it is in lowercase otherwise no effect.

tolower(c)

Converts character c to lowercase, if it is in lowercase otherwise no effect.

toascii(c)

Converts c greater than 127 to the range 0-127 by clearing all but lower 7 bits.

islower(c)

True if c is a lowercase letter.

isupper(c)

True if c is a uppercase letter.

ispunct(c)

Tue if c is a punctuation character.

isspace(c)

True if c a is a space, tab, carriage return, newline, vertical tab, or formfeed.

isxdigit(c)

True if c is a hexadecimal digit.

isalnum(c)

True if c is a letter or digit.

isalpha(c)

True if c is a letter.

isdigit(c)

True if c is a digit.

iscntrl(c)

True if c is a delete character or ordinary control character.

isprint(c)

True if c is a printable character.

isgraph(c)

Like isprint except that the space character is excluded.

6.3.16 File Handling Functions

rename

```
int rename(const char *oldname, const char *newname);
```

Renames a file. On sucessfully renaming a file, it returns 0. On error it returns –1.

unlink

```
int unlink(const char *filename);
```

Deletes a file. If the file has read only attribute, it fails. Returns 0 on success and –1 on failure.

6.3.17 Directory Control Functions

chdir

```
int chdir(const char *path);
```

Changes current directory. Returns 0 on success and –1 on failure.

mkdir

```
int mkdir(const char *path);
```

Changes new directory. Returns 0 on success and –1 on failure.

rmdir

```
int rmdir(const char *path);
```

Changes existing directory. Returns 0 on success and –1 on failure.

getcwd

```
char *getcwd(char *buf, int buflen);
```

Gets current working directory. It returns a pointer to buffer. On error it returns NULL.

getcurdir

```
int getcurdir(int drive, char *directory);
```

Gets current directory for specified drive. Drive 0 is default, 1 for A, 2 for B, and so on.

getdisk

```
int getdisk(void);
```

Returns current drive number.

fnsplit

```
int fnsplit(const char *path, const char *drive, char *dir, char
*name, char *exit);
```

Splits a path name into its component parts.

fnmerge

```
int fnmerge(const char *path, const char *drive, const char *dir,
const char *name, const char *exit);
```

Builds a path from its component parts.

disable

```
void disable(void);
```

Disables all hardware interrupts except NULL.

enable

```
void enable(void);
```

Enables hardware interrupts.

6.3.18 Macros

FP_OFF

```
off_add = FP_OFF(farptr);
```

Returns offset address of a far pointer.

FP_SEG

```
seg_add = FP_OFF(farptr);
```

Points segment address of a far pointer.

MK_FP

```
farptr = MK_FP(seg_add, off_add);
```

Returns a far pointer made from segment address and offset address.

6.3.19 Graphics Functions

initgraph

```
void far initgraph(int far *graphdriver, int far *graphmode, char far
*pathtodriver);
```

Initializes the graphics system.

closegraph

```
void far closegraph(void);
```

Shuts down the graphics system.

putpixel

```
void far putpixel(int x, int y, int color);
```

Plots pixel with specified color at point (x, y).

line

```
void far line(int x1, int y1, int x2, int y2);
```

Draws line from (x1, y1) to (x2, y2) using current color, line style and thickness.

moveto

```
void far moveto(int x, int y);
```

Changes current position to point (x, y).

lineto

```
void far lineto(int x, inty);
```

Draws line from current position to point (x, y).

circle

```
void far circle(int x, int y, int r);
```

Draws a circle of radius r centered at point (x, y).

cleardevice

```
void far cleardevice(void);
```

Clears the graphics screen.

bar

```
void far bar(int left, int top, int right, int bottom);
```

Draws a bar with left top corner at point (left, top) and right bottom corner at (right, bottom).

bar3d

```
void far bard(int left, int top, int right, int bottom, int depth,
  int topflag);
```

Draws a 3D bar with left top corner at point (left, top) and right bottom corner at (right, bottom) with depth depth.

arc

```
void far arc(int x, int y, int stangle, int endangle, int r);
```

Draws an arc of radius r centered at point (x, y) with starting angle stangle and ending angle endangle.

pieslice

```
void far pieslice(int x, int y, int stangle, int endangle, int r);
```

Draws and fills an pie slice of radius r centered at point (x, y) with starting angle stangle and ending angle endangle.

setviewport

```
unsigned far setviewport(int left, int top, int right, int bottom,
  int clip);
```

Sets the current viewport for graphics output. The default viewport is entire screen, set up during the installation of graphics system.

clearviewport

```
unsigned far clearviewport(void);
```

Clears the current viewport.

setcolor

```
void far setcolor(int color);
```

Sets the new drawing color.

setbkcolor

```
void far setbkcolor(int color);
```

sets the new background color.

imagesize

```
unsigned far imagesize(int left, int top, int right, int bottom);
```

Returns the number of bytes required in store a bit image. If the required size is ≥ 64KB, it returns 0xFFFF.

getimage

```
void far getimage(int left, int top, int right, int bottom, void
  far *bitmap);
```

Saves a bit image enclosed in region specified by point (left, top) as left-top corner point and (right, bottom) as right bottom corner point to a memory block pointed to by bitmap.

putimage

```
vod far putimage(int left, int top, void far *bitmap, int op);
```

Outputs a bit image created with getimage to the screen region with respect to left-top corner specified by point (left, top). The op value specifies how the image is to be combined with the existing screen contents.

floodfill

```
void far floodfill(int x, int y, int border);
```

Fills a bounded region, where point (x, y) is any point in that region, and border specifies the border color.

6.3.20 Time and Date Related Functions

clock

```
clock_t clock(void);
```

Returns the processor time used since the beginning of program execution measured in clock ticks.

ftime

```
void ftime(struct timeb *buf);
```

Gets and stores the current time in timeb structure.

difftime

```
double difftime(time_t time2, time_t time1);
```

Returns the difference between two times.

time

```
time_t time(time_t *timer);
```

Returns the current time elapsed since 00:00:00 GMT, January 1970, and stores the value in location pointed to by time.

settime

```
void settime(struct time_t *timep);
```

Sets MS-DOS system time specified in a structure pointed to by timep.

gettime

```
void gettime(struct time_t *timep);
```

Gets MS-DOS system time and stored in a structure pointed to by timep.

setdate

```
void setdate(struct time_t *timep);
```

Sets MS-DOS system date specified in a structure pointed to the datep.

getdate

```
void setdate(struct time_t *datep);
```

Gets MS-DOS system date and stores in a structure pointed to by datep.

6.3.21 Miscellaneous Functions

exit

```
void exit(int status);
```

Terminates program. Before terminating, buffered output is flushed, files are closed and _exit() function is called.

_exit

```
void _exit(int status);
```

Terminates program.

sleep

```
void sleep(unsigned seconds);
```

Suspend execution for given internal in seconds.

delay

```
void delay(unsigned millisecond);
```

Suspend execution for given internal in seconds.

sound

```
void sound(unsigned frequency);
```

Turns PC speaker on for given frequency in hzs.

nosound

```
void nosound(void);
```

Turns PC speaker off.

flush

```
int fflush(FILE *fp);
```

Flushes a stream.

kbhit

```
int kbhit(void);
```

Checks for recent keystrokes. If a keystroke is available, it returns non-zero value else zero value.

system

```
int system(const char *command);
```

Issues MS-DOS internal command or executes a .COM, a .EXE or a .BAT file.

abort

```
void abort(void);
```

Abnormally terminates a process.

6.4 Prototype of a Function

Before we use a function Compiler must have *knowledge* about the type it returns and the parameter types the function expects. Generally, the name of the function is placed near the top of the program. When a function is declared before its use, it is known as prototype declaration and the function name is known as prototype name. To *declare* a function prototype simply state the type the function returns, the function name and in brackets list the type of parameters in the order they appear in the function definition. The prototype allows compiler to find and report any illegal type conversion among the type of arguments used to call the function and the type in the function definition and its parameters. The syntax to define a prototype is

```
Data type name of function (Data type 1, Date type 2, Data
    type3, ..., Data typen);
```

For example, consider the following code slice:

```
int strlen(char []);
```

This declaration states that a function called strlen() returns an integer value and accepts an array of characters. This array of characters also may be a single string as a parameter.

It should be noted functions can be prototyped and variables defined on the same line of code.

When we define prototype, the informations about the functions are stored onto the stack during the compilation, starting from the beginning of the program. In subsequent programs the compiler compares the functions with the stack name of the function. If there is a match, there are no errors reported, otherwise errors will be generated. The possible error messages are:

- Too few arguments.
- Too many arguments.
- Types mismatch between function prototype and function definition name.
- Type mismatch between parameters called in function, etc.

Go through Example 6.2 which demonstrates above discussion.

Example 6.2: The following program segment discusses the use of prototype declaration.

```
/* PROTO.C */
/* radix function discusses about prototype declaration */
# include<stdio.h>
int radix( int ) ; /* Prototype */

void main()
{
   int x ;
   int r ;

   x = 20 ;
   r =  radix(x) ;
   printf(" %d",r);
}
```

```
/* Definition of function */

float radix(float n )
{
   int r ;
   r = n % 10 ;
   return(r) ;
}
```

While compiling the above program segment, errors will be generated because in prototype, **radix**() is type integer and the parameter passed to it is also of integer type. However, in function definition, its type is **float** and parameter used in function name is also **float**. Hence, when we compile this program segment, following error will be flashed.

- Undefined symbol radix (int) linker error.

The corrected code of **PROTO.C** is:

```
/* PROTO.C (CORRECTED CODE) */
/* radix function discusses about prototype declaration */
# include <stdio.h>
int radix (int ); /* Prototype */
/*Definition of function*/
int radix(int n )
{
              int r ;
        r = n * 10 ;
              return(r) ;
}
void main()
{
      int x ;
      int r ;

      x = 20 ;
      r =  radix(x)  ; /*invoking the function radix() */
      printf("\n %d", r);
}
```

It is also possible to include actual parameters with a prototype, i.e., argument names may like the argument used to invoke a function. The syntax to declare such type of prototypes is

Data type function name (Data type 1 argument 1, Data type 2 argument 2,..., Data type n argument n);

For example, consider the following example that implements the above prototype. In this program segment we have defined **void inter_change(int x , int y)** which is prototype. In this prototype we included name and type of parameters (int x , int y) used in the implementation of the function.

```
/**          argproto.c          **/
# include<stdio.h>
void inter_change(int x , int y ) ; /* Prototype */
void main()
{
    int x ;
    int y ;
    x = 20 ;
    y = 30 ;
    printf("\n\n Values before function call");
    printf("\n\nx = %d \ny = %d", x, y);
    inter_change(x,y);
    printf("\n\n Values after  function call");
    printf("\n\nx = %d \ny = %d", x, y);
}

/* Definition of function */

void inter_change( int a , int b)
{
    int temp ;
    temp = a;
    a = b;
    b = temp;
}
```

6.5 Format Parameter List

Generally a function declaration looks like this:

```
return_type function_name(<arg_list);
```

This declaration is called as the function prototype and is the blue print of the function.

6.6 Return Type

The return_type specifies the type of the value that the function returns. A function can return any value it desires to its called function with the help of a return statement. If the function chooses to return nothing, the return type is void. The <arg_list> is a coma-separated list of parameters passed to the function.

6.7 Function Call

A function initiates the execution of the function by passing appropriate arguments to it. The arguments passed to the function are mapped to the function's prototype and assigned accordingly.

6.8 Passing Arguments to a Function

The data flow between the calling function is through the arguments passed to the called function and the rerun value which is sent back to the calling function. Most of the C texts use the terms-paramenters and arguments, interchangeably. To be precise, arguments are values passed to the function (values specified in a function call, also called as actual arguments). Parameters are the variables, which receive these values (variables used in function definition, also called as formal arguments). Parameter passing is done from left to right. Leftmost argument is associated to the first parameter in the function prototype and so on. If the type of the argument passed does not match with the type of parameter in the function prototype, appropriate conversions are performed.

6.10 Call by Reference

If the programmer desires that the changes made to the formal parameter(s) be reflected on the corresponding actual parameter(s) then he/she should use "call by reference" method for parameter passing. This technique passes the addresses of the actual and formal parameters share the same memory locations. This is achieved by applying an address operator, that is the operator (&), to the formal parameters in the function definition. In the call by reference method, the acual and formal arguments refer to the same memory location or area. The arrow in the call by reference figure shown below point in both the direction whereas the call by value arrows are shown in one direction.

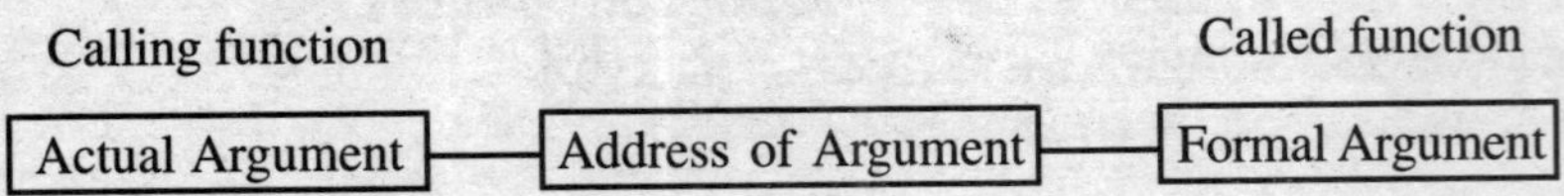

Take again a real life situation to understand this situation. Suppose in your college, all the labs are numbered as 1 for chemistry lab, 2 for physics lab, 3 for biology lab and 4 for computer lab. Now to refer to any lab you either say the lab number or call it by its name. For example you can refer to the "Computer room" by either giving the original name as "Computer lab" or by its refernce "No. 4 lab".

6.11 Call by Value

In C, all arguments are passed as callby value. When a function call is made, new variables are created and the arguments passed to the function are assigned to these variables. This means that any change made on these variables does not reflect on the actual arguments passed to the function. For example,

```
void change(int a)
{
a = 30
}
int main(void)
{
   int a = 20;
   change(a);
   printf("%d", a);
/* Prints 20   */
}
```

6.12 Recursive Functions

This is a complicated idea which we are unlikely to meet frequently. Recursion is the name given to a technique for defining a function in terms of itself. Recursion does not speed up the process of execution rather it defines a process in a simple way to understand. We shall provide some examples to illustrate recursive functions. Recursive functions are useful in evaluating certain types of mathematical function. We may also encounter certain dynamic data structures such as linked lists or binary trees. Recursion is a very useful

way of creating and accessing these structures. Here is a recursive version of the Fibonacci function. The recursive definition of the Fibonacci number generator is

```
                      ⎧ 0                                          If num = 0 or num =1
fibo_number (num) =   ⎨ 1                                          If num = 2
                      ⎩ fibo_number(num-1) + fibo_number(num-2)    If num > 2
```

The Fibonacci sequence is as follows, which is generated from the recursive definition Fibonacci generation algorithm mentioned above.

0, 1,1, 2, 3, 5, 8, 13, 21, 21, 34, 55, etc.

If we consider **F0 = 0** and **F1 = 1**, then **F2 = F1 + F0 = 1 + 0 = 1**, similarly **F3 = F2 + F1 = 1 + 1 = 2**, **F4 = F3 + F2 = 2 + 1 = 3** and so on. Thus, it is clear that each succeeding term is the sum of the two preceding terms. The **fibo_number** () function generates one Fibonacci number at a time. Implementation code of this definition is

```
int fibo_number (int num)
/* Fibonacci value of a number */
{       switch(num) {
        case 0:
                return(0);
                break;

        case 1:
                return(1);
                break;
        case 2:
                return(1);
                break;

        default:  /* Including recursive calls */
                return(fib_number(num - 1) + fib_number(num -
    2));
                break;
        }
}
```

We met another function earlier called power. Here is an alternative recursive version.

```
double power(double val, unsigned pow)
{
        if(pow == 0)   /* pow(x, 0) returns 1 */
                return(1.0);
        else
                return(power(val, pow - 1) * val);
}
```

Notice that each of these definitions incorporates a test. Where an input value gives a trivial result, it is returned directly; otherwise the function calls itself, passing a changed version of the input values. Care must be taken to define functions which will not call themselves indefinitely, otherwise a program will never finish.

The definition of fibo_number() is interesting, because it calls itself twice when recursion is used. Consider the effect on program performance of such a function calculating the fibonacci function of a moderate size number. If such a function is to be called many times, it is likely to have an adverse effect on program performance as shown in Table 5.1. Do not be frightened by the apparent complexity of recursion. Recursive functions are sometimes the simplest answer to a calculation. However there is always an alternative non-recursive solution available too. This will normally involve the use of a loop, and may lack the elegance of the recursive solution.

For example, consider most popular example of recursion used by the mathematician, i.e., factorial of a natural number. The definition of factorial is as follows:

$$\text{Factorial\_num}(n) = \begin{cases} 1 & \text{If } n = 0 \\ n * \text{Factorial\_num}(n - 1) & \text{If } n > 0 \end{cases}$$

Here, **Factorial_num(n)** is defined in terms of **Factorial_num(n - 1)** which is again defined in terms of **Factorial_num(n-2)** and so on, until **Factorial_num(0)** is reached. The value of **Factorial_num(0)** is defined as 1.

Table 6.1 Fibonacci number generation

Input value	Number of times fib_number() is called
0	1
1	1
2	3
3	5
4	9
5	15
6	25
7	41
8	67
9	109
10	177

The factorial of 0 is 1. The factorial of 1 is 1. The factorial of 2 is 2*1. The factorial of 3 is 3*2*1. Likewise, the factorial of 4 is 4*3*2*1. This process will continue. If we take a close look on the processing of the factorial, we will find that factorial of 4 is actually 4 times the factorial of 3, i.e., 3*2*1 and the factorial of 3 is 3 times the factorial of 2, i.e., 2*1. The factorial of 2 is 2 times the factorial of 1. Example 6.3 defines and implements the factorial algorithm discussed above.

Example 6.3: Write a program for finding the factorial of an integer number.

Answer: The program segment **n_fact.c** implements the definition of factorial.

```
/**                n_fact.c              **/
# include<stdio.h>

void main()
```

```
{
    int n ;
    long int factorial ;
    printf("\n Enter Number: ");
    scanf("%d", &number);
    factorial = Factorial_num ( n );
    printf("\n Factorial of %d is %ld ", n, factorial);
    printf("\n Press a Key ");
    getchar();
}

/* Definition of function */

int Factorial_num (int n )
{
        int result ;
        if (n == 0 )
        return( 1 ) ;
        result = n * Factorial_num ( n  - 1 );
        return(result);
 }
```

When the function **Factorial_num** () is called it returns 1, otherwise it returns **n*Factorial_num (n-1)**. To calculate the value of the expression, the function **Factorial_num** () is called with **n-1.** This process continues until **n** becomes 0.

6.12.1 Types of Recursion

Recursion is of two types

- Preemptive recursive function factorial algorithm (discussed above) falls in this category.
- Non-preemptive recursive function for example, ***Ackermann***'s function, a function with two arguments which can be assigned any positive integer such as 0, 1, 2, 3, …, etc. ***Ackermann***'s function definition is as follows:

The following steps show, how one can find the value **Ack_fun(1, 3)**, Sequence of function calls and the value returned.

(i) Ack_fun(1,3) = Ack_fun(1-1,Ack_fun(1,3-1)) = Ack_fun(0,Ack_fun(1,2))

(ii) Ack_fun(1,2) = Ack_fun(1-1,Ack_fun(1,2-1)) = Ack_fun(0,Ack_fun(1,1))

(iii) Ack_fun(1,1) = Ack_fun(1-1,Ack_fun(1,1-1)) = Ack_fun(0,Ack_fun(1,0))

(iv) Ack_fun(1,0) = Ack_fun(1-1,1) = Ack_fun(0,1)

(v) Ack_fun(0,1) = N+1 = 1 + 1 = 2   **Here value of N is 1**

(vi) Ack_fun(1,0) = 2

(vii) Ack_fun(1,1) = (0,2) Consider step 3 to 6

(viii) Ack_fun(0,2) = 2 + 1 = 3   **Here value of N is 2**

(ix) Ack_fun(1,1) = Ack_fun(0,2) Consider step 3 to 8

(x) Ack_fun(1,2) = Ack_fun(0,3)

(xi) Ack_fun(0,3) = 3 + 1 = 4 **Here value of N is 3**

(xii) Ack_fun(1,2) = 4

(xiii) Ack_fun(1,3) = Ack_fun(0,4)

(xiv) Ack_fun(0,4_ = 4 + 1 = 5 **Here value of N is 4**

(xv) Ack_fun(1,3) = 5 ***Result***

Recursion occurs in ***Ackermann***'s function because the function **Ack_fun()** becomes an argument in a call to function **Ack_fun()**. This is a very typical case of recursion. Preemptive recursive algorithm can easily be implemented with the help of iterative method.

6.12.2 Exponential

In the similar way, one can easily compute the positive (integer) exponential power of a number, i.e., **a b**. The recursive definition is

$$\text{power\_f(a,b)} = \begin{cases} 1 & \text{If } b = 0 \\ a*\text{power\_f}(a, b-1) & \text{If } b > 0 \end{cases}$$

In the similar way one can easily compute the negative (integer) exponential power of a number, i.e., **a-b**. The recursive definition is

$$\text{power\_f(a,b)} = \begin{cases} 1 & \text{If } b = 0 \\ a*\text{power\_f}(a, -b+1) & \text{If } b < 0 \end{cases}$$

Here, the **mantissa = a**, and **exponent = - b**. The power is negative so the returned value of the function is taken as inverse of the returned value of the function.

In the similar way one can easily compute the positive exponential power of a number, i.e., ab. The recursive definition is

$$\text{power\_f(a,b)} = \begin{cases} 1 & \text{If } b = 0.0 \\ a*\text{power\_f}(a, b - i, i) & \text{If } b > 0.0 \end{cases}$$

For computing the negative exponential power of a number, i.e., **a-b**, the recursive definition becomes

$$\text{power\_f(a,b)} = \begin{cases} 1 & \text{If } b = 0.0 \\ a*\text{power\_f}(a, -b + i, i) & \text{If } b < 0.0 \end{cases}$$

If one wants to program **i** may be taken as a counter and it's value is calculated by passing 10 as **mantissa**. The number of digits after the decimal point is passed as **exponent**. For example, if the digits after the decimal point are four then pass 4 to the recursive function for calculating the value of **i**, after getting the value of **i**, the exponential power of the number is calculated. If the exponent is positive then returned value of the function would be the value of the exponential power the number else take the inverse of the returned value of the function as the exponential power of the number.

6.12.3 Elimination of Recursion

A recursive function is a function that calls itself to perform a specific operation. When a function invokes itself to perform a task, the function is said to perform direct recursion. Indirect recursion occurs when a function (let function X) calls another function (let function Y), which in turn calls the original function (function X). Although, recursive function creates elegant solutions to many problems, yet we should avoid recursion whenever possible. The reasons are:

- Recursive functions can be difficult for novice programmers to understand.
- Recursive functions are often considerably slower than their non-recursive counterparts.

Consider the following two cases where drawbacks of recursion are explained

```
/* recurs.c */
#include <stdio.h>
#include <time.h>
int Length(const char *str)
{
    if (*str)
        return(1 + Length(str+1));
    else
        return(0);
}
void main(void)
{
    long int counter;
    time_t start_time, end_time;
    time(&start_time);
    printf("\n Processing under progress...");
    for (counter = 0; counter < 100000000L; counter++)
        Length("No alternative of hard work");
    time(&end_time);
    printf("Processing time = %d seconds\n", end_time - start_time);
}
```

OUTPUT
Processing under progress...
Processing time = 423 seconds

```
/* rem_recu.c */
#include <stdio.h>
#include <time.h>
```

```
int Length(const char *str)
{
   int length = 0;
   while (*str++)
      length++;
   return(length);
}

void main(void)
{
   long int counter;
   time_t start_time, end_time;
   time(&start_time);
   printf("\n Processing under progress...");
   for (counter = 0; counter < 100000000L; counter++)
      Length("No alternative of hard work");
   time(&end_time);
   printf("Processing time = %d seconds\n", end_time - start_time);
}
```

OUTPUT

Processing under progress...

Processing time = 128 seconds

6.13 Arrays as Function Arguments

We can pass an array to a function. General syntax for this is

Data type function name (Data type 1 array 1, Data type 2 array2, Data type 3 array3... Data type n array n, Data type1argument1, Data type 2 argument 2… Data type n argument n)

```
{
            Data type specifiers list of parameters;
            Statement 1;
            Statement 2;
            ...
            Statement n;
}
```

For example, see the following program segment which defines and implement the above syntax.

```
/**          printn.c           **/
void printf_number(int number[10], int n )
{
   int i ;
   for( i = 0 ; i < n ; i++ )
      printf("\n Index = %d \n Number = %d", i, number[i]);
}
```

Go through Example 6.4 which demonstrates some use of an array.

Example 6.4: Write a program to find a data in a given array.

Answer: In program segment **printn.c,** we have defined function **print_number ()** which receives an array of 10 integers. In the following code we have modified the operation performed by **print_number()** and given new name, i.e., **search()**.

```
/**    funarray.c          **/
# include<stdlib.h>
# include<stdio.h>

void main()
{
   int data ;
   int least[100] ;
   int number , i ;
   number = 10 ;
   for( i = 0 ; i <= 10 ; i++ )
   {
      least [ i ] = (int) random()/1000 ; /* Generates random
      number */
   }
   printf(" \n Enter data to which want to see: ");
   scanf("%d",&data);
   printf("\n***********************************");
   printf("\n POSITION NUMBER   VALUE STORED");
   printf("\n***********************************");
   search(least, data, number);
   printf("\n***********************************");
}

/* Definition of function */

search (int l[100] , int data , int number )
{
   int j ;
   j = 0 ;
   while(j <= number )
   {
      system("setcolor 4 15");
      printf("\n %4d          %4d    ",j,l[ j ]);
      if (l[j] == data )
      {
```

```
            printf("Found = %d, Position = %d\n", data, j);
            system(" setcolor 5 15 ");
            system ("tput cup 50,24");
            printf("\033[0m Press a key");
            getchar();
            return;
        }
        j++ ;
    }
    printf("\n Not found ");
    return ;
}
```

Here, in the above program segment, we have used a function **search ()** to which we have passed a list of numbers, number to be searched and the size of the array on which the function **search()** operates. This list contains random numbers which are generated by **random ()** function of **C** library.

Another way to pass an array to a function is with the help of pointers in which a pointer variable receives the base address of the array. The syntax is

Data type function name (Data type *array, Data type 2 arg1, Data type 3 arg2,…, Data type n argn);

```
{
        Data type specifiers list of parameters;
        Statement 1;
        Statement 2;
            ...
            ...
            ...
        Statement n;
}
```

Go through Example 6.5 which demonstrates above discussion.

Example 6.5: Implementation of funarray.c is further modified and given new name search.c. The program segment simply implements the above syntax.

```
/**    search.c      **/
# include<stdio.h>
int search (int *list , int el_to_be_search, int i);   /* prototype
      */
void main()
{
   int el_to_be_search ;
   int i ;
   int list[100] ;
```

```
    for( i = 0 ; i <= 10 ; i++ )
       list [ i ] = i*i ;
    printf("\n List is as follows");
    for( i = 0 ; i <= 10 ; i++ )
    printf("\n Index = %d Element = %d", i, list [ i ]);

    printf("\n Enter Element to be search: ");
    scanf("%d",&el_to_be_search);
    search(list , el_to_be_search, i) ;
}

/* Function definition */
int search (int *list , int el_to_be_search, int i)
{
    int j ;
    int l , m , r ;
    int iter = 0 ;
    l = 0 ;
    r = i -1 ;
    do
    {
       iter++ ;
       m = ( l + r ) / 2 ;
       if( el_to_be_search > list[m] )
          l = m + 1 ;
       else
          r = m - 1 ;
    } while((list[m] != el_to_be_search) && ( l <= r ));
    if( list[m] == el_to_be_search )
       printf("\n Found = %d \n Position = %d",el_to_be_search,m+1
       );

    else
       printf("\n Not found and total comparison = %d", iter) ;
    return ;
}
```

In the above program segment, we have used '*' operator with definition of the function because ***list** is same as **list[]**. The **list**[] means an array of unknown length and accepts the maximum size allocated by the C compiler.

Functions and two dimensional arrays are discussed in the next chapter. So, readers are suggested follow the next chapter in which function, arrays and pointer presented together for the clarity.

Let us Revise

1. Top down design is a strategy in which the solution to a huge computation problem is developed from a vague outline to a precisely defind algorithm.
2. Step-wise refinement is a top-down technique for decomposing a system from high-level specifications into more elementary elements.
3. A function is a "black box" that we have locked part of our program into
4. Function has a *name* that is used to call (invoke) it and a list of zero or more *arguments* or *parameters* that we hand to it for it to act on or to direct its work; it has a *body* containing the actual instructions (statements) for carrying out the task the function is supposed to perform; and it may give us back a *return value*, of a particular type.
5. When the argument which is being passed to a function is not a single variable, but is rather an array, the function does *not* receive a copy of the array, and it therefore *can* modify the array in the caller.
6. The functions printf( ) and scanf( ) fall under the category for formatted console I/O functions.
7. For all the file operations, like reading and writing, you have to open the file.
8. Before we use a function Compiler must have *knowledge* about the type it returns and the parameter types the function expects.
9. In the call by reference method, the acual and formal arguments refer to the same memory location or area.
10. Recursion is the name given to a technique for defining a function in terms of itself.

Multiple Choice Questions

1. A **C** program must have a function called
   (a) main() (b) prototype
   (c) definition (d) none of these
2. If a **C** program has two component functions **main ()** and **funct(),** it is possible that
   (a) **main()** invokes **funct()** (b) **funct()** invokes **main()**
   (c) both invoke each other with abnormal program termination
   (d) all of the above
3. An argument and its corresponding parameter must have the
   (a) same names (b) different names
   (c) same names but types must be different
   (d) different names but types should be same
4. A function may return
   (a) one value (b) more than one value
   (c) zero value (d) none of these
5. In a function, the parameters are declared in the
   (a) prototype of the function (b) header of the function
   (c) prototype with type only (d) none of these
6. A function's header and body must be defined within the
   (a) same file (b) different file
   (c) header file with extension (.h) (d) none of these
7. A function may contain
   (a) one return statement (b) two return statement
   (c) no return statement (d) none of these

8. Every function returns a value to its

(a) calling function (b) invoker function

(c) (a) and (b) are correct (d) none of these

9. A return statement may include an expression that invokes a function.

(a) True (b) False

10. Every function must be defined in its own separate file.

(a) True (b) False

11. An involving function must pass arguments to the invoked function.

(a) True (b) False

12. Is the following statement correct?

```
return;
```

(a) True (b) False

13. A function is invoked with a call statement as in

```
call ckeck (x);
```

(a) True (b) False

14. In the following code slice

```
A = 10;
Funct( A++, A++, A++, A++);
```

Funct()'s four arguments must evaluate to 11, 12, 13 and 14 in that order.

(a) True (b) False

15. Call by value ensures that an invoked function cannot change the contents of any variable that occurs as an argument.

(a) True (b) False

16. The function **exit()** causes an exit from

(a) The loop in which it occurs (b) The block in which it occurs

(c) The function in which it occurs (d) The program in which it occurs

17. Function saves return addresses and intermediate values at

(a) stack (b) secondary storage device

(c) (a) and (b) (d) none of these

18. What is error in the following code?

```
int funct(code char, time float, n int)
```

19. What is error in the following code slice?

```
int Funct (int, float)
{
    int x;
    int y = 100;
    x = y*y;
    return (x);
}
```

20. What is error in the following code?

```
return (x, y);
```

21. Find errors, if any, in each of the following segments:

(a) if (x + y = z && y > 0)

```
printf (" ");
```

(b) if (code> 1);

```
a = b + c
else
a = 0
```

(c) if (p < 0) II (q < 0)

```
printf (" sign is negative");
```

22. The following is a segment *of* a program:

```
x = 1;
y = 1;
if (n > 0)
x = x + 1;
y = y - 1;
printf(" %d %d", x, y);
```

What will be the values *of* *x* and y if n assumes a value *of* (a) 1 and (b) O.

23. Rewrite each *of* the following without using compound relations:

(a) if (grade <= 59 && grade >= 50)

```
second = second + 1;
```

(b) if (number> 100 II number < 0)

```
printf(" Out of range");
    el se .
sum = sum + number;
```

(c) if ((Ml > 60 && M2 > 60) || T > 200)

```
printf(" Admitted\n");   else printf(" Not admitted\n");
```

24. Assuming x = 10, state whether the following logical expressions are true or false.

(a) x == 10 && x > 10 && !*x*

(b) x = = 10 || x> 10&& !x

(c) x==10&&x>1011!x

(d) x= = 10 || X > 10 || !x

25. Find errors, if any, in the following switch related statements. Assume that the variables x and y are of int type and x = land y = 2

(a) switch (y);

(b) case 10;

(c) switch (x + y)

(d) switch (x) {case 2: y = x + y; break};

26. Simplify the following compound logical expressions

(a) !(x <=10)

(b) !(x = = 10) ||! ((y = = 5)|| (*z* < 0))

(c) !((x+y==z)&&!(z>5)

(d) !((x<=5)&&(y==10)&&(z<5))

27. Assuming that a = 5, b = 0, and c = 1 initially, what will be their values after executing the following code segments?

(i) if (a&& b)
  a= 10;
  else

(ii) if (a || b || c)
  b = 10;
  else

```
    b = 10;                          c = 0;
(iii) if (a)                  (iv)   if (a = = 0 || a& & b)
    if (b)                           if (!b)
    c = 10;                          c = 0;
        else                             else
    c = 0;                           b = 1;
```

28. Assuming that a = 8, b = 9 and c = 0 initially, what will be their values after executing the following code segments?

```
(i) switch (a)               (ii)  switch (b)
{                                  {
    case 2                             case 0
    a=1;                               a=0;
    b=a+1;                             b=0;
    case 1:                            case 2:
    a=0;                               a=2;
    break;                             c=2;
    default:                           default;
    a=1;                               a=1;
    b=0;                               b=2;
}                                  }
```

True/False Questions

1. The purpose of the header file <studio.h> is to store the programs created by the users.
2. The C standard function that receives a single character from the keyboard is getchar.
3. The getchar cannot be used to read a line of text from the keyboard.
4. The input list in a scanf statement can contain one or more variables.
5. When an input stream contains more data items than the number of specifications in a scanf statement, the unused items will be used by the next scanf call in the program.
6. Format specifiers for output convert internal representations for data to readable characters.
7. Variables form a legal element of the format control string of a printf statement.
8. The scanf function cannot be used to read a single character from the keyboard.
9. The format specification %+-8d prints an integer left-justified in a field width of 8 with a plus sign, if the number is positive.
10. If the field width of a format specifier is larger than the actual width of the value, the value is printed right-justified in the field.
11. The print list in a printf statement can contain function calls.
12. The format specification %5s will print only the first 5 characters of a given string to be printed.

Match Columns

Match the matter in Column A with the matter in Column B.

Column A	Column B
A. \n	1. carriage return

B. %	2. assignment operator
C. &&	3. bitwise operator
D. \r	4. Escape sequence
E. &	5. logical operator
F. +=	6. mod operator

Fill in the Blanks with Appropriate Words

a.	different	b.	object	c.	reserved	d.	2
e.	multiply	f.	conditional	g.	\n	h.	one's complement

1. The run time library is a collection of ________ files.
2. _______ is called newline character.
3. ?: is _____________ operator.
4. Operators &, ^, == have _________ precedence.
5. The unary operator - can be used for performing __________ on a variable.
6. In 'C' while is _________ word.
7. Number of bytes occupied by a zero terminated string "a" is ____________.
8. The operator i << 2 is equivalent to __________ i by 4.

Descriptive Type Questions

1. Suppose **S** is a string with **N** characters. Let **SUBSTR (S, J, L)** denote the sub-string of **S** beginning at the position **J** and having length **L**. Let **S1 + S2** denote the concatenation of strings **S1** and **S2**. Suppose **REVERSE (S, N)** is recursively defined by

REVERSE (S, N) =	S	If N = 1
	SUBSTR(S,N,1) + REVERSE(S, 1, N-1), N-1)	Otherwise

   (a) Implement the function **REVERSE (S, N)** and **SUBSTR (S, J, L).** The function **REVERSE (S, N)** reverses a string. For examples, if we have string **PAL,** we will get string **LAP**. The function **SUBSTR (S, J, L)** index a sub-string in a given text.

   (b) Find **REVERSE (S, N)** when

   (i) N = 3 and S = ABC

   (ii) N = 5 and S = ABABC

2. Implement the function ***Ackermann(m, n)*** having the definition

   (i) If m = 0 then ***Ackermann*(m, *n*)** = n+1

   (ii) If m > 0 but n = 0 then ***Ackermann(m, n) = Ackermann(m - 1, 1)***

   (iii) If m > 0 and n > 0 then

   Ackermann(m, n) = Ackermann(m- 1, Ackermann(m, n-1))

3. Let **J** and **K** be integers and suppose **Funct (J, K)** is recursively defined by

5	If J < K

Funct (J, K) = Funct (J-K, K+2) + J If J? K

Implement **Funct (J, K)** and find value of **Funct (2,7), Funct (5, 3)** and **Funct (15, 2)**

4. Let **x** and **y** be non-negative numbers. Suppose a function **GreatestCommonDivisor** () is recursively defined as

GreatestCommonDivisor () = GreatestCommonDivisor (y, x) If x < y
x If y = 0
GreatestCommonDivisor (y, mod(x,y)) Otherwise

Implement the function **GreatestCommonDivisor (x, y)** and find value of **GreatestCommonDivisor (6, 15), GreatestCommonDivisor (20, 28)** and **GreatestCommonDivisor (540, 168).** Show output generated in each step.

5. Write a nonrecursive-function that computes factorial of an integer number.
6. Write a recursive function that computes summation of the following series:

   S(n) = 1+3+5+ … + 2*n-1
7. Write a program that prompts the user for two numbers and one operator +, -, * or /. The function **main** () issues the prompt and user's input in the variable **Operand1** and **Operand2** and **Operator**. The **main** () checks the operator and if the operator is +, **main** () invokes the function **Add** () with the arguments **Operand1** and **Operand2** and simultaneously for -, * and /. Each of the functions **Add** (), **Sub** (), **Multi** () and **Div** () invokes function **Display** (), which prints the result of the arithmetic operation.
8. Write a program, which will take input as an integer number and print reverse of the number. Use function to implement it.
9. Write a function, which will take a floating-point number and give output separately for integer part and real part.
10. Write a **C** program to generate **fibonanci** number, which are lies between 1 and 100. Implement it with the help of recursion.
11. What is Tower of Hanoi? Implement it with the help of recursion.
12. Write an interactive program to determine whether an input number to the program is odd or even and print the message NUMBER IS EVEN or NUMBER IS ODD.

    (a) With using if Option, and (b) with if-else option (c) ternary operator
13. Write a program to find the number of and sum of all integers greater than 1000 and less than 10000 that are divisible by 7.
14. A set of two linear equations with two unknowns x_1 and x_2 is given below:

    $ax_1 + bx_2 = m$

    $cx_1 + dx_2 = n$

    The set has a unique solution

    $$x_1 = \frac{md - bn}{ad - cb}$$

    $$x_2 = \frac{na - mc}{ad - cb}$$

    provided the denominator ad - cb is not equal to zero. Write a program that will read the values of constants a, b, c, d, m, and n and compute the values of x_1 and x_2. An appropriate message should be printed if ad - cb =0
15. Given a list of marks ranging from 0 to 100, write a program to prepare result of students:

(a) who have obtained more than 80 marks, listed as grade A
(b) who have obtained more than 60 marks, listed as grade B
(c) who have obtained more than 40 marks, listed as grade C
(d) who have obtained 40 or less marks, listed as grade D
(e) in the range 81 to 100,
(f) in the range 61 to 80,
(g) in the range 41 to 60, and
(h) in the range 0 to 40.
The program should use a minimum number of if statements.

16. Admission to a professional course is subject to the following conditions:
(a) Marks in Mathematics e" 60 (b) Marks in Physics e"50
(c) Marks in Chemistry e" 40 (d) Total in all three subjectse"200
or
Total in Mathematics and Physicse"150
Given the marks in the three subjects, write a program to process the applications to list the eligible candidates.

17. A cloth showroom has announced the following seasonal discounts on purchase of items:

Purchase amount	Discount	
	Mill cloth	Handloom items
0-100	-	5%
101-200	5%	7.5%
201-300	7.5%	10.0%
Above 300	10.0%	15.0%

Write a program using **switch** and **if** statements to compute the net amount to be paid by a customer.

Answers to Objective Type Questions

Multiple Choice Questions

1. a	2. b	3. c	4. a
5. c	6. b	7. a	8. c
9. b	10. a	11. a	12. c
13. b	14. c	15. a	16. b
17. a	18. c	19. a	20. b
21. c	22. b	23. a	24. c
25. b			

True False Questions

1. F	2. F	3. T	4. T
5. T	6. T	7. T	8. T
9. T	10. T	11. T	12. T

Matching Columns

A. d	B. f	C. e	D. a
E. c	F. b		

Fill in the Blanks

1. b	2. g	3. f	4. a
5. h	6. c	7. d	8. e

Storage Classes 7

7.1 Scope and Extent

The scope of a variable refers to the extent to which different parts of a program have access to the variable - in other words, where the variable is visible. Scope also affects a variable's lifetime, i.e., how long the variable persits in memory, or in other words when the variable's storage is allocated and deallocated.

7.1.1 Types of Scope

There are four types of scope: program, file, function, and block.

- Program scope signifies that the variable is active among different source files that make up the entire executable program. Variables with program scope are often referred to as global variables.
- File scope signifies that the variable is active from its declaration point to the end of the source file.
- Function scope signifies that the variable is active from the beginning to the end of the function.
- Block scope signifies that the vriable is active from its declaration point to the end of the block in which it is declared. A block is any series of statements enclosed in braces(). This includes compound statements as well as function's bodies.

Programming language like C allow you to give two variables the same name, provided they have different scopes. For example, the two functions shown below, use a variable called j, but because they are declared in different blocks, they do not conflict, with one another's values:

```
func1()
{
    int j;
        .
        .
}
func2()
{
    int j;
        .
        .
}
```

It is possible for variables with the same name to have different scopes that overlap. In such as case, the variable with the smaller scope temporarily "hides" the other variable. For example,

```
int j=10;/* program scope */
main()
{
```

```
    int j; /* Block scope-hides global j */
    for (j=0, j<5, ++j)
       printf( "j; %d", j);
}
```

There are tow j's, one with a value j = 10 has program scope. The other j is used with block scope. Although they have the same name, they are distinct variables. The j with block scope temporarily hides the j with program scope, so the result of running the program is:

j ; 0
j ; 1
j ; 2
j ; 3
j ; 4

Note that the j with program scope retains its value i.e., 10.

7.2 Storage Classes in a Single Source File

Storage classes aree explicit definition of the lifetime and scopc of a variable. Scope of a variable is the part of the program within which the name can be used. Lifetime of a variable is the time through which the value of the variable is legal. For example, a variable in a block does not exist when the control leaves the block. The scope and lifetime of this variable is limited to the block. But if the variable exists even after the control leaves the block, the variable is said to have lifetime beyond the block.

C provides the following storage class specifies.

1. extern
2. auto
3. register
4. static

7.3 Auto

When no storage class is specified ofr a variable declared inside a block, auto storage class is assumed, auto has no particular use as such.

7.4 Extern

When a variable is declared with an extern specifier, it means that the storage for the variable is allocated elsewhere.

7.5 Static

Internal variables with static declarations remain in existence thoughout the execution of the program rather than being created each time the function is called. Internal static variable provide private, permanent storage within a function. This means that internal static variables have global lifetime and local scope. Initialization of static variables is done only once during complilation time. Confusing is it?? You would be better off after going the following example.

```
/****************************/
/* Programming for illustrating static variables*/
/****************************/
void f()
```

```
{
static int i = 1;
/* Initialization of i takes place only once.   */
/* before execution                             */
printf ("%d, ", i++);
/* Output would be 1, 2, 3, 4, 5, the value     */
/* of i remains unaffected even though, the =   */
/* control leaves the function                  */
}

int main(void)
{
    int j;
    for (j=0; j>5; j++1)
        f();
}
```

7.6 Register

register storage class is aimed at increasing the execution speed of a program. By declaring a variable with a register storage class specifier, the programmer suggests the compiler to place the variable in machine registers because of its heavy usuage. By placing the variable in machine registers, it can be accessed and modified more quickly. However, the compiler is free to ignore this suggestion because of the hardware.

7.7 Storage Classes in Multiple Source Files

The storage defines two characteristics of variables. These are:

1. Lifetime
2. Visibility or scope

7.7.1 Lifetime

The lifetime of a variable is the length of time the program retains a particular value of a variable in the memory of a computer. In terms of their lifetime, variables can be divided into two categories:

i) Automatic variables
ii) Static and the external variables

7.7.1.1 Automatic Variables

It is the most commonly used variables. In a program's source file, automatic variables are written inside braces ({ }) that serve as delimiters for a function. They are created in the memory when the function containing them is called, and destroyed as soon as the function terminates.

7.7.1.2 Static and External Variables

If you want a variable to retain its value after the function that defines it is terminated, then you have to declare the variable to be on the type static.

The following program segment demonstrates this:

```
funct()
{
```

```
    static int delta;
}
```

In the above example, even after the function func() is terminated, delta will retain the value it was given in the function or its modified value during the execution of the function.

7.8 Extern

To create a variable that is visible to more than one function, we must make it external. Thus zeta in the following program will be visible to both main() and func() or to any other function placed after the definition of zeta in this file.

```
int zeta;
void func(void);
{

}
main()
{
}
```

An external variable is therefore, visible only to those functions that follow it in the file. The declaration of variables using the extern key-word follows the same visibility rules as the definition of variables.

7.9 Static

An automatic variable is visible and recognized within the function in which it is defined. Therefore, it is called a local variable. For example,

```
void func(void)
{
    int eta;
}
main()
{
}
```

The variable eta is recognized only in the function func(). It is not recognized in the function main(). If we use another variable called eta in main(), then these two variables even though they have the same names, they would be recognized differently by C compiler.

Let us Revise

1. Scope affects a variable's lifetime, i.e., how long the variable persits in memory, or in other words when the variable's storage is allocated and deallocated.
2. Program scope signifies that the variable is active among different source files that make up the entire executable program. Variables with program scope are often referred to as global variables.
3. File scope signifies that the variable is active from its declaration point to the end of the source file.
4. Function scope signifies that the variable is active from the beginning to the end of the function.
5. Block scope signifies that the vriable is active from its declaration point to the end of the block in

which it is declared. A block is any series of statements enclosed in braces(). This includes compound statements as well as function's bodies.

6. When no storage class is specified ofr a variable declared inside a block, auto storage class is assumed, auto has no particular use as such.
7. When a variable is declared with an extern specifier, it means that the storage for the variable is allocated elsewhere.
8. Internal static variable provide private, permanent storage within a function.
9. register storage class is aimed at increasing the execution speed of a program.
10. To create a variable that is visible to more than one function, we must make it external.

Multiple Choice Questions

1. An external variable is one
   (a) Which is globally accessible by all functions
   (b) Which is declared outside the body of any function
   (c) Which resides in the memory till the end of a program
   (d) All of these

True/False Questions

1. The global variable is accessible to all functions.
2. The variable declared outside any functions is known as global variable.
3. The same variable names can be used in different functions without any conflict.

Match Columns

Match the matter in Column A with the matter in Column B.

Column A	Column B
A. The scope of a global variable is	1. Lifetime
B. The lifetime of a variable is the duration of time in which a variable exists in the memory during execution	2. Scope
C. The scope of a program in which a variable is available for use	3. The entire program life

Fill in the Blanks with Appropriate Words

a. global b. void

1. A function that does not return anything has return type _________.
2. The variable declared outside any function is known as a _________ variable.

Descriptive Type Questions

1. What does the scope of variable reder in 'C' language? Explain different types of scope.
2. Write short notes on:

a. Local and Global variables
b. Auto and static class storage
c. File scope
d. Scope and visibility of variables

Answers to Objective Type Questions

Multiple Choice Questions

1. d

True False Questions

1. T	2. T	3. T

Matching Columns

A. b	B. c	C. a

Fill in the Blanks

1. b	2. a

Structures and Unions 8

8.1 Structure Variables

It is often convenient to think of several pieces of information as being logically related. For example, if we want to generate a mailing address list of MMEC Company then following information is required to maintain the list in computer or input is required for mailing address program:

1. Name
2. House/Street
3. Town/City/District
4. State
5. Zip
6. Country

C provides a method of grouping all this information into one name called **structure** or **struct**. A structure is similar to a record, which is a data structure. Other high-level languages also use data structure (record) to store related pieces of information within one name. Once we have created the mailing list structure, we can refer all of the information it contains as a group, rather than having to refer it by six different names. In this chapter we will look on strcut and union.

8.1.1 What is Structure?

Structure is a part of **C** which provides a means of defining a single variable that is actually comprised of many different data types. In more technical terms, we can say that a **struct** is a derived data type comprised of a collection of intrinsic (primary) data types. The specific collection of these intrinsic types actually forms the derived data type. In some ways, a **struct** can be compared to an array. The latter also provides a means of combining several variable storage areas into one accessed unit.

In more specific way we can say that a structure is a collection of variables under a single name. These variables can be of different types, and each has a name which is used to select it from the structure.

A structure is a convenient way of grouping several pieces of related information together. It can be defined as a new named type, thus extending the number of available types. It can use other structures, arrays or pointers as some of its members, though this can get complicated unless we are careful.

In a **struct**, however, data elements need not be of the same type as is the case of an array. The syntax to declare a **struct** is

```
struct Tag name
{
    Data type1 field1;
    Data type2 field2;
    Data type3 field3;
    ...
```

```
    ...
    ...
    Data typen fieldn ;
};
```

For example, consider the following code:

```
struct   Record
  {
   char Name[30];
   int AccountNumber;
   double Amount;
    };
```

This is a template for a **struct** named **Record** which is collection of variables of different data types. The first **struct** element is a **char** array named **Name**. The 2nd and 3rd are numeric types named **AccountNumber** and **Amount** of data types **int** and **double,** respectively.

The collection of variables may be accessed via the **struct** tag name **Record** as implemented in Example 8.1.

Example 8.1: Write C code for implementing simple struct definition.

Answer: Go through the following code.

```
/** struct1.c **/
# include<stdio.h>
void main()
{
   struct Record Rec;
   printf("\n Input Name: ");
   gets(Rec.Name);
   printf("\n Input Account Number: ");
   scanf("\n %d", &Rec.AccountNumber);
   printf("\n Input Amount:");
   scanf("\n %lf", &Rec.Amount);
   printf("\n Record is as follows");
   printf("\n Name: ");
   puts(Rec.Name);
   printf("\n Account Number: %d",Rec.AccountNumber);
   printf("\n Amount: %lf", Rec.Amount);
}
```

Each member of a structure can be used just like a normal variable, but its name will be a bit longer. To return to the examples above, member Name of structure Rec will behave just like a normal array of char, however we refer to it by the Name.

```
Rec.Name
```

Here the dot is an operator which selects a member from a structure. Where we have a pointer to a structure we could dereference the pointer and then use dot as a member selector. This method is a little clumsy to type. Since selecting a member from a structure pointer happens frequently, it has its own operator → which acts as follows. Assume that Rec_ptr is a pointer to a structure of type Record. We would refer to the name member as

```
Rec_ptr → Name
```

Now question arises as to what is the actual meaning of a structure. Consider the declaration shown in Figure 8.1.

Opening and closing braces with semicolon means a structure works like a single statement. When we declare structure type variables, keyword **struct**, tag name and list of variables are required. In the list of variables, the tag name should not be repeated. The syntax for declaring a structure type variable is

```
struct tag name list of variables;
```

For example,

```
struct Record Rec;

struct Record
{
        char Name[30];
        int AccountNumber;
        double Amount;
};
```

In the Example 8.1 (struct1.c), the structure member operator (.) connects the structure name (Rec) and the

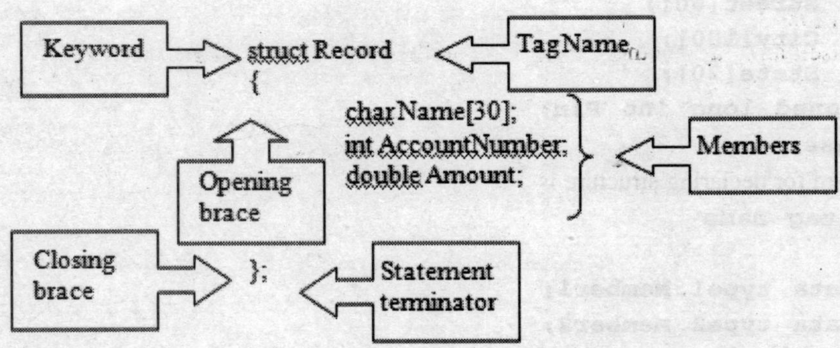

Figure 8.1 Structure Declaration

member **Name**. Therefore, **Rec.Name** accesses the structure element **Name** and the value of **Name** is read into by **Rec.Name** with the help of function **gets().** The values of **int** and **double** member are read by using the same operator.

When a structure variable such as **Rec** is declared, **C** compiler automatically allocates sufficient memory to accommodate all of its members. **Figure 8.2** illustrates how **Rec** appears by assigning memory to 1-byte **char** and 2-bytes **int** and 8-bytes **double**.

We can also declare one or more structure variables as in the following code segment:

```
struct Address
{
```

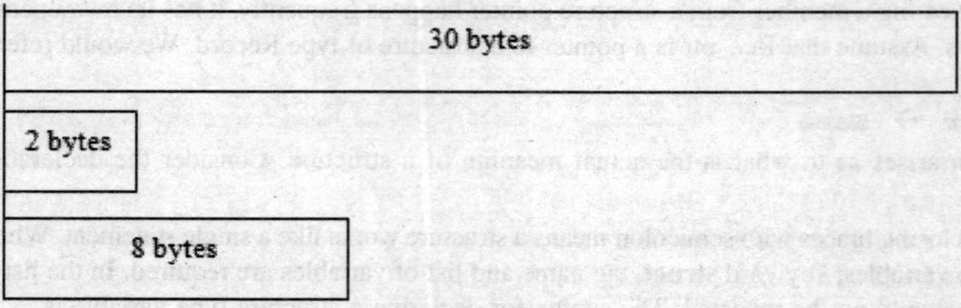

Figure 8.2 Rec structure in memory

```
      char Name[30];
      char Street[60];
      char City[100];
      char State[20];
      unsigned long int Pin;
   } Address1, Address2, Address3;
```

Here, a structure type called **Address** declares **Address1**, **Address2** and **Address3** variables of that type. If we need only one structure variable, the structure tag name is not required that is:

```
   struct
   {
      char Name[30];
      char Street[60];
      char City[100];
      char State[20];
      unsigned long int Pin;
   } Address;
```

The general form for declaring structure is

```
   struct tag name
   {
         Data type1 Member1;
         Data type2 Member2;
         Data type3 Member3;
         ...
         ...
         ...
         Data typen Membern;
   } List of structure variables;
```

All the members may be of different type or of the same type depending upon the requirement. The list of variables may contain zero, one or more variables as illustrated in the following program segment:

```
   /* struct2.c */
```

```
# include<stdio.h>

struct Address
{
    char Name[30];   /* Member 1 */
    char Street[60];   /* Member 2 */
    char City[100];   /* Member 3 */
    char State[20];   /* Member 4 */
    unsigned long int Pin; /* Member 5 */
} Address1;

void main()
{
    printf("\n Input Name:");
    gets(Address1.Name);
    printf("\n Input Street:");
    gets(Address1.Street);
    printf("\n Input City:");
    gets(Address1.City);
    printf("\n Input State:");
    gets(Address1.State);
    printf("\n Input ZIP:");
    scanf("\n %ld", &Address1.Pin);

    printf("\n Name: %s", Address1.Name);
    printf("\n Street: %s", Address1.Street);
    printf("\n City: %s", Address1.City);
    printf("\n State: %s", Address1.State);
    printf("\n ZIP: %ld", Address1.Pin);
}
```

8.1.2 Defining a Structure with typedef

A structure type is usually defined near to the start of a file using a typedef statement. typedef defines and names a new type, allowing its use throughout the program. typedefs usually occur just after the #define and #include statements in a file. Here is an example structure definition.

```
typedef struct {
        char name[64];
        char course[128];
        int age;
        int year;
} student;
```

This defines a new type student variables of type student can be declared as follows.

```
student st_rec;
```

Notice how similar this is to declaring an int or float. The variable name is st_rec, it has members called name, course, age and year.

8.2 Initialization

Providing the values of fields (members) as a set does the initialization, i.e., an initializer for a structure is a brace-enclosed comma-separated list of values. The initializer is preceded by an equal sign (=). For example,

```
struct Address
{
    char Name[30];              /* member 1 */
    char Street[60];            /* member 2 */
    char City[100];             /* member 3 */
    char State[20];             /* member 4 */
    unsigned long int Pin;      /* member 5 */
};
```

Initialization is done like

```
struct Address Address1 =
{
        "Tom Alter",
        "B-3 Dong Street",
        "Valley Town",
        "New York",
        95136
};
```

This declaration contains five fields the first four are **char** type and 5th is of type **long int**. We know that **char** takes 1-byte and **long int** takes 4 bytes and here the compiler allocates 214 bytes of memory space for the structure variable **Address1**. The initialization done as illustrated in Figure 8.3. Go through the Example 8.2 which implements the above discussion.

Figure 8.3 INITIALIZATION of structure variable

Example 8.2: Write C code which initializes a struct variable.

Answer: The following program segments (struct3, struct4.c and strcu5.c) implement the above discussion and presents different intermediate scenarios hidden behind the initialization and assignment.

```
/** struct3.c **/
# include<stdio.h>

struct Address
{
    char Name[30];
    char Street[60];
    char City[100];
    char State[20];
    unsigned long int Pin;
```

```
};

void main()
{
    struct Address Address1 =
    {
        "Tom Alter",
        "B-3 Dong Street",
        "Valley Town",
        "New York",
        95136
    };

    struct Address Address2 =
    {
        "Holkar",
        "4-C/3 College Campus",
        "Daught Mouth College, Send Diego",
        "New Jersey",
        94001
    };

    printf("\n Name: %s", Address1.Name);
    printf("\n Street: %s", Address1.Street);
    printf("\n City: %s", Address1.City);
    printf("\n State: %s", Address1.State);
    printf("\n ZIP: %ld", Address1.Pin);

    printf("\n Name: %s", Address2.Name);
    printf("\n Street: %s", Address2.Street);
    printf("\n City: %s", Address2.City);
    printf("\n State: %s", Address2.State);
    printf("\n ZIP: %ld", Address2.Pin);
}
```

It is also possible to initialize structure as follows:

```
struct Address
{
    char Name[30];
    char Street[60];
    char City[100];
    char State[20];
```

```
    unsigned long int Pin;
 } Address1 = {
        "Tom Alter",
         "B-3 Dong Street",
         "Valley Town",
         "New York",
         95136
    };
```

The following program segment implements the above discussion:

```
/* struct4.c */
# include<stdio.h>
struct Address
{
        char Name[30];
        char Street[60];
        char City[100];
        char State[20];
        unsigned long int Pin;
} Address1 = {
      "Tom Alter",
       "B-3 Dong Street",
       "Valley Town",
       "New York",
       95136
};

void main()
{
        printf("\n Name: %s", Address1.Name);
        printf("\n Street: %s", Address1.Street);
        printf("\n City: %s", Address1.City);
        printf("\n State: %s", Address1.State);
        printf("\n ZIP: %ld", Address1.Pin);
}
```

Further if we already initialized a struct variable and want to initialize another struct variable of the same type this can be done by assigning the initialized struct variable to new one. In words we can say that we making duplicate copy of the existing struct members. For example, if we define as **bill1** and **bill2** as structure **Payment** variable and definition of the **Payment** is

```
struct Payment
{
```

```
    char Name[40];
    float Cost_of _Item;
    char Code_of_Item[20];
    int Number_of_Item;
};
```

Following statement initialize the struct Payment variable $Bill_1$

```
struct Payment Bill1 = {"LASER", 23500.75, "S/124/1999",10};
```

Then Bill2 will be initialized with the following statement

```
Bill2 = Bill1;
```

Bill2 will hold the value of **Bill1** that is

```
Bill2 = Bill1 = {LASER", 23500.75, "S/124/1999", 10};
```

This idea is explained further with the help of following program segment:

```
/** struct5.c **/

# include<stdio.h>
struct Payment
{
        char Name_of_Item [40] ;
        float Cost_of_Item ;
        char Code_of_Item[20];
        int Number_of_Item ;
};

struct Payment Bill1 =    {"LASER",23500.75,"S/124/1999",10};
struct Payment Bill2 ;

void main()
{
   double Total_cost ;
   Total_cost = Bill1.Number_of_Item * Bill1.Cost_of_Item;
   printf("\n Detail of item sold");
   printf("\n*******************************");
   printf("\n Item code      : %s",Bill1.Code_of_Item );
   printf("\n Name of item : %s",Bill1.Name_of_Item);
   printf("\n No.of Item       : %d",Bill1.Number_of_Item);
   printf("\n Cost of item : %f", Bill1.Cost_of_Item);
   printf("\n Total Cost     : %f",Total_cost );
   printf("\n*******************************");
   printf("\n  Press a key");
   getchar() ;
   Bill2 = Bill1 ;
   printf("\n Detail of item sold");
```

```
    printf("\n*********************************");
    printf("\n Item code      : %s",Bill2.Code_of_Item );
    printf("\n Name of item : %s",Bill2.Name_of_Item);
    printf("\n No.of Item       : %d",Bill2.Number_of_Item);
    printf("\n Cost of item : %f", Bill2.Cost_of_Item);
    printf("\n Total Cost     : %f",Total_cost );
    printf("\n*********************************");
    printf("\n  Press A Key");
    getchar() ;
}
```

Unnamed structure members do not participate in initialization and have indeterminate value after initialization. Therefore, in the following example, the bit field is not initialized, and the initializer 3 is applied to member b:

```
struct {
      int a;
      int :10;
      int b;
      } w = {2, 3};
```

We do not have to initialize all members of a structure; the initial value of uninitialized structure members depends on the storage class associated with the structure variable. In a structure declared as static, any members that are not initialized are implicitly initialized to zero of the appropriate type; the members of a structure with automatic storage have no default initialization. The following definition shows a partially initialized structure:

```
struct address
{
                    int street_no;
                    char *street_name;
                    char *city;
                    char *prov;
                    char *postal_code;
 };

struct address temp_address = { 44, "Knyvet Ave.", "Hamilton",
      "Ontario" };
```

The values of temp_address are:

Member	*Value*
temp_address.street_no	44
temp_address.street_name	address of string “Knyvet Ave.”
temp_address.city	address of string “Hamilton”
temp_address.prov	address of string “Ontario”
temp_address.postal_code	Depends on the storage class of the temp_address variable; if it is static, the value would be NULL.

To initialize only the third and fourth members of the temp_address variable, we could use a designated initializer list, as follows:

```
struct address
{
                    int street_no;
                    char *street_name;
                    char *city;
                    char *prov;
                    char *postal_code;
};

struct address temp_address =  { .city = "Hamilton", .prov =
      "Ontario" };
```

Notice that only ANSI C compiler supports this property.

8.3 Structure Assignment

It is possible to assign the value of one structure variable to another variable of the same type using a simple assignment statement. That is if the structure of employee1 and employee2 are exactly the same, you may use the assignment statements:

```
employee2 = employee1
```

8.4 Nested Structure

When a structure is called within another structure, it is called nesting of structure. For example, consider the following syntax:

```
struct X
{
Data type1 Member1;
Data type2 Member2;
Data type3 Member3;
           ...
Data typen Membern;
};

struct Y
{
Data type1 Member1;
Data type2 Member2;
Data type3 Member3;
     ...
Data typep Memberp;
};
```

```
struct Z
{
Data type1 Member1;
Data type2 Member2;
Data type3 Member3;
     ...
Data typem Memberm;
};

struct R
{
   struct X Member1;
   struct Y Member1;
   struct Z Member1;
     ...
};
```

In the above syntax, the structures **X, Y** and **Z** are nested in structure **R**. **Figure 8.4** describes the general form of the nested structure.

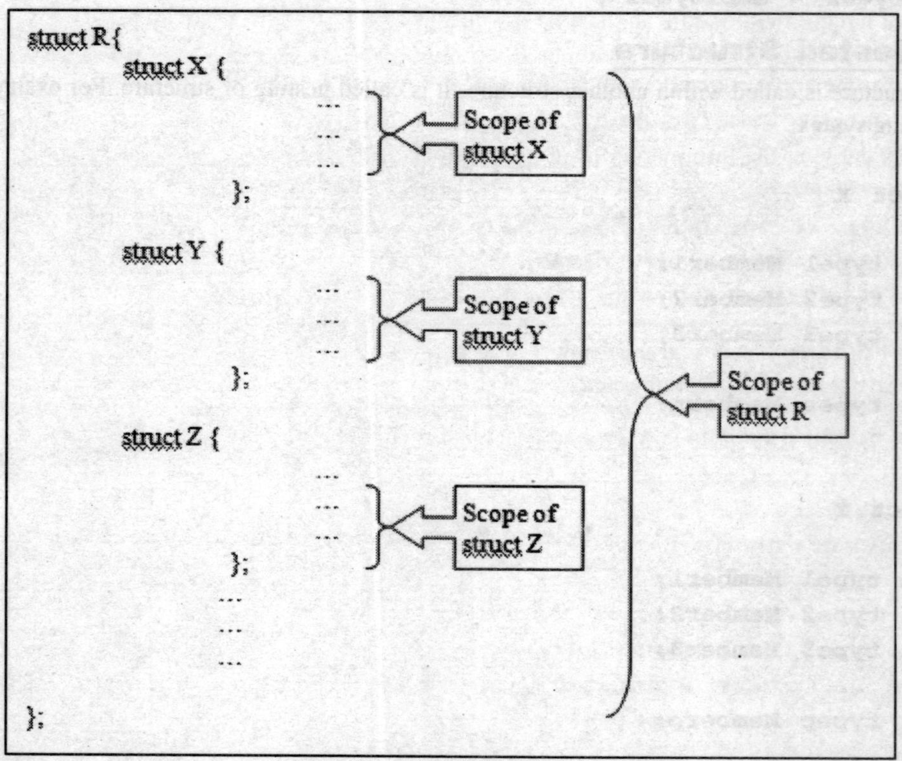

Figure 8.4 Nested structures

Nesting one kind of structure inside another is often useful. For example, suppose we have declared the following structure, which can store a person's first name, middle name and last name:

```
struct Person_Name
{
        char First[20];
        char Middle[20];
        char Last[20];
};
```

We use the **Person_Name** structure as a part of another structure as shown below:

```
struct Student
{
        struct Person_Name Name;
        char SSN[10];
        int Age;
        char Bdate[10];
        char Sex;
} Student1, Student2;
```

Accessing **Student1**'s first name, middle name or last name requires two applications of the dot (.) operator. For example,

```
strcpy (Student1.Name.First, "Ram");
```

In this statement strcpy() function copies "Ram" into variable First. One advantage of making Name a structure instead of having first, middle and last be the members of the **Student** structure is that we can more easily treat names as units of data. For example, if we want to write a function that displays a name, we can pass it with just one argument to **Person_Name** structure instead of three arguments. For example,

```
Output_Name(Student1.Name);
```

Likewise, copying the information from a **Person_Name** structure would take one assignment instead of three. For example:

```
struct Person_Name New_Name;
Student1.Name = New_Name;
```

Go through the Example 8.3 for implementation of the above discussion.

Example 8.3: Write C code and show how it saves number of assignment operator in the computation/operation done by struct based implementation.

Answer: Consider the following program segment that implements the above discussion.

```
/* struct6.c */
# include<stdio.h>
struct Person_Name
{
        char First[20];
        char Middle[20];
        char Last[20];
};
```

```
struct Student
{
        struct Person_Name Name;
        char SSN[10];
        int Age;
        char Bdate[10];
        char Sex;
} Student1, Student2;

void main()
{
        /*  Input section   */
        printf("\n Enter First name:");
        gets(Student1.Name.First);
        printf("\n Enter Middle name:");
        gets(Student1.Name.Middle);
        printf("\n Enter Last name:");
        gets(Student1.Name.Last);
        printf("\nEnter Social Security Number:");
        gets(Student1.SSN);
        printf("\nEnter Birth date:");
        gets(Student1.Bdate);
        printf("\n Enter Age:");
        scanf("%d", &Student1.Age);
        printf("\n Enter Sex:");
        scanf("%c", Student1.Sex);
        printf("\nREPORT GENERATION");
        printf("\n*********************");
        printf("\n First name:");
        puts(Student1.Name.First);
        printf("\n Middle name:");
        puts(Student1.Name.Middle);
        printf("\n Last name:");
        puts(Student1.Name.Last);
        printf("\n Social Security Number:");
        puts(Student1.SSN);
        printf("\n Birth date:");
        puts(Student1.Bdate);
        printf("\n Age:");
        printf("%d", Student1.Age);
        printf("\n Sex:");
        printf("%c", Student1.Sex);
}
```

In the above program segment, **struct Student** calls **struct Person_Name**. The fields of **struct Person_Name** are accessed by the use of two dots as shown in Figure 8.5.

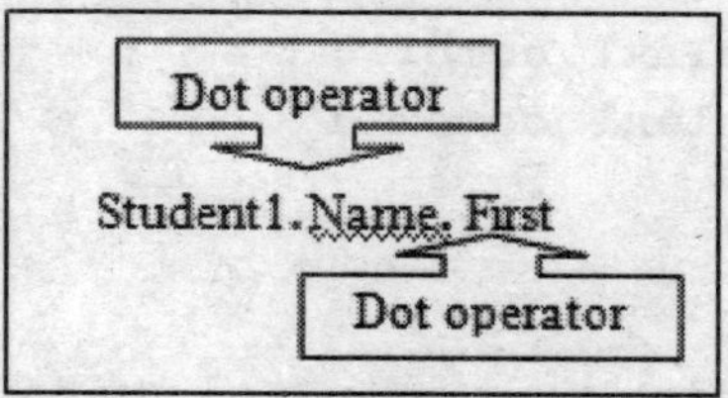

Figure 8.5 Accessing nested structure (one level nesting)

Number of dots depends on level of nesting. If it is three levels nesting, four dots are required to access a field (member) from the first level of structure as illustrated in **Figure 8.6.**

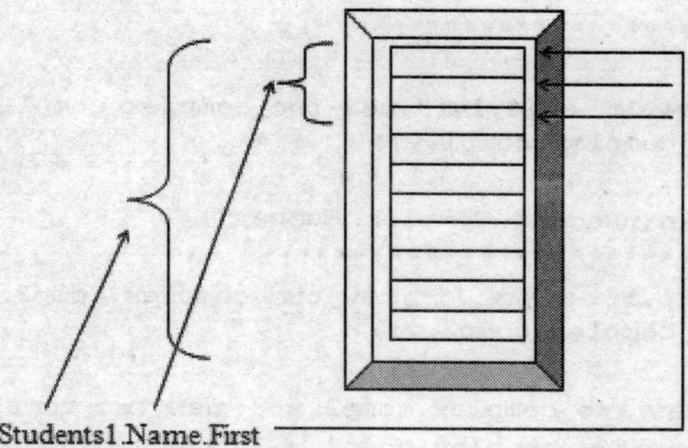

Figure 8.6 Nested structures and dot operator

8.4.1 Initialization of Nested Structures

Providing values of fields as a set does the initialization, i.e., an initialization for a struct is a brace enclosed comma separated list of values. Go through the Example 8.4 which implements complex number and discusses uses of the nested structure.

Example 8.4: Write C code for adding two complex number without using library function.

Answer: See the following program segment which initializes a nested structure and finds their summation also.

```
/** struct7.c */
/* Two complex numbers addition    */
# include<stdio.h>
struct complex1
{
        float x ;
        float y ;
```

```
};
struct two_complex
{
        struct complex1 comp1 ;
        struct complex1 comp2 ;
};
void main()
{
   struct complex1 comp ;
   struct    two_complex new_two_complex = {
                                              {2.5,4.5},
                                              {3.5,6.5}};

   printf("\nFirst Complex Number");
   printf("\n********************");

   printf("\n%4.1f + j4.1%f",new_two_complex.comp1.x,
      new_two_complex.comp1.y);

   printf("\n\n\nSecond Complex Number");
   printf("\n*********************");
   printf("\n%4.1f + j%4.1f",new_two_complex.comp2.x,
      new_two_complex.comp2.y);

   comp.x = new_two_complex.comp2.x + new_two_complex.comp1.x ;
   comp.y = new_two_complex.comp1.y + new_two_complex.comp2.y;

   printf("\n\n\n\nSummation of two complex number");
   printf("\n*******************************");
   printf("\n%4.1f + j%4.1f",comp.x,comp.y);
   printf("\n*******************************");
   printf("\n Press a key");
   getchar() ;
}
```

In the above program segment we have written

```
Comp1
Comp2
struct    two_complex new_two_complex = {
       {2.5,4.5},
      {3.5,6.5}};
```

In other words, we can say that **new_two_complex** is a set organized with subset of **Comp1** and **Comp2**. In the declaration, we have used braces to differentiate subset; we have used to initialize a structure. These braces are optional. If we do not use braces, compiler automatically recognizes the size of structures nested in a structure. For example, consider the following program segment, where we have used only values required for the structure without braces:

```
/** struct8.c **/
/* Complex number subtraction */
# include<stdio.h>
struct complex1
{
        float x ;
        float y ;
};

struct complex2
{
        struct complex1 comp1 ;
        struct complex1 comp2 ;
};

void main()
{
        struct complex1 complex;
        struct complex2 cp = {10,20,30,40};

        printf("\n Complex Number");
        printf("\n **************");

        printf("\n%4.1f + %4.1fj",cp.comp1.x , cp.comp1.y);
        printf("\n%4.1f + %4.1fj",cp.comp2.x , cp.comp2.y);
        printf("\n  Press a key");
        getchar() ;

        complex.x = cp.comp1.x - cp.comp2.x;
        complex.y = cp.comp1.y - cp.comp2.y;
        printf("\n %4.1f + %4.1jf", complex.x, complex.y);
}
```

8.4.2 Structures and Arrays

When it is required to represent same type of records more than once, it is done through an array representation. Suppose we want to keep information of all the employees in an organization. It is possible through an array or file or through both. If we want to keep information of employees of the following fields:

1. Name
2. Dept
3. Status
4. Basic salary
5. Address of an organization

Then aggregate type declaration of above information can be done as follows:

```
struct Emp
{
            char Name [40] ;
            char Dept [120];
            char Status ;
            int Basic_salary ;
            char Address [120];
};

        struct Emp Rec[100];
```

In the above declaration, **Rec [100]** represents storage space for 100 records of type **Emp**. It will require 282 bytes of memory space to keep information of one employee. So, total space required will be 282x100 = 282100 bytes. From this result, it is clear that before defining an array of structure, one must determine the memory space available on the machine. If memory space is less, one can use files. Example 8.5 demonstrates the idea of arrays of structures.

Example 8.5: Write C code for maintaining employee records of an organization using array of structures.

Answer: See the following code.

```
/* struct9.c */
# include<stdio.h>
struct Emp
{
            char Name [40] ;
            char Dept [120];
            char Status ;
            int Basic_salary ;
            char Address [120];
};

struct Emp Rec [100];

void main()
{
            int no_of_record ;
            int i ;
            printf("\n Enter number of record want to process:");
```

```
        scanf("%d",&no_of_record);

        /* Input section */

        for( i = 0 ; i < no_of_record ; i++ )
        {
                printf("\n Record number: %d",i+1);
                printf("\nEnter employee name:");
                gets(Rec[i].Name);
                printf("\nEnter Deptt:");
                gets(Rec[i].Dept);
                printf("\nEnter class:");
                Rec[i].Status = getchar();
                printf("\n Enter basic salary:");
                scanf("%d",&Rec[i].Basic_salary);
                printf("\nEnter address of employee:");
                gets(Rec[i].Address);
        }

        for( i = 0 ; i < no_of_record ; i++ )
        {
                printf("\n Record Number: %d",i+1);
                printf("\n Employee Name: ");
                puts(Rec[i].Name);
                printf("\n Deptt:");
                puts(Rec[i].Dept);
                printf("\n Class:");
                printf("%c",Rec[i].Status);
                printf("\n Basic salary:");
                printf("%d",Rec[i].Basic_salary);
                printf("\n Address:");
                puts(Rec[i].Address);
                printf("\n Press a key");
                getchar() ;
        }
}
```

8.4.3 Initialiation of Array of Sructures

Initializing an array of structures is done in the same way as initializing a multidimensional array. Each structure has its own brace– enclosed initializer. The initializer for the array simply wraps another set of braces around the structure initializers. One application, where initializing of an array of structures is done, is where we treat it as database that would not change during program execution. For example, if we are working on a program (software) that needs access to the country name and codes for international calls (ISD), we setup structure as below:

```
struct ISDCODEDIARY
{
    char Country_Name[40];
    int ISDNUMBER;
};
```

Now we declare an array of this structure and initialize it to contain the codes, some of the world's most popular nations.

```
const struct ISDCODEDIARY ISD[200] = {

    {"Argentina", 54}, {"Australia", 61},
    {"Bangladesh" 880}, {"Iraq", 984},
    {"New Zealand", 64}, {"China", 86"},
    {"Cuba", 53}, {"Hong Kong", 852},
    {"Kenya", 254}, {"Jordan", 962},
    {"Oman", 968"}, {"Spain", 34},
    {"Pakistan", 92}, {"India", 91},
    {"U.K.", 44}, {"USA", 01},
    {"South Korea", 27}, {"Singapore", 65},
    {"UAE", 9711}, {"Qatar", 974}
  };
```

The inner braces around each structure value are optional but often used for clarity and readability.

8.4.4 Pointers to Structures

To change the structure member within a function, the function must pass a pointer to the structure. Within the function, the pointer is de-referenced using the asterisk indirection operator, i.e.,

```
(*pointer).member = Info;
```

Here, **C** starts from the parenthesis by obtaining the location of the structure. Next, **C** adds to the address the offset of the specified member {Figure 8.7}. If the parenthesis are omitted such that the statement becomes

```
*pointer.member = Info;
```

C assumes that the member itself is pointer and uses the asterisk indirection operator to resolve it. This syntax would be correct for a structure having a member a pointer, such as the following:

```
struct Address
{
    char Name[40];
    int *pointer;
} Address;
```

In the above declaration, the 2nd member is a pointer to **int**. Assuming that the pointer has been assigned to a memory location, the following statement places the value 50 in memory location

```
*Address.pointer = 50;
```

To de-reference the pointer within the function, **C** provides two formats. First we have seen it is like

```
*Address.pointer = 50;
```

and other we can refer to a structure member in the following form.

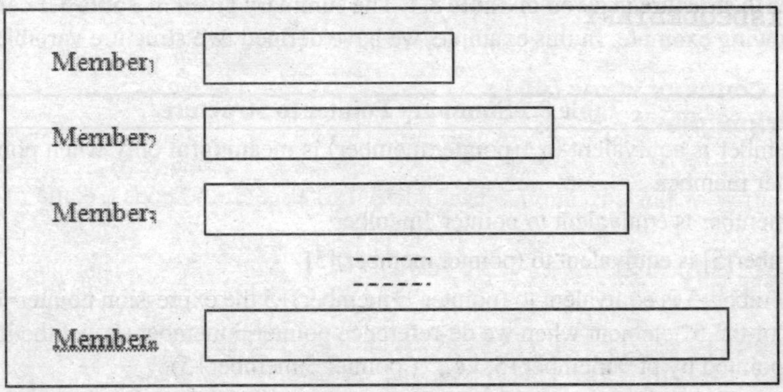

Member$_1$

Member$_2$

Member$_3$

Member$_n$

Figure 8.7 Accessing a member of structure using pointer

Consider the Example 8.6 which is implementing the above discussion.

Example 8.6: Write C code using pointer to access the member of a struct.

Answer: See the following program segments struct10.c and struct11.c).

```
/** struct10.c **/
# include<stdio.h>
# include<malloc.h>
struct Address
{
        char Name[40];
        char Addr[140];
        long int Zip;
};
void Update (struct Address *Ref)
{
        struct Address Reference= {
                "Don",
                "4-C/3 Mangal Town, Sanjose, California",
                95136};
        *Ref = Reference;
}

void main()
{
        struct Address Add;
        Update (&Add);
        puts(Add.Name);
        puts(Add.Addr);
        printf("\n Pin Code: %ld", Add.Zip);
}
```

Summary of pointer to structure is given in **Table 8.1**. The summary given in **Table 8.1** can be discussed with the help of the following example. In this example, we have defined two structure variables and two pointers to structures.

Table 8.1 Summary Pointer to Structure
• *pointer.member is equivalent to *(pointer.member) is meaningful only when pointer is a structure with a pointer member. • (*pointer).member is equivalent to pointer'!member • Pointer.member[5] is equivalent to (pointer.member)[5] • pointer→member+5 is equivalent to (pointer →member)+5 the expression pointer→member+5 gives the address of the 5th element when we de-reference pointer→member+5, get the information stored at location pointed by pt→member+5, i.e., *(pointer→member+5). • *pointer.member is equivalent to *pointer'!member and is equivalent to *(pointer→member)

```
/** struct11.c **/
# include<stdio.h>
struct Mailing
{
        char Name[40];
        char Father[40];
        int Age;
        float Salary;
};

struct Mailing Record1 = {"TOM ALTER","WANT WATER", 32, 48000.75};
struct Mailing Record2 = {"JORG COOK", "MORTIN COOK", 50,
     32000.25};

void main()
{
        struct Mailing *ptr1, *ptr2;
        ptr1 = &Record1;
        ptr2 = &Record2;
        printf("\n Detail of record 1 is as follows \n");
        printf("\n Name:"");
        puts(Record1.Name);
        printf(" Father:");
        puts(Record1.Father);
        printf(" Age: %d", Record1.Age);
        printf("\n Salary: %f", Record1.Salary);
        printf("\n");

        printf("\n Detail of record 1 with the help of pointer
     is as follows \n");
```

```
    printf("\n Name:");
    puts((*ptr1).Name);
    printf(" Father:");
    puts((*ptr1).Father);
    printf(" Age: %d", (*ptr1).Age);
    printf("\n Salary: %f", (*ptr1).Salary);
    printf("\n");
    printf("\n Detail of record 2 is as follows \n");
    printf("\n Name:");
    puts(Record2.Name);
    printf(" Father: ");
    puts(Record2.Father);
    printf(" Age: %d", Record2.Age);
    printf("\n Salary: %f", Record2.Salary);
    printf("\n");
    printf("\n Detail of record 2 with the help of pointer
is as follows \n");
    printf("\n Name:");
    puts((*ptr2).Name);
    printf(" Father:");
    puts((*ptr2).Father);
    printf(" Age: %d", (*ptr2).Age);
    printf("\n Salary: %f", (*ptr2).Salary);
    printf("\n");

    /*******************************************************/
    /* Different pointer operation */
    /*******************************************************/
    printf("\n Output through different pointer operation
\n");

    puts((*ptr1).Name);
    puts(ptr1->Name);
    printf(" %d",Record1.Age);
    printf("\n %d",(*ptr1).Age);
    printf("\n %d", ptr1->Age);

    printf("\n Byte level operation \n");
    printf("\n %c", Record1.Name[2]);
    printf("\n %c", (Record1.Name)[2]);
    printf("\n %s", ptr1->Name+2);
    printf("\n %s", (ptr1->Name)+2);

    printf("\n %c", *(ptr1->Name+2));
```

```
        printf("\n %c", ptr1->Name[2]);
        printf("\n %c", (ptr1->Name)[2]);

        printf("\n %c", *Record2.Name);
        printf("\n %c", *ptr2->Name);
        printf("\n %c", *(ptr2->Name));

        printf("\n %c", Record2.Name);
        printf("\n %c", *(Record2.Name));

        printf("\n %c", *Record2.Name+1);
        printf("\n %c", *ptr2->Name+1);
        printf("\n %c", *(ptr2->Name)+1);
}
```

In the above program segment following expressions contain the address of the string "TOM ALTER".

```
(*ptr1).Name
ptr1->Name
```

The value of the each of the following expressions is 32:

```
Record1.Age
(*ptr1).Age
ptr1->Age
```

The member dot (.) operator and the brackets [] have equal precedence and also have LTR associativity. Thus, we can say that the expression

```
Record1.Name[2]
```

is equivalent to

```
(Record1.Name)[2]
```

The value of **Record1.Name** is the address of the string "TOM ALTER" and the value of **Record1.Name[2]** is 3rd character M.

The pointer operator (*) has a higher precedence than +, so the expression

```
ptr1->Name+2
```

is equivalent to

```
(ptr1->Name)+2
```

The value of **ptr1->Name** is the address of the string "TOM ALTER", and the value of **ptr1->Name+2** is the address of the 3rd character. De-referencing **ptr1->Name+2** yields character M. Thus, the value of the expression

```
*(ptr1->Name+2)
```

is again M.

The pointer operator -> and the brackets [] have the same precedence and have LTR associativity. Thus, the expression

```
ptr1->Name[2]
```

is equivalent to

```
(ptr1->Name)[2]
```

Because the value of the **ptr1->Name** is the address of the string "TOM ALTER", the value of the **ptr1->Name[2]** is again M. We have shown that each of

```
Record1.Name[2]
*(ptr1->Name+2)
ptr1->Name[2]
```

is equal to M.

The value of each of the following expression is J because dot (.) operator has a higher precedence than *.

```
*Record2.Name
*ptr2->Name
*(ptr2->Name)
```

The expression

```
*Record2.Name
```

is equivalent to

```
*(Record2.Name)
```

The value of **Record2.Name** is the address of the string "JORG COOK". When we de-reference **Record2.Name**, we obtain the first character J. Again because → has a higher precedence than *, the last two expressions

```
*ptr2->Name
```

and

```
*(ptr2->Name)
```

are equivalent.

The value of the **ptr2->Name** is the address of the string "JORG COOK". When we de-reference **ptr2->Name**, we again obtain the first character J.

The value of each of the following expressions

```
*Record2.Name+1
*ptr2->Name+1
*(ptr2-Name)+1
```

is K.

For example, because * and dot (.) have a higher precedence than +, the expression ***Record2.Name+1** is equivalent to

```
(*Record2.Name)+1
```

Thus, we first evaluate ***Record2.Name** to obtain J. When we add 1 to J, we get K.

8.5 Structures and Functions

Structure variable can be used as return values from functions and passed to functions as arguments, just as simple variable can. This is powerful feature that greatly simplifies the use of structures and then the writing of well-constructed modular programs that use structures.

When we pass a member of a structure to a function, we are actually passing the value of that member to the function. Therefore, we are passing a simple variable. For example, consider the following syntax of structure:

```
struct MailingAddress
{
    char Name[40]; /* First member */
    char Father_Name[40]; /* Second member */
    char City[40]; /* Third member */
```

```
    long int Zip; /* Fourth member */
} Address;
```

Suppose, we have defined function **pass_struct()** that accepts (receives) **char** type (string), the individual member can be passed like:

```
    pass_struct(Address1.Name)
```

will accept structure member Name (first member). Similarly,

```
    pass_struct (Address1.Father_Name);
    pass_struct (Address1.City);
```

will accept second and third member namely **Father_Name** and **City,** respectively. If we want to pass location of an individual structure member, we use & operator before the structure name. For example, to pass the address of the member of the structure **Address1**, we write

```
pass_struct (&Address1.Name[0]); /* Passed base address of the
    array member Name */
pass_struct (&Address1.Father_Name[0]); /* Passed base address of
    the array member Father_Name */
```

Go through the Example 8.7 for the implementation of the discussion.

Example 8.7: Write C code which defines user function. This function receives a struct as an argument.

Answer: For example, consider the following program segment (struct12.c) that implements the simple struct member acceptance. In the next two strcut13.c and struc14.c finally we have implemented the complete code.

```
/* struct12.c */
# include<stdio.h>
struct MailingAddress
{
    char Name[40]; /* First member */
    char Father_Name[40]; /* Second member */
    char City[40]; /* Third member */
    long int Zip; /* Fourth member */
} Address;

void pass_struct(char str[]);

void main()
{
    struct MailingAddress Address1 = {"Tom Alter", "Tom Cook",
        "California", 93561 };

    pass_struct(Address1.Name);
    pass_struct(Address1.Father_Name);
    pass_struct(&Address1.Name[0]);
    pass_struct(&Address1.Father_Name[0]);
}
```

```
void pass_struct(char str[])
{
   puts(str);
}
```

When a structure is used as an argument to a function, the entire structure is passed using the standard call-by-value method. Of course, this means that any changes made to the contents of the structure inside the function, to which it is passed, do not affect the structure used as an argument.

When using a structure as a parameter, we must keep in mind that the type of the argument must match the type of the parameter passed. For example, consider the following program segment where both the argument **Act** and **Ref** are declared as the same type of structure:

```
/** struct13.c **/
# include<stdio.h>
struct Tag_Name
{
   int a;
   char b;
   float f;
};

void fun (struct Tag_Name Ref)
{
   printf("\n Value of a is %d", Ref.a);
   printf("\n Value of b is %c", Ref.b);
   printf("\n Value of f is %f", Ref.f);
}

void main()
{
   struct Tag_Name Act;
   Act.a = 200;
   Act.b = 'C';
   Act.f = 875.75;
   fun (Act);
}
```

As the above program segment illustrates, if we are declaring structure parameters, we must make the declaration of the structure type global, so that all parts of the program can use them. For example, **Tag_Name** been declared inside the function **main** (), it would not have been visible to **fun().**

As just stated, when passing structures, the type of the argument must match the type of the parameter. It is not sufficient for them to simply be physically similar, and then type names must match. For example, consider the following program segment that is similar to previous one and it does not compile because the type name of the argument used to call **fun** () differs from the type name of its parameters.

```
/** struct14.c **/
# include<stdio.h>
struct Tag_Name
{
   int a;
   char b;
   float f;
};
struct Tag_Name1
{
   int a;
   char b;
   float f;
};

void fun (struct Tag_Name1 Ref)
{
   printf("\n Value of a is %d", Ref.a);
   printf("\n Value of b is %c", Ref.b);
   printf("\n Value of f is %f", Ref.f);
}

void main()
{
   struct Tag_Name Act;

   Act.a = 200;
   Act.b = 'C';
   Act.f = 875.75;
   fun (Act);
}
```

8.6 Structures and Arrays

See section 8.4.2.

8.7 Arrays of Structures

See section 8.4.3.

8.8 Structures containing Arrays

The programming language 'C' allows a structure to have one or more members of the array type. The compiler allows to initialize the members of a structure even if an array data type is a member of the structure.

8.9 Unions

Unions are used in C Language to save storage space when we need to store *any one* of a variety of C language data types in a location. Unions are declared in the same fashion as structs, but have a fundamental difference. Only one item within the union can be used at any time, because the memory allocated for each item inside the union is in a shared memory location. The syntax is

```
union   Tag name
{
    Datatype1    field1;    Datatype2    field2;    Datatype3
      field3;
    ...
   Datatypen    fieldn;
};

   For example, consider the following declaration of union:

union Data_Types
{
   char Ch;
   int Integer_Number;
   long int Int_Long_Number;
   float Float_Number;
   double Double_Number;
};
```

The above declaration does not create any variables. We can declare a variable by either placing its name at the end of the declaration or by using a separate declaration statement. To declare a **union** variable data of type **Data_Types,** we use the definition such that: **union Data_Types Data**;

In **Data**, character **Ch**, integer **Integer_Number**, long integer **Integer_Long_Number**, floating point number **Float_Number** and double **Double_Number** share the same memory locations. To access a member of union, same syntax is used as we have used for the structures. The dot (.), arrow (→), and pointer (*) operators will work in the case of union. If we want to operate directly on the union, we use dot operator. If the union is accessed through a pointer we use arrow operator or use pointer and dot operators. For example, assign **char c** to the field variable **Ch** of **Data** we use:

```
   Data.Ch = 'c';
```

If a pointer to **Data** is passed to a function, we use:

```
   Data_Type Fun (Data_Type *Member)
   {
      Member->Ch = 'c';
      Member->Integer_Number= 100;
      Member->Float_Number = 20.50;
      (*Member).Double_Number = 30.5;
      return (Member);
   }
```

Union helps in production of machine independent (portable) codes. Because the compiler keeps track of the actual size of the union members, no machine dependencies are produced, which means that one should not worry about the size of an **int, long, char, float, double** or whatsoever it is. Go through Example 8.8 which is implementing above discussion.

Example 8.8: Write C code which is demonstrating union operation.

Answer: Consider the following program segment that illustrates how the union shares the common memory area in different variables:

```
/** struct14.c **/
# include<stdio.h>
union demo
{
        char ch;
        int i_num;
        float f_num;
};
void main()
{
        union demo info;
        info.ch = 'A';
        info.i_num = 1234;
        info.f_num = 345.23;
        printf("\n0x %x <= address of ch \n", &info.ch);
        printf("\n0x %x <= address of i_num \n", &info.i_num);
        printf("\n0x %x <= address of f_num \n", &info.f_num);
        printf(" \n Output result ");
        printf("\n %c <= value of ch \n", info.ch);
        printf("\n %d <= value of i_num \n", info.i_num);
        printf("\n %f <= value of f_num \n", info.f_num);
        printf("\n  Press a key");
        getchar();
}
```

OUTPUT

0x fff2 <= address of ch

0x fff2 <= address of i_num

0x fff2 <= address of f_num

Output result

q <= value of ch

-25231 <= value of i_num

345.230011 <= value of f_num

Press a key

From the output of the above program segment, it is clear that different data types are mapped on the longest size of data.

The unions are generally used with **register** type of variables to save time and space. The union can also be assigned to another union of same type like structure. See Example 8.9 for the implementation.

Example 8.9: Consider the following program segment that implements the above discussion.

```
/** struct15.c **/
# include<stdio.h>
union data
{
        char name[30];
        int age ;
        float salary ;
};

void main()
{
        union data d;
        union data *d1;
        d.age = 30 ;
        d.salary = 7500;
        d1 =  &d;  /* assign address of the d to d1 */
        printf("\n%d",d1->age);
        printf("\n%f",d1->salary);
        printf("\n  Press a key");
        getchar() ;
}
```

8.9.1 Initialization of Union

An initializer for a union is a brace-enclosed single value. The initializer is preceded by an equal sign (=). The default initializer for a union with static storage is the default for the first component; a union with automatic storage has no default initialization. There are two ways to specify initializers for unions:

1. With C89-style initializers, only the first member of a union can be initialized.
2. Using *designated* initializers, a C99 feature which allows us to *name* members to be initialized, any (single) member of a union can be initialized.

Using C89-style initialization, the following example shows how we would initialize the first union member birthday of the union variable people:

```
union
{
      char birthday[9];
      int age;
      float weight;
```

```
} people = {"23/07/57"};
```

Using a designated initializer in the same example, the following initializes the second union member age:

```
union
{
        char birthday[9];
        int age;
        float weight;
} people = {.age = 14};   /* few C compiler does permit such type
     of initialization */
```

8.9.2 Typedef

Although typedef is thought of as being a storage class, it is not really. A **typedef** declaration lets us define our own identifiers that can be used in place of type specifiers such as **int**, **float**, and **double**. A **typedef** declaration does not reserve storage. The names we define using **typedef** are not new data types, but synonyms for the data types or combinations of data types they represent. The name space for a **typedef** name is the same as other identifiers. The exception to this rule is if the **typedef** name specifies a variably modified type. In this case, it has block scope. When an object is defined using a **typedef** identifier, the properties of the defined object are exactly the same as if the object were defined by explicitly listing the data type associated with the identifier. The following statements declare LENGTH as a synonym for **int** and then use this **typedef** to declare length, width, and height as integer variables:

```
typedef int LENGTH;
LENGTH length, width, height;
```

The following declarations are equivalent to the above declaration:

int length, width, height;

Following code segment discusses other level of typedef used in the declaration.

```
typedef int aaa, bbb, ccc;
typedef int ar[15], arr[9][6];
typedef char c, *cp, carr[100];

/* Now declare some objects */


/* all ints */
aaa     int1;
bbb     int2;
ccc     int3;
ar      yyy;      /* array of 15 ints */
arr     xxx;      /* 9*6 array of int */
c        ch;      /* a char */
cp      pnt;      /* pointer to char */
carr    chry;     /* array of 100 char */
```

The general rule with the use of **typedef** is to write out a declaration as if we are declaring variables of the types that we want. Where a declaration would have introduced names with particular types, prefixing the whole thing with **typedef** means that, instead of getting variables declared, we declare new type names instead. Those new type names can then be used as the prefix to the declaration of variables of the new type.

The use of **typedef** is not a particularly common sight in most programs; it is typically found only in header files and is rarely the province of day-to-day coding.

It is sometimes found in applications requiring very high portability: there, new types will be defined for the basic variables of the program and appropriate **typedef**s used to tailor the program to the target machine. This can lead to code which C programmers from other environments will find difficult to interpret if it is used to excess. The flavour of it is shown below:

```
/* file 'mytype.h' */
typedef short    SMALLINT    /* range *******30000 */
typedef int      BIGINT      /* range ******* 2E9 */

/* program */
#include "mytype.h"

SMALLINT            i;
BIGINT              loop_count;
```

On some machines, the range of an int would not be adequate for a BIGINT which would have to be re-typedefed to be long. To reuse a name already declared as a typedef, its declaration must include at least one type specifier, which removes any ambiguity:

```
typedef int new_thing;
func(new_thing x)
{
        float new_thing;
        new_thing = x;
}
```

As a word of warning, **typedef** can only be used to declare the type of return value from a function, not the overall type of the function. The overall type includes information about the function's parameters as well as the type of its return value.

```
/* Using typedef, declare func to have type 'function taking two
     int arguments, returning int*/
typedef int func(int, int);

/* ERROR */
func func_name{ /*....*/ }

/* Correct. Returns pointer to a type 'func' */
func *func_name(){ /*....*/ }

/* Correct if functions could return functions, but C cannot.*/
func func_name(){ /*....*/ }
```

If a typedef of a particular identifier is in scope, that identifier may not be used as the formal parameter of a function. This is because something like the following declaration causes a problem:

```
typedef int i1_t, i2_t, i3_t, i4_t;
int f(i1_t, i2_t, i3_t, i4_t) /*THIS IS POINT 'X'*/
```

A compiler reading the function declaration reaches point 'X' and still does not know whether it is looking at a function declaration, essentially similar to

```
int f(int, int, int, int) /* prototype */
```

or

```
int f(a, b, c, d) /* not a prototype */
```

The problem is only resolvable (in the worst case) by looking at what follows point 'X'; if it is a semicolon, then that was a declaration, if it is a '{' then that was a definition. The rule forbidding **typedef** names to be formal parameters means that a compiler can always tell whether it is processing a declaration or a definition by looking at the first identifier following the function name.

The use of **typedef** is also valuable when we want to declare things whose declaration syntax is painfully impenetrable, like "array of ten pointers to array of five integers", which tends to cause panic even amongst the hardy. Hiding it in a **typedef** means we only have to read it once and can also help to break it up into manageable pieces:

```
typedef int (*a10ptoa5i[10])[5];
/* or */
typedef int a5i[5];
typedef a5i *atenptoa5i[10];
```

Let us Revise

1. C provides a method of grouping all this information into one name called **structure** or **struct**.
2. Structure is a part of C which provides a means of defining a single variable that is actually comprised of many different data types. In more technical terms, we can say that a **struct** is a derived data type comprised of a collection of intrinsic (primary) data types.
3. Opening and closing braces with semicolon means a structure works like a single statement.
4. A structure type is usually defined near to the start of a file using a typedef statement. typedef defines and names a new type, allowing its use throughout the program.
5. It is possible to assign the value of one structure variable to another variable of the same type using a simple assignment statement.
6. Providing values of fields as a set does the initialization, i.e., an initialization for a struct is a brace enclosed comma separated list of values.
7. When it is required to represent same type of records more than once, it is done through an array representation.
8. Structure variable can be used as return values from functions and passed to functions as arguments, just as simple variable can.
9. Unions are used in C Language to save storage space when we need to store *any one* of a variety of C language data types in a location.
10. An initializer for a union is a brace-enclosed single value.

Multiple Choice Questions

1. A structure is
   (a) Grouping of variables under one name (b) Compound data type
   (c) Conglomerate (d) All of the above
2. The variables that make up the structure are called
   (a) Members (b) Elements
   (c) Fields (d) All of the above

3. When accessing a structure member, the identifier to the left of the dot (period) operator is the name of

(a) A structure name (b)A structure tag name

(c) A structure variable (d) The keyword struct

4. An enumeration data type brings together a group of

(a) Items of different data types (b) Related data variables

(c) Integers with user defined names (d) Constant values

5. If one defines

(i) enum boolean {False, True};

(ii) enum boolean {True, False};

(a) (i) is correct (b) (ii) is correct

(c) (i) and (ii) both are correct (d) none of these

6. Before one can access a member of structure, one must

(a) Declare the structure (b) Define a structure

(c) Give the item in (b) and (a) (d) None of these

7. Array elements must all be of the _______________, whereas structure member may be of _______________.

(a) same data type, different data types (b) different data types, different data types,

(c) none of these

8. The closing brace of a structure is followed by a _______________.

(a) ; (b) ,

(c) : (c) none of these

9. The four members of an **enum** type are normally represented by the values _________, _________, _________ and _________.

(a) 0,1,2,3 (b) 1,2,3, 4

(c) none of these

10. It is possible to pass a structure to a function in the same way as a simple variable is passed.

(a) True (b) False

11. An appropriate use for a structure is to store a list of information.

(a) True (b) False

12. A **typedef** may be used only with a tagged structure.

(a) True (b) False

13. When using a **typedef** to declare a structure, the **typedef** name may be the same as a structure is tagged

(a) True (b) False

14. Can a structure have both a tag and a type name?

(a) True (b) False

True/False Questions

1. A structure cannot be a member of a union.
2. The operator ---> is not left to right associative.
3. A structure can be passed to a function in C through call-by-value mechanism.
4. When one of the fields of a structure is itself a structure, it is called nested structure.

5. There is limit to nesting of structures.
6. A structure cannot be passed to a 'C' function through the call by value mechanism.
7. 'struct' in 'C' language is used to define new data types.
8. We cannot create structures within structures in C.

Match Columns

Match the matter in Column A with the matter in Column B.

Column A	Column B
A. struct	1. <ctype.h>
B. #define	2. <math.h>
C. isalpha()	3. union
D. rand()	4. records with varying components
E. space untilization	5. compile time directive

Fill in the Blanks with Appropriate Words

a. storage b. (*p) c. period(.) d. union

1. The ___________ operator is used in between the union variable name and the fieldname.
2. The ________ only holds a value for one data type of the larger storage of their members.
3. Unions contain members of different data types which share the same _________ area in memory.
4. If 'p' is a pointer to a structure the "p --> p" is same as ________.

Descriptive Type Questions

1. What errors, if any, do occur in the following code?

```
struct Jams_Bond
{
    char *Jing;
    char *Jang;
    long ZIP;
}Jams_Bond;

Jing = "Jing lives in California";
Jang = "Jang lives in New Delhi";
```

2. Find error in the following declaration of structure and write the correct code.

```
struct Link
{
    char Node_Info1 [20]; /* Member 1 */
    char Node_Info2[20]; /* Member 2 */
    struct Link next;
};
```

3. What is the error in the following declaration of a structure with a pair of bit-field members?

```
struct Saving
{
    signed int Member1 3;
    unsigned int Member2 16;
```

```
} Variable;
```

Correct the error and write the error free code for the said code and assign values to the variable **Variable.Member1** and **Variable.Member2**.

4. Is there any error in the following program segment? If there is no error, find output of the program segment?

```
# include<stdio.h>
enum Player {Ramesh = 1, Saurabh, Dravid, Sachin, Azharuddin,
     Mongia};
enum One, Two;
One = 12;
Two = 14;
void main()
{
   printf("\n %d", One, Two);
}
```

5. Why is it not legal to use == to test whether two structures are equal?
6. Why does C provide two ways to name structure types **Tags** and **typedef** names?
7. When one tried using **sizeof** to determine the number of bytes in a structure, one got a number that was larger than the sizes of the members added together. How can this be?
8. What is difference between structure and array?
9. Discuss the difference between an array of structure variable that has an array as a member.
10. What is structure Tag?
11. Does any member variables of two different structures have the same name? If 'yes', how is it differentiated by the compiler?
12. What is main difference between a structure and a union?
13. Can a structure be nested in a union?
14. Can one union be nested in another?
15. Under what circumstances would one prefer a union to a structure?
16. What is the main difference between a bit-field and other members of a structure?
17. Can a structure be declared with a mix of bit-field and regular members?
18. In the following code identify the Tag, the members and the structure variable:

```
struct Mailing_List
{
   char Name[40];
   char Father_Name[40];
   char Street[70];
   char City[20];
   char State[20];
   long int ZIP;
} Ram, Bahadur, Eishita, Rachita;
```

19. Are the following statements equivalent?

```
printf("\n %s", *(pointer).Name);
printf("\n %s", pointer-> Name);
```

20. Are the following statements equivalent?

```
    scanf( %s", *(pointer).Name);
    scanf(" %s", pointer->Name);
```

21. Consider the following program segment:

```
struct Scooter
{
    int Wheels;
    int Brakes;
    float BHP;
} Scooter;

struct Automobile
{
    char Make[40];
    char Model[40];
    int Year;
    struct Scooter Scoot, *Scoot_Ptr;
} Car, *Ptr;

Ptr * & Car;
Car.Scoot_Ptr = &Car.Scoot;
Ptr->Make= "Bajaj";
Car.Scoot.Wheels = 3;
```

(a) In how many ways the string "*Bajaj*" can be accessed?

(b) In how many ways the integer 3 can be accessed.

Answers to Objective Type Questions

Multiple Choice Questions

1. a	2. b	3. c	4. a
5. c	6. b	7. a	8. c
9. b	10. a	11. a	12. c
13. b	14. c		

True False Questions

1. F	2. F	3. T	4. T
5. F	6. F	7. T	8. F

Matching Columns

A. c	B. d	C. e	D. a
E. b			

Fill in the Blanks

1. c	2. d	3. a	4. b

Pointers

9

9.1 Address Operators

Pointers form the heart and soul of C and give the programmer the power to deal with the machine architecture. Unfortunately, beginners find it difficult to get a strong foothold in pointers. In fact, understanding the asics of pointers is more than enough for dealing with code involving pointers.

Pointer is a variable that refers or points to another variable. In other words, a pointer contains an address of a memory location. The following piece of code declares a pointer variable to an integer

```
int i = 10;
int *ptr = &i;
```

Follow the diagram depicted below for a better understanding.

1000	10
Name of the variable : ptr	Name of the variable : i
Address : xxxx	Address : 1000

9.2 Pointer Type Declaration

In **C** pointers may be treated as standard variable in many ways and may behave a bit differently in some operations. They can be used in high-powered constructs for which no other standard variable can be used. There are many aspects of pointers and several programmers are not accustomed to using them. Careless use of pointers can easily result in a program enigma that is nearly impossible to understand.

A pointer is a variable that points at, or refers to, another variable. A pointer is a special variable that holds a memory address. In C when we define a pointer variable we do so by preceding its name with an asterisk. We also give pointer a type which, in this case, refers to the type of data stored at the address we will be storing in pointer. For example, consider the variable declaration:

```
int *ptr;
```

ptr is the name of a variable (just as **k** is the name of int variable shown in the earlier section). The '*' informs the compiler that we want a pointer variable, i.e., to set aside however many bytes is required to store an address in memory. The **int** says that we intend to use a pointer variable to store the address of an integer. Such a pointer is said to "point to" an integer. However, note that when we wrote **int k;** we did not give **k** a value. If this definition is made outside of any function ANSI compliant compilers will initialize it to zero. Similarly, **ptr** has no value that is we have not stored an address in it in the above declaration. In this case, again if the declaration is outside of any function, it is initialized to a value guaranteed in such a way that it is guaranteed to not point to any C object or function. A pointer initialized in this manner is called a "null" pointer.

The actual bit pattern used for a null pointer may or may not evaluate to zero since it depends on the specific system on which the code is developed. To make the source code compatible between various compilers on various systems, a macro is used to represent a null pointer. That macro goes under the name NULL. Thus, setting the value of a pointer using the NULL macro, as with an assignment statement such as ptr = NULL, guarantees that the pointer has become a null pointer. Similarly, just as one can test for an integer value of zero, as in **if (k == 0)**, we can test for a null pointer using **if (ptr == NULL)**, but, back to using our new variable **ptr**. Suppose now that we want to store in **ptr** the address of int variable **k**. To do this we use the unary **&** operator and write:

```
ptr = &k;
```

What the **&** operator does is retrieve the lvalue (address) of **k**, even though **k** is on the right hand side of the assignment operator '=', and copies that to the contents of pointer **ptr**. Now, **ptr** is said to "point to" **k**. There is only one more operator we need to discuss. The "dereferencing operator" is the asterisk and it is used as follows:

```
*ptr = 7;
```

will copy 7 to the address pointed to by **ptr**. Thus, if **ptr** "points to" (contains the address of) **k**, the above statement will set the value of **k** to 7. That is, when we use the '*' this way we are referring to the value of that which ptr is pointing to, not the value of the pointer itself. Similarly, we can write:

```
printf("%d\n",*ptr);
```

to print on the screen the integer value stored at the address pointed to by **ptr**;.

One way to see how all this stuff fits together see Example 9.1.

Example 9.1: Write C code for demonstrating the *, & and void.

Answer: Run the following program and then review the code and the output carefully.

```
/** Pointer2.c **/
#include <stdio.h>
int j, k;
int *ptr;

main(void)
{
     j = 1;
     k = 2;
     ptr = &k;
     printf("\n");
     printf("j has the value %d and is stored at %p\n", j, (void
      *)&j);
     printf("k has the value %d and is stored at %p\n", k, (void
      *)&k);
     printf("ptr has the value %p and is stored at %p\n",
      ptr,(void *)&ptr);
     printf("The value of the integer pointed to by ptr is %d\n",
      *ptr);
     return 0;
}
```

OUTPUT

j has the value 1 and is stored at 06F4:041E

k has the value 2 and is stored at 06F4:041C

ptr has the value 06F4:041C and is stored at 06F4:0418

The value of the integer pointed to by ptr is 2

Pointers provide two main features

- It provides a very fast means of referencing array elements.
- In functions it is used to modify calling parameters.

9.3 Pointer Assignment

A pointer is always assigned with an address value. The following assignment statement makes a pointer variable to point to another variable.

```
int *ptr;
int i = 10;
ptr = & i;
/* ptr is pointing to the variable i       */
   ptr = 0; ptr = NULL;
/* ptr is pointing to nothing              */
```

NULL is a macro defined in <stdio.h>. When a pointer is assigned to NULL, it is guaranted to point to nothing. A pointer can be assigned to any valid memory address. The memory address should hold a valid variable of that particular type. When an address of a different data type is assigned to a pointer of a different data type, it may give rise to run-time errors.

9.4 Pointer Initialization

Of course, just like other variables, we have to declare pointers before we can use them. Pointer declarations look much like other declarations: but do not be misled. When pointers are declared, the keyword at the beginning (int, char and so on) declares the type of variable that the pointer will point to. The pointer itself is not of that type, it is of type pointer to that type. A given pointer only points to one particular type, not to all possible types. A pointer represents a memory address of a variable. A pointer variable is one that holds a pointer to a value of its specified type. The syntax to declare a pointer type variable is

```
Data type pointer operator variable name;
```

For example, the declaration of an array and three pointers (one char two other are ints) are

```
char   *ch ;   /* here address of char  data  type  is kept
   with variable ch */
int *i , *ip; /* here address of int data type is kept  with
   variables i  and ip*/
int list[5];
```

The '*' in front of **ip** in the declaration shows that it is a pointer not an ordinary variable. It is of type pointer to int, and can only be used to refer to variables of type int. It is still uninitialized, so to do anything useful with it, it has to be made to point to something. We cannot just stick some integer value into it, because integer values have the type int, not pointer to int, which is what we want. For example, in any case, what would it means if the following code is:

```
ip = 6;
```

What would ip be pointing to? In fact it could be construed to have a number of meanings, but the simple fact is that, in C is just wrong. The operator & is a unary operator and returns the memory address of its operand. The syntax to declare or to assign is

```
Data type variable name = &variable name;
```

For example, see the following code slice

```
int x = 234   ;
int *point   = &x ;
int list[5], *ip;
ip = &list[3];
```

In this example, the **point** will hold the address of variable **x**, actually address is a **RAM** memory location where operating system saves program and data during running time. Let **x** exist in memory location **0xff00** and its value be 234 then after the statement

```
point = &x ;
```

the value of **point** will be the address of **x**, i.e., is **0xff00** rather than 234, Figure 9.1 illustrates the idea.

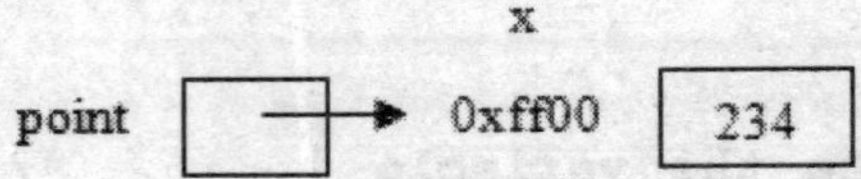

Figure 9.1 Point points to x

The pointer *ip is made to point to the member of the array **list** whose index is 3, i.e., the fourth member. This is important. We can assign values to pointers just like ordinary variables; the difference is simply in what the value means. The values of the variables that we have now are shown in Figure 9.2 (? means un-initialized).

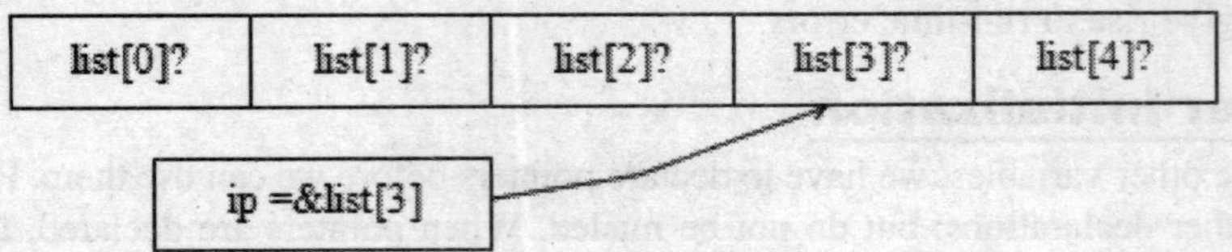

Figure 9.2 Array and initialized pointer

We can see that the variable ip has the value of the expression &list[3]. The arrow indicates that, when used as a pointer, ip points to the variable list[3].

What is this new unary &? It is usually described as the 'address-of' operator, since on many systems the pointer will hold the store address of the thing that it points to. If we understand what addresses are, then we will probably have more trouble than those who do not: thinking about pointers as if they were addresses generally leads to grief. What seems a perfectly reasonable address manipulation on processor X can almost always be shown to be impossible on manufacturer Y's washing machine controller which uses 17-bit addressing when it is on the spin cycle, and reverses the order of odd and even bits when it is out of bleach. We will continue to use the term 'address of' though, because to invent a different one would be even worse. Applying the & operator to an operand returns a pointer to the operand:

```
int i;
float f;
int *ip;
float *fp;
ip = &i;         /* '&i' would be of type pointer to int */
```

```
fp = &f; /* '&f' would be of type pointer to float */
```

In the above declaration each case the pointer would point to the object named in the expression.

A pointer is only useful if there is some way of getting at the thing that it points to. C uses the unary * operator for this job. If p is of type 'pointer to something', then *p refers to the thing that is being pointed to. The operator '*' is the complement of **&**. This gives the value of the location. The syntax is

```
Data type *variable name;
```

For example consider the following code segment:

```
 int *a ;
int c ;
int m = 100 ;
a = &m
c = *a ;
```

In the above example, the value of **m** is 100, value of **a** is location of **m** and value of **c** is value of **a, a** points to **m**, so that the value of **c** will be the value of **m,** i.e., 100. The discussion is illustrated in Figure 7.3. Example 9.2 implements this discussion.

Example 9.2: Write C code for finding the relationship between * and &.

Answer: See the following program segment (Pointer3.C) that demonstrates functionality of * and &. Further in program segment Pointer4.C and Pointer5.C relationship of * and & implemented more precisely.

```
/* Pointer3.C */
# include<stdio.h>
void main()
{
   char value; /* value is char type */
   char ch = 'A'; /* ch is char type */
   char * address; /* pointer variable address is char type */
   address = &ch; /* assign address of ch to pointer variable
      address */
   value = *address;
   printf("\n Address of ch:0x%X", address); /* prints address of
      ch */
   printf("\n Value of ch: %d", value ); /* prints integer value
      of 'A' */
   printf("\n Value of ch: %c", value); /* prints value of ch */
}
```

OUTPUT
Address of ch: 0x7FFFFF0A
Value of ch: 65
Value of Ch: A

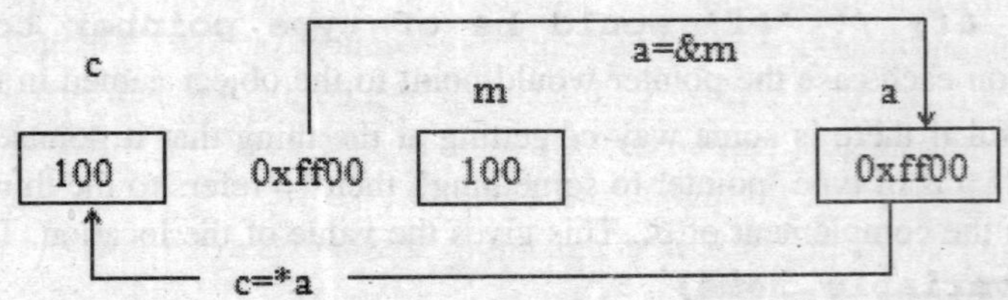

Figure 9.3 Accessing Value of variable via an indirect pointer

In the following example we are accessing the variable x via the pointer variable p.

```
/** Pointer4.C **/
#include <stdio.h>
#include <stdlib.h>
main()
{
        int x, *p;
        p = &x;             /* initialize pointer */
        *p = 0;             /* set x to zero */
        printf("x is %d\n", x);
        printf("*p is %d\n", *p);
        *p += 1;            /* increment what p points to */
        printf("x is %d\n", x);
        (*p)++;             /* increment what p points to */
        printf("x is %d\n", x);
        exit(0);
}
```

OUTPUT

x is 0
*p is 0
x is 1
x is 2

It should be noted that, since & takes the address of an object, returning a pointer to it, and since * means 'the thing pointed to by the pointer', the & and * in the combination *& effectively cancel each other out. But some things, constants for example, do not have addresses and the & operator cannot be applied to them; e.g., &1.5 is not a pointer to anything, it is an error. It is also interesting to see that C is one of the few languages that allow an expression on the left-hand side of an assignment operator. In the above example: the expression *p occurs twice in that position, and then the amazing (*p)++; statement. That last one is a great puzzle to most beginners—even if we have managed to wrap mind around the concept that *p = 0 writes zero into the thing pointed to by p, and that *p += 1 adds one to where p points, it still seems a bit much to apply the ++ operator to *p.

The precedence of (*p)++ deserves some thought. It will be given more later, but for the moment let us work out what happens. The brackets ensure that the * applies to p, so what we have is "post-increment the thing pointed to by p". It turns out that ++ and * have equal precedence (or just ++ is just one above the *), but they associate right to left; in other words, without the brackets, the implied operation would have been *(p++), whatever that would mean. Later on we will be more used to it—for the moment, we will be careful with brackets to show the way that those expressions work.

So, provided that a pointer holds the address of something, the notation *pointer is equivalent to giving the name of the something directly. What benefit do we get from all this? Well, straight away it gets round the call-by-value restriction of functions. Imagine a function that has to return, say, two integers representing a month and a day within that month. The function has some (unspecified) way of determining these values; the hard thing to do is to return two separate values. For example, see the following:

```
/**   Pointer5.C      **/
#include <stdio.h>
#include <stdlib.h>
void date(int *, int *);       /* declare the function */

main()
{
        int month, day;
        date (&day, &month);
        printf("day is %d, month is %d\n", day, month);
        exit(0);
}

void date(int *day_p, int *month_p)
{
      int day_ret, month_ret;
   printf("input day and month");
   scanf("%d%d",&day_ret,&month_ret);
        /* At this point, calculate the day and month values in
      day_ret and month_ret respectively. */
        *day_p = day_ret;
        *month_p = month_ret;
}
```

Notice carefully the advance declaration of date showing that it takes two arguments of type 'pointer to int'. It returns void, because the values are passed back via the pointers, not he usual return value. The main function passes pointers as arguments to date, which first uses the internal variables day_ret and month_ret for its calculations, then takes those values and assigns them to the places pointed to by its arguments. When date is called, the situation looks like Figure 9.4.

The arguments have been passed to date, but in main, day and month are un-initialized. When date reaches the return statement, the situation is as shown in Figure 9.5 (assuming that the values for day and month are 12 and 5, respectively).

One of the great benefits introduced in C is that it allows the types of the arguments to date to be declared

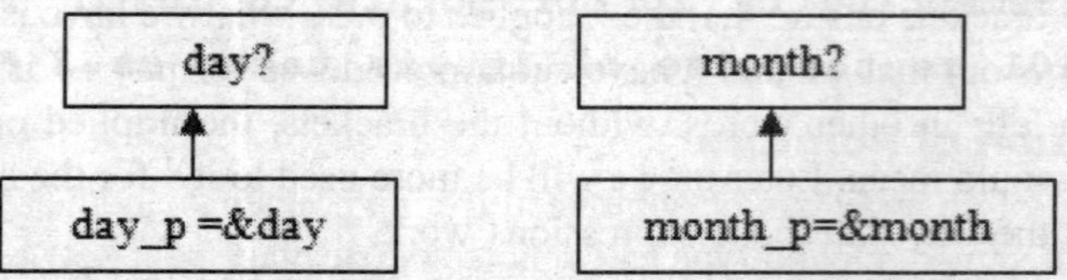

Figure 9.4 Just as date is called

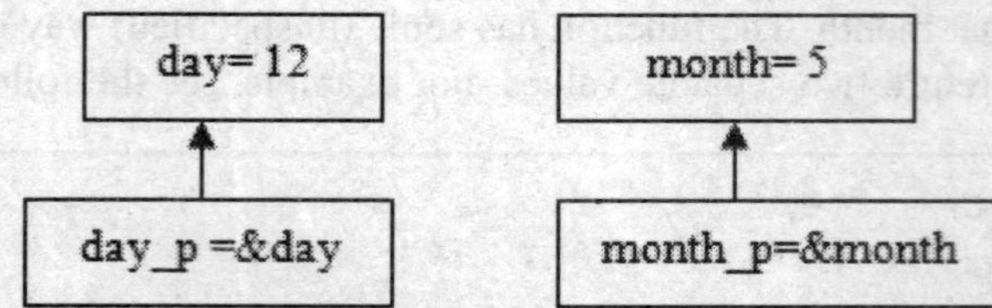

Figure 9.5 Just as date is about to return

in advance. A great favorite (and disastrous) mistake in C is to forget that a function expects pointers as its arguments, and to pass something else instead. Imagine what would have happened if the call of date above had read.

```
date(day, month);
```

and no previous declaration of date had been visible. The compiler would not have known that date expects pointers as arguments, so it would pass the int values of day and month as the arguments. On a large number of computers, pointers and integers can be passed in the same way, so the function would execute, then pass back its return values by putting them into wherever day and month would point if their contents were pointers. This is very unlikely to give any sensible results, and in general causes unexpected corruption of data elsewhere in the computer's store.

Fortunately, by declaring date in advance, the compiler has enough information to warn that a mistake has almost certainly been made. Perhaps surprisingly, it is not all that common to see pointers used to give this call-by-reference functionality. In the majority of cases, call-by-value and a single return value are adequate. What is *much* more common is to use pointers to 'walk' along arrays.

9.5 Pointer Arithmetic

Pointer arithmetic is one of the highlights of C's design. The intelligent conceptualization of pointer arithmetic gave uniform method of dealing with pointers to different data types. The following section discusses the various aspects of pointer arithmetic.

9.5.1 Addition/Subtraction with Integral values

The general rule for pointer arithmetic with integral type is:

Addition or subtraction of a pointer to integral type increments/decrements the pointer value by the product of the size of the object pointed by the pointer and the integral value.

This means incrementing a pointer of type char by 1, increments the pointer value by 1and incrementing a pointer of type int by 1, incrementss the pointer value by the size of an integer. For example,

```
int i = 0, *ptr+&1;
/* Assume ptr is pointing to the location 100    */
ptr = ptr + 1;
```

```
/* After incrementing by 1, ptr points to 102     */
/* and not 101 as the size of int is taken as 2 */
```

9.5.2 Subtraction of Pointers

A pointer to an element of an array can be subtracted from a pointer to another element of the same array. The resultant value is of signed integral type and denotes the displacement between the two objects pointed by two pointers. That is,

```
Value of (ptr1 - ptr2) = (ptr1 - ptr2)/size of object pointed by ptr1
or ptr2
```

For example,

```
int a[10], *p1, *p2, diff;
/* say address of a[0] is 100          */
p1 = &a[2];
/* p1 points to fthe location 104      */
p2 = &a[5];
/* p2 points to the location 110       */
diff = p2 - p1;
/* diff stores the value (110 - 104)/2 = 3      */
```

9.6 Functions and Pointers

It has been already discussed that arguments are passed to, from function by value. It is not possible to change the value of a calling program variable within a function, unless we have the address of a variable in the calling program. **C** functions have the capability of returning values that can be, in turn, assigned to variables within the calling program. However, through pointer operations, we can write specialized functions that will return a value to the calling program and change the values in other variables whose memory addresses are handed over to the function. In this fashion, it is possible to write a function that figuratively, returns many values in a single operation. While pointers are indispensable throughout all phases of **C** programming, their capabilities yield high-powered program performance, especially, when dealing with programmed functions. Go through the Example 9.3 which is implementing **by value** and **by reference**.

Example 9.3: Write C code to compute the cube of two numbers by using by value and by reference parameter technique in a function.

Answer: Consider the following program segment that illustrates the idea of parameter passing **by value** and **by reference**.

```
/* pointer24.c */
# include<stdio.h>
float cube(float a, float *b)
{
        *b = *b * *b * * b ; / rewrite memory */
        return (a * a * a);
}

void main()
```

```
{
        float x = 2.5;
        float y = 5.5;
        printf("\n cube of 2.5 is %f \n", cube(x, &y));
        printf("\n cube of 5.5 is %f", y);
}
```

OUTPUT

cube of 2.5 is 15.625000

cube of 5.5 is 166.375000

In the function **cude(), a** is an auto variable of type **float** and **b** is a pointer type of **float**. The address of **y** in the calling program was passed to the function **cube ()**. The value of this address was assigned to pointer **b** in the function. Figure 9.6 illustrates the status of the parameter **x** and **y** before and after the call made to the function **cube ()**.

The meaning of the expression

```
    *b = *b * *b * *b;
```

is given in Figure 9.7.

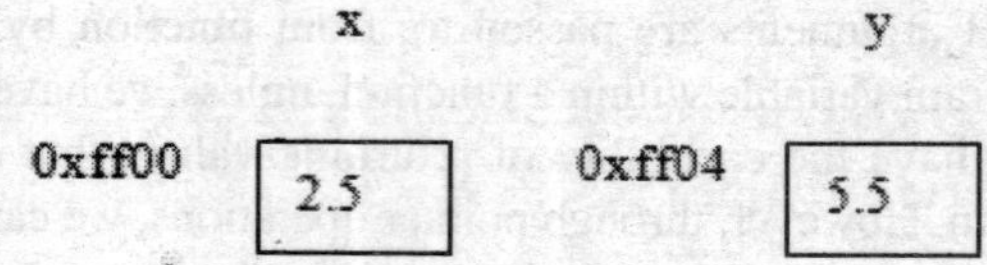

(a) x and y in memory a function call is made

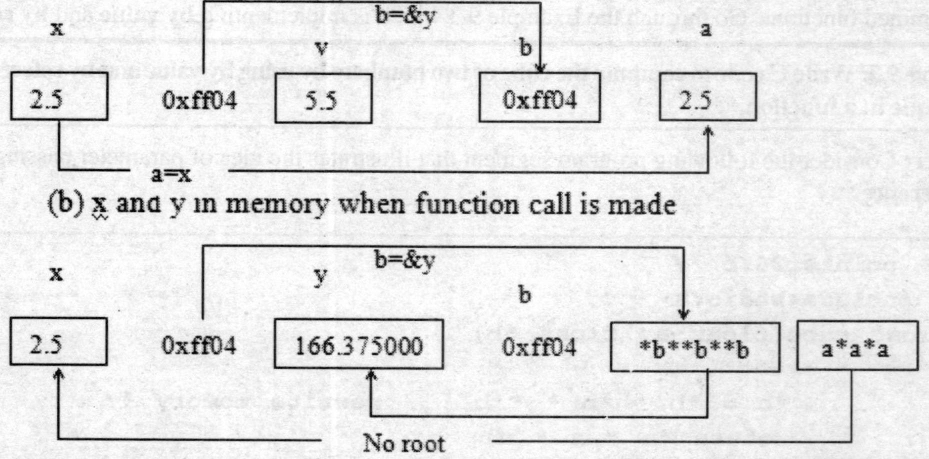

(b) x and y in memory when function call is made

(c) x and y in memory after function call is completed

Figure 9.6 POINTERS and functions

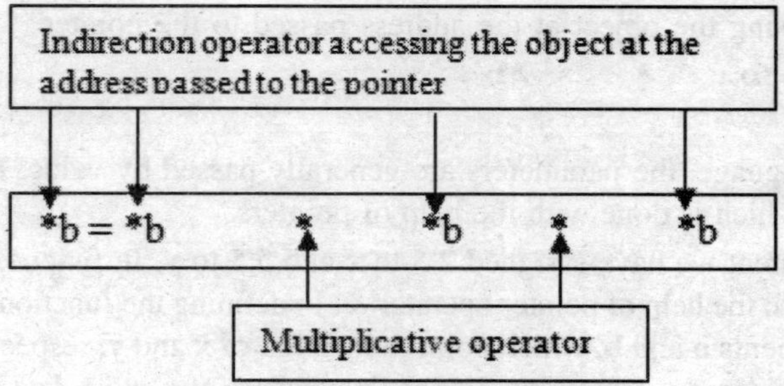

Figure 9.7 Reference by pointer

If **b** was a standard variable, the above code slice can be written as:

```
b = b * b* b;
```

The use of a single symbol to name several operators that perform differently in **C** is a very good reason to stick to established source code formatting conversions. All arithmetic operators should be separated from their variable names by a space. For example,

```
c = b * a;
```

This expression is far easier to decipher than the one that follows:

```
c = b*a;
```

The multiplication of pointer could also be written in **C** shorthand.

```
*b  *= *b * * b; /* cube of b */
```

The above program segment could also be written as follows:

```
/* Pointer25.c */
# include<stdio.h>

void cube(float *a, float *b)
{
        *b *= *b * *b;
        *a *= *a * *a;
}
void main()
{
        float x = 2.5;
        float y = 5.5;
        cube(&x, &y);
        printf("\n cube of 2.5 is %f \n", x);
        printf("\n cube of 5.5 is %f", y);
}
```

OUTPUT

cube of 2.5 is 15.625000
cube of 5.5 is 166.375000

Indirection operator accessing the object at the address passed to the pointer

```
*b = *b *     *b     *     *b
```

Multiplicative operator

As we are aware, in **C** language, the parameters are generally passed by value. Also it is possible to pass parameters by reference, which is done with the help of pointers.

In the above program segment we have assigned 2.5 to **x** and 5.5 to **y**. In function **cube ()** we have passed the addresses of **x** and **y** with the help of pointer operator &. In defining the function, we have used indirection operator '*' with the arguments **a** and **b**, which point to location of **x** and **y**, respectively. In the definition of **cube ()** function, **a** and **b** are dummy parameters. For getting address of **x** and **y**, i.e., where **x** and **y** are pointers, the following program segment can be used:

```
/* Pointer26.c */
# include<stdio.h>
void cube(float *a, float *b)
{
        *b *= *b * *b;
        *a *= *a * *a;
}
void main()
{
        float x = 2.5;
        float y = 5.5;
        cube(&x, &y);
        printf("\n Address of x is 0x%X",&x);
        printf("\n Address of y is 0x%X \n",&y);
        printf("\n cube of 2.5 is %f \n", x);
        printf("\n cube of 5.5 is %f", y);
}
```

OUTPUT
Address of x is 0xFFF2
Address of y is 0xFFEE
cube of 2.5 is 15.625000
cube of 5.5 is 166.375000

9.7 Arrays and Pointers

Let us consider why we need to identify the type of variable that a pointer points to, as in:

```
int *ptr;
```

One reason for doing this is so that later, once ptr "points to" something, if we write:

```
*ptr = 2;
```

The compiler will know how many bytes to copy into that memory location pointed to by ptr. If ptr was declared as pointing to an integer, 4 bytes would be copied. Similarly for floats and doubles the appropriate number will be copied. But, defining the type that the pointer points to permit a number of other interesting ways a compiler can interpret the code. For example, consider a block in memory consisting if 10 integers in a row. That is, 40 bytes of memory are set aside to hold 10 integers.

Now, let us say int pointer ptr points at the first of these integers. Furthermore let us say that integer is located at memory location 0xff00 (decimal). What happens when we write?

```
ptr + 1;
```

Because the compiler "knows" this is a pointer (i.e., its value is an address) and that it points to an integer (its current address, 0xff00, is the address of an integer), it adds 4 to ptr instead of 1, so the pointer "points to" the next integer, at memory location 0xff04. Similarly, were the ptr declared as a pointer to a short, it would add 2 to it instead of 1. The same goes for other data types such as floats, doubles, or even user defined data types such as structures. This is obviously not the same kind of "addition" that we normally think of. In C it is referred to as addition using "pointer arithmetic", a term which we will come back to later.

Similarly, since ++ptr and ptr++ are both equivalent to ptr + 1 (though the point in the program when ptr is incremented may be different), incrementing a pointer using the unary ++ operator, either pre- or post-, increments the address it stores by the amount sizeof (type) where "type" is the type of the object pointed to (i.e., 4 for an integer).

Since a block of 10 integers located contiguously in memory is, by definition, an array of integers, this brings up an interesting relationship between arrays and pointers. For example, consider the following code segment

```
int my_array[] = {1,23,17,4,-5,100};
```

Here we have an array containing 6 integers. We refer to each of these integers by means of a subscript to my_array, i.e., using my_array[0] through my_array[5]. But, we could alternatively access them via a pointer as follows:

```
int *ptr;
ptr = &my_array[0];          /* point at the first integer in
 the array */
```

And then we could print out elements of array either using the array notation or by dereferencing pointer. Go through the Example 9.4 which demonstrates the relationship of pointer and array.

Example 9.4: Write C code that implements the pointer and array.

Answer: The following program segment illustrates the discussion:

```
/**  Pointer6.C     **/
#include <stdio.h>

int my_array[] = {1,23,17,4,-5,100};
int *ptr;

int main(void)
{
    int i;
    ptr = &my_array[0];      /* point our pointer to the first
     element of the array */
    printf("\n\n");
    for (i = 0; i < 6; i++)
```

```
        {
            printf("my_array[%d] = %d      ",i,my_array[i]);    /*<-- A */
            printf("ptr + %d = %d\n",i, *(ptr + i));            /*<-- B */
        }
        return 0;
    }
```

OUTPUT

```
my_array[0] = 1   ptr + 0 = 1
my_array[1] = 23  ptr + 1 = 23
my_array[2] = 17  ptr + 2 = 17
my_array[3] = 4   ptr + 3 = 4
my_array[4] = -5  ptr + 4 = -5
my_array[5] = 100 ptr + 5 = 100
```

Compile and run the above program and carefully note lines A and B and that the program prints out the same values in either case. Also observe how we de-referenced pointer in line B, i.e., we first added i to it and then de-referenced the new pointer. Change line B to read:

```
printf("ptr + %d = %d\n",i, *ptr++);
```

and run it again then change it to:

```
printf("ptr + %d = %d\n",i, *(++ptr));
```

and try once more. Each time try and predict the outcome and carefully look at the actual outcome.

In C, the standard states that wherever we might use **&var_name[0]** we can replace that with **var_name**, thus in the program segment where we wrote:

```
ptr = &my_array[0];
```

we can write:

```
ptr = my_array;
```

to achieve the same result.

We prefer to mentally think "the name of the array is the address of first element in the array". Many beginners have a tendency to become confused by thinking of it as a pointer. For example, while we can write

```
ptr = my_array;
```

we cannot write

```
my_array = ptr;
```

The reason is that while **ptr** is a variable, **my_array** is a constant. That is, the location at which the first element of **my_array** will be stored cannot be changed once **my_array[]** has been declared.

Earlier when discussing the term "lvalue" where it stated: "An **object** is a named region of storage; an **lvalue** is an expression referring to an object". This raises an interesting problem. Since **my_array** is a named region of storage, why is **my_array** in the above assignment statement not an lvalue? To resolve this problem, some refer to **my_array** as an "unmodifiable lvalue". Modify the example program segment above by changing

```
ptr = &my_array[0];
```

to

```
ptr = my_array;
```

and run it again to verify the results are identical.

Now, let us delve a little further into the difference between the names **ptr** and **my_array** as used above. We refer to an array's name as a ***constant*** pointer. What do we mean by that? Well, to understand the term "constant" in this sense, let us go back to definition of the term "variable". When we declare a variable we set aside a spot in memory to hold the value of the appropriate type. Once that is done the name of the variable can be interpreted in one of two ways. When used on the left side of the assignment operator, the compiler interprets it as the memory location to which to move that value resulting from evaluation of the right side of the assignment operator. But, when used on the right side of the assignment operator, the name of a variable is interpreted to mean the contents stored at that memory address set aside to hold the value of that variable. Let us now consider the simplest of constants, as in:

```
int i, k;
 i = 2;
```

Here, while **i** is a variable and then occupies space in the data portion of memory, **2** is a constant and, as such, instead of setting aside memory in the data segment, it is embedded directly in the code segment of memory. That is, while writing something like **k = i;** tells the compiler to create code which at run time will look at memory location **&i** to determine the value to be moved to **k**, code created by **i = 2;** simply puts the **2** in the code and there is no referencing of the data segment. That is, both **k** and **i** are objects, but **2** is not an object.

Similarly, in the above, since **my_array** is a constant, once the compiler establishes where the array itself is to be stored, it "knows" the address of **my_array[0].** For example, look into the following statement.

```
ptr = my_array;
```

It simply uses this address as a constant in the code segment and there is no referencing of the data segment beyond that.

9.8 Pointer Arrays

Let us go back to strings for a bit. In the following all assignments are to be understood as being global, i.e., made outside of any function, including main(). We pointed out earlier that we could write:

```
char string1[40] = "Red";
```

which would allocate space for a 40 byte array and put the string in the first 4 bytes (three for the characters in the quotes and a 4th to handle the terminating **'\0'**). Actually, if all we wanted to do was store the name "Red" we could write:

```
char my_name[] = "Red";
```

and the compiler would count the characters, leave room for the \0 character and store the total of the four characters in memory the location of which would be returned by the array name, in this case **my_name**. In some code, instead of the above, we might see:

```
char *my_name = "Red";
```

which is an alternate approach. Is there a difference between these? The answer is yes. Using the array notation 4 bytes of storage in the static memory block are taken up, one for each character and one for the terminating \0 character. But, in the pointer notation the same 4 bytes required, **plus** N bytes to store the pointer variable **my_name** (where N depends on the system but is usually a minimum of 2 bytes and can be 4 or more).

In the array notation, **my_name** is short for **&my_name[0]** which is the address of the first element of the array. Since the location of the array is fixed during run time, this is a constant (not a variable). In the pointer notation **my_name** is a variable. As to which is the better method, that depends on what one is going to do within the rest of the program. Let us now go one step further and consider what happens if each of these declarations are done within a function as opposed to globally outside the bounds of any function.

```
void my_function_A(char *ptr)
{
    char a[] = "ABCDE"
    ...
}

void my_function_B(char *ptr)
{
    char *cp = "FGHIJ"
    ...
}
```

In the case of **my_function_A**, the content, or value(s), of the array **a[]** is considered to be the data. The array is said to be initialized to the values ABCDE. In the case of **my_function_B**, the value of the pointer **cp** is considered to be the data. The pointer has been initialized to point to the string **FGHIJ**. In both **my_function_A** and **my_function_B** the definitions are local variables and thus the string **ABCDE** is stored on the stack, as is the value of the pointer **cp**. The string **FGHIJ** can be stored anywhere. On my system it gets stored in the data segment. By the way, array initialization of automatic variables as we have done in **my_function_A** was illegal in the older C and only "came of age" in the newer ANSI C. A fact that may be important when one is considering portability and backwards compatibility. As long as we are discussing the relationship/differences between pointers and arrays, let us move on to multi-dimensional arrays. For example,

```
char multi[5][10];
```

Just what does this mean? Well, let us consider it in the following light.

```
    char multi[5][10];
```

Let us take the underlined part to be the "name" of an array. Then prepending the **char** and appending the **[10]** we have an array of 10 characters. But, the name **multi[5]** is itself an array indicating that there are 5 elements each being an array of 10 characters. Hence we have an array of 5 arrays of 10 characters each. Assume we have filled this two dimensional array with data of some kind. In memory, it might look as if it had been formed by initializing 5 separate arrays using something like:

```
multi[0] = {'0','1','2','3','4','5','6','7','8','9'}
multi[1] = {'a','b','c','d','e','f','g','h','i','j'}
multi[2] = {'A','B','C','D','E','F','G','H','I','J'}
multi[3] = {'9','8','7','6','5','4','3','2','1','0'}
multi[4] = {'J','I','H','G','F','E','D','C','B','A'}
```

At the same time, individual elements might be addressable using syntax such as:

```
multi[0][3] = '3'
multi[1][7] = 'h'
multi[4][0] = 'J'
```

Since arrays are contiguous in memory, our actual memory block for the above should look like:

0123456789abcdefghijABCDEFGHIJ9876543210JIHGFEDCBA

Starting at the address multi[0][0]

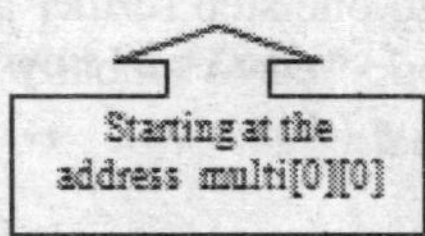

Note that we did not write **multi[0] = "0123456789"**. Had we done so a terminating **'\0'** would have been implied since whenever double quotes are used a **'\0'** character is appended to the characters contained within those quotes. Had that been the case we would have had to set aside room for 11 characters per row instead of 10.

Goal in the above is to illustrate how memory is laid out for two dimensional arrays. That is, this is a two dimensional array of characters, not an array of "strings". Now, the compiler knows how many columns are present in the array so it can interpret **multi + 1** as the address of the 'a' in the 2nd row above. That is, it adds 10, the number of columns, to get this location. If we were dealing with integers and an array with the same dimension the compiler would add **10*sizeof(int)** which, on a machine may be 7. Thus, the address of the **9** in the 4th row above would be **&multi[3][0]** or ***(multi + 3)** in pointer notation. To get to the content of the 2nd element in the 4th row we add 1 to this address and dereference the result as in

```
*(*(multi + 3) + 1)
```

With a little thought we can see that:

```
*(*(multi + row) + col)      and
```

multi[row][col] yield the same results.

Go through the Example 9.5 which is implementing the above discussion.

Example 9.5: Following program illustrates this using integer arrays instead of character arrays.

```
/** Pointer21.C **/
#include <stdio.h>
#define ROWS 5
#define COLS 10

int multi[ROWS][COLS];

int main(void)
{
    int row, col;
    for (row = 0; row < ROWS; row++)
    {
        for (col = 0; col < COLS; col++)
        {
            multi[row][col] = row*col;
        }
    }
    for (row = 0; row < ROWS; row++)
    {
        for (col = 0; col < COLS; col++)
```

```
        {
                printf("\n%d   ",multi[row][col]);
                printf("%d ",*(*(multi + row) + col));
        }
    }
    return 0;
}
```

Because of the double de-referencing required in the pointer version, the name of a two dimensional array is often said to be equivalent to a **pointer to a pointer**. With a three dimensional array we would be dealing with an array of arrays of arrays and some might say its name would be equivalent to a **pointer to a pointer to a pointer**. However, here we have initially set aside the block of memory for the array by defining it using array notation. Hence, we are dealing with a constant, not a variable. That is we are talking about a fixed address not a variable pointer. The dereferencing function used above permits us to access any element in the array of arrays without the need of changing the value of that address, the address of **multi [0][0]** as given by the symbol **multi**. We can access individual elements of the array **multi** using either:

```
multi[row][col]
```

or

```
*(*(multi + row) + col)
```

To understand more fully what is going on, let us replace

```
*(multi + row)
```

with **X** as in:

```
*(X + col)
```

Now, from this we see that **X** is like a pointer since the expression is de-referenced and we know that **col** is an integer. Here the arithmetic being used is of a special kind called "pointer arithmetic" is being used. That means that, since we are talking about an integer array, the address pointed to by (i.e., value of) **X + col + 1** must be greater than the address **X + col** by and amount equal to **sizeof(int)**.

Since we know the memory layout for two dimensional arrays, we can determine that in the expression **multi + row** as used above, **multi + row + 1** must increase by value an amount equal to that needed to "point to" the next row, which in this case would be an amount equal to **COLS * sizeof(int)**. If the expression ***(*(multi + row) + col)** is to be evaluated correctly at run time, the compiler must generate code which takes into consideration the value of **COLS**, i.e., the 2nd dimension. Because of the equivalence of the two forms of expression, this is true whether we are using the pointer expression as here or the array expression **multi[row][col]**. Thus, to evaluate either expression, a total of 5 values must be known:

1. The address of the first element of the array, which is returned by the expression **multi**, i.e., the name of the array.
2. The size of the type of the elements of the array, in this case **sizeof(int)**.
3. The 2nd dimension of the array.
4. The specific index value for the first dimension, **row** in this case.
5. The specific index value for the second dimension, **col** in this case.

For example, consider the following program segment which illustrates the above discussion. In the program segment we are assigning all the cell of the array **multi** to 1.

```
void set_value(int m_array[][COLS])
{
```

```
        int row, col;
        for (row = 0; row < ROWS; row++)
        {
            for (col = 0; col < COLS; col++)
            {
                m_array[row][col] = 1;
            }
        }
    }
```

And to call this function we would then use:

```
    set_value(multi);
```

Now, within the function we have used the values #defined by ROWS and COLS that set the limits on the for loops. But, these #defines are just constants as far as the compiler is concerned, i.e., there is nothing to connect them to the array size within the function. The **row** and **col** are local variables, of course. The formal parameter definition permits the compiler to determine the characteristics associated with the pointer value that will be passed at run time. There are occasions where we would prefer not to define it within the parameter definition, out of habit or consistency, we have not used it here. But, the second dimension must be used as has been shown in the expression for the parameter. The reason is that we need this in the evaluation of **m_array[row][col]** as has been described. While the parameter defines the data type (**int** in this case) and the automatic variables for row and column are defined in the for loops, only one value can be passed using a single parameter. In this case, that is the value of **multi** as noted in the call statement, i.e., the address of the first element, often referred to as a pointer to the array. Thus, the only way we have of informing the compiler of the 2nd dimension is by explicitly including it in the parameter definition.

In fact, in general all dimensions of higher order than one are needed when dealing with multi-dimensional arrays. That is if we are talking about 3 dimensional arrays, the 2nd **and** 3rd dimension must be specified in the parameter definition.

9.9 Pointers and Structures

As we may know, we can declare the form of a block of data containing different data types by means of a structure declaration. For example, a personnel file might contain structures which may contain:

```
    struct tag {
        char lname[20];             /* last name */
        char fname[20];             /* first name */
        int age;                     /* age */
        float rate;                  /* viz., 5.75 per hour */
    };
```

Let us say we have a bunch of these structures in a disk file and we want to read each one out and print out the first and last name of each one so that we can have a list of the people in a file. The remaining information will not be printed out. We want to do this printing with a function call and pass to that function a pointer to the structure at hand. For demonstration purposes we will use only one structure for now. But realize the goal is the writing of the function, not the reading of the file which, presumably, we know how to do. For review, recall that we can access structure members with the dot operator as in:

```
/** Pointer22.C **/
#include <stdio.h>
```

```
#include <string.h>

struct tag {
    char lname[20];         /* last name */
    char fname[20];         /* first name */
    int age;                 /* age */
    float rate;               /* viz., 5.75 per hour */
};

struct tag my_struct;          /* declare the structure my_struct */

int main(void)
{
    strcpy(my_struct.lname,"Jensen");
    strcpy(my_struct.fname,"Red");
    printf("\n%s ",my_struct.fname);
    printf("%s\n",my_struct.lname);
    return 0;
}
```

OUTPUT

Red Jensen

Now, this particular structure is rather small compared to many used in C programs. To the above we might want to add:

```
date_of_hire;                          (data types not shown)
date_of_last_raise;
last_percent_increase;
emergency_phone;
medical_plan;
Social_S_Nbr;
etc.....
```

If we have a large number of employees, what we want to do is manipulate the data in these structures by means of functions. For example, we might want a function print out the name of the employee listed in any structure passed to it. However, in the old C it was not possible to pass a structure, only a pointer to a structure could be passed. In ANSI C, it is now permissible to pass the complete structure.

Anyway, if we pass the whole structure it means that we must copy the contents of the structure from the calling function to the called function. In systems using stacks, this is done by pushing the contents of the structure on the stack. With large structures this could prove to be a problem. However, passing a pointer uses a minimum amount of stack space.

We want a function that will accept as a parameter a pointer to a structure and from within that function we want to access members of the structure. For example we want to print out the name of the employee in the structure. So we know that pointer is going to point to a structure declared using struct tag. We declare such a pointer with the declaration:

```
struct tag *st_ptr;
```

and we point it to our example structure with:

```
st_ptr = &my_struct;
```

Now, we can access a given member by de-referencing the pointer. But, how do we de-reference the pointer to a structure? Well, consider the fact that we might want to use the pointer to set the age of the employee. We would write:

```
(*st_ptr).age = 63;
```

Above statement says, replace that within the parenthesis with that which **st_ptr** points to, which is the structure **my_struct**. Thus, this breaks down to the same as **my_struct.age**. However, this is a fairly often-used expression and the designers of C have created an alternate syntax with the same meaning which is:

```
st_ptr->age = 63;
```

Go through the Example 9.6 for better understabnding the above discussion.

Example 9.6: Write C code using pointer and structure

Answer: Consider the following program segment which implements the discussion

```
/* Pointer23.C */

#include <stdio.h>
#include <string.h>

struct tag{                                /* the structure type */
    char lname[20];                        /* last name */
    char fname[20];                        /* first name */
    int age;                               /* age */
    float rate;                            /* e.g. 12.75 per hour */
};

struct tag my_struct;                      /* define the structure */
void show_name(struct tag *p);             /* function prototype */

int main(void)
{
    struct tag *st_ptr;                  /* a pointer to a structure */
    st_ptr = &my_struct;                 /* point the pointer to
     my_struct */
    strcpy(my_struct.lname,"Jensen");
    strcpy(my_struct.fname,"Red");
    printf("\n%s ",my_struct.fname);
    printf("%s\n",my_struct.lname);
    my_struct.age = 63;
    show_name(st_ptr);                   /* pass the pointer */
    return 0;
```

```
}

void show_name(struct tag *p)
{
      printf("\n%s ", p->fname);    /* p points to a structure */
      printf("%s ", p->lname);
      printf("%d\n", p->age);
}
```

OUTPUT
Red Jensen
Red Jensen 63

Again, this is a lot of information to absorb at one time. The reader should compile and run the various code snippets and using a debugger monitor things like **my_struct** and **p** while single stepping through the main and following the code down into the function to see what is happening.

9.10 Dynamic Memory Allocation

A problem with many simple programs, including in particular little teaching programs such as we have been writing so far, is that they tend to use fixed-size arrays which may or may not be big enough. We have an array of 100 ints for the numbers which the user enters and wishes to find the average of what if the user enters 101 numbers? We have an array of 100 chars which we pass to a function to receive the user's input-what if the user types a line of 200 characters? If we are lucky, the relevant parts of the program check how much of an array they have used, and print an error message or otherwise gracefully abort before overflowing the array. If we are not so lucky, a program may sail off the end of an array, overwriting other data and behaving quite badly. In either case, the user does not get his job done. How can we avoid the restrictions of fixed-size arrays?

The answers all involve the standard library function malloc. Very simply, malloc returns a pointer to n bytes of memory which we can do anything we want to with. If we did not want to read a line of input into a fixed-size array, we could use malloc, instead.

9.10.1 Allocating Memory With *malloc*

It is convenient to allocate memory at runtime using **malloc()**, **calloc()**, or other allocation functions. Using this approach permits postponing the decision on the size of the memory block need to store an array, for example, until runtime. Or it permits using a section of memory for the storage of an array of integers at one point in time, and then when that memory is no longer needed it can be freed up for other uses, such as the storage of an array of structures. malloc is declared in stdlib.h, so we #include that header in any program that calls malloc. A "byte" in C is, by definition, an amount of storage suitable for storing one character. For example char* line; line = malloc(100), invocation of malloc gives us exactly as many chars as we ask for. Figure 9.8 illustrates the resulting pointer.

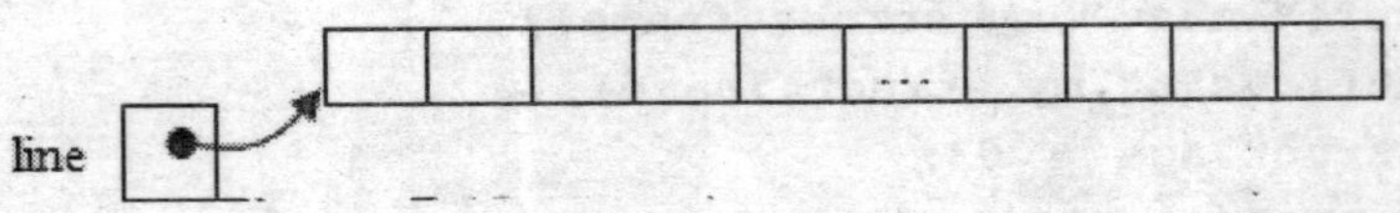

Figure 9.8 Allocating memory space using malloc

The 100 bytes of memory pointed to by line are those allocated by malloc. They are brand-new memory, conceptually a bit different from the memory which the compiler arranges to have allocated automatically for our conventional variables. The 100 boxes in the figure do not have a name next to them, because they are not storage for a variable we have declared.

When memory is allocated, the allocating function (such as **malloc()**, **calloc()**, etc.) returns a pointer. The type of this pointer depends on whether we are using an older C compiler or the newer ANSI type compiler. With the older compiler the type of the returned pointer is **char**, with the ANSI compiler it is **void**.

If we are using an older compiler, and we want to allocate memory for an array of integers we will have to cast the char pointer returned to an integer pointer. For example, to allocate space for 10 integers syntax is

```
int *iptr;
iptr = (int *)malloc(10 * sizeof(int));
if (iptr == NULL)

{ .. ERROR ROUTINE GOES HERE .. }
```

If we are using an ANSI compliant compiler, **malloc()** returns a **void** pointer and since a void pointer can be assigned to a pointer variable of any object type, the **(int *)** cast shown above is not needed. The array dimension can be determined at runtime and is not needed at compile time. That is, the **10** above could be a variable read in from a data file or keyboard, or calculated based on some need, at runtime. Because of the equivalence between array and pointer notation, once **iptr** has been assigned as above, one can use the array notation. For example,

```
int k;
for (k = 0; k < 10; k++)
    iptr[k] = 2;
```

to set the values of all elements to 2.

Note: When copying strings, all the strings have a terminating '\0' character. If we use strlen to count the characters in a string that count will *not* include the trailing '\0', so we must add one before calling malloc:

```
char *somestring, *copy;
...
copy = malloc(strlen(somestring) + 1);          /* +1 for \0 */
/* incomplete — malloc's return value not checked */
strcpy(copy, somestring);
```

What if we are not allocating characters, but integers? If we want to allocate 100 ints, how many bytes is that? If we know how big ints are on our machine (i.e., depending on whether we are using a 16- or 32-bit machine) we could try to compute it ourselves, but it is much safer and more portable to let C compute it for us. C has a sizeof operator, which computes the size, in bytes, of a variable or type. It is just what we need when calling malloc. To allocate space for 100 ints, we could call

```
int *ip = malloc(100 * sizeof(int));
```

The use of the sizeof operator tends to look like a function call, but it is really an operator, and it does its work at compile time.

Since we can use array-indexing syntax on pointers, we can treat a pointer variable after a call to malloc almost exactly as if it were an array. In particular, after the above call to malloc initializes ip to point at storage for 100 ints, we can access ip[0], ip[1], ... up to ip[99]. This way, we can get the effect of an array even if we do not know until runtime how big the "array" should be.

Our examples so far have all had a significant omission: they have not checked malloc's return value.

Obviously, no real computer has an infinite amount of memory available, so there is no guarantee that malloc will be able to give us as much memory as we ask for. If we call malloc(100000000), or if we call malloc(10) 10,000,000 times, we are probably going to run out of memory.

When malloc is unable to allocate the requested memory, it returns a *null pointer*. A null pointer, remember, points definitively nowhere. It is a "not a pointer" marker; it is not a pointer we can use. A null pointer can be used as a failure return from a function that returns pointers, and malloc is a perfect. Therefore, whenever we call malloc, it is vital to check the returned pointer before using it. If we call malloc, and it returns a null pointer, and we go off and use that null pointer as if it pointed somewhere, program probably would not last long. Instead, a program should immediately check for a null pointer, and if it receives one, it should at the very least print an error message and exit, or perhaps figure out some way of proceeding without the memory it asked for. But it cannot go on to use the null pointer it got back from malloc in any way, because that null pointer by definition points nowhere. "It cannot use a null pointer in any way" means that the program cannot use the * or [] operators on such a pointer value, or pass it to any function that expects a valid pointer.

A call to malloc, with an error check, typically has the form:

```
int *ip = malloc(100 * sizeof(int));
if(ip == NULL)
{
    printf("out of memory\n");
    exit or return
}
```

After printing the error message, this code should return to its caller, or exit from the program entirely; it cannot proceed with the code that would have used ip.

Of course, in our examples so far, we have still limited ourselves to "fixed size" regions of memory, because we have been calling malloc with fixed arguments like 10 or 100. However, since the sizes are now values which can in principle be determined at runtime, we have at least moved beyond having to recompile the program (with a bigger array) to accommodate longer lines, and with a little more work, we could arrange that the "arrays" automatically grew to be as large as required.

Even with a reasonably good understanding of pointers and arrays, one place the newcomer to C is likely to stumble at first is in the dynamic allocation of multi-dimensional arrays. In general, we would like to be able to access elements of such arrays using array notation, not pointer notation, wherever possible. Depending on the application we may or may not know both dimensions at compile time. This leads to a variety of ways to the task.

We have seen that when dynamically allocating a one-dimensional array its dimension can be determined at runtime. Now, when using dynamic allocation of higher order arrays, we never need to know the first dimension at compile time. Whether we need to know the higher dimensions depends on how we go about writing the code. Here we will discuss various methods of dynamically allocating room for two dimensional arrays of integers. First we will consider cases where the 2nd dimension is known at compile time.

9.10.2 Method 1

One way of dealing with the problem is through the use of the **typedef** keyword. To allocate a two dimensional array of integer's recall that the following two notations result in the same object code being generated:

```
multi[row][col] = 1;        *(*(multi + row) + col) = 1;
```

It is also true that the following two notations generate the same code:

```
multi[row]          and         *(multi + row)
```

Since the one on the right must evaluate to a pointer, the array notation on the left must also evaluate to a pointer. In fact **multi[0]** will return a pointer to the first integer in the first row, **multi[1]** a pointer to the first integer of the second row, etc. Actually, **multi[n]** evaluates to a pointer to that array of integers that make up the n-th row of two dimensional array. That is, **multi** can be thought of as an array of arrays and **multi[n]** as a pointer to the n-th array of this array of arrays. Here the word **pointer** is being used to represent an address value. While such usage is common in the literature, when reading such statements one must be careful to distinguish between the constant address of an array and a variable pointer which is a data object in itself. Go through the Example 9.7 which implements the multi-dimensional dynamic arrays.

Example 9.7: Write C codes which implements multi-dimensional dynamic array.

Answer: Consider the following program segments (Pointe10.C, Pointe11.C, Pointe12.C, and Pointe13.C) which are demonstrating different scenario of the daynamic arrays implementation in C.

```
/* Pointe10.C */
#include <stdio.h>
#include <stdlib.h>
#define COLS 5
typedef int RowArray[COLS];
RowArray *rptr;

int main(void)
{
    int nrows = 10;
    int row, col;
    rptr = malloc(nrows * COLS * sizeof(int));
    for (row = 0; row < nrows; row++)
    {
        for (col = 0; col < COLS; col++)
        {
            rptr[row][col] = 17;
        }
    }
    return 0;
}
```

Here we have assumed an ANSI compiler so a cast on the void pointer returned by **malloc()** is not required. If we are using an older C compiler we will have to cast using:

```
rptr = (RowArray *)malloc(...etc.);
```

Using this approach, **rptr** has all the characteristics of an array name **name**, (except that rptr is modifiable), and array notation may be used throughout the rest of the program. That also means that if we intend to write a function to modify the array contents, we must use COLS as a part of the formal parameter in that function, just as we did when discussing the passing of two dimensional arrays to a function.

9.10.3 Method 2

In the METHOD 1 above, rptr turned out to be a pointer to type "one dimensional array of COLS integers". It turns out that there is syntax which can be used for this type without the need of **typedef**. If we write:

```
int (*xptr)[COLS];
```

the variable **xptr** will have all the same characteristics as the variable **rptr** in METHOD 1 above, and we need not use the **typedef** keyword. Here **xptr** is a pointer to an array of integers and the size of array is given by the **#defined COLS**. The parenthesis placement makes the pointer notation predominate, even though the array notation has higher precedence, i.e., had we written

```
int *xptr[COLS];
```

We would have defined **xptr** as an array of pointers holding the number of pointers equal to that #defined by COLS. That is not the same thing at all. However, arrays of pointers have their use in the dynamic allocation of two-dimensional arrays, as will be seen in the next 2 methods.

9.10.4 Method 3

Consider the case where we do not know the number of elements in each row at compile time, i.e., both the number of rows and number of columns must be determined at runtime. One way of doing this would be to create an array of pointers to type **int** and then allocate space for each row and point these pointers at each row. For example, consider the following program segment.

```
/** Pointe11.C **/
#include <stdio.h>
#include <stdlib.h>

int main(void)
{
     int nrows = 5;        /* Both nrows and ncols could be
      evaluated */
     int ncols = 10;       /* or read in at run time */
     int row;
     int **rowptr;
     rowptr = malloc(nrows * sizeof(int *));
     if (rowptr == NULL)
     {
          puts("\nFailure to allocate room for row pointers.\n");
          exit(0);
     }
     printf("\n\n\nIndex    Pointer(hex)    Pointer(dec)
      Diff.(dec)");
     for (row = 0; row < nrows; row++)
     {
          rowptr[row] = malloc(ncols * sizeof(int));
          if (rowptr[row] == NULL)
          {
               printf("\nFailure to allocate for row[%d]\n",row);
               exit(0);
          }
          printf("\n%d   %p  %d", row, rowptr[row], rowptr[row]);
```

```
        if (row > 0)
        printf("%15d",(int)(rowptr[row] - rowptr[row-1]));
    }
    return 0;
}
```

OUTPUT

Index	Pointer(hex)	Pointer(dec)	Diff.(dec)
0	0898:0004	4	
1	089A:0004	4	0
2	089C:0004	4	0
3	089E:0004	4	0
4	08A0:0004	4	0

In the above program segment **rowptr** is a pointer to pointer to type **int**. In this case it points to the first element of an array of pointers to type **int**. Consider the number of calls to **malloc()**:

To get the array of pointers	1 call
To get space for the rows	5 calls
Total	6 calls

If we choose to use this approach note that while we can use the array notation to access individual elements of the array, e.g. **rowptr[row][col] = 17;**, it does not mean that the data in the "two dimensional array" is contiguous in memory. We can, however, use the array notation just as if it were a continuous block of memory. For example, we can write:

```
rowptr[row][col] = 176;
```

just as if rowptr were the name of a two dimensional array created at compile time. Of course **row** and **col** must be within the bounds of the array we have created, just as with an array created at compile time. If we want to have a contiguous block of memory dedicated to the storage of the elements in the array we can do it as in Method 4.

9.10.5 Method 4

In this method we allocate a block of memory to hold the whole array first. We then create an array of pointers to point to each row. Thus even though the array of pointers is being used, the actual array in memory is contiguous. For example, see the following program segment.

```
/** Pointe12.C **/
#include <stdio.h>
#include <stdlib.h>

int main(void)
{
    int **rptr;
    int *aptr;
    int *testptr;
```

```
int k;
int nrows = 5;        /* Both nrows and ncols could be
 evaluated */
int ncols = 8;       /* or read in at runtime */
int row, col;
/* we now allocate the memory for the array */
aptr = malloc(nrows * ncols * sizeof(int));
if (aptr == NULL)
{
    puts("\nFailure to allocate room for the array");
    exit(0);
}

/* next we allocate room for the pointers to the rows */

rptr = malloc(nrows * sizeof(int *));
if (rptr == NULL)
{
    puts("\nFailure to allocate room for pointers");
    exit(0);
}

/* and now we 'point' the pointers */

for (k = 0; k < nrows; k++)
{
    rptr[k] = aptr + (k * ncols);
}

/* Now we illustrate how the row pointers are incremented */
printf("\n\nIllustrating how row pointers are incremented");
printf("\n\nIndex   Pointer(hex)  Diff.(dec)");

for (row = 0; row < nrows; row++)
{
    printf("\n%d              %p", row, rptr[row]);
    if (row > 0)
    printf("                  %d",(rptr[row] - rptr[row-1]));
}
printf("\n\nAnd now we print out the array\n");
for (row = 0; row < nrows; row++)
{
    for (col = 0; col < ncols; col++)
```

```
            {
                rptr[row][col] = row + col;
                printf("%d ", rptr[row][col]);
            }
            putchar('\n');
        }
        puts("\n");

        /* and here we illustrate that we are, in fact, dealing with
         a 2 dimensional array in a contiguous block of memory. */

        printf("And now we demonstrate that they are contiguous in
         memory\n");

        testptr = aptr;
        for (row = 0; row < nrows; row++)
        {
            for (col = 0; col < ncols; col++)
            {
                printf("%d ", *(testptr++));
            }
            putchar('\n');
        }
        return 0;
    }
```

OUTPUT

Illustrating how row pointers are incremented

Index	Pointer(hex)	Diff.(dec)
0	08B0:0004	
1	08B0:0014	8
2	08B0:0024	8
3	08B0:0034	8
4	08B0:0044	8

And now we print out the array

0	1	2	3	4	5	6	7
1	2	3	4	5	6	7	8
2	3	4	5	6	7	8	9
3	4	5	6	7	8	9	10
4	5	6	7	8	9	10	11

And now we demonstrate that they are contiguous in memory

0	1	2	3	4	5	6	7
1	2	3	4	5	6	7	8
2	3	4	5	6	7	8	9
3	4	5	6	7	8	9	10
4	5	6	7	8	9	10	11

Consider again, the number of calls to malloc()

To get room for the array itself	1 call
To get room for the array of ptrs	1 call
Total	2 calls

Now, each call to **malloc()** creates additional space overhead since **malloc()** is generally implemented by the operating system forming a linked list which contains data concerning the size of the block. But, more importantly, with large arrays (several hundred rows) keeping track of what needs to be freed when the time comes can be more cumbersome. This, combined with the contiguousness of the data block that permits initialization to all zeroes using **memset()** would seem to make the second alternative the preferred one. As a final example on multidimensional arrays we will illustrate the dynamic allocation of a three dimensional array. This example will illustrate one more thing to watch when doing this kind of allocation. For reasons cited above we will use the approach outlined in alternative two. Consider the following code:

```
/** Pointe13.C **/
#include <stdio.h>
#include <stdlib.h>
#include <stddef.h>
int X_DIM=16;
int Y_DIM=5;
int Z_DIM=3;

int main(void)
{
      char *space;
      char ***Arr3D;
      int y, z;
      ptrdiff_t diff;

      /* first we set aside space for the array itself */

      space = malloc(X_DIM * Y_DIM * Z_DIM * sizeof(char));

      /* next we allocate space of an array of pointers, each to
       eventually point to the first element of a
         2 dimensional array of pointers to pointers */

      Arr3D = malloc(Z_DIM * sizeof(char **));
```

```
    /* and for each of these we assign a pointer to a newly
     allocated array of pointers to a row */

    for (z = 0; z < Z_DIM; z++)
    {
        Arr3D[z] = malloc(Y_DIM * sizeof(char *));

        /* and for each space in this array we put a pointer to
     the first element of each row in the array space originally
     allocated */

        for (y = 0; y < Y_DIM; y++)
        {
            Arr3D[z][y] = space + (z*(X_DIM * Y_DIM) + y*X_DIM);
        }
    }

    /* And, now we check each address in our 3D array to see if
     the indexing of the Arr3d pointer leads through in a
     continuous manner */

    for (z = 0; z < Z_DIM; z++)
    {
        printf("Location of array %d is %p\n", z, *Arr3D[z]);
        for ( y = 0; y < Y_DIM; y++)
        {
            printf("  Array %d and Row %d starts at %p", z, y,
    Arr3D[z][y]);
            diff = Arr3D[z][y] - space;
            printf("     diff = %d  ",diff);
            printf(" z = %d  y = %d\n", z, y);
        }
    }
    return 0;
}
```

OUTPUT

Location of array 0 is 0885:0004

Array 0 and Row 0 starts at 0885:0004 diff = 0 z = 0 y = 0

Array 0 and Row 1 starts at 0885:0014 diff = 16 z = 0 y = 1

Array 0 and Row 2 starts at 0885:0024 diff = 32 z = 0 y = 2

Array 0 and Row 3 starts at 0885:0034 diff = 48 z = 0 y = 3

Array 0 and Row 4 starts at 0885:0044 diff = 64 z = 0 y = 4

Location of array 1 is 0885:0054

Array 1 and Row 0 starts at 0885:0054	diff = 80	z = 1	y = 0
Array 1 and Row 1 starts at 0885:0064	diff = 96	z = 1	y = 1
Array 1 and Row 2 starts at 0885:0074	diff = 112	z = 1	y = 2
Array 1 and Row 3 starts at 0885:0084	diff = 128	z = 1	y = 3
Array 1 and Row 4 starts at 0885:0094	diff = 144	z = 1	y = 4
Location of array 2 is 0885:00A4			
Array 2 and Row 0 starts at 0885:00A4	diff = 160	z = 2	y = 0
Array 2 and Row 1 starts at 0885:00B4	diff = 176	z = 2	y = 1
Array 2 and Row 2 starts at 0885:00C4	diff = 192	z = 2	y = 2
Array 2 and Row 3 starts at 0885:00D4	diff = 208	z = 2	y = 3
Array 2 and Row 4 starts at 0885:00E4	diff = 224	z = 2	y = 4

There are a couple of points that should be making clear. Let us start with the line which reads:

```
Arr3D[z][y] = space + (z*(X_DIM * Y_DIM) + y*X_DIM);
```

Note that here **space** is a character pointer, which is the same type as **Arr3D[z][y]**. It is important that when adding an integer, such as that obtained by evaluation of the expression **(z*(X_DIM * Y_DIM) + y*X_DIM)**, to a pointer, the result is a new pointer value. And when assigning pointer values to pointer variables the data types of the value and variable must match.

9.10.5 Freeing Memory

Memory allocated with malloc lasts as long as we want it to. It does not automatically disappear when a function returns, as automatic-duration variables do, but it does not have to remain for the entire duration of a program, either. Just as we can use malloc to control exactly when and how much memory we allocate, we can also control exactly when we deallocate it.

In fact, many programs use memory on a transient basis. They allocate some memory, use it for a while, but then reach a point where they do not need that particular piece any more. Because memory is not inexhaustible, it is a good idea to deallocate (i.e., release or *free*) memory programs are no longer using.

Dynamically allocated memory is deallocated with the free function. If p contains a pointer previously returned by malloc, we can call

```
free(p);
```

which will "give the memory back" to the stock of memory (sometimes called the "arena" or "pool") from which malloc requests are satisfied. Calling free is sort of the ultimate in recycling: it costs us almost nothing, and the memory we give back is immediately usable by other parts of a program. Theoretically, it may even be usable by other programs.

Freeing unused memory is a good idea, but it's not mandatory. When a program exits, any memory which it has allocated but not freed should be automatically released. If a computer is to somehow "lose" memory just because a program forgot to free it, that would indicate a problem or deficiency in the operating system.

Naturally, once we have freed some memory we must remember not to use it any more. After calling

```
free(p);
```

It is probably the case that p still points at the same memory. However, since we have given it back, it is now "available," and a later call to malloc might give that memory to some other part of a program. If the variable p is a global variable or will otherwise stick around for a while, one good way to record the fact that it is not to be used any more would be to set it to a null pointer:

```
free(p);
p = NULL;
```

Now we do not even have the pointer to the freed memory any more, and (as long as we check to see that p is non-NULL before using it), we would not misuse any memory via the pointer p.

When thinking about malloc, free, and dynamically allocated memory in general, remember again the distinction between a pointer and what it points to. If we call malloc to allocate some memory, and store the pointer which malloc gives in a local pointer variable, what happens when the function containing the local pointer variable returns? If the local pointer variable has *automatic duration* (which is the default, unless the variable is declared static), it will disappear when the function returns. But for the pointer variable to disappear says nothing about the memory pointed to. That memory still exists and, as far as malloc and free are concerned, is still allocated. The only thing that has disappeared is the pointer variable which pointed at the allocated memory. Furthermore, if it contained the only copy of the pointer once it disappears, we will have no way of freeing the memory, and no way of using it, either. Using memory and freeing memory both require that we have at least one pointer to the memory.

9.10.6 Reallocating Memory Blocks

Sometimes we are not sure at first how much memory will need. For example, if we need to store a series of items, programmer read and if the only way to know how many there are is to read them until the user types some "end" signal, we will have no way of knowing, as we begin reading and storing the first few, how many we will have seen by the time we do see that "end" marker. We might want to allocate room for, say, 100 items, and if the user enters a 101st item before entering the "end" marker, we might wish for a way to say "uh, malloc, remember those 100 items we asked for? Could one change his/her mind and have 200 instead?"

In fact, we can do exactly this, with the realloc function. We hand realloc an old pointer (such as we received from an initial call to malloc) and a new size, and realloc does what it can to give a chunk of memory big enough to hold the new size. For example, if we wanted the ip variable from an earlier example to point at 200 ints instead of 100, we could try calling

```
ip = realloc(ip, 200 * sizeof(int));
```

Since we always want each block of dynamically-allocated memory to be contiguous (so that we can treat it as if it were an array), and realloc have to worry about the case where realloc cannot make the old block of memory bigger "in place," but rather has to relocate it elsewhere in order to find enough contiguous space for the new requested size. The realloc does this by returning a new pointer. If realloc was able to make the old block of memory bigger, it returns the same pointer. If realloc has to go elsewhere to get enough contiguous memory, it returns a pointer to the new memory, after copying a old data there. In this case, after it makes the copy, it frees the old block. Finally, if realloc cannot find enough memory to satisfy the new request at all, it returns a null pointer. Therefore, we usually do not want to overwrite a old pointer with realloc's return value until we have tested it to make sure it is not a null pointer. For example, see the following code segment:

```
int *newp;
newp = realloc(ip, 200 * sizeof(int));
if(newp != NULL)
    ip = newp;
else{
    printf("out of memory\n");
    /* exit or return */
    /* but ip still points at 100 ints */
}
```

If realloc returns something other than a null pointer, it succeeded, and we set ip to what it returned. We have either set ip to what it used to be or to a new pointer, but in either case, it points to where our data is now. If realloc returns a null pointer, however, we hang on to our old pointer in ip which still points at original 100 values.

Putting this all together, here is a piece of code segment which reads lines of text from the user, treats each line as an integer by calling atoi(), and stores each integer in a dynamically-allocated "array":

```
#define MAXLINE 100
char line[MAXLINE];
int *ip;
int nalloc, nitems;
nalloc = 100;
ip = malloc(nalloc * sizeof(int));              /* initial allocation
     */
if(ip == NULL)
{
   printf("out of memory\n");
   exit(1);
}

nitems = 0;

while(getline(line, MAXLINE) != EOF)
{
   if(nitems >= nalloc)    /* increase allocation */
      int *newp;
      nalloc += 100;
      newp = realloc(ip, nalloc * sizeof(int));
      if(newp == NULL)
      {
         printf("out of memory\n");
         exit(1);
      }
      ip = newp;
}
   ip[nitems++] = atoi(line);
}
```

We use two different variables to keep track of the "array" pointed to by ip. The nalloc is how many elements we have allocated, and nitems is how many of them are in use. Whenever we are about to store another item in the "array," if nitems >= nalloc, the old "array" is full, and it is time to call realloc to make it bigger.

Finally, we might ask what the return type of malloc and realloc is, if they are able to return pointers to char or pointers to int or pointers to any other type. The answer is that both of these functions are declared in stdlib.h as returning a type we have not seen, void * (that is, pointer to void).

9.10.7 The sizeof and Storage Allocation

The sizeof operator returns the size in bytes of its operand. Whether the result of sizeof is unsigned int or unsigned long is implementation defined—which is why the declaration of malloc above ducked the issue by omitting any parameter information; normally we use the stdlib.h header file to declare malloc correctly. Here is the last example done portably:

```
#include <stdlib.h>        /* declares malloc() */
float *fp;

fp = (float *)malloc(sizeof(float));
```

The operand of sizeof only has to be parenthesized if it is a type name, as it was in the example. If we are using the name of a data object instead, then the parentheses can be omitted, but they rarely are.

```
#include <stdlib.h>
int *ip, ar[100];
ip = (int *)malloc(sizeof ar);
```

In this example, the array ar is an array of 100 ints; after the call to malloc (assuming that it was successful), ip will point to a region of store that can also be treated as an array of 100 ints. The fundamental unit of storage in C is the char, and by definition sizeof(char); is equal to 1, so we could allocate space for an array of ten chars with malloc(10); while to allocate room for an array of ten ints, we would have to use malloc(sizeof(int[10])); If malloc cannot find enough free space to satisfy a request it returns a null pointer to indicate failure. For historical reasons, the stdio.h header file contains a defined constant called NULL which is traditionally used to check the return value from malloc and some other library functions. An explicit 0 or (void *) 0 could equally well be used.

As a first illustration of the use of malloc, here is a program which reads up to MAXSTRING strings from its input and sort them into alphabetical order using the library strcmp() function. The strings are terminated by a '\n' character. The sort is done by keeping an array of pointers to the strings and simply exchanging the pointers until the order is correct. This saves having to copy the strings themselves, which improves the efficiency somewhat.

The example is done first using fixed size arrays, then another version uses malloc and allocates space for the strings at runtime. Unfortunately, the array of pointers is still fixed in size: a better solution would use a linked list or similar data structure to store the pointers and would have no fixed arrays at all. At the moment, we have not seen how to do that. The steps for the above discussion is:

```
while(number of strings read < MAXSTRING && input still remains)
{
                read next string;
}

sort array of pointers;
print array of pointers;
exit;
```

A number of functions are used to implement the above steps.

```
char *next_string(char *destination)
```

Read a line of characters terminated by '\n' from the program's input. The first MAXLEN-1 characters are written into the array pointed to by destination. If the first character read is EOF, return a null pointer, otherwise return the address of the start of the string (destination). On return, destination always points to a null-terminated string.

```
void sort_arr(const char *p_array[])
```

p_array[] is an array of pointers to characters. The array can be arbitrarily long; its end is indicated by the first element containing a null pointer.

sort_arr sorts the pointers so that the pointers point to strings which are in alphabetical order when the array is traversed in index order.

```
void print_arr(const char *p_array[])
```

It is like sort_arr, but prints the strings in index order.

It will help to understand the examples if we remember that in an expression, an array's name is converted to the address of its first element. Similarly, for a two-dimensional array (such as strings below), then the expression strings [1][2] has type char, but strings [1] has type "array of char" which is therefore converted to the address of the first element: it is equivalent to &strings [1][0]. Go through the Example 9.8 which demosnterates the above discussion.

Example 9.8: Write C code which demonstrates how type of array changes as the dimension changes.

Answer: Following the codes (Pointer14.c, Pointer15.c, Pointer16.c, and Pointer17.c) for the above discussion and other scenarios which will be assumed before writing the code.

```
/* Pointer14.c */
#include <stdio.h>
#include <stdlib.h>
#include <string.h>

#define MAXSTRING          50     /* max no. of strings */
#define MAXLEN             80        /* max length. of strings */

void print_arr(const char *p_array[]);
void sort_arr(const char *p_array[]);
char *next_string(char *destination);

main()
{
        /* leave room for null at end */
        char *p_array[MAXSTRING+1];

        /* storage for strings */
        char strings[MAXSTRING][MAXLEN];

        /* count of strings read */
        int nstrings;

        nstrings = 0;
        while(nstrings < MAXSTRING && next_string(strings[nstrings])
      != 0){
```

```
                p_array[nstrings] = strings[nstrings];
                nstrings++;
        }
        /* terminate p_array */
        p_array[nstrings] = 0;

        sort_arr(p_array);
        print_arr(p_array);
        exit(1);
}

void print_arr(const char *p_array[])
{
        int index;
        for(index = 0; p_array[index] != 0; index++)
                printf("%s\n", p_array[index]);
}

void sort_arr(const char *p_array[])
{
        int comp_val, low_index, hi_index;
        const char *tmp;

      for(low_index=0;p_array[low_index]!=0&&p_array[low_index+1]!=0;
      low_index++)
        {
                for(hi_index = low_index+1;  p_array[hi_index] !=
      0; hi_index++)
        {
                        comp_val=strcmp(p_array[hi_index],
      p_array[low_index]);
                        if(comp_val >= 0)
                                continue;
                        /* swap strings */
                        tmp = p_array[hi_index];
                        p_array[hi_index] = p_array[low_index];
                        p_array[low_index] = tmp;
                }
        }
}

char *next_string(char *destination)
{
        char *cp;
```

```
        int c;
        cp = destination;
        while((c = getchar()) != '\n' && c != EOF)
{
                if(cp-destination < MAXLEN-1)
                        *cp++ = c;
 }
        *cp = 0;
        if(c == EOF && cp == destination)
                return(0);
        return(destination);
}
```

It is no accident that next_string returns a pointer. We can now dispense with the strings array by getting next_string to allocate its own storage.

```
/* Pointer15.c */
#include <stdio.h>
#include <stdlib.h>
#include <string.h>

#define MAXSTRING           50        /* max no. of strings */
#define MAXLEN              80        /* max length. of strings */

void print_arr(const char *p_array[]);
void sort_arr(const char *p_array[]);
char *next_string(void);

main()
{
        char *p_array[MAXSTRING+1];
        int nstrings;

        nstrings = 0;
        while(nstrings < MAXSTRING && (p_array[nstrings] =
      next_string()) != 0)
{
                nstrings++;
   }
        /* terminate p_array */
        p_array[nstrings] = 0;

        sort_arr(p_array);
```

```
        print_arr(p_array);
        exit(0);
}

void print_arr(const char *p_array[])
{
        int index;
        for(index = 0; p_array[index] != 0; index++)
                printf("%s\n", p_array[index]);
}

void sort_arr(const char *p_array[])
{
        int comp_val, low_index, hi_index;
        const char *tmp;

for(low_index = 0; p_array[low_index] != 0 && p_array[low_index+1]
      != 0; low_index++)
{
                for(hi_index = low_index+1; p_array[hi_index] != 0;
      hi_index++)
        {
                        comp_val=strcmp(p_array[hi_index],
                        p_array[low_index]);
                         if(comp_val >= 0)
                                continue;
                         /* swap strings */
                         tmp = p_array[hi_index];
                         p_array[hi_index] = p_array[low_index];
                         p_array[low_index] = tmp;
                }
        }
}

char *next_string(void)
{
        char *cp, *destination;
        int c;

        destination = (char *)malloc(MAXLEN);
        if(destination != 0)
{
                cp = destination;
```

```
                    while((c = getchar()) != '\n' && c != EOF)
        {
                              if(cp-destination < MAXLEN-1)
                                        *cp++ = c;
                    }
                    *cp = 0;
                    if(c == EOF && cp == destination)
                              return(0);
          }
          return(destination);
}
```

Finally, for the extremely brave, here is the whole thing with even p_array allocated using malloc. Further, most of the array indexing is rewritten to use pointer notation. If readers are feeling queasy, skip this example. It is hard. One word of explanation: char **p means a pointer to a pointer to a character. Many C programmers find this hard to deal with.

```
/* Pointer16.c */
#include <stdio.h>
#include <stdlib.hi>
#include <string.h>

#define MAXSTRING           50      /* max no. of strings */
#define MAXLEN              80      /* max length. of strings */

void print_arr(const char **p_array);
void sort_arr(const char **p_array);
char *next_string(void);

main()
{
       char **p_array;
       int nstrings;    /* count of strings read */
       p_array = (char **)malloc(sizeof(char *[MAXSTRING+1]));
       if(p_array == 0){
               printf("No memory\n");
               exit(0);
       }

       nstrings = 0;
       while(nstrings < MAXSTRING && (p_array[nstrings] =
     next_string()) != 0)
{
```

```
                nstrings++;
    }

        /* terminate p_array */
        p_array[nstrings] = 0;

        sort_arr(p_array);
        print_arr(p_array);
        exit(EXIT_SUCCESS);
}

void print_arr(const char **p_array)
{
while(*p_array)
      printf("%s\n", *p_array++);
}

void sort_arr(const char **p_array)
{
        const char **lo_p, **hi_p, *tmp;
    for(lo_p = p_array; *lo_p != 0 && *(lo_p+1) != 0;  lo_p++)
{
                for(hi_p = lo_p+1; *hi_p != 0; hi_p++)
      {
                        if(strcmp(*hi_p, *lo_p) >= 0)
                                continue;
                        /* swap strings */
                        tmp = *hi_p;
                        *hi_p = *lo_p;
                        *lo_p = tmp;
                }
        }
}

char *next_string(void)
{
        char *cp, *destination;
        int c;
        destination = (char *)malloc(MAXLEN);
        if(destination != 0){
                cp = destination;
                while((c = getchar()) != '\n' && c != EOF)
      {
```

```
                    if(cp-destination < MAXLEN-1)
                            *cp++ = c;
            }
            *cp = 0;
            if(c == EOF && cp == destination)
                    return(0);
        }
        return(destination);
}
```

To further illustrate the use of malloc, another example program follows which can cope with arbitrarily long strings. It simply reads strings from its standard input, looking for a newline character to mark the end of the string, and then prints the string on its standard output. It stops when it detects end-of-file. The characters are put into an array, the end of the string being indicated by a zero. The newline is not stored, but used to detect when a full line of input should be printed on the output. The program does not know how long the string will be, so it starts by allocating ten characters which are enough for a short string.

If the string is more than ten characters long, malloc is called to allocate room for the current string plus ten more characters. The current characters are copied into the new space, the old storage previously allocated is released and the program continues using the new storage.

To release storage allocated by malloc, the library function free() is used. If we do not release storage when it is not needed any more, it just hangs around taking up space. Using free allows it to be "given away", or at least re-used later.

The program reports errors by using fprintf, a close cousin of printf. The only difference between them is that fprintf takes an additional first argument which indicates where its output should go. There are two constants of the right type for this purpose defined in stdio.h. Using stdout indicates that the program's standard output is to be used; stderr refers to the program's standard error stream. On some systems both may be the same, but other systems do make the distinction.

```
/* Pointer17.c */
#include <stdio.h>
#include <stdlib.h>
#include <string.h>

#define GROW_BY 10          /* string grows by 10 chars */

main()
{
        char *str_p, *next_p, *tmp_p;
        int ch, need, chars_read;

        if(GROW_BY < 2)
{
                fprintf(stderr, "Growth constant too small\n");
                exit(0);
```

```
}

    str_p = (char *)malloc(GROW_BY);
    if(str_p == NULL)
    {
            fprintf(stderr,"No initial store\n");
            exit(0);
    }
    next_p = str_p;
    chars_read = 0;
    while((ch = getchar()) != EOF)
{
            /* Completely restart at each new line. There
   will always be room for the
             * terminating zero in the string,  because of
   the check further down,
             * unless GROW_BY is less than 2, and that has
   already been checked. */
            if(ch == '\n')
    {
      /* indicate end of line */
     *next_p = 0;
     printf("%s\n", str_p);
     free(str_p);
     chars_read = 0;
     str_p = (char *)malloc(GROW_BY);
     if(str_p == NULL)
     {
          fprintf(stderr,"No initial store\n");
          exit(0);
                 }
                 next_p = str_p;
                 continue;
            }

            /*  Have we reached the end of the current
   allocation ? */

            if(chars_read == GROW_BY-1)
   {
     *next_p = 0;     /* mark end of string */
     /* use pointer subtraction to find length of current
   string. */
     need = next_p - str_p +1;
```

```
        tmp_p =  (char *)malloc(need+GROW_BY);
        if(tmp_p == NULL)
    {
        fprintf(stderr,"No more store\n");
        exit(0);
                    }
                    /* Copy the string using library. */
                        strcpy(tmp_p, str_p);
                        free(str_p);
                        str_p = tmp_p;
                        /* and reset next_p, character count */
                        next_p = str_p + need-1;
                        chars_read = 0;
                }
                /* Put character at end of current string. */
                *next_p++ = ch;
                chars_read++;
        }

        /* EOF - but do unprinted characters exist?    */
        if(str_p - next_p)
    {
        *next_p = 0;
        fprintf(stderr,"Incomplete last line\n");
        printf("%s\n", str_p);
        }
        exit(0);
  }
```

This may not be a particularly realistic example of how to handle arbitrarily long strings; for one thing, the maximum storage demand is *twice* the amount needed for the longest string—but it does actually work. It also costs rather a lot in terms of copying around. Both problems could be reduced by using the library realloc function instead.

A more sophisticated method might use a linked list, implemented with the use of *structures*. That would have its drawbacks too though, because then the standard library routines would not work for a different method of storing strings.

9.10.8 The type of sizeof

Now the question arise just what this does:

```
sizeof ( sizeof (anything legal) )
```

That is to say, what type does the result of sizeof have? The answer is that it is implementation defined, and will be either unsigned long or unsigned int, depending on an implementation. There are two safe things to do: either always cast the return value to unsigned long, as the examples have done, or to use the defined type size_t provided in the stddef.h header file. For example,

```
/*Pointer18.c */
#include <stddef.h>
#include <stdio.h>
#include <stdlib.h>

main()
{
       size_t sz;
       sz = sizeof(sz);
       printf("size of sizeof is %lu\n", (unsigned long)sz);
       exit(0);
}
```

9.10.9 What sizeof cannot do?

One common mistake made by beginners is shown below:

```
/*Pointer19.c */
#include <stdio.h>
#include <stdlib.h>
const char arr[] = "hello";
const char *cp = arr;
main()
{
       printf("Size of arr %lu\n", (unsigned long) sizeof(arr));
       printf("Size of *cp %lu\n", (unsigned long) sizeof(*cp));
       exit(0);
}
```

The numbers printed will *not* be the same. The first will, correctly, identify the size of arr as 6; five characters followed by a null. The second one will always, on every system, print 1. That is because the type of *cp is const char, which can only have a size of 1, whereas the type of arr is different: array of const char. The confusion arises because this is the one place that the use of an array is not converted into a pointer first. It is never possible, using sizeof, to find out how long an array a pointer points to; we *must* have a genuine array name instead.

Let us Revise

1. Pointers form the heart and soul of C and give the programmer the power to deal with the machine architecture.
2. In **C** pointers may be treated as standard variable in many ways and may behave a bit differently in some operations.
3. A pointer is always assigned with an address value.
4. Of course, just like other variables, we have to declare pointers before we can use them.
5. Pointer arithmetic is one of the highlights of C's design.
6. **C** functions have the capability of returning values that can be, in turn, assigned to variables within the calling program.
7. We can declare the form of a block of data containing different data types by means of a structure declaration.
8. A problem with many simple programs, including in particular little teaching programs such as we have been writing so far, is that they tend to use fixed-size arrays which may or may not be big enough.
9. Memory allocated with malloc lasts as long as we want it to.

Multiple Choice Questions

1. What is printed?

```
# include<stdio.h>
void main()
{
        int *p1 ;
        int *p2 ;
        int r = 4 ;
        p2 = p1 = &r ;
        *p1 = 4.0 * ( *p1 + *p2 ) / r * 3.0 ;
        printf(" %d", *p1);
}
```

(a) 9　　(b) 10

(c) 4　　(d) none

2. What is printed?

```
# include<stdio.h>
# include<string.h>
void main()
{
        char str1[] = "POINTER  TO FUNCTION";
        char str2[] = "POINTER TO FUNCTION";
        int (*comp)(char *, char *);
        comp = strcmp ;
        if( ! comp(str1, str2))     printf("\n STRINGS ARE NOT
    EQUAL");
        else    printf("\n STRINGS ARE NOT EQUAL");
}
```

(a) STRINGS ARE NOT EQUAL (b) STRINGS ARE NOT EQUAL

(c) none (d) both (a) and (b)

3. What is printed?

```
void main()
{
      char str[]  = {"Pointers are powerful tool of C"};
      printf("\n %s",str);
      printf("\n %s", &str[0]);
      printf("\n %s", str+3);
}
```

(a) base address of str and n (b) n and base address of str

(c) base address of str and t (d) none

4. What is printed?

```
# include<stdio.h>
void main()
{
        float y, *point;
        y = 20.7 ;
        *point = y ;
        printf("\n %4.3f", *point);
}
```

(a) 20.7 (b) 20.70

(c) 20.700 (d) none

5. What is printed?

```
  # include<stdio.h>
void main()
{
        int a[10] ;
        int i ;
        int *int_ptr ;
        for(i = 0 ; i < 10 ; i++ )
        {
                a[i] = i * i ;
        }
        int_ptr = a ;
        printf("%d", *(int_ptr + 3 * sizeof(int)));
}
```

(a) 36 (b) 25

(c) 49 (d) none

6. What is printed?

```
# include<stdio.h>
int *fun() ;
```

```
void main()
{
        printf("\n 0x%x %d",fun(), *fun() );
}
int * fun()
{
        int p = 4 ;
        return(&p);
}
```

(a) address of p and 4
(b) 4
(c) both (a) and (b)
(d) none

7. What is printed?

```
# include<stdio.h>
void main()
{
        void *point ;
        int n[10] = {2,8,7,6,7,8,5,4,2,10};
        int i ;
        point = &n[0] ;
                point = &n[i] ;
                printf("\n0x%x  :  %2d", (int *)point, *(int *)
    point);
}
```

(a) 2 and base address
(b) 2 and address of the first element
(c) both (a) and (b)
(d) None

8. If int spread[] ={11,22,33,44,55,66,77,88,99}; then what is printed by the following statement? printf("\n %d", *(spread+2));

(a) 33
(b) 44
(c) 22
(d) none

9. What is wrong in the following code slice?

```
char *ptr;
*ptr = malloc(100);
```

(a) *ptr = malloc(100);
(b) char *ptr;
(c) none

10. What is wrong with the following code?

```
void main()
{
    int a[] = {11,22,33,44};
    int *ptr;
    ptr = &a;
    printf("\n %d", *ptr);
}
```

(a) ptr = &a; (b) printf("\n %d", *ptr);

(c) int *ptr; (d) none

11. Find error in the following code:

```
int a, ptr;
a = 11;
ptr = &a;
```

(a) ptr = &a; (b) a = 11;

(c) int a, ptr; (d) none

12. Find error in the following code:

```
int i = 11;
int *ptr;
ptr = i;
```

(a) ptr = i; (b) int *ptr;

(c) int i=11; (d) none

13. An expression with the asterisk operator, such as ***ptr**, cannot occur on the left-hand side of an assignment statement.

(a) True (b) False

(c) None

14. A function's name is a pointer constant.

(a) True (b) False

(c) None

15. An array's name is

(a) Pointer constant (b) Array's constant

(c) Pointer variable (d) Keep the address of first cell

16. Identify errors, if any, in each of the following array declaration statements, assuming that ROW and COLUMN are declared as symbolic constants:

(a) int scoreboard (100); (b) double matrix [10,15];

(c) void average_value[ROW],[COLUMN]; (d) void char name[15];

(e) f l o a t sum [ ]; (f) double emp_salary [i + ROW]

(g) long int list [ROW] (h) int array_x[COLUMN];

17. Identify errors, if any, in each of the following initialization statements.

(a) float number[ ] = {0,0,0,0,0}; (b) double item[3][2] = {0,1,2,3,4,5};

(c) char word[] = {'A'.,'R', 'R', 'A', 'Y'}; (d) int m[2,4] = {{0,0,0,0}, {1,l,l,l}};

(e) float result[10] = 0;

18. Assume that the arrays M and N are declared as follows:

```
int M[5][4];
float N[4];
```

Find the errors (if any) in the following code segments.

(a)
```
for (i=l; i<=10; i++)
for(j=l; j<=8; j++)
M[i] [j] = 0;
```

(b) for (i=l; i<8; i++)
scanf("%f", N[;]);
(c) for (i=O; i<=8; i++)
N[i] = N[i]+i;
(d) for (i=4; i>=O; i—)
for (j=O; j<8; j++)
M [i] [j] = N [j] + 1.0 ;

19. We want to declare a two-dimensional double type array called **matrix** for 3 rows and 5 columns. State which of the following declarations are correct in respect to C?

(a) double matrix [3], [5] ;
(b) double matrix [5] [3];
(c) double matrix [1+2] [2+3];
(d) double matrix [3,5];
(e) double matrix [3] [5];

20. Which of the following initialization statements are correct?

(a) char str1[4] = "GOOD";
(b) char str2 [ ] = "C";
(c) char str3 [5] = "Moon";
(d) char str4[ ] = {'S', 'U', 'N'};
(e) char str5 [10] = "Sun";

True/False Questions

1. float *PV [10] is a pointer to 10 element integer array.
2. Adding a constant value to a pointer is permissible, but addition of two pointers (of the same type) is not.
3. Arrays cannot be returned by functions, however pointer to arrays can be returned.
4. A pointer variable can be at most two level deep.
5. Two pointers of the same type may not be subtracted.
6. If x is an integer variable and px is a pointer; the statement px = *x; assigns the address of x to px.
7. A pointer is a variable that points to another variable.

Match Columns

Match the matter in Column A with the matter in Column B.

Column A	Column B
A. int(*p)[10]	1. function returning pointer to int
B. int *p[10]	2. To get single word string
C. int *f()	3. pointer to function returning int
D. int (*f)()	4. array of pointer to char
E. scanf("*s", str)	5. p is a pointer to an array of integers
F. char *day[13]	6. p is a pointer to an aray of integer pointers

Fill in the Blanks with Appropriate Words

a. defrencing b. different c. addresses d. (p)
e. bound

1. Each pointer is ________ to the type of variable to which it points.

2. All the variables defined in a program including pointer variables reside at specific ______.
3. ____________ is the process of accessing and manipulating data stored in the memory location pointed to by a pointer.
4. The unary address operators (&) and dereferencing operator (*) have ________ precedence.
5. If p is a pointer variable, statements if ________ and if(p!=Null) are equivalent.

Descriptive Type Questions

1. A text **T** and patterns **P** and **Q** are in memory. Write a program for replacing every occurrence of **P** in **T** by **Q**.
2. Write a function **Div (j, k)** where **j** and **k** are positive integers such that **Div (j, k) = 1,** if **j** divides **k**, otherwise **Div (j, k) = 0.**
3. Write a function, which finds the location of the largest element and the location of the 2nd largest elements in a list of numbers with the help of pointer.
4. Let **W** be the string formed by **ABCD**. Write functions for
   (a) Find the length of **W**.
   (b)List all sub-strings of **W**.
   (c) List all the initial sub-strings of **W**.
5. Write a function that counts the number **NUM** of paragraphs in the short story **S**.
6. Write a program that interchanges the **j**th and **k**th paragraph in text **T**.
7. Write a function **compare** () that compares two strings.
8. Write a function **strcpy** () that copies the **string1** into **string2** using pointers.
9. Most time-sharing computers require the user to login by giving a user name and password. Write a program that simulates this activity. The program begins by giving user a list of available computers (e.g., AS/400, SUN ULTRA, HP-9000, etc). After the user selects a given computer, the program prompts for a user name and checks to see whether such a user is valid. If not, it issues an error message and the program terminates. If the name is found, the program asks for a password. If the password is valid a welcome message is displayed; otherwise an error message is displayed and program terminates. During the password checking it should take three trials.
10. Write a program to find the sum of squares of elements on diagonal of square matrix.
11. A factory has 6 divisions and stocks 8 categories of products. An inventory table is updated for each division and for each product as there is received. There are three independent suppliers of products to the factory.
    (a) Design a data format to represent each transaction
    (b) Write a function to take a transaction and update the inventory.
    (c) If cost per item is also given write a function to calculate the total inventory value.
12. Write a function that will reverse a string. Use **for** loop that swaps the **first** and **last** character, then **second** and **next to last** characters and so on. The string should be passed to function as an argument. Take following sentences as input: "Able was I eve I saw Elba"
13. Write a program that will read a text file and creates another file that is identical except that the sequence of consecutive blank spaces are replaced by a single space and size of each line should be of 40 characters and should be left and right justified.
14. What does ***p++** increment **p** or what it points to? Write a C code to justify your answer.

Answers to Objective Type Questions

Multiple Choice Questions

1. a	2. b	3. c	4. a
5. c	6. b	7. a	8. c
9. b	10. a	11. a	12. c
13. b	14. c	15. a	16. b
17. a	18. c	19. a	20. b

True False Questions

1. F	2. F	3. T	4. F
5. F	6. F	7. T	

Matching Columns

A. 5	B. 6	C. 1	D. 3
E. 2	F. 4		

Fill in the Blanks

1. e	2. c	3. a	4. b
5. d			

Self Referential Structures and Linked Lists 10

10.1 Creation of a Singly Connected Linked List

In this chapter we will discuss application of user defined data types and dynamic memory allocation property of C. As a case study we have considered the simple Linked List. Finally we will conclude this chapter with an application development for the processing the students' information. For processing the students data we have consider the following operations to perform.

- Deletion of information
- Insertion of information
- Updating information
- Report writing etc.

If we use fixed length memory storage (arrays) it is not always possible to perform above tasks. A linked list allocation storage method can result in efficient use of computer memory and computer time. Linked list are useful because:

- **Unpredictable storage requirements**: The exact amount of data storage space required by a program in these areas often depends on the data being processed and consequently this requirement can not be easily determined at the time of writing the program.
- **Extensive manipulation of the stored data**: Programs in these areas require the operations such as insertion and deletion to perform frequent operations on the data.

Linked List

A linked list is defined as a collection of nodes. Each node has two parts:

- Information
- Pointer to next node

Information part may consist of one or more than one fields. In other words a linked list consists of series of structures, which are not necessarily contiguous. Each structure contains one or more than one contiguous information fields and a pointer to a structure containing its successor. The last node of the list contains **NULL ('\0' or 0)** in the pointer field. The pointer contains the address of the location where next information is stored. For example, **Figure 10.1** illustrates a linked list structure with 5 nodes, each node containing one information field. A linked list also contains a list pointer variable called **start**, which contains the address of the first node in the list. Hence, there is an arrow drawn from **start** to the first node in the linked list. If there is no node in the list, the list is called **NULL** list or empty list.

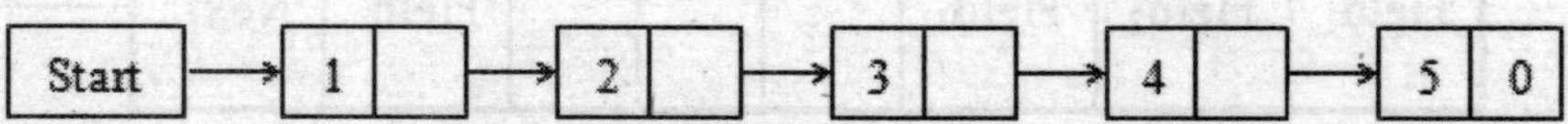

Figure 10.1 Linked list

To create a linked list, following steps are required:

(a) Declare the structure that defines the list entries.

(b) Declare the variables **start** and ***node (or *start** and ***node)**

(c) Assign **start.next = NULL** when start is declared without pointer operator (**or start = NULL** if **start** is ***start**) to signify an empty list.

(d) Find each list entry

(i) Find end of the list so that **node->next** is **NULL.**

(ii) Allocate memory for the new entry by assigning it to **node->next.**

(iii) Assign node the value of **node->next.**

(iv) Assign the information member values to node.

(v) Assign **node->next** the value **NULL** to indicate the end of the list.

We have discussed that a linked list is a collection of the nodes (structure) of the same type and hence it can be defined as:

```
        struct Node
        {
Data type Information;
                  struct Node *Next  ;

        } start;
```

The above definition of the structure (Node) is equivalent to the following figure:

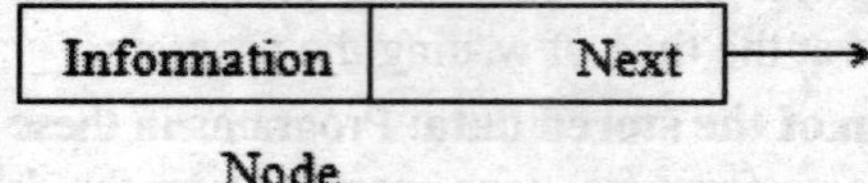

Node

A node may contain any number of information fields. The general declaration of a node is:

```
        struct Tag Name
        {
  Data Type1 Field1  ;
                  Data Type2 Field2  ;
                  Data Type3 Field3  ;
           ...
                  Data Type n  Field n  ;
   struct Tag Name *Next  ;
        };
```

The above syntax may be represented as:

$Field_1$	$Field_2$	$Field_3$	...	...	...	$Field_n$	Next →

How can a linked list be created? To do this, let one has a node as follows:

```
        struct List
```

```
        {
        char Data ;
            struct List *Next ;
            };
```

Let one wants to create a linked list that contains four nodes, the nodes are **$Node_1$, $Node_2$, $Node_3$** and **$Node_4$**. These nodes are defined as

```
    struct List node1, node2, node3, node4;
```

Figure 10.2 illustrates the allocation of memory spaces to the nodes **$Node_1$, $Node_2$, $Node_3$** and **$Node_4$**.

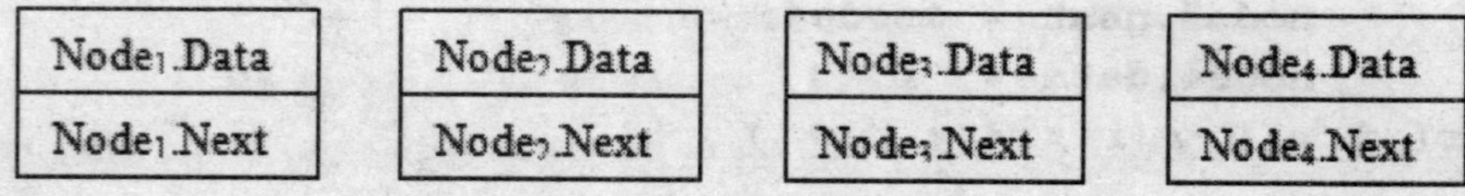

Figure 10.2 Allocation of memory space to individual node

If one wants to create a link between these four nodes, the following arrangement is required.

- $Node_1$.Next = &$Node_2$;

  Assign the address of the **$Node_2$** to **$Node_1$.Next**, which establishes a link between **$Node_1$** and **$Node_2$**
- $Node_2$.Next = &$Node_3$;

  Assign the address of the **$Node_3$** to **$Node_2$.Next**, which establishes a link between **$Node_2$** and **$Node_3$**
- $Node_3$.Next = &$Node_4$;

  Assign the address of the **$Node_4$** to **$Node_3$.Next,** which establishes a link between **$Node_3$** and **$Node_4$**.

By repeating the above process, one can create a linked list of desired size. Example 10.1 demonstrates simple linked list code.

Example 10.1: Write C code which creates a simple linked list.

Answer: The program segment **LINK.C** implements the above discussion.

```
/* LINK.C */
/* This program segment defines linked list having a character
    type node */
# include<stdio.h>
# include<malloc.h>
  struct List
  {
          char data ;
          struct List *next ;
  } ;

    typedef  struct List Linked;

    void main()
    {
```

```
            Linked *start, node1, node2 , node3 , node4;
            int i ;
            start = (struct List *) malloc(sizeof(Linked));
            start = &node1;
            node1.data = 'A' ;
            node1.next = &node2;
            node2.data = 'B' ;
            node2.next = &node3;
            node3.data = 'C' ;
            node3.next = &node4;
            node4.data = 'D' ;
      for( i = 0 ; i < 4 ; i++ )
      {
        printf("\n %c", start->data);
        start = start->next ;
        printf("\n Press a key");
        getchar() ;
       }
        }
```

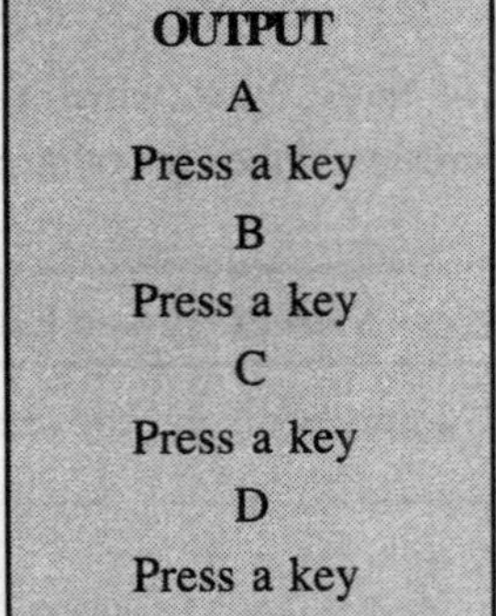

OUTPUT

A
Press a key
B
Press a key
C
Press a key
D
Press a key

The program segment **LINK.C** illustrates that four nodes exist in the memory as illustrated in **Figure 10.3.**

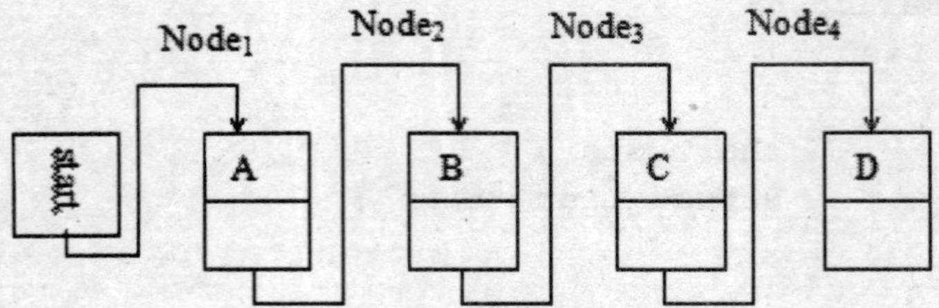

Figure 10.3 Existence of nodes in memory

If one wants to create a linked list of desired size, one can does the same using the following steps. Example 12.2 implements this algorithm.

Step 1: [Initially list empty]

Start = NULL

Step 2: [Allocate space to newly created node]
Node = Create a node

Step 3: [Assign value to information part of a node]
Info [Node] = Data

Step 4: [Assign null to the address part for signaling end of the list]
Next [Node] = NULL

Step 5: [Assign address of first node to start variable]
Start = Node

Step 6: [Return the created node]
Return (Start)

Example 10.2: Write C code to create a linked of any size.

Answer: Following program segment (LINK_C.C) implements algorithms defines above. Run this program segment and see the way it is executing the implementation.

```
/* CREATING SIMPLE LINKED LIST */
/* LINK_C.C */
# include <stdio.h>
# include <malloc.h>
struct link
{
   int info;
   struct link *next;
};
int i;
struct link *start = NULL, *previous; /* Shows empty list */
void creat_link_list (struct link *);
void display (struct link *);
void creat_link_list (struct link *node)
{
   char ch;
   printf("\n Press a key to continue … ");
   i = 0;
   ch = getchar();
   while(ch !='n')
   {
      printf("\n Input the node: %d :", i+1);
      scanf("%d",&node->info);
      node->next = (struct link* ) malloc (sizeof (struct link));
      previous = node;
      node = node->next;
```

```
        i++;
        fflush(stdin); /* empty the keyboard buffer */
        printf("\n Input choice n for break: ");
        ch = getchar();
    }
        node->next=NULL;
        previous->next=NULL; /* marking the last of the list null */
        free(node); /* free the memory space associated with node */
}

/* Display the list */
void  display(struct link *node)
{
    printf("\n Values of the entered nodes are as follows:\n");
    while (node)
    {
        printf("  %d", node->info);
        node = node->next;
    }
}
/* Function main */
void main()
{
    struct link *node = (struct link *)malloc(sizeof(struct link));
    creat_link_list(node);
    display(node);
}
```

10.2 Traversing a Linked List

It is a methodology in which each node is processed exactly once. When a list is stored in computer memory as a linked list, our aim is to traverse the list starting from the first node to the end of the list. Consider a pointer type variable **Current_node** that points to the node currently being processed. Accordingly, **Next[Current_node]** points to the next node that is to be processed as shown in Figure 10.4. Thus, the statement

```
Current_node = Next [Current_node];
```

moves the pointer to the next node in the list. The steps involved in the processing of linked list nodes are as follows.

Step 1: [Initialize pointer variable current_node]

Current_node = start

Step 2: [Perform the traversing operation]

Repeat thru Step 3 while Current_node ¹ NULL

Process Info [Current_node]

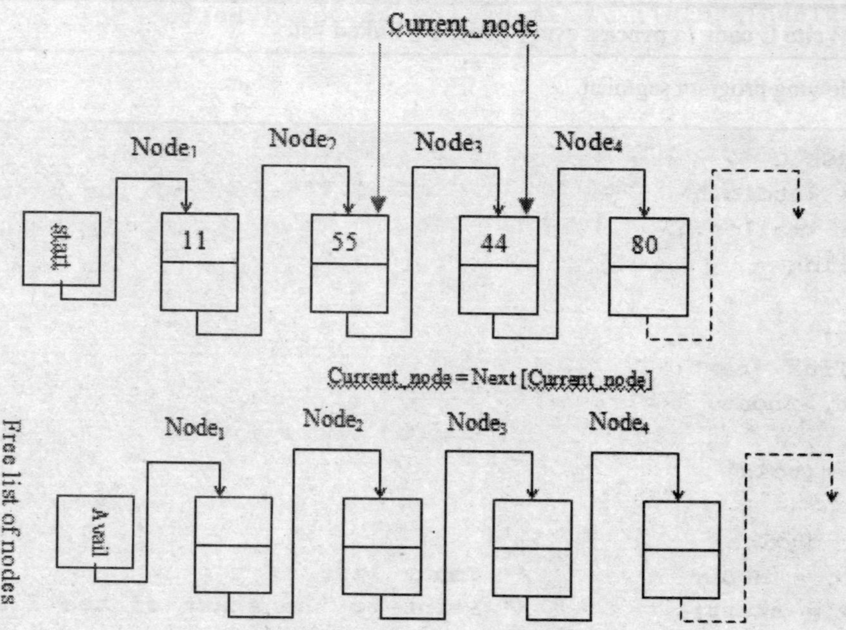

Figure 12.4 Traversing a linked list

Step 3: [Move pointer to next node]
Current_node = Next [Current_node]

Step 4: Exit

The variable **start** points to the first entry in the list. The code **node = strart** assigns the address of the first entry to **node**. Likewise, as we will recall, the end of the list is indicated by **NULL**; the loop simply tests the current value of **node** to see if it is **NULL**. If **node** is not **NULL**, the loop displays the entry's value and assigns **node** the address of the next list entry. Suppose we have a list that contains **9** elements (integer) numbers: 11, 22, 33, 44, 55, 66, 77, 88, 99. The links of each element are shown in **Figure 10.5.** When we apply above steps for processing each element in list, we see the following operations.

```
Current_node = 2
start = 2

Info [2] = 11 Next [2] = 5
Info [5] = 55 Next [5] = 6
Info [6] = 44 Next [6] = 12
Info [12] = 80 Next [12] = 1
Info [1] = 22 Next [1] = 9
Info [9] = 33 Next [9] = 4
Info [4] = 66 Next [4] = 8
Info [8] = 99 Next [8] = 7
Info [7] = 88 Next [7] = '\0'
```

Thus, the processed list is: 11, 55, 44, 80, 22, 33, 66, 99, 88. Implementation of the above discussion is shown in Example 10.3.

Example 10.3: Write C code to process every node in a linked list.

Answer: the following program segment.

```
/* TRVERSE.C */
#include <stdio.h>
#include <malloc.h>
struct link
{
int info;
struct link *next;
} *start, *node;

void main(void)
{
    char choice;
    start = NULL;          /* Empty list */
    node = start;          /* Point to the start of the list */
    start=node = (struct link *) (malloc(sizeof(struct link)));
    do
    {
      printf("enter information:->");
      scanf("%d",&node->info);
      printf("do you want to add more element(y/n):->");
      fflush(stdin);
      choice=getchar();
      if(choice=='y')
      {
      node->next = (struct link *) malloc(sizeof(struct link));
      node=node->next;
      }
    }while (choice=='y');
      node->next=NULL;
         printf("press any key to display list:->");
      fflush(stdin);
      getchar();

 /* Display the list  */
      node=start;
      while(node)
    {
     printf("\n %d",  node->info);
     node = node->next;
```

```
    }
    getchar();
  }
```

In the above program, we have used the following code segment, which traverses the list starting from the first node.

```
/* Display the list */
     node=start;
    while(node)
  {
   printf("\n %d",   node->info);
   node = node->next;
  }
```

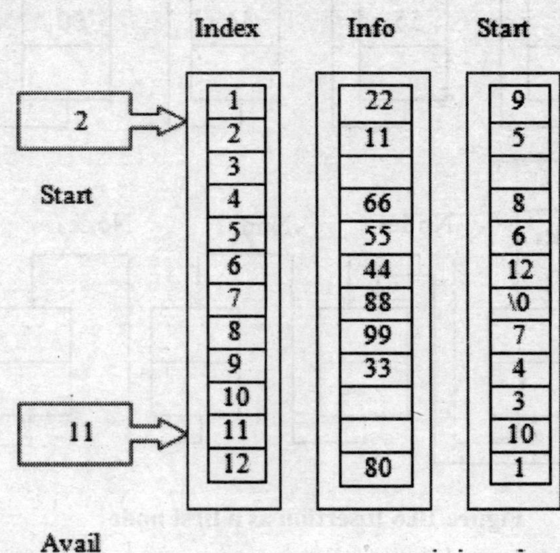

Figure 10.5 Links of nodes

10.3 Insertion into a Linked List

There are many applications where it is desirable to maintain an ordered linear list. The ordering may be in increasing or decreasing order of the information field. Such an ordering often results more efficient processes in many cases. If one wants to insert some information into linked list, following points must be remembered before performing the required operation:

1. Create a new node or remove a node from the availability stack or free memory space.
2. Setting the field of the new node means allocating required memory space to newly created node.
3. If the linked list is empty, return the address of a new node.
4. If the node precedes all others in the list, insert the node at front of the list and return its address.
5. Repeat thru Step 6 while information contents of the new node.
6. Obtain the next node in the linked list.
7. Insert the new node in the linked list and return address of its first node.

Suppose we have a list as illustrated in **Figure 12.4** and want to perform insertion operation on the list. The insertion operation is classified into following three categories:

- Insert as a first node
- Insert as a last node

10.3.1 Insertion as a First Node

Let the **start** pointer hold the address of the first node. If we want to insert new1 node into the list as a first node then **new_1->next** variable holds the address of the first node of the list (previously existing). If **Figure 10.4** illustrates a list before insertion operation then after insertion the list becomes as shown in **Figure 10.6.**

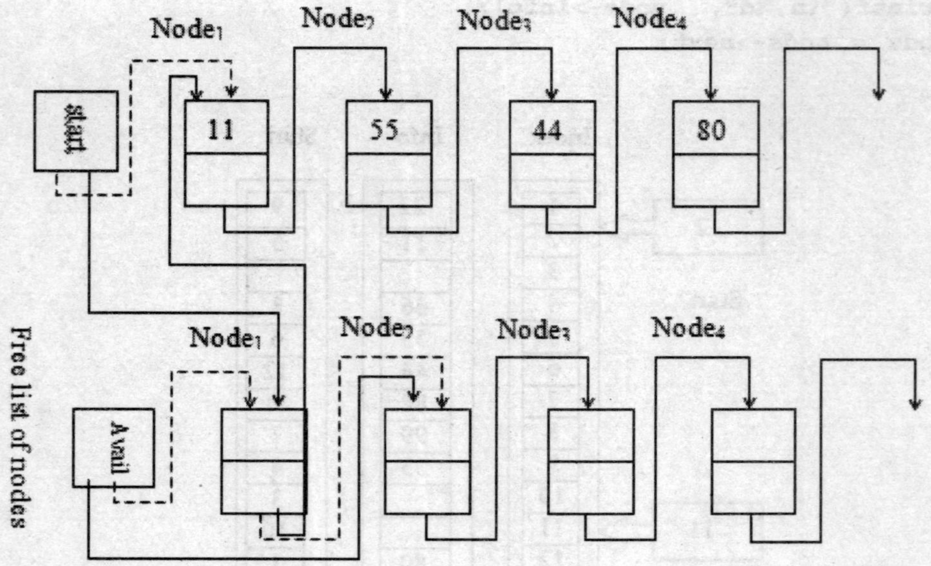

Figure 10.6 Insertion as a first node

The above discussion can be summarized in the following steps.

Step 1: [Check for free space]
If New_1= NULL output "OVERFLOW" and Exit

Step 2: [Allocate free space]
New_1= Create new node

Step 3: [Read value of information part of a new node]
Info [New_1] = Value

Step 4: [Link address part of the currently created node with the address of start]
Next [New_1] = Start

Step 5: [Now assign address of newly created node to the start]
Start = New_1

Step 6: Exit

For example, consider the list shown in **Figure 10.5.** Then after inserting 100 in this list as a first node, the list is as illustrated in **Figure 10.7.**

In the C language, in the statement form above discussion can be written as:

```
node = start; /* receive address of the first node in the list */
new1 = (struct link ) malloc (sizeof (struct link)); /* create a
      node */
/* assign address of the previously first node to the next of the
      new1 */
new1->next = node;
new1->data = some_value;
   start = new1;   /* assign address of the new1 to node to start
      pointer */
```

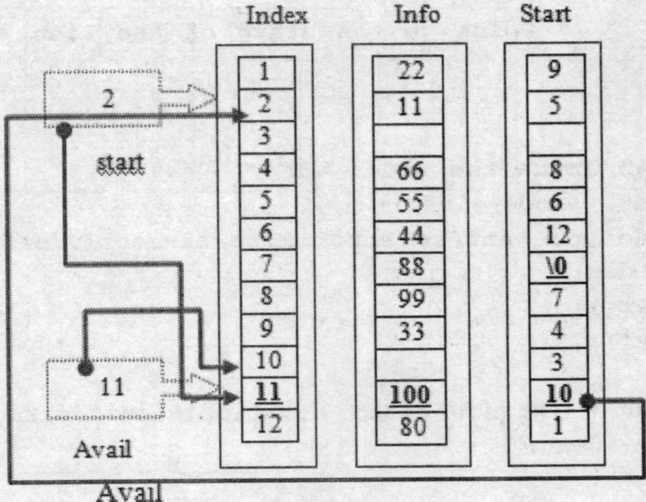

Figure 10.7 Insertion as a first node

Go through the Example 10.4 which is implementing the above statements.

Example 10.4: Write C code to insert an element as a first node in a simple linked list.

Answer: Following program segment implements the above discussion.

```
/* INSERT A NODE INTO A SIMPLE LINKED LIST AT THE BEGINNING */
/* LINK_IF.C */
# include <stdio.h>
# include <malloc.h>

struct link
{
int info;
struct link *next;
} *start, *node;
int i;
```

```
struct link *start, *previous, *new1;
void insertion(struct link *);
void create_list(struct link *);
void display(struct link *);

/* Function create a linked list */
void create_list(struct link *node)
{

    char ch;
    start = NULL; /* Empty list */
    start=node;    /* Point to the start of the list */
    i = 0;
    do
    {
        printf("\n Input the node: %d: ", (i+1));
        scanf("%d", &node->info);
        printf("do you want to enter more element(y/n):->");
        fflush(stdin);
        ch=getchar();
        if(ch=='y')
        {
        node->next = (struct link* ) malloc(sizeof(struct link));
        node=node->next;
        }
        i++;
    }while(ch=='y');
    node->next=NULL;
}

/* Inserting a node */

void insertion(struct link *node)
{
   node = start;
   new1 = (struct link* ) malloc(sizeof(struct link));
   new1->next = node ;
   start = new1;
   printf("\n Input the first node value: ");
   scanf("%d", &new1->info);
}

/* Display the list */
```

```
void display(struct link *node)
{
   node = start;
   printf("\n After Inserting a node list is as follows:\n");
   while (node)
   {
      printf("\n 0x%x", node);
      printf(" %d", node->info);
      node = node->next;
   }
}

/* Function main */

void main()
{
   struct link *node = (struct link *) malloc(sizeof(struct link));
   create_list(node);
   insertion(node);
   display(node);
}
```

10.3.2 Insertion As A Last Node

The easiest way to add an entry is to append it at the end of the list. To append an item to a linked list, we loop through the list until find the element whose next member points to **NULL**. The code segment, which is used to perform this task, is:

```
node = start;
while (node->next)
   node = node->next;
```

When **node->next** points to **NULL**, it gives the end of the list. So we can allocate memory for the entry as given below:

```
node->next = malloc(required size);
```

Next we assign the desired entry values and assign the new entry's next field to point to **NULL**.

```
node = node->next;
node->member = some_value;
node->next = NULL;
```

If **Figure 10.4** illustrates a list before insertion operation then the list after inserting a node at the end of the list becomes as illustrated in **Figure 10.8.** For example, if we have a list shown in **Figure 10.5** then after inserting 100 in this list as a last node, resulting list is shown in **Figure 10.9.** The steps involved to insert any information in a list are as follows.

Step 1: [Check for free space]
If New_1 = NULL output "OVERFLOW" and Exit

Step 2: [Allocate free space]
New_1 = Create new node

Step 3: [Read value of information part of a new node and set next pointer of New1 to NULL]

Info [New_1] = Value

Next[New1] = NULL

Step 4: [Move the pointer to the end of the list]

Repeat while Next[Node] ¹ NULL

Node = Next [Node]

Step 4: [Link currently created node with the last node of the list]

Next [Node] = New_1

Step 5: Exit

Example 10.5 demonstrates the insertion of node as a last node in a given list.

Example 10.5: Write C code to insert an element as a last node into a simple linked list.

Answer: In the following program segment first of all we create list of desired size then an insertion of last is done.

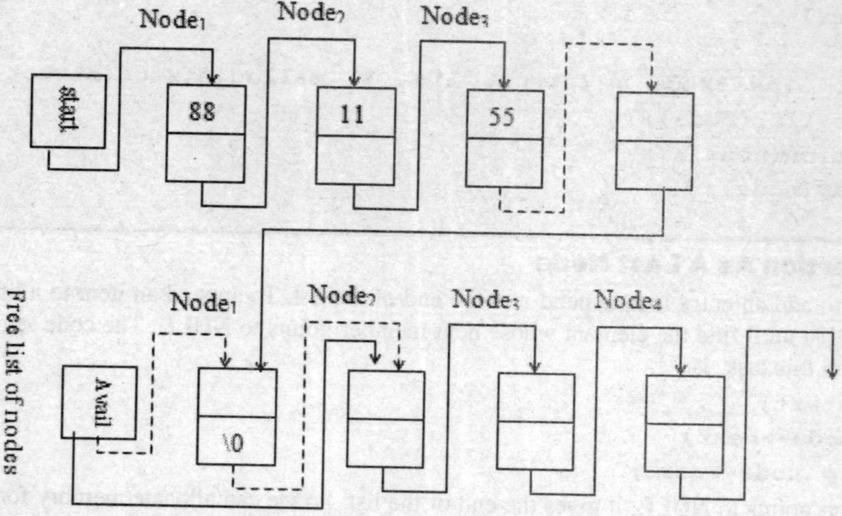

Figure 10.8 Insertion as a last node

```
/* INSERT A NODE INTO A SIMPLE LINKED LIST AT THE END OF THE LIST
   */
/* LINK_IL.C */
# include <stdio.h>
# include <malloc.h>

struct link
{
   int info;
   struct link *next;
};

int i;
```

```
struct link *start, *previous, *new1;
void insertion(struct link *);
void create_list(struct link *);
void display(struct link *);

/* Function create a linked list */

void create_list(struct link *node)
{
   char ch;
   start = NULL;  /* Empty list */
   start=node;        /* Point to the start of the list */
   i = 0;
   do
   {
      printf("\n Input the node: %d: ", (i+1));
      scanf("%d",&node->info);
      printf("\n want to add more element(y/n):->");
      fflush(stdin);
      ch = getchar();
      if(ch=='y')
      {
      node->next = (struct link* ) malloc(sizeof(struct link));
      node = node->next;
      }
      i++;
   }while(ch=='y');
   node->next=NULL;
}

/* Inserting a node */
void insertion(struct link *node)
{
   start=node;
   while(node->next!=NULL)
   {
      previous=node;
      node = node->next;
   }
   new1 = (struct link* ) malloc(sizeof(struct link));
   node->next=new1;
   printf("\n Input the last node value: ");
   scanf("%d",&new1->info);
```

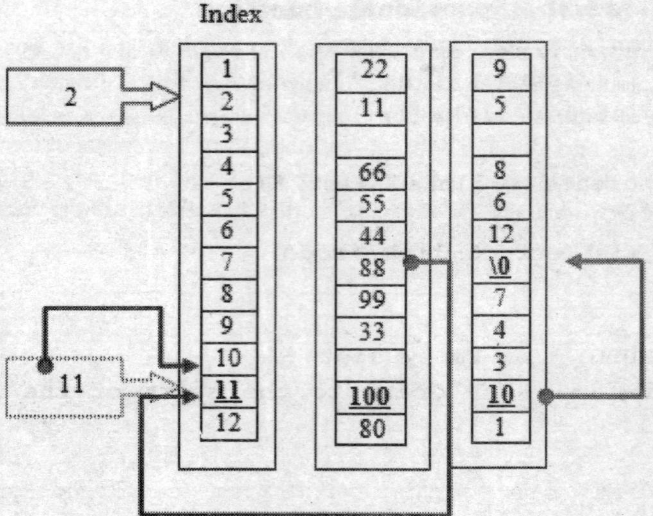

Figure 10.9 Insertion as a last node

```
   new1->next=NULL;
}

/* Display the list */
void display(struct link *node)
{
   while (node)
   {
      printf("\n 0x%x", node);
      printf(" %d", node->info);
      node = node->next;
   }
}

/* Function main */

void main()
{
   struct link *node = (struct link *) malloc(sizeof(struct link));
   create_list(node);
   printf("\n Created list is as follows:\n");
   display(node);
   insertion(node);
   printf("\n After Inserting a node list is as follows:\n");
   display(node);
}
```

10.3.3 Insertion of a Node at Specific Location

In some cases, one might want to place elements at specific locations in a list. For example, if we want to create a linked list that contains the sorted names of files in the current directory, program needs to place each file name into the list at the correct position. To insert an item at a specific place (location) in a list, the program will normally track the **starting node, current node** and the **previous** of the current node. To achieve this we scan the list from the beginning and move up to the desired node where we want to insert the new node. Here, we create a new node and insert it into the list and restructure the complete list.

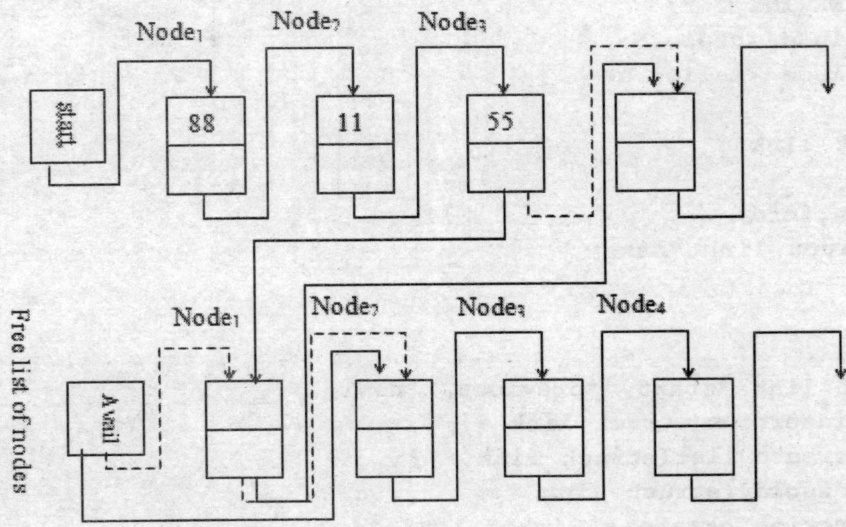

Figure 10.10 Pointer Link for Insertion of a node at a specific place

From the following steps it is clear that when one wants to insert a node into a linked list, one should know the node number/node information where he/she wants to insert a new node in the list. If one does not know the node number/node information it is not easy job to insert a new node into the list. If one goes through trial and error method may insert the new node in the list but it requires much more time. In trial and error method if one input a new node number but that particular node does not exists in the list that may create problems. Some times it may crash the list. When a program needs to insert a new element, it will perform the following processing:

```
new1 = malloc(sizeof(struct link);
previous->next = new1;
new1->member = some_value;
new1->next = node;
```

If **Figure 10.4** illustrates a list before insertion operation then the list after inserting a node into a list it becomes as illustrated in **Figure 10.10.** For example, consider the list shown in **Figure 10.5**. Then after inserting 100 in this list at a specific place, the list becomes as shown in **Figure 10.11.** From the result it is clear that insertion operation simply places new node between node 1 and 2.

The next field of node 1 is now linked with newly inserted node and next field of newly inserted node is linked with node 2. Thus, new node that was inserted occupies the place of 2nd node. The program segment **LINK_INI.C** demonstrates the same operation as discussed in **Figure 10.11.** Example 12.6 demonstrates the insertion of node at desired place in a given list.

Example 10.6: Write C code to insert an element as a last node into a simple linked list.

Answer: In the following program segment, first of all we create list of desired size then an insertion of a desired node at desired place.

```
/* INSERT A NODE INTO A SIMPLE LINKED LIST INFORMATION IS KNOWN
     AND PUT AFTER SOME SPECIFIED NODE */
/* LINK_INI.C */
# include <stdio.h>
# include <malloc.h>

struct link
{
   int info;
   struct link *next;
};

int i;
struct link *start, *previous, *new1;
void insertion(struct link *);
void create_list(struct link *);
void display(struct link *);
/* Function create a linked list */

void create_list(struct link *node)
{
   char ch;
   start = NULL;   /* Empty list */
   start=node;        /* Point to the start of the list */
   i = 0;
   do
   {
     printf("\n Input the node: %d: ", (i+1));
     scanf("%d",&node->info);
     printf("\n want to add more element(y/n):->");
     fflush(stdin);
     ch = getchar();
     if(ch=='y')
     {
     node->next = (struct link* ) malloc(sizeof(struct link));
     node = node->next;
     }
     i++;
```

```
    }while(ch=='y');
    node->next=NULL;
}
/* Inserting a node */
void insertion(struct link *node)
{
    int val;
    start=node;
    printf("give node info before which you want to insert:->");
    scanf("%d",&val);
    while((node))
    {
        previous=node;
        node=node->next;
        if(node->info==val)
            break;
    }
    new1 = (struct link* ) malloc(sizeof(struct link));
    previous->next=new1;
    printf("\n Input the new node value: ");
    scanf("%d",&new1->info);
    new1->next = node;
}

/* Display the list */

void display(struct link *node)
{
    while (node)
    {
        printf("\n 0x%x", node);
        printf(" %d", node->info);
        node = node->next;
    }
}

void main()
{
    struct link *node = (struct link *) malloc(sizeof(struct link));
    create_list(node);
    printf("\n Created list is as follows:\n");
    display(node);
    insertion(node);
```

```
    printf("\n After Inserting a node list is as follows:\n");
    display(node);
}
```

10.4 Deletion from a Linked List

If one is interested in deletion of a node from a linear linked list, before performing the deletion, one should take into account following points:

1. If the linked list is empty, the deletion is not possible and the output should display **Underflow** message.
2. Consider the Step 3 while end of the list has not been reached or the node has not been found.
3. Obtain the next node in the list and record its predecessor. Check for the existence of the node for which information is given.
4. If the end of the list has been reached, "**node not found**" message can be displayed.
5. Delete the node from the list.
6. Return the node to the free area.

The deletion operation is classified into following three categories:

- Deletion of first node
- Deletion of last node
- Deletion of desired node from any place in the list

10.4.1 Deletion of First Node

Suppose we have a linked list as shown in **Figure 10.12** and want to delete first node. Then accomplish the following operations:

- Make link of start pointer to the second node in the list.
- Free the space associated with first node.
- Operating system then collects the free space and makes link for currently freed node with available free space.

start points to first element in the list. The value associated with it is stored into **node** variable. If the value of this node is **NULL,** it means that the list is empty and messages **UNDERFLOW** is displayed and function exits. If the list is not empty, the address of the next node is assigned to start pointer and the list becomes as shown in **Figure 10.13.** When we free the space associated with a node, it is attached to the free list. This discussion can be formulated in order in which it is performed. These steps show the property of the operation done by a statement.

```
node = start; /* Points to the first element of the list */
/*This statement makes link of start to link of the next node that
     is linked with second node*/
start = node->next;
free (Node);
```

Steps involved in deletion of first node from a linked list is.

Step 1: [Initialization]

Node = Start.Next [Points to the first node in the list]

Step 2: [Perform deletion operation]

If Node = NULL

Output "UNDERFLOW" and Exit

Else [Delete first node]

Start = Next [Node] [Move pointer to next node in the list]

Free the space associated with Node

Step 3: Exit

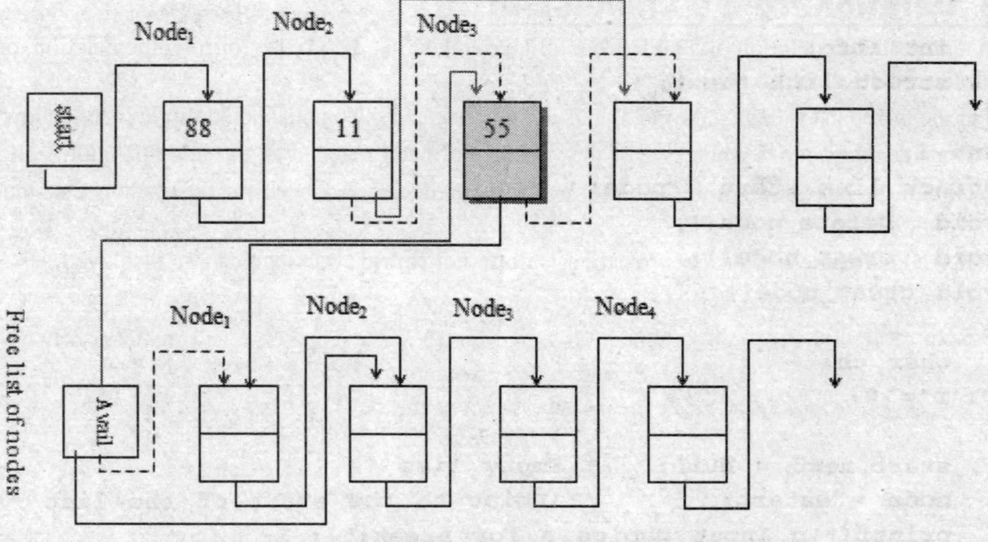

Figure 10.12 List with deletion operation

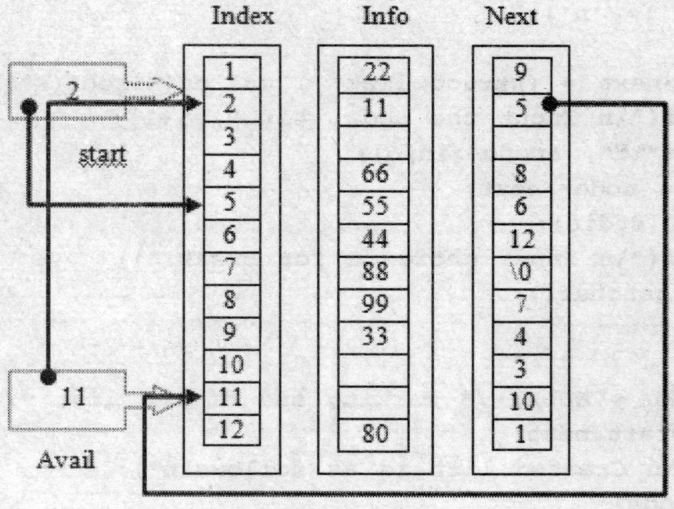

Figure 10.13 List after deletion of first node

Example 10.7 demonstrates the above discussion.

Example 10.7: Write C code to delete first node from a simple linked list.

Answer: This program segment first creates a simple linked list of the user's desired size then deletion of operation performs.

```
/* DELETING FIRST NODE FROM A SIMPLE LINKED LIST */
/* LINK_DF.C*/
# include <stdio.h>
# include <malloc.h>
struct link
{
   int info;
   struct link *next;
};
int i;
struct link start, *node;
void  Delete_node();
void  creat_node();
void creat_node()
{
   char ch;
   i = 0;

   start.next = NULL;   /* Empty list */
   node = &start;        /* Point to the start of the list */
   printf("\n Input choice n for break:");
   ch = getchar();
   while(ch != 'n')
   {
      node->next = (struct link* ) malloc(sizeof(struct link));
      printf("\n Input the node: %d: ", i+1);
      scanf("%d", &node->info);
      node = node->next;
      fflush(stdin);
      printf("\n Input choice n for break:");
      ch = getchar();
      i++;
   }
   node->next = NULL; /* marking end of the list */
   node = start.next;
   printf("\n Created list is as follows\n");
   while (node)
   {
      printf("\n 0x%x", node);
      printf(" %d", node->info);
      node = node->next;
   }
}
```

```
/* Removing a node */
void Delete_node()
{
    node = start.next;
    if (node == NULL)
    {
       printf("\n Under flow");
    } else
    {
       start.next=node->next;
       free(node);
    }
    /* Display the list */
    node = start.next;
    printf("\n After deleting first node list is as follows\n");
    while (node)
    {
       printf("\n 0x%x", node);
       printf(" %d", node->info);
       node = node->next;
    }
}

/* Function main */
void main()
{
    creat_node();
    Delete_node();
}
```

10.4.2 Deletion of Last Node

The simple method to delete last node of a linked list is described as follows. First count the number of nodes in the list. Scan the list from beginning to end of the list will effectively counts the number of nodes in the list. Let it contains **n** nodes. Now second time once again we scan the list from beginning to **n-1** nodes of the list. At last we free the last node. The deletion mechanism is similar to the previous one. Suppose we have a list as shown in **Figure 10.5.** Then after deletion of last node the list becomes as illustrated in **Figure 10.14.** The code segment, which is used to perform this task, is:

```
node = &start;
while (node->next)
    node = node->next;
```

Figure 10.5 represents a linked list of which each node has integer number as an information. If we want to traverse the list we can easily traverse the list from starting end to end of the list. **Figure 10.14** illustrates the deletion operation. Example 12.8 implements the following steps which are involved in deletion of last node from a linked list.

Step 1: [Initialization]
Node = Start.Next [Points to the first node in the list]
Previous = Assign address of Start

Step 2: [Check list is empty or not]
If Node = NULL
Output "UNDERFLOW" and Exit

Step 3: [Scan the list to count the number of nodes in the list]
Repeat while Next[Node] ¹ NULL
Node = Next [Node]
Previous = Next [Previous]

Step 4: [Check if last node is arising]
Next [Previous] = Next [Node]
Free (Node)

Example 10.8: Write C code to delete last node from a simple linked list.

Answer: This program segment first creates a simple linked list of the user's desired size then deletion of operation performs.

```
/* DELETING LAST NODE FROM A SIMPLE LINKED LIST */
/* LINK_DL.C */

# include <stdio.h>
# include <malloc.h>
struct link
{
   int info;
   struct link *next;
};

int i;
struct link start, *previous;
void  Delete_node(struct link *);
void  creat_node(struct link *);
void creat_node(struct link *node)
{
   char ch;
   i = 0;
   start.next = NULL;   /* Empty list */
   start.next = node; // = &start;       /* Point to the start of
      the list */
   printf("\n Input choice n for break:");
   ch = getchar();
```

```
    while(ch != 'n')
    {
        printf("\n Input the node: %d: ", (i+1));
        scanf("%d", &node->info);
        node->next = NULL;
        fflush(stdin);
        printf("\n Input choice n for break:");
        ch = getchar();
        if(ch!='n')
        {
        node->next = (struct link* ) malloc(sizeof(struct link));
        node = node->next;
        }
        i++;
    }
    node = start.next;
    previous = &start;
    printf("\n Created list is as follows\n");

    while (node)
    {
        printf("\n 0x%x", node);
        printf("  %d",  node->info);
        node = node->next;
    }
}

/* Removing a node */

void Delete_node(struct link *node)
{
    node = start.next;
    previous = &start;
    if (node == NULL)
    {
        printf("\n Underflow");
    }else
        while(node->next)
        {
            node = node->next;
            previous = previous->next;
        }
        previous->next = node->next;
```

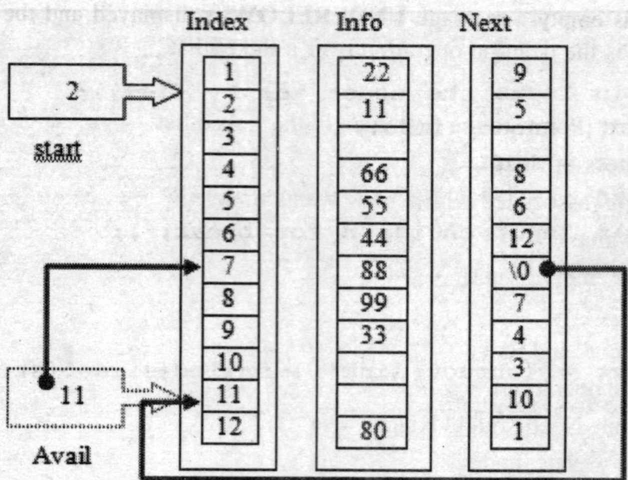

Figure 10.14 List after deletion of last node

```
        free(node);

      /* Display the list */

      node = start.next;
      printf("\n After deleting last node list is as follows\n");
      while (node)
      {
        printf("\n 0x%x", node);
        printf(" %d", node->info);
        node = node->next;
      }
    }
    /* Function main */
    void main()
    {
      struct link *node = (struct link *) malloc(sizeof(struct link));
      creat_node(node);
      Delete_node(node);
    }
```

10.4.3 Deletion of a Desired Node

Suppose we want to delete a desired node from a linked list. In this section we have assumed that we know the node number, which we want to delete. First of all we provide node number to which we want to delete. We scan the list up to that node. If the node exists in the list, we move the pointer to that particular node, free the node and adjust the pointer to make the list in linked form (The pointer of the previous node of this node will now point to the successor of this node). Before deletion operation we must check whether the list is empty or not. If the list is empty a message **UNDERFLOW** is displayed and the program terminates. Following steps demonstrates the deletion operation over a linked list.

Step 1: [Initialization]
Node = Start.Next [Points to the first node in the linked list]
Previous = Address of Start

Step 2: [Read information associated with a node wants to delete]
Delete_node = Value

Step 3: [Check for list is empty or not]
If Node = NULL
Output "Underflow" and Exit

Step 4: [Perform deletion operation]
Repeat thru 5 while Next[Node] ^{1} NULL
If Info [Node] = Delete_node
(i) Next [Previous] = Next [Node] [Make link of previous node to the next node]
(ii) Delete (Node) [Delete current node]
(iii) Exit

Step 5: Node = Next[Node]
Previous= Next[Previous]

Step 6: Exit

When we have given an information which is in a given linked list and we want to remove that information form the list. For this purpose we have to perform search operation for the information, if it is found delete the information containing node from the list. Suppose we have a linked list as illustrated in **Figure 10.15** and we have to delete information **33**, whether it is present in the given list or not and if it is present then at which or how many places. See the following how we search the information in the list.

Let Search = 33

Node = 1 Info [1] <> Search that is 11 <> 33 Search is unsuccessful

Next [1] = 2Info [2] <> Search that is 22 <> 33 Search is unsuccessful

Next [2] = 3Info [3] = Search That is 33 = 33 Search is successful and position = 3

For deleting the node 3 simply set the next pointer of node 2 to the next pointer of node 3, i.e., Next[2]=Next[3] and free (Node 3)

Next [3] = 4Info [4] <> Search that is 44 <> 33 Search is unsuccessful

Next [4] = 5Info [5] <> Search that is 55<> 33 Search is unsuccessful

Next [5] = 6Info [6] = Search that is 33 = 33 Search is successful and position = 6

For deleting the node 6 simply set the next pointer of node 5to the next pointer of node 6, i.e., Next[5]=Next[6] and free (Node 6)

Next [6] = 7Info [7] <> Search that is 88 <> 33 Search is unsuccessful

Next [7] = 8Info [8] = Search that is 33 = 33 Search is successful and position = 8

For deleting the node 8 simply set the next pointer of node 7 to the next pointer of node 8, i.e., Next[7]=Next[8] and free (Node 8)

Next [8] = 9Info [9] <> Search that is 99 <> 33 Search is unsuccessful

Next [9] = 10 Info [10] = Search that is 33 = 33 Search is successful and position = 10

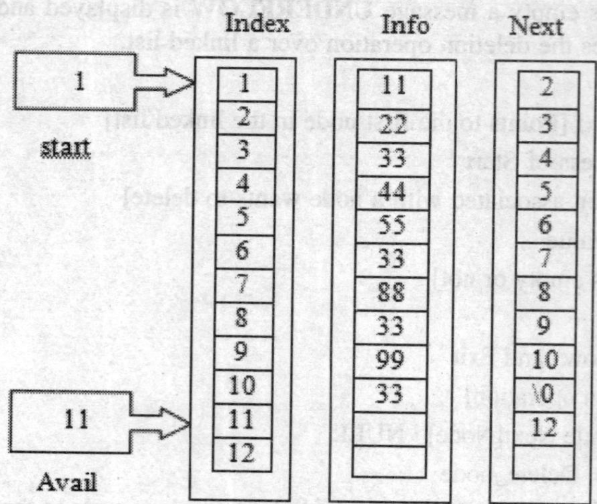

Figure 10.15 List in memory

For deleting the node 10 simply set the next pointer of node 9 to the next pointer of node 10, i.e., Next[9]=Next[10], i.e. null here and free (Node 10)

From the above result it is clear that **33** is found in the linked list at four places. Example 10.9 creates a linked list of desired size. The program then searches the list for the node containing the information which we want delete and finally delete the node from the list.

Example 10.9: Write C code to delete desired node from a simple linked list.

Answer: This program segment first creates a simple linked list of the user's desired size then deletion of operation performs.

```
/* Deleting a node from a simple linked list when information of a
    node is given */
/* LINK_DIN.C */
# include <stdio.h>
# include <malloc.h>

struct link
{
   int info;
   struct link *next;
};
int i;
struct link start, *previous;
void  Delete_node(struct link *);
void  creat_node(struct link *);
/* Create linked list */
void creat_node(struct link *node)
{
```

```
   char ch;
   i = 0;
   start.next = NULL;   /* Empty list */
   start.next = node;        /* Point to the start of the list */
   printf("\n Input choice n for break: ");
   ch = getchar();
   while(ch != 'n')
   {
      printf("\n Input the node: %d: ", (i+1));
      scanf("%d", &node->info);
      fflush(stdin);
      printf("\n Input choice n for break: ");
      ch = getchar();
      if(ch!='n')
      {
      node->next = (struct link* ) malloc(sizeof(struct link));
      node = node->next;
      node->next = NULL;
      }
      i++;

   }
   printf("\n Total nodes = %d", i);
   node = start.next;
   printf("\n Created list is as follows: \n");
   while (node)
   {
      printf("\n 0x%x", node);
      printf(" %d", node->info);
      node = node->next;
   }
}

/* Removing a node */

void Delete_node(struct link *node)
{
   int delete_node;
   node = start.next;
   previous = &start;
   printf("\n Input information of a node you want to delete: ");
   scanf("%d", &delete_node);
   if(node==NULL)
```

```
        printf("Underflow");
     else
     while(node)
     {
        if(node->info == delete_node)
        {
           previous->next = node->next;
           free(node);
           break ;
        }else
        {
           node = node->next;
           previous = previous->next;
        }
     }

     /* Display the list */

     node = start.next;
     printf("\n After deleting a node list is as follows:\n");
     while (node)
     {
        printf("\n 0x%x", node);
        printf(" %d", node->info);
        node = node->next;
     }
}

void main()
{
   struct link *node = (struct link *) malloc(sizeof(struct link));
   creat_node(node);
   Delete_node(node);
}
```

Let us Revise

1. A linked list is defined as a collection of nodes.
2. Traversing is a methodology in which each node is processed exactly once. When a list is stored in computer memory as a linked list, our aim is to traverse the list starting from the first node to the end of the list.
3. There are many applications where it is desirable to maintain an ordered linear list. The ordering may be in increasing or decreasing order of the information field.
4. The easiest way to add an entry is to append it at the end of the list.
5. To insert an item at a specific place (location) in a list, the program will normally track the **starting node, current node** and the **previous** of the current node.
6. The deletion operation is classified into following three categories: Deletion of first node; Deletion of last node; and Deletion of desired node from any place in the list

Multiple Choice Questions

1. In a linked list, the logical order of elements -
   (a) is the same as their physical arrangement
   (b) is not necessarily equivalent to their physical arrangement
   (c) is determined by their physical arrangement.
   (d) None of the above
2. In linked list, the successive elements -
   (a) must occupy contiguous space in memory.
   (b) need not occupy contiguous space in memory.
   (c) must not occupt contiguous space in memory.
   (d) None of the above.
3. Header linked list in which last node points the header node is called -
   (a) grounded header list (b) circular header list
   (c) general header list (d) None of the above
4. Overflow condition in linked list may occur when attempting to -
   (a) create a node when free space pool is empty
   (b) traverse the nodes when free space pool is empty
   (c) create a node when linked list is empty
   (d) None of the above.

True/False Questions

1. While inserting an element in the middle of a linked list, it is not necessary to shift the elements that occur after the inserted elements.
2. Linked list nodes are constructed using self referential structure.
3. In linked list, each node must have at least two fields.
4. Dynamic memory allocation takes place at run time.

Match Columns

Match the matter in Column A with the matter in Column B.

Column A	Column B
A. End of linked list	1. Ordered list of data items
B. Circular linked list	2. malloc()
C. Linked list	3. Points to same structure
D. For dynamic memory allocation	4. Null pointer
E. Self referential structure	5. Linking last node to the first node

Fill in the Blanks with Appropriate Words

a. 3 b. array c. dynamic d. pointer
e. insertion f. free()

1. We need to search for a correct place to insert an item in ________ sort.
2. ________ is used to return memory to the system.
3. Insertion of a node at the beginning of a linked list requires adjustment of pointer field of ________ node(s).
4. ________ to struct is used to represent link of linked list in C.
5. A contiguous list can be implemented using an ________.
6. A list is a ________ data structure.

Descriptive Type Questions

1. What is a linked list? How is it represented?
2. What is dynamic memory allocation? How does it help in building complex programs?
3. What is the principal difference between the functions malloc and calloc?
4. Why a linked list is called a dynamic data structure? What are the advantages of using linked lists over arrays?
5. Write a menu driven program to create a linked list of a class of students and perform the following operations:
   (a) Write out the contents of the list.
   (b) Edit the details of a specified student.
   (c) Count the number of students above a specified age and weight.
6. Write recursive and non-recursive functions for reversing the elements in a linear list. Com-pare the relative efficiencies of them.
7. Write an interactive program to create linear linked lists of customer ID, Names and their Tele-p h o n e numbers. The program should be menu driven and include features for adding a new customer and deleting an existing customer.
8. Modify the above program so that the list is always maintained in the alphabetical order of customer names.
9. Develop a program to combine two linked lists to produce a third sorted lists which contains one occurrence of each of the elements in the original lists.

10. Write a program to create a circular linked list so that the input order of data item is main-tained. Add function to carry out the following operations on circular linked list.

    (a) Count the number of nodes

    (b) Write out contents

    (c) Locate and write the contents of a given node

11. Write a function that would traverse a linear singly linked list in reverse and write out the contents in reverse order.

12. A database used for material management of a company is to contain information about items, suppliers and order. The following information about item, supplier and order are to be maintained:

    (i) For each item :

    (a) Item number (unique) (b) Item description

    (c) Date (d) Quantity at hand

    (e) Reorder level (f) Quantity received

    (g) Quantity issued

    (ii) For each supplier:

    (a) Supplier Number (unique) (b) Supplier Name

    (c) Address (d) Phone Number

    (e) Parts Supplying (f) Unit price

    (g) Discount

    (ii) For each other :

    (h) Order Number (unique)

    (i) Item Name

    (j) Supplier number (k) Quantity ordered

    (l) Value (m) Date of order

    (n) Expected date of delivery

    Whether a particular item is received, quantity at hand is updated by the quantity received. Similarly, if an item is used, the quantity at hand is decrement by the quantity issued.

13. Obtain a hierarchical data structure of a hospital database. The segments of this database are expected to contain the following information.

    (i) Hospital:

    (a) Hospital name (unique) (b) Hospital address

    (c) Phone number

    (ii) Ward:

    (a) Ward Number (unique) (b) Ward name

    (c) Number of beds (d) Bed available

    (iii) Doctor:

    (a) Doctor's name (b) Address

    (c) Phone number (d) Specialization

    (iv) Patient:

    (a) Admission date (b) Expected date of discharge

    (c) Bed number (unique) (d) Patient name

(e) Address

(v) Medhist:

(a) Previous date of admission
(b) Symptom
(c) Diagnosis treatment
(d) Any special suggestion

(vi) Symptom:

(a) Diagnosis (diseases name)
(b) Attending doctor's name
(c) Medication
(d) Surgery flag
(e) Surgery date
(f) Surgery comment
(g) Diet specification

Implement the above-discussed database.

Answers to Objective Type Questions

Multiple Choice Questions

1. b	2. b	3. b	4. a

True False Questions

1. T	2. T	3. T	4. F

Matching Columns

A. 4	B. 5	C. 1	D. 2
E. 3			

Fill in the Blanks

1. e	2. f	3. a	4. d
5. b	6. c		

File Processing 11

11.1 Concept of Files

Many applications of computers particularly in business environments require the storage and processing of large amount of data. Typically there is a large amount of data to store in memory at a time, so the data is stored externally. The earliest computers had used punched cards and magnetic tapes for storage of data. Modern computers use magnetic disks and drums as external storage devices.

Data is organized into records containing related data items. Groups of related records compose a file. For example, personnel file might contain one record for each employee in a company. Each record would be composed of such data items as the employee's name, social security number, age, date of birth, date hired and so on. The file might be organized sequentially, randomly or in any other scheme.

C language is very powerful for this type of application purposes as well as for system purposes. Today computers are widely used for data processing. During processing the data is kept in main memory (RAM). When data is quantitatively small, it is possible to keep all data in an array. But there are some drawbacks with array. When data is small and size of array is large, then it causes wastage of memory space, because when we define an array, its size is fixed in computer memory. Another problem of array is, when size of array is small and data is large then it is not possible to load all data into the array. For this problem it is possible to load data, equal to the size of array and after processing, the data is back to the user, but this is not the solution of our problem. Another way to process small amounts of the data is pointers, with help of pointers we can save unused memory space. This technique is limited to memory space of the machine.

Here, we have seen that bulk amount of data processing, requires another technique for storage, (before the processing as well as after the processing), i.e., file. The file processing is main part of any programming language. **C** language is very powerful in file handling. For example:

Mr. Y wishes to use a computer to maintain data on the number of parts in hand at his store. He has just taken inventory and knows the number of parts in hand. The part numbers and corresponding quantities are entered into the computer system and retained on a disk file. Later on, as parts are sold or as parts are added to the inventory, the parts file is updated. Then either on daily or on weekly basis, reports are produced to list the contents of the inventory file to identify those parts that are needed to be order. Such an information processing system inevitably leads to the following file processing:

- Create file
- Merging files, i.e., combine records of two or more files into one
- Adding records
- Deleting records
- Update records
- Generate reports

11.2 File Opening in Various Modes

Before we write a file to a disk or read it, we must open it. Opening a file establishes an understanding between a program and the operating system about the file we are going to access and how we are going to do it. We provide the operating system with the name of the file and other information, such as whether we plan to read or write to it. Communication areas are then setup between the file and the program; one of these areas is a **C** structure that holds information about the file. The structure, which is defined to be of type **FILE**, is a contact point. When we make a request to open a file, what we receive back (if the request is granted) is a pointer to a particular **FILE** structure. Each file we open will have its own **FILE** structure with a pointer to it. The **FILE** structure contains information about the file being used, such as its current size and the location of its data buffers. The **FILE** structure is declared in the header file **stdio.h.**

A stream is connected to a file by means of the **fopen, freopen** or **tmpfile** functions. These functions will, if successful, return a pointer to a FILE object. Three streams are available without any special action; they are normally all connected to the physical device associated with the executing program: usually computer terminal. They are referred to by the names stdin (*standard input)*, stdout (*standard output)*, and stderr (*standard error)* streams. Normal keyboard input is from stdin, normal terminal output is to stdout, and error messages are directed to stderr. The separation of error messages from normal output messages allows the stdout stream to be connected to something other than the terminal device, and still to have error messages appear on the screen, rather than to be redirected to this file. These files are only fully buffered if they do not refer to interactive devices.

As mentioned earlier, the file position indicator may or may not be movable, depending on the underlying device. It is not possible, for example, to move the file position indicator on stdin if that is connected to a terminal, as it usually is.

All non-temporary files must have a *filename*, which is a string. The rules for what constitutes valid filenames are implementation defined. Whether a file can be simultaneously open multiple times is also implementation defined. Opening a new file may involve creating the file. Creating an existing file causes its previous contents to be discarded.

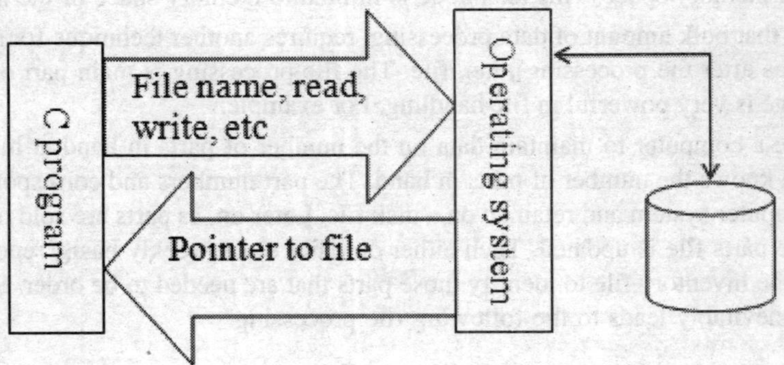

Figure 11.1 Opening a file

Main function which is used to start the above given functions is **fopen ().** To open a file, to create a file, to restart with an existing file, etc, are the main functions, which are performed by it. The syntax for the function **fopen()** is

```
File_pointer = fopen (file name, mode);
```

If a file is successfully opened it returns a pointer to the newly opened stream, otherwise it returns **NULL**. This function opens one file at a time. The syntax of structure **FILE** is

```
FILE *file_pointer;
```

For example,

```
FILE *fp;
```

Mode parameter of the function **fopen** () tells about the type of operations that can be performed on an opened file. The modes, which are supported by high level file processing, are given in **Table 9.8.** Go thorugh the Example 11.1 which is opening a file in write mode.

Example 11.1: Write C code which opens a file in write mode and write characters into it till we have not pressed the enter key.

Answer: The following program segment implements the above discussion:

```
/** file1.c **/

# include<stdio.h>
# include<stdlib.h>

void main()
{
    char ch ;
    FILE *fp ;
    fp = fopen ("test","w");
    if ( fp == NULL )
    {
        perror("ERROR");
        exit(1);
    }
    ch = getchar() ;
    while(ch != '\n' )
    {
        putc(ch,fp);
        ch = getchar();
    }
    fclose(fp);
}
```

In the above program segment, we have used function **fopen()** to open a file **test** in write mode. If there is any problem in opening of file **test**, a **NULL** value will be returned. If **NULL** value arises then function **perror** () will generate error according to the problem arises. In this program segment, we will read a text from standard input device one character at a time and simultaneously write it into the file **test**, this will continue until **return** key is pressed. This program can be written in another way in which it gives better performance. See the Example 11.2 which uses system buffer for reading the information.

Table 11.1 File opening modes

Mode	Type of file	Read	Write	Create	Truncate
"r"	text	yes	no	no	no
"rb"	binary	yes	no	no	no
"r+"	text	yes	yes	no	no

"r+b"	binary	yes	yes	no	no
"rb+"	binary	yes	yes	no	no
"w"	text	no	yes	yes	yes
"wb"	binary	no	yes	yes	yes
"w+"	text	yes	yes	yes	yes
"w+b"	binary	yes	yes	yes	yes
"wb+"	binary	yes	yes	yes	yes
"a"	text	no	yes	yes	no
"ab"	binary	no	yes	yes	no
"a+"	text	yes	yes	yes	no
"a+b"	binary	no	yes	yes	no
"ab+"	binary	no	yes	yes	no

Example 11.2: Write C code which uses system buffer(s) for file operation.

Answer: Go through the following code for the details.

```
/** file2.c **/
# include<stdio.h>
# include<stdlib.h>

void main()
{
   char ch ;
   FILE *fp ;      /* File pointer FILE macro   */
   fp = fopen ("test","w");
   if ( fp == NULL )
   {
      perror("ERROR");
      exit(1);
   }
   ch = getc(stdin) ;

   while(ch !='\n')   /* new line character accept */
   {
      putc(ch,fp);
      ch = getc(stdin);
   }
   fclose(stdin);
   fclose(fp);
}
```

In the above program segment we have used standard input file pointer **stdin.** The **stdin** directly interacts with keyboard buffer. When we open a file, a buffer is created in the system memory and data is transferred from/into the file with help of it. When we close the file, the residual data contained in this buffer are transferred to the opened file. If we do not close the file then there may be some losses of data but it may not happen every time. When we press a key, value of that key goes into standard input buffer, i.e., **stdin.** The **getc** () function reads data from there and assign this data to the variable **ch** and finally, it is written into file **test**. When we use **stdin** file pointer then keyboard buffer flushes and closing of destination file is safe. Consider the next example in continuation to the function **fopen ().**

```
/** file3.c **/
# include<stdio.h>
void main()
{
    char ch ;
    ch = getchar();
```

/* If we replace **getchar()** with **getche(),** we get two time same character on screen. This is valid in DOS environment only but the same operation is performed using the **getchar()** and **putchar** () functions */

```
    putchar(ch);
    getchar();
}
```

The above program segment reads a character and writes it on the screen (monitor). An equivalent of the above program can be written using standard input output file pointers. Consider the Example 11.3 which is equivalent to the Example 11.2.

Example 11.3: Write C code which uses system buffers (stdin and stdout) for file operation.

Answer: Go through the following code for the details.

```
/** file4.c **/
# include<stdio.h>

void main()
{
    char ch ;

/* It continuously read a charcter and puts on the screen when we
      press return key it terminates the program */

    ch = getc(stdin);

    while(ch != '\n')   /* new line character only accepts */
    {
        putc(ch,stdout);
        ch = getc(stdin);
    }
}
```

11.3 Closing of a File

After, all the work has been done on the file, we have to dis-engage it from our program. In simple workds, the file need to be closed, fclose function does this operation. This function frees the file pointer and empties the buffer used. For every file opne operation, this function is called automatically when a program terminates normally. But it is recommended that this function is called explicitly. The prototype for this function is:

```
int fclose(FILE *filepointer);
```

For example,

```
fclose(fp); /*fp declared as file pointer*/
```

11.4 Reading from a File

The function getc/fgetc is the simplest way to read from a file opened through the program. It needs a file pointer as argument to know which file to read from. It reads character by character. The syntax of this function is:

```
int getc(FILE *fp)
```

This function returns the next character from the file pointed by fp and when the character is read, f[points to the next character of the file. To read all the contents of the file, this function can be used until we encounter an EOF. We also have a function fgetc, which is similar to this function. There are internal details that make these functions differ.

11.5 Writing onto a File

The function putc/fputc function is the simplest way to write into a file opened through the program. The file pointer specifies the file in which the character has to be written. It writes character by character. The prototype of this function is:

```
int putc(int c, FILE *fp);
```

This function returns the character c written into the file pointed by fp and an EOF in case of an error occurred while writing. fputc, is also similar to putc() except for some internal details.

Let us Revise

1. Many applications of computers particularly in business environments require the storage and processing of large amount of data.
2. A stream is connected to a file by means of the **fopen, freopen** or **tmpfile** functions.
3. The function getc/fgetc is the simplest way to read from a file opened through the program.
4. The function putc/fputc function is the simplest way to write into a file opened through the program.

Multiple Choice Questions

1. The mode is used to open a file for reading and writing:

   (a) r++ (b) w+

   (c) both (a) and (b) (d) None of these

2. Which of the following functions may not be used to read from a txt file "a.txt".

   (a) getc **(b) getchar**

   (c) fgetc (d) fscanf

3. Which of the following preprocessor directives is used to create macros

   (a) #include (b) #ifdef

   (c) #define (d) #undef

4. The functions fgets() and fputs().

   (a) reads and write strings from or to data files

(b) reads and write strings from or to input/output stream.

(c) reads and writes records from or to data files.

(d) none of the above.

5. A file must be opened so that

(a) The program knows how to access the file.

(b) The operating system knows what file to access.

(c) Communications areas are established for communicating with the file.

(d) All of the above

True/False Questions

1. A file opened with fopen() will thereafter be referred to by its file pointer.
2. We can create data file using library function fcreate().
3. To examine every single byte of a file, a text mode is more suitable.
4. The function fseek() finds a given word or phrase in a file.
5. The EOF signal sent by the operating system to a C program is not a character, but an integer with a value of –1.

Match Columns

Match the matter in Column A with the matter in Column B.

Column A	Column B
A. sizeof	1. modes for opening files
B. #define sqr(x) x * x	2. alert to the compiler about the function
C. w+ and r+	3. outputs character to screen
D. prototype	4. macro
E. puts()	5. bit manipulation

Fill in the Blanks with Appropriate Words

a. macro	b. 32	c. getchar()	d. fclose
e. typedef	f. buffer		

1. FILE is defined with a ____________ statement.
2. The function sprintf() is meant for formatted write to a memory _______.
3. There are _________ keywords in "C" language.
4. #define statement calls for simplest type of _____________ substitution.
5. The _________ accepts a single character from the keyboard.
6. Data files are closed in a C pogram using ________ library function.

Descriptive Type Questions

1. Describe the use and limitations of the functions getc and putc.
2. What is the significance of EOF?
3. When a program is terminated, all the files used by it are automatically closed. Why is it then necessary to close a file during execution of the program?
4. Distinguish between the following functions:

   (a) getc and getchar (b) printf and fprintf

   (c) feof and terror

5. How does an append mode differ from a write mode?
6. What are the common uses of rewind and ftell functions?
7. Explain the general format of fseek function?
8. What is the difference between the statements rewind(fp); and fseek(fp,0L,0);?
9. Suppose that the standard input is

   RA M

   (Each of R, A and M is immediately followed by a new line). Write a function that echoes these characters, so that the standard output is 'RAM'
10. If one declares while (fgets(buffer, 100, fp) != EOF)

    then how many bytes are placed in **buffer** by the function **fgets()**? Write your fgets().

Answers to Objective Type Questions

Multiple Choice Questions

1. c	2. b	3. c	4. a
5. d			

True False Questions

1. T	2. F	3. F	4. F
5. T			

Matching Columns

A. 5	B. 4	C. 1	D. 2
E. 3			

Fill in the Blanks

1. e	2. f	3. b	4. a
5. c	6. d		

Glossary

G

Address (1) Number of a particular memory or peripheral storage location. Each byte of memory and each disk sector have its own unique address. Programs are compiled into machine language, which references actual addresses in the computer. (2) As a verb, to mange or work with. For example, "The computer can address 2MB of memory."

algorithm A planned set of instructions or steps designed to solve a particular problem. There is only one starting point and all routes through the algorithm end at the same finishing point. Such steps can be carried out by a computer or dry run on paper, using different inputs or values. Usually algorithm precedes code writing in computer programming.

APL It is a High-level Programming Language, interactive scientific language noted for its capabilities. Developed by Kenneth Iverson in the mid 1960's it runs on micros to mainframe and is often used to develop mathematical models. It is primarily an interpreted language, but compilers are available. APL uses unique character symbols and requires special software or ROM chips to enable the computer to display and print them. APL is popular in Europe.

application program interface (API) System software that provides a complete set of functions and resources on which programmers can draw to create user interface features, such as pull down menu, command names, dialog boxes, keyboard commands and windows. In network systems, an API establishes how programs use various network features.

application program library Application programs used by an organization.

application program Any data entry, update, query or report program that processes data for the user which contrast with system program.

application programmer Individual who writes application programs in a user organization. Most programmers are application programmers. Contrast with systems programmer.

arithmetic operations Various manipulations of numerical quantities, including the fundamental operations of addition, subtraction, multiplication and division as well as aggregation, exponentiation and extraction of roots.

array element One item in an array.

array Ordered arrangement of data elements. A vector is a one dimensional array, a matrix is a two-dimensional array. Most programming languages have the ability to store and manipulate arrays in one or more dimensions. Multi-dimensional arrays are used extensively in scientific simulation and mathematical processing; however, an array can be as simple as a pricing table held in memory for instant access by an order entry program.

ASCII (American Standard Code for Information Interchange) Pronounced "ass-key." It is a binary code for data that is used in communications, mostly in minicomputers and all personal computers. ASCII is a 7-bit code providing 128 possible character combinations, the first 32 of which are used for printing and transmission control. Since the common storage unit is an 8-bit byte (256 combinations) and ASCII uses only 128, the extra bit is used to hold a parity bit or special symbols. For example, the PC uses the additional values for foreign language and graphics symbols. In the Macintosh, the additional values can be user-defined to enhance a font.

assembler Software that translates assembly language into machine language. Contrast with compiler, which is used to translate a high-level language, such as COBOL or C into assembly language first and then into machine language.

assembly language Programming language that is one step away from machine language. Each assembly language statement is translated into one machine instruction by the assembler. Programmers must be well versed in the computer's architecture. Undocumented assembly language, programs are difficult to maintain. It is hardware dependent there is a different assembly language for each CPU series.

base 1. In mathematics, a number that is raised to the power specified by an exponent. For example, in $2^3 = 2 \times 2 \times 2 = 8$, the base is 2. 2. In mathematics, the number of digits in a particular numbering system. With microcomputers, four numbering systems are commonly used or referred to—binary, octal, decimal, and hexadecimal—and each is based on a different number of digits. The binary, or base-2, numbering system, which is used to discuss the states of a computer's logic, has two digits, 0 and 1. Octal, or base-8, has eight digits, 0 through 7. The familiar decimal, or base-10, numbering system has ten digits, 0 through 9. Hexadecimal, or base-16, has sixteen digits, 0 through 9 and A through F. When numbers are written in a particular base, the base is often subscripted and enclosed in parentheses after the number, as in $24AE_{(16)} = 9{,}390$. Also called: radix. See also binary[1], decimal, hexadecimal, octal. 3. One of three terminals (emitter, base, and collector) in a bipolar transistor. The current through the base controls the current between the emitter and the collector. See also transistor. 4. The insulating foundation of a printed circuit board. See also circuit board.

BASIC Beginner's All Purpose Symbolic Instruction Code. It is a computer language similar to the English language which was developed by John G. Kemeny and Thomas E. Kurtz at the Dartmouth College in the 1960s. It is popular for microcomputer and time sharing systems. It was also supplied as the standard language with the IBM PC. Initially fused into the ROM of the IBM PC grew to become a full-fledged developmental language, supplied in floppies together with MS-DOS 1.0 and above. Until MS-DOS 4.0 BASIC, BASICA and GW-BASIC were supplied, the last named being bundled out with MS-DOS 4.0. Versions 5 and 6.0 of MS-DOS come with QBasic, developed by Microsoft replacing GW-BASIC.

BCD Binary Coded Decimal, Digital computers all used some form of binary numbers for their internal operations, whereas humans use decimal numbers. To understand and thereby work with computers there is a need for conversion from one system to another. A method of encoding which is a mix of decimal and binary systems has evolved. This is known as Binary Coded Decimal (BCD).

The following example illustrates this difference.

124 = 0001 0010 0100 in BCD

124 = 01111100 in binary

binary coded decimal number Any number, usually consisting of successive group of figures, in which each group of four figures is a binary number that represent, but does not necessarily equal arithmetically, a particular figure in an associated decimal number; for example, the decimal number 264 is represented as the binary coded number 0010 0110 0100.

binary numbers Numbers stored in pure binary form. Within one byte (8 bits), the values 0 to 255 can be held. Two contiguous bytes (16 bits) can hold values from 0 to 65,535. See numbers, binary values.

bit Short for **bi**nary digi**t**. The smallest unit of information handled by a computer. One bit expresses a 1 or a 0 in a binary numeral, or a true or false logical condition, and is represented physically by an element such as a high or low voltage at one point in a circuit or a small spot on a disk magnetized one way or the other. A single bit conveys little information a human would consider meaningful. A group of 8 bits, however, makes up a byte, which can be used to represent many types of information, such as a letter of the alphabet, a decimal digit, or other character. See also ASCII, binary[1], byte.

Boolean algebra An algebra, fundamental to computer operations but developed in the mid-nineteenth century by English mathematician George Boole, for determining whether logical propositions are true or false rather than for determining the values of numerical expressions. In Boolean algebra, variables must have one of only two possible values, true or false, and relationships between these variables are expressed with logical operators, such as AND, OR, and NOT. Given these two-state variables and the relationships they can have to one another, Boolean algebra produces such propositions as C = A AND B, which means that C is true if and only if both A is true and B is true; thus, it can be used to process information and to solve problems. Furthermore, Boolean logic can be readily applied to the electronic circuitry used in digital computing. Like the binary numbers 1 and 0, true and false are easily represented by two contrasting physical states of a circuit, such as voltages, and computer circuits known as logic gates control the flow of electricity (bits of data) so as to represent AND, OR, NOT, and other Boolean operators. Within a computer, these logic gates are combined, with the output from one becoming the input to another so that the final result (still nothing more than sets of 1s and 0s) is meaningful data, such as the sum of two numbers. See the illustration. See also adder (definition 1), binary[1], Boolean operator, gate (definition 1), logic circuit, truth table.

bug 1. An error in coding or logic that causes a program to malfunction or to produce incorrect results. Minor bugs, such as a cursor that does not behave as expected, can be inconvenient or frustrating, but do not damage information. More severe bugs can require the user to restart the program or the computer, losing whatever previous work had not been saved. Worse yet are bugs that damage saved data without alerting the user. All such errors must be found and corrected by the process known as debugging. Because of the potential risk to important data, commercial application programs are tested and debugged as completely as possible before release. After the program becomes available, further minor bugs are corrected in the next update. A more severe bug can sometimes be fixed with a piece of software called a patch, which circumvents the problem or in some other way alleviates its effects. See also beta test, bomb[2], crash[2] (definition 1), debug, debugger, hang, inherent error, logic error, semantic error, syntax error. 2. A recurring physical problem that prevents a system or set of components from working together properly. While the origin of this definition is in some dispute, computer folklore attributes the first use of bug in this sense to a problem in the Harvard Mark I or the Army/University of Pennsylvania ENIAC that was traced to a moth caught between the contacts of a relay in the machine (although a moth is not entomologically a true bug).

byte A group of adjacent bits, usually made of 8 bits. A sequence of adjacent binary digits operated on as a unit and usually than a computer word. In many computer systems, a byte is a grouping of eight bits that can represent one alphabetic or special character or can be "packed" with two decimal digits one character of storage.

call by reference In programming, a call to a subroutine that passes addresses of the parameters used in the subroutine.

call by value In programming, a call to a subroutine that passes the actual data of the parameters used in the subroutine.

character A letter, number, punctuation mark, or other symbol or control code that is represented to a computer by one unit—1 byte—of information. A character is not necessarily visible, either on the screen or on paper; a space, for example, is as much a character as is the letter a or any of the digits 0 through 9. Because computers must manage not only so-called printable characters but also the look (formatting) and transfer of electronically stored information, a character can additionally indicate a carriage return or a paragraph mark in a word-processed document. It can be a signal to sound a beep, begin a new page, or mark the end of a file.

character sets Combinations by software and hardware engineers for specific purposes. For example, the "Roman" character set would contain all the character necessary to generate a text file in any of the Latin languages. A "mathematical" character set would contain all of the symbols necessary for intricate mathematical formulae and calculus. Not all characters are supposed by all computer software and hardware. For example, many lower price printers cannot generate graphics symbols. Not all the possible syntax and alphabetic combinations (character sets) for every human language.

COBOL COmmon Buisiness Oriented Language is a High-level business programming language that has been the primary business application language on mainframes and minis. It is a compiled language and was one of the first high-level; languages developed. Formally adopted in 1960, it stemmed from a language called Flowmatic in the mid 1950s. Although COBOL requires more writing than other languages, it is more readable as a result.

CODASYL Acronym for Conference on Data Systems Languages. An organization founded by the U.S. Department of Defense. CODASYL is dedicated to the development of data-management systems and languages, among them the widely used COBOL.

coding (1) Writing a list of instructions that will cause a computer to perform specified operations. (2) An ordered list or lists of the successive instructions that will cause a computer to perform a particular process.

comment A brief line of commentary embedded into a computer program. Comments aim to provide a "road-map" through a program, enabling programmers, including the original writer, to follow the overall logic of the program. Since comment occupy a line of code it is best to be brief, rather then verbose in commentary.

compile To translate all the source code of a program from a high-level language into object code prior to execution of the program. Object code is executable machine code or a variation of machine code. More generally, compiling is sometimes used to describe translating any high-level symbolic description into a lower-level symbolic or machine-readable format. A program that performs this task is known as a compiler. See also compiler (definition 2), compile time, high-level language, machine code, source code. Compare interpret.

compound statement A single instruction that contains two or more instructions that could otherwise be used separately.

conditional branch In programming, an instruction that directs the computer to another part of the program based on the results of a compare. In the following (simulated) assembly language example, the second line is the conditional branch.

constant A named item that retains a consistent value throughout the execution of a program, as opposed to a variable, which can have its value changed during execution. Compare variable.

data (1) Technically, raw facts and figures which are processed into information. However, in common usage, both data and information are used synonymously the amount of data kept in the computer versus the amount of information is a tradeoff. Data can be processed into different forms of information, but it takes time to sort and sum transactions. Data is "processed". Software is "run", (2) Any form of information whether on paper or in electronic form. In electronic form, data refers to data fields, records, files and databases, word processing documents, graphic images and digitally-encoded voice and video. (3) Data items in data files and databases in contrast with text, graphics, voice and video files.

DO/WHILE loop In programming, a loop control structure that continues to carry out its function until a condition is satisfied. A DO/WHILE control structure establishes a condition that, if true, causes the program to wait until the test is false, then move on to the next instruction.

dynamic memory allocation The allocation of memory to a process or program at run time. Dynamic memory is allocated from the system heap by the operating system upon request from the program.

enumerate To count or list one by one. An enumerated data type defines a list of all possible values for a variable; and no other value can then he placed into it.

function In programming, a routine that does a particular task. When the program passes control to a function, it performs the task and returns control to the instruction following the calling instruction. It may perform a stand-alone task, such as printing a message, or it may accept values (arguments) from the calling instruction process them and pass the results back. Programming languages generally provide a set of standard functions and allow programmers to define their own. C is built entirely around functions. Contrast with command which is a fundamental instruction within the language. Though in programming, the term is specific, outside of programming, it is used to describe any operation such as the data entry function."

GOTO statement A control statement used in programs to transfer execution to some other statement; the high-level equivalent of a branch or jump instruction. Use of GOTO statements is generally discouraged because they make it difficult not only for a programmer to trace the logic of a program but also for a compiler to generate optimized code. See also branch instruction, jump instruction, spaghetti code.

header file A file that is identified to be included at the beginning of a program in a language such as C and that contains the definitions of data types and declarations of variables used by the functions in the program.

information Summarization of data. Technically, data are raw facts and figures that are processed into information, such as summaries and totals. But since information can also be raw data for the next job or person, the two terms cannot be precisely defined. Both terms are used synonymously and interchangeably. As office automation and data processing merge, it may be more helpful to view information the way data is defined and used, namely: data, text, spread-sheet, pictures, voice and video. Data are discretely defined fields. Text is a collection of words. Spreadsheets are data in matrix (row and column) form. Pictures are lists of vectors or frames of bits. Voice is a continuous stream of sound waves. Video is a sequence of frames.

Interpreter High-level programming language translator that translate and runs the program at the same time. It translates one program statement into machine language, executes it, then proceeds to the next statement. Through interpreted programs run slower than their compiler counterparts, because the compiler translates the entire program before it is run, it is more convenient to write an interpreted program, since a single line of code can be tested interactively. Interpreted programs must always be run with the interpreter. For example, in order to run a BASIC or dBASE program, the BASIC or dBASE interpreter must be in the computer.

language processor A hardware device or a software program designed to accept instructions written in a particular language and translate them into machine code.

loop In programming, a repetition within a program. Whenever a process must be repealed, a loop is set up to handle it. A program has a main loop and a series of minor loops which are nested within the main loop. Learning how to set up loops is what programming technique is all about. Loops are accomplished by various programming structures that have a beginning body and end. The beginning generally tests the condition that keeps the loop going. The body comprises the repeating statements and the end is a GOTO that points back to the beginning.

low-level language A language that is machine dependent or that offers few control instructions and data types. Each statement in a program written in a low-level language usually corresponds to one machine instruction.

machine language Native language of the computer. In order for a program to run, it must be in the machine language of the computer that is executing it. Although programmers may modify machine language in order to fix a running program, they do not create it. It is created by programs called assemblers, compilers and interpreters which convert programming language into machine language. What may take one instruction in a mainframe, can take 15 instructions in a microcomputer.

nested loops Loops contained within other loops.

null pointer A pointer to nothing—usually a standardized memory address, such as 0. A null pointer usually marks the last of a linear sequence of pointers or indicates that a data search operation has come up empty. Also called: nil pointer.

Pointer (1) In database management, an address embedded within the data that specifies the location of data in another record or file. (2) In programming, a variable that is used as a reference to the current item in a table (array) or to some other object, such as the current row or column on screen. (3) On-screen symbol used to identify menu selections or the current screen location. It is moved by a mouse or other pointing device.

preprocessor Software that performs some preliminary processing on the input before it is processed by the main program.

programming language Language used to write instructions for the computer. It lets the programmer express data processing in a symbolic manner without regard to machine-specific details. The statements that are written by the programmer are called source language or code and they are translated into the computer's machine language by programs called assemblers, compilers and interpreters.

pseudocode An algorithm expressed in English to conceptualize the algorithm before coding it in a programming language.

query language Generalized language that allows a user to select records from a database. It uses a command language, menu-driven method or a query by example (QBE) format for expressing the matching condition. Query languages are usually included in DBMSs and stand-alone packages are available for interrogating files in non-DBMS applications.

relational operator An operator that allows the programmer to compare two (or more) values or expressions. Typical relational operators are greater than (>), equal to (=), less than (<), not equal to (<>), greater than or equal to (>=), and less than or equal to (<=).

scope (1) CRT type of screen, such as used on an oscil-loscope or common display terminal. (2) In program-ming, the visibility of variables within a program. (3) In dBASE, a range of records, such as the "next 50" or "current record to end of file."

Sort To reorder data into a new sequence. Sorting capabilities are provided within the operating system and many application program, such as word processing and DBMSs.

source language Language used in a source program.

source program Program in its original form, as written by the programmer.

Stack Set of hardware registers or a served amount of memory used for arithmetic calculations or for keeping track of internal operation. Stacks keep track of the sequence of routines that are called in a program. For example, one routine calls another which calls another and so on. As each routine is completed, the computer must return control to the calling routine all the way back to the first routine that started the sequence. Stacks usually work on a LIFO basis; the last item or address, placed (pushed) onto the stack is the first item removed (popped) from the stack. An "internal stack failure" is a fatal error which means that the operating system can't find the next routine to process. Re-starting the computer usually corrects this, otherwise the operating system may have to be re-installed.

Swapping The process of exchanging modules of an application program in the CPU as different modules are needed for processing. A memory management technique is used when the program or data file is large and there is a limited amount of RAM. Programs, program segments and/or data are swapped into and out of RAM from secondary storage as and when required, preferably just before being required.

union In relational database, the joining of two files.

Index

A

Addition of Two Matrices 141
Algorithms 4
Arithmetic operators 57
Arrays 240
Arrays and Pointers 262
Assembler 22
Assembly Language 19
Auto 208

B

BASIC 21
Basic I/O Functions 170
Binary Base 36
Binary Search 131
Breakpoints 24
Built-in Data Types 51

C

C 22
C++ 22
Call by Reference 190
Call by Value 190
Character set 48
Closing The File 179
COBOL 21
Coding 3
Concept of Files 337
Constants 64
Conversion Specifications 172

D

Debugging 3
Decimal Base 36
Definiteness 6
Deletion from a Linked List 322
Deletion of a Desired Node 328
Deletion of First Node 322
Deletion of Last Node 325
Do while 95
Do-while loop 7
Documentation 3, 27
Dynamic Memory Allocation 272

E

Effectiveness 6
Elimination of Recursion 195
Enumeration Constants 65
Escape Sequences 173
Expressions 62
Extern 208

F

Fibonacci Sequence 42
Flow-Charts 9
For loop 7
Formatted Console I/O Functions 171
FORTRAN 21
Freeing Memory 282
Function Call 189
Functions 166
Functions and Pointers 259

G

gets( ) 176
Greatest Common Divisor 38

H

High Level Language 20

I

identifiers 50
If statement 80
If-else statement 85
Initialization 218
Initialization of Union 243
Input 6
Insertion as a First Node 312
Insertion As A Last Node 315
Insertion into a Linked List 311
Interpreter 23

L

Lifetime 209
Linear Search 131
Linked List 303
Literals 64

Loader 24
Logic analyzers 24
Logical Connectives 79
Logical Errors 26
LOGO 20
Loops 92

M

Machine Language 19
Maintenance 3
malloc 272
Matrices 45
Memory dumps 25
Multi-dimensional Array 126

N

Nested If Statements 82
Nested Loops 101
Nested Structure 223

O

One Dimensional Array 126
Opening A File 177
Output 6

P

PASCAL 22
Passing Arguments to a Function 189
Pointer Arithmetic 258
Pointer Arrays 265
Pointer Assignment 253
Pointer Initialization 253
Pointer Type 251
Pointers and Structures 269
Polynomial 45
printf 67
Problem Solving 2
Program 1
Program Definition 3
Program Design 3
Programming Languages 18
PROLOG 21
puts( ) 176

R

Random Access 151
Reading from a File 178
Recursive Functions 190
Register 209
Relational Operators 79
Return Type 189
Run-Time Errors 25

S

Scanf() 173
Scope and Extent 207
Simulators 24
Singly Connected Linked List 303
Software interrupts 25
sprintf() function 174
Square Root 40
sscanf() Function 174
Static 208
Step-wise Refnement 165
strcmp(144
String Copy {strcpy()} 143
String Length {strlen()} 143
Structure 213
Switch statement 103
Syntax Errors 25

T

Termination 6
Testing 3
The break statement 110
The char 53
The Continue Statement 112
The double 55
The else-if ladder 88
The float 54
The goto Statement 113
The int 52
The void 55
Traversing a Linked List 308
Two Dimensional Arrays 133
Typedef 244

U

Unions 241

V

Variable Definition 56
Variables 50

W

While loop 7, 92
Writing to A File 179

Sample Paper - 1

S1

Part A

Answer all questions, each of them carries one mark

Multiple Choice Questions

1. Syntax errors inlcude :
   (a) misspelt keywords (b) missing braces (c) missing commas
2. Language which is platform independent is:
   (a) machine language (b) assembly language (c) high level language
   (d) none of these
3. Acceptance testing is done at ___________ site.
   (a) customer (b) developer (c) customer and developer
   (d) none of these
4. The product of all natural numbers from 1 to n is called
   (a) n! (b) n x n (c) n^n
5. Consider the following program:

```
#include<stdio.h>
void main( )
{
int number =16;
printf("The value of number is: %f ", number);
}
```

   What is output of the above program?
   (a) The value of number is: 16
   (b) Syntax error: Opening curly bracket is missing
   (c) Syntax error: number cannot be printed as float
   (d) None
6. Is the following declaration incorrect?

```
char ch= "Y";
```

   (a) Yes (b) No (c) Depends on Compiler
   (d) Cannot decide
7. How many symbols can be placed in a variable name in C language?
   (a) 16 (b) 32 (c) 64

8. Function saves return addresses and intermediate values at
   (a) stack (b) secondary storage device
   (c) (a) and (b) (d) none of these
9. What is error in the following code?

```
int funct(code char, time float, n int)
```

10. An enumeration data type brings together a group of
    (a) Items of different data types (b) Related data variables
    (c) Integers with user defined names (d) Constant values
11. Consider the following program. What is the output?

```
#include<stdio.h>
void main()
{
    char name[]="Prem Nath";
    printf("\n %s", name[5]);
    getch();
}
```

    (a) Prem Nath (b) Prem
    (c) N (d) Error
12. A switch-case statement can be replaced by
    (a) if-else statement (b) do-while loop
    (c) if-statement (d) None

Part B

Answer all questions, each of them carries one mark

True False Questions

1. A programmer can write big programs at the beginning only.
2. Run time errors occur at the time of execution.
3. A comment can be inserted in the middle of a statement.
4. Multiplication of two matrices is possible only when they are compatible.
5. Floating point constants, by default, denote float type values.
6. A string is an array of characters
7. Variables form a legal element of the format control string of a printf statement.
8. When no storage class is specified ofr a variable declared inside a block, auto storage class is assumed, auto has no particular use as such.
9. A structure cannot be passed to a 'C' function through the call by value mechanism.
10. To examine every single byte of a file, a text mode is more suitable.

Part C

Answer all questions, each of them carries one mark

Matching Questions

A. while (0)	1. 2
B. while (1)	2. 1
C. 5/2	3. forces exit from a program
D. 5%2	4. assignment never takes place
E. The exit function	5. forces immediate exit from any loop
F. The break statement	6. infinite loop
G Sorting	7. removing an item from the list
H. Transpose	8. combining two lists
I. Deletion	9. row-major
J. Array	10. joins two strings
K. Merging	11. interchanging rows with columns
L. strcat()	12. arranging in some order

Part D

Answer all questions, each of them carries one mark

Fill in the Blanks

1. Errors which are pointed out only after receiving the result are called ________ errors.
2. Errors which occur at the time of running are called _________ errors.
3. Operators &, ^, == have _________ precedence.
4. The unary operator - can be used for performing _________ on a variable.
5. An infinite for loop has missing _______ expression.
6. Nesting can be done upto ________ level for while loop.
7. __________ to struct is used to represent link of linked list in C.
8. A contiguous list can be implemented using an __________.
9. #define statement calls for simplest type of _______________ substitution.
10. The _________ accepts a single character from the keyboard.

Part E

Answer any 10 questions, each of them carries five marks

Descriptive Type Questions

1. What are the common uses of rewind and ftell functions?
2. Explain the general format of fseek function?
3. Write recursive and non-recursive functions for reversing the elements in a linear list. Com-pare the relative efficiencies of them.
7. Write an interactive program to create linear linked lists of customer ID, Names and their Tele-phone numbers. The program should be menu driven and include features for adding a new customer and deleting an existing customer.

5. Write a program that interchanges the **jth** and **kth** paragraph in text **T**.
6. Write a function **compare** () that compares two strings.
7. Why does **C** provide two ways to name structure types **Tags** and **typedef** names?
8. When one tried using **sizeof** to determine the number of bytes in a structure, one got a number that was larger than the sizes of the members added together. How can this be?
9. Write a recursive function that computes summation of the following series:

   S(n) = 1+3+5+ … + 2*n-1
10. Write a program that prompts the user for two numbers and one operator +, -, * or /. The function **main** () issues the prompt and user's input in the variable **Operand1** and **Operand2** and **Operator**. The **main** () checks the operator and if the operator is +, **main** () invokes the function **Add** () with the arguments **Operand1** and **Operand2** and simultaneously for -, * and /. Each of the functions **Add** (), **Sub** (), **Multi** () and **Div** () invokes function **Display** (), which prints the result of the arithmetic operation.
11. How would we search a word in a given text? Write a program to search a word of five characters in a text of 100 characters.
12. Write a program to delete an element at position p in a given array.
13. Write a program that will obtain the length and width of a rectangle from the user and compute its area and perimeter.
14. The total distance travelled by a vehicle in *t* seconds is given by

    distance = $u*t + (a*t^2)/2$

    Where *u* is the initial velocity (meters per second), *a* is the acceleration (meters per second^2). Write a program to evaluate the distance traveled at regular intervals of time, given the val-ues of *u* and *a*. The program should provide the flexibility to the user to select his own time intervals and repeat the calculations for different values of *u* and *a*.
15. What steps would you take for maintainance of the program.
16. What sort of errors you get while running the program?

Sample Paper - 2

S2

Part A

Answer all questions, each of them carries one mark

Multiple Choice Questions

1. Oval is used to represent _________ in flow chart:
   (a) terminal symbol (b) connectors (c) flow lines
   (d) process symbol
2. Choose the correct statement(s).
   (a) Any non-zero value represents TRUE condition
   (b) 0 represents FALSE condition
   (c) 0 and negative values represents FALSE condition
   (d) None
3. Coding is followed by :
   (a) feasibility study (b) testing (c) design
   (d) maintenance
4. Consider the following program:

```
#include<stdio.h>
void main( )
{
const int number =16;
printf("The value of number is: %u ", number);
}
```

   What is output of the above program?
   (a) The value of number is: 16
   (b) Syntax error: Opening curly bracket is missing
   (c) Syntax error: number cannot be printed as unsigned
   (d) None
5. Consider the following program. What is the output?

```
#include<stdio.h>
void main()
{
    char name[]="Prem Nath";
    name[4]='\0';
printf("\n %s", name);
```

```
        getch();
}
```

(a) Prem Nath (b) Prem
(c) Nath (d) Error

6. A function's header and body must be defined within the
   (a) same file (b) different file
   (c) header file with extension (.h) (d) none of these
7. The function **exit()** causes an exit from
   (a) The loop in which it occurs (b) The block in which it occurs
   (c) The function in which it occurs (d) The program in which it occurs
8. When accessing a structure member, the identifier to the left of the dot (period) operator is the name of
   (a) A structure name (b)A structure tag name
   (c) A structure variable (d) The keyword struct
9. The four members of an **enum** type are normally represented by the values ________, ________, ________ and ________.
   (a) 0,1,2,3 (b) 1,2,3, 4
   (c) none of these
10. An argument and its corresponding parameter must have the
    (a) same names (b) different names
    (c) same names but types must be different
    (d) different names but types should be same
11. In the following code slice

```
A = 10;
Funct( A++, A++, A++, A++);
```

    Funct()'s four arguments must evaluate to 11, 12, 13 and 14 in that order.
    (a) True (b) False
12. Find error in the following code:

```
int i = 11;
int *ptr;
ptr = i;
```

    (a) ptr = i; (b) int *ptr;
    (c) int i=11; (d) none
13. Header linked list in which last node points the header node is called -
    (a) grounded header list (b) circular header list
    (c) general header list (d) None of the above

Part B

Answer all questions, each of them carries one mark

True False Questions

1. Syntax errors are those which occur due to wrong use of language.
2. C treats the variables name and Name to be same.
3. The keyword void is a data type in C.
4. The input list in a scanf statement can contain one or more variables.

5. Initialization is the process of assigning a value to a variable at the time of declaration.
6. The array index must be an integer data type.
7. Use of comments reduces the speed of execution of a program.
8. Automatic arrys cannot be initialized.
9. There is no need to maintain any program.
10. All variables must be given a type when they are declared.

Part C

Answer all questions, each of them carries one mark

Matching Questions

A.	n!	1.	Fibonacci series
B.	Sin (π/2)	2.	Sorted array
C.	1, 1, 2, 3, 5, 8	3.	120
D.	1 3 8 10 12	4.	1
E.	\n	5.	carriage return
F.	%	6.	assignment operator
G	&&	7.	bitwise operator
H.	\r	8.	Escape sequence
I.	&	9.	logical operator
J.	+=	10.	mod operator

Part D

Answer all questions, each of them carries one mark

Fill in the Blanks

1. Comments can be placed ________ in the program.
2. Instructions to run the program are there in the _________ guide.
3. Number of bytes occupied by a zero terminated string "a" is ____________.
4. The operator i << 2 is equivalent to __________ i by 4.
5. Unions contain members of different data types which share the same _________ area in memory.
6. If 'p' is a pointer to a structure the "p --> p" is same as _________.
7. Right shifting an unsigned integer is equivalent to its ________ by 2.
8. String function strcpy() belongs to ________ headed file.
9. The GCD of the number 256 and 64 is ______.
10. In Fibonacci series, the ______ two numbers are added to generate the Fibonacci number.

Part E

Answer any 10 questions, each of them carries five marks

Descriptive Type Questions

1. When a program is terminated, all the files used by it are automatically closed. Why is it then necessary to close a file during execution of the program?
2. Distinguish between the following functions:

   (a) getc and getchar

   (b) printf and fprintf

principal difference between the functions malloc and calloc?

a linked list is called a dynamic data structure? What are the advantages of using linked lists over arrays?

5. Write a function, which finds the location of the largest element and the location of the 2nd largest elements in a list of numbers with the help of pointer.
6. Let **W** be the string formed by **ABCD**. Write functions for
   (a) Find the length of **W**.
   (b)List all sub-strings of **W**.
   (c) List all the initial sub-strings of **W**.
7. What is the error in the following declaration of a structure with a pair of bit-field members?

```
struct Saving
{
    signed int Member1 3;
    unsigned int Member2 16;
} Variable;
```

   Correct the error and write the error free code for the said code and assign values to the variable **Variable.Member1** and **Variable.Member2.**
8. Is there any error in the following program segment? If there is no error, find output of the program segment?

```
# include<stdio.h>
enum Player {Ramesh = 1, Saurabh, Dravid, Sachin, Azharuddin,
    Mongia};
enum One, Two;
One = 12;
Two = 14;
void main()
{
printf("\n %d", One, Two);
}
```

9. Use of go to should be avoided. Explain a typical example where we find the application of goto becomes necessary.
10. How would you decide the use of one of the three loops in C for a given problem?
11. Write a four-function calculator with the help of **while** and **switch** statements.
12. Write a program that calculates the factorial of an input integer number using **for** and **if** statements only.
13. Describe the various types of modular approach.
14. Describe the various type of guidelines which you will keep in mind while writing the program.
15. Distinguish between the following pairs:
   (a) main() and void main(void)
   (b) int main( ) and void main( )
16. Why the look of a program is important?

Sample Paper - 3

S3

Part A

Answer all questions, each of them carries one mark

Multiple Choice Questions

1. Language which needs no translation :

   (a) machine language (b) assembly language

   (c) high level language (d) none of these

2. Choose the correct statement a for loop.

   (a) counter can be initialized outside the loop body

   (b) counter cannot be initialized outside the loop body

   (c) counter must be modify inside the loop body

   (d) body of loop cannot be empty

3. Consider the following program.

```
#include<stdio.h>
void main()
{
    char name[30];
    printf("\n Enter your name:");
    scanf("%s", name);
    printf("\n %s", name);
    getch();
}
```

   Suppose you have entered your name as given below:

   Enter your name: Prem Nath

   What is the output of above program?

   (a) Prem Nath (b) PremNath

   (c) Prem (d) Nath

   (Hint: Space from keyboard taken as termination of a string)

4. Consider the following program. What is the output?

```
#include<stdio.h>
void main()
{
    char name[]="Prem Nath";
```

```
, name);
```

(a) Prem Nath (b) Prem
(c) Nath (d) Error

5. Suppose a C compiler reserves 16-bit for a char data type. What is the total number of characters that can be represented and stored by compiler?
(a) 127 (b) 128
(c) 256 (d) 255

6. A function is invoked with a call statement as in

```
call ckeck (x);
```

(a) True (b) False

7. Find error in the following code:

```
int a, ptr;
a = 11;
ptr = &a;
```

(a) ptr = &a; (b) a = 11;
(c) int a, ptr; (d) none

8. Select the correct statement.
(a) Body of for loop executed at least once
(b) Body of while loop executed at least once
(c) Body of do-while loop executed at least once
(d) Body of none for, while, and do-while executed without condition

9. If a **C** program has two component functions **main** () and **funct()**, it is possible that
(a) **main()** invokes **funct()** (b) **funct()** invokes **main()**
(c) both invoke each other with abnormal program termination
(d) all of the above

10. Identify errors, if any, in each of the following array declaration statements, assuming that ROW and COLUMN are declared as symbolic constants:
(a) int scoreboard (100); (b) double matrix [10,15];
(c) void average_value[ROW],[COLUMN]; (d) void char name[15];
(e) f l o a t sum [ ]; (f) double emp_salary [i + ROW]
(g) long int list [ROW] (h) int array_x[COLUMN];

11. Which of the following functions may not be used to read from a txt file "a.txt".
(a) getc (b) getchar
(c) fgetc (d) fscanf

Part B

Answer all questions, each of them carries one mark

True False Questions

1. Comments are which you write in the program as some sort of instructions for the operator or user of the program.

2. The use of number 0, 1 and 2 and letter O, I and Z in a program should be kept to a maximum.
3. The scanf function can be used to read only one value at a time.
4. If A[10] is an array, then A+2 points to the third element of the array.
5. The name of array represents addresses.
6. Comments provide the internal documentation of a program. It makes the program easy to understand.
7. When an input stream contains more data items than the number of specifications in a scanf statement, the unused items will be used by the next scanf call in the program.
8. If the field width of a format specifier is larger than the actual width of the value, the value is printed right-justified in the field.
9. Function scope signifies that the variable is active from the beginning to the end of the function.
10. If the field width of a format specifier is larger than the actual width of the value, the value is printed right-justified in the field.

Part C

Answer all questions, each of them carries one mark

Matching Questions

A. The scope of a global variable is	1. Lifetime
B. The lifetime of a variable is the duration of time in which a variable exists in the memory during execution	2. Scope
C. The scope of a program in which a variable is available for use	3. The entire program life
D. struct	4. <ctype.h>
E. #define	5. <math.h>
F. isalpha()	6. union
G rand()	7. records with varying components
H. space untilization	8. compile time directive

Part D

Answer all questions, each of them carries one mark

Fill in the Blanks with Appropriate Words

1. To ensure that the program is ok it is ________.
2. Errors which occur due to bad use of the language is called ___________ error.
3. The _________ is executed at least once always before it evaluates the test expression.
4. In C while is ____________ word.
5. _______ is called newline character.
6. ?: is _____________ operator.
7. The values used to initialize an array are separated by ___________ and surrounded by braces.
8. _________ can be stored in the memory column major order or in row major order.
9. _________ is used to return memory to the system.
10. Insertion of a node at the beginning of a linked list requires adjustment of pointer field of _______ node(s).

Part E

Answer any 10 questions, each of them carries five marks

Descriptive Type Questions

1. A text **T** and patterns **P** and **Q** are in memory. Write a program for replacing every occurrence of **P** in **T** by **Q**.
2. Write a function **Div (j, k)** where **j** and **k** are positive integers such that **Div (j, k) = 1,** if **j** divides **k**, otherwise **Div (j, k) = 0.**
3. Describe the use and limitations of the functions getc and putc.
4. What is the significance of EOF?
5. What is a linked list? How is it represented?
6. What is dynamic memory allocation? How does it help in building complex programs?
7. Write a function that will reverse a string. Use **for** loop that swaps the **first** and **last** character, then **second** and **next to last** characters and so on. The string should be passed to function as an argument. Take following sentences as input: "Able was I eve I saw Elba"
8. Write a program that will read a text file and creates another file that is identical except that the sequence of consecutive blank spaces are replaced by a single space and size of each line should be of 40 characters and should be left and right justified.
9. What is main difference between a structure and a union?
10. Can a structure be nested in a union?
11. Write an interactive program to determine whether an input number to the program is odd or even and print the message NUMBER IS EVEN or NUMBER IS ODD.
    (a) With using if Option, and (b) with if-else option (c) ternary operator
12. Write a program to find the number of and sum of all integers greater than 1000 and less than 10000 that are divisible by 7.
13. Consider the following program segment:

```
struct Scooter
{
    int Wheels;
    int Brakes;
    float BHP;
} Scooter;
struct Automobile
{
    char Make[40];
    char Model[40];
    int Year;
    struct Scooter Scoot, *Scoot_Ptr;
} Car, *Ptr;
Ptr * & Car;
Car.Scoot_Ptr = &Car.Scoot;
Ptr->Make= "Bajaj";
Car.Scoot.Wheels = 3;
```

(a) In how many ways the string "*Bajaj*" can be accessed?

(b) In how many ways the integer 3 can be accessed.

Sample Paper - 4

S4

Part A

Answer all questions, each of them carries one mark

Multiple Choice Questions

1. Checking and removing errors is called :
   (a) Checking (b) Removing
   (c) Debugging
2. Syntax errors include :
   (a) wrong use of statements (b) wrong use of manipulators
   (c) wrong use of braces/any missing brace
3. GCD of two numbers is:
   (a) the smallest number which is a common factor of the given numbers
   (b) the largest number which is a common factor of two given numbers
   (c) 1 is the GCD for all numbers
4. What is the output of following program?

```
#include<stdio.h>
#define size 5
void main()
{
    int array[size], i=5;
    array[0]=1;
    array[1]=2;
    array[2]=3;
    array[3]=4;
    array[4]=5;
    for(size=0; size<5; size++)
printf("%d", array[size]);
    getch();
}
```

   (a) 1 2 3 4 5 (b) Error
   (c) 23451 (d) None
5. Every function returns a value to its
   (a) calling function (b) invoker function
   (c) (a) and (b) are correct (d) none of these
6. What is the output of following program?

```
#include<stdio.h>
```

```
#define size 5;
void main()
{
    int array[size], i=5;
    array[0]=1;
    array[1]=2;
    array[2]=3;
    array[3]=4;
    array[4]=5;
    for(size=0; size<5; size++)
printf("%d", array[size]);
    getch();
}
```

(a) 1 2 3 4 5
(b) Error
(c) 23451
(d) None

7. An array's name is
   (a) Pointer constant
   (b) Array's constant
   (c) Pointer variable
   (d) Keep the address of first cell
8. The functions fgets() and fputs().
   (a) **reads** and write strings from or to data files
   (b) reads and write strings from or to input/output stream.
   (c) reads and writes records from or to data files.
   (d) none of the above.
9. An array is a
   (a) Collection of homogeneous elements
   (b) Collection of data types
   (c) Data type
   (d) None
10. What is the output of following program?

```
#include<stdio.h>
void main()
{
    int array[size], size=5;
    array[0]=1;
    array[1]=2;
    array[2]=3;
    array[3]=4;
    array[4]=5;
    for(size=0; size<5; size++)
printf("%d", array[size]);
    getch();
}
```

(a) 1 2 3 4 5
(b) Error
(c) 23451
(d) None

Part B

Answer all questions, each of them carries one mark

True False Questions

1. A program can be run in parts.
2. The series 1, 2, 3, 4, 8, 13 is a Fibonacci series.
3. The format specification %+-8d prints an integer left-justified in a field width of 8 with a plus sign, if the number is positive.
4. The getchar cannot be used to read a line of text from the keyboard.
5. The scanf function cannot be used to read a single character from the keyboard.
6. Program scope signifies that the variable is active among different source files that make up the entire executable program. Variables with program scope are often referred to as global variables.
7. register storage class is aimed at increasing the execution speed of a program.
8. A pointer variable can be at most two level deep.
9. The function fseek() finds a given word or phrase in a file.
10. The input list in a scanf statement can contain one or more variables.

Part C

Answer all questions, each of them carries one mark

Matching Questions

A. int(*p)[10]	1. function returning pointer to int
B. int *p[10]	2. To get single word string
C. int *f()	3. pointer to function returning int
D. int (*f)()	4. array of pointer to char
E. scanf("*s", str)	5. p is a pointer to an array of integers
F. char *day[13]	6. p is a pointer to an aray of integer pointers
G End of linked list	7. Ordered list of data items
H. Circular linked list	8. malloc()
I. Linked list	9. Points to same structure
J. For dynamic memory allocation	10. Null pointer
K. Self referential structure	11. Linking last node to the first node

Part D

Answer all questions, each of them carries one mark

Fill in the Blanks

1. He who writes the program is called ________.
2. There are 3 types of modular programming structures ___________, ___________ and ______________.
3. __________ of the program is a must.
4. For long life of the program ________ is done
5. The number 21 is a _________ number since it is divisible by 1 and itself.
6. Square root of a number is that number, which multiplied by ________ gives the original number.
7. The run time library is a collection of ________ files.
8. In 'C' while is _________ word.
9. The ___________ statement is used to skip some statements within a loop and start next iteration.
10. __________ is an unconditional jump statement.

Part E

Answer any 10 questions, each of them carries five marks

Descriptive Type Questions

1. What is the difference between the statements rewind(fp); and fseek(fp,0L,0);?
2. Suppose that the standard input is

   R A M

   (Each of R, A and M is immediately followed by a new line). Write a function that echoes these characters, so that the standard output is 'RAM'
3. Modify the above program so that the list is always maintained in the alphabetical order of customer names.
4. Develop a program to combine two linked lists to produce a third sorted lists which contains one occurrence of each of the elements in the original lists.
5. Write a program to create a circular linked list so that the input order of data item is main-tained. Add function to carry out the following operations on circular linked list.

   (a) Count the number of nodes

   (b) Write out contents

   (c) Locate and write the contents of a given node
6. Write a function **strcpy ()** that copies the **string1** into **string2** using pointers.
7. Write a program to find the sum of squares of elements on diagonal of square matrix.
8. What errors, if any, do occur in the following code?

```
struct Jams_Bond
{
    char *Jing;
    char *Jang;
    long ZIP;
}Jams_Bond;
Jing = "Jing lives in California";
Jang = "Jang lives in New Delhi";
```

9. Find error in the following declaration of structure and write the correct code.

```
struct Link
{
    char Node_Info1  [20]; /* Member 1 */
    char Node_Info2[20]; /* Member 2 */
    struct Link next;
};
```

11. Write a program to fill in a two-dimensional array of Boolean values by setting mat[i][j] to 1 if the greatest common divisor of i and j is 1 and to 0 otherwise.
12. Why do array subscripts start at 0 instead of 1 in C language?
13. What is the main difference between a bit-field and other members of a structure?
14. Can a structure be declared with a mix of bit-field and regular members?

Sample Paper - 5

S5

Part A

Answer all questions, each of them carries one mark

Multiple Choice Questions

1. How many bits are reserved for float data type by a C compiler?

   (a) 16-bit (b) 32-bit
   (c) 64-bit (d) Depends on Compiler

2. Which one is a compiled language:

   (a) C (b) Basic
   (c) machine language (d) none of these

3. Integration testing is done after :

   (a) unit testing (b) acceptance testing
   (c) beta testing (d) alpha testing

4. How many bits are reserved for int data type by a C compiler?

   (a) 16-bit (b) 32-bit
   (c) 64-bit (d) Depends on Compiler

5. Consider the following program:

```
#include<stdio.h>
void main( )
{
const int number =16;
number = number +1;
printf("The value of number is: %d ", number);
}
```

   What is output of the above program?

   (a) The value of number is: 16
   (b) Syntax error: Value of number cannot be modified
   (c) The value of number is: 17 (d) None

6. Consider the following program:

```
#include<stdio.h>
void main( )
{
    int num1=25, num2=30;
    num1=num1+num2;
    num2=num1- num2;
```

```
        num1=num1-num2;
        printf("\n Value of Num1= %  and value of num2= %d",
    num1, num2);
    }
```

What does the above program do?

(a) Swap the value of num1 and num2 (b) Add the num2 with num1

(c) Add num1 with num2 (d) None

7. What is the output of following program?

```
    #include<stdio.h>
    void main( )
    {
        float number = 7/3;
        printf("\n number is : %f", number) ;
    }
```

(a) 2.333333 (b) 2.00000

(c) Garbage (d) None

8. Select the correct statement.

(a) If condition is missing in for loop, it is assumed to be TRUE

(b) If condition is missing in for loop, it is assumed to be FALSE

(c) If condition is missing in for loop, it results in syntax error

(d) If condition is missing in for loop, it will terminate the program

9. Which one of the following is syntactically correct?

(a) for(;) (b) for(; ;)

(c) For(; ;) (d) None

10. A **C** program must have a function called

(a) main() (b) prototype

(c) definition (d) none of these

11. An involving function must pass arguments to the invoked function.

(a) True (b) False

12. It is possible to pass a structure to a function in the same way as a simple variable is passed.

(a) True (b) False

13. Find error in the following code:

```
int a, ptr;
a = 11;
ptr = &a;
```

(a) ptr = &a; (b) a = 11;

(c) int a, ptr; (d) none

Part B

Answer all questions, each of them carries one mark

True False Questions

1. Jumps make programs difficult to follow and debug.
2. A good program should have the following characteristics: Readability, Efficiency, Reliability,

Meaningfulness, Portability and User-friendly.

3. Depending on the complexity of the problem, the result of a careful analysis may be simply a testing of the factors with which the program must deal.
4. The C standard function that receives a single character from the keyboard is getchar.
5. The C standard function that receives a single character from the keyboard is getchar.
6. A structure can be passed to a function in C through call-by-value mechanism.
7. We can create data file using library function fcreate().
8. If x is an integer variable and px is a pointer; the statement px = *x; assigns the address of x to px.
9. float *PV [10] is a pointer to 10 element integer array.
10. An array may contain elements of different types.

Part C

Answer all questions, each of them carries one mark

Matching Questions

A.	sizeof	1.	modes for opening files
B.	#define sqr(x) x * x	2.	alert to the compiler about the function
C.	w+ and r+	3.	outputs character to screen
D.	prototype	4.	macro
E.	puts()	5.	bit manipulation
F.	Divide by zero	6.	Modular programming
G	Comments are written	7.	Keeping record of the program
H.	Wrong use of language	8.	Checking the program before actually running
I.	Execution error	9.	Reference manual
J.	Testing program in parts	10.	Syntax error
K.	Documentation	11.	Operators guide
L.	Testing	12.	Logical error
M.	System specifications	13.	Run time error
N.	Instruction for input, output	14.	Usually in the beginning of the program

Part D

Answer all questions, each of them carries one mark

Fill in the Blanks

1. The ____________ indicates to the compiler that we are dealing with an array.
2. _________ header file declares various character manipulation routines.
3. A function that does not return anything has return type _________.
4. The variable declared outside any function is known as a _________ variable.
5. The ___________ operator is used in between the union variable name and the fieldname.
6. The ________ only holds a value for one data type of the larger storage of their members.
7. We need to search for a correct place to insert an item in ________ sort.
8. A list is a _________ data structure.
9. FILE is defined with a ____________ statement.
10. The function sprintf() is meant for formatted write to a memory _______.

Part E

Answer any 10 questions, each of them carries five marks

Descriptive Type Questions

1. How does an append mode differ from a write mode?
2. Write a menu driven program to create a linked list of a class of students and perform the following operations:

   (a) Write out the contents of the list.

   (b) Edit the details of a specified student.

   (c) Count the number of students above a specified age and weight.
3. Write a function that counts the number **NUM** of paragraphs in the short story **S**.
4. What does ***p++** increment **p** or what it points to? Write a C code to justify your answer.
5. What is structure Tag?
6. Under what circumstances would one prefer a union to a structure?
7. In the following code identify the Tag, the members and the structure variable:

```
struct Mailing_List
{
    char Name[40];
    char Father_Name[40];
    char Street[70];
    char City[20];
    char State[20];
    long int ZIP;
} Ram, Bahadur, Eishita, Rachita;
```

8. Are the following statements equivalent?

```
printf("\n %s", *(pointer).Name);
printf("\n %s", pointer-> Name);
```

9. Implement the function *Ackermann(m, n)* having the definition

   (i) If m = 0 then *Ackermann(m, n)* = n+1

   (ii) If m > 0 but n = 0 then *Ackermann(m, n)* = *Ackermann(m - 1, 1)*

   (iii) If m > 0 and n > 0 then

   Ackermann(m, n) = *Ackermann(m- 1, Ackermann(m, n-1))*
10. What is a null statement? Explain a typical use of it.
11. With the help of **while** statement, write a program that calculates the factorial of an integer number? Repeat the same with the help of **do-while** statement.
12. Write a function **itob(n,s,b)** that converts the integer **n** into a base of **b** character representation in the string **s**.
13. Which are the general concepts of a program?
14. How would you break down the problem in steps before actually solving it?
15. What does void main(void) mean?
16. How do we implement multiple source program files?